THE DEREGULATED MUSE

Also by Sean O'Brien

The Indoor Park (Bloodaxe Books, 1983)
The Frighteners (Bloodaxe Books, 1987)
HMS Glasshouse (Oxford University Press, 1991)
Ghost Train (Oxford University Press, 1995)

SEAN O'BRIEN

the DEREGULATED MUSE

BLOODAXE BOOKS

ISBN: 1 85224 281 7 hardback edition
1 85224 282 5 paperback edition

First published 1998 by
Bloodaxe Books Ltd,
P.O. Box 1SN,
Newcastle upon Tyne NE99 1SN.

Bloodaxe Books Ltd acknowledges
the financial assistance of Northern Arts.

Cover printing by J. Thomson Colour Printers Ltd, Glasgow.

Printed in Great Britain by
Cromwell Press Ltd, Trowbridge, Wiltshire.

In memory
of
Anne Wardle

ACKNOWLEDGEMENTS

Acknowledgements are due to the editors of the following publications in which some of these essays first appeared: *Bête Noire*, *The North*, *The Oxford Companion to Twentieth Century Poetry*, *Poetry Wales*, *Sunk Island Review* and *The Times Literary Supplement*.

CONTENTS

PREFACE

> Who would not say that commentaries increase doubt and ignorance, since there is no book to be found, human or divine, in which the world has any business, in which the difficulties are cleared up by interpretation?
>
> MONTAIGNE, *Essays*[1]

A few words about what this book is and is not. Firstly, what it's not. It's not a history or a comprehensive account of contemporary poetry in Britain and Ireland. That would be a life's work and will need to be done by others at a later period, when some of the dust has settled, and the nine days' wonder has separated out from more enduring material – though many of the poets discussed here will surely outlive the immediate present, and this is a particularly interesting poetic moment.

The last claim is part of the reason for the book's title. At present it is not clear where authority in poetic matters resides. This may not be an historically unique state of affairs, since shifts of taste, interest and literary power may always be marked by an interregnum, but our situation is at any rate complex, in that the very *variousness* of contemporary poetry seems to prevent, or any rate dispute, the emergence of a dominant line. The variousness is something I try to bear out in the essays, though I am aware on the one hand that for some readers my idea of variety will be their idea of homogeneity. I look forward to reading their accounts of the matter.

Although at present there may be an inclination to view ourselves as waiting at the end of an ideological phase, deregulation has been and goes on being a significant theme in recent political history in Britain – in obvious ways as applied to the financial market and to the management, ownership and function of public utilities and services, more largely in the resulting questions raised about citizenship, subjection and the role of the state. It has figured in the psychology (or maybe the psychiatry) of the nation as a whole. In the last generation it has become possible, and legitimate, and in some quarters certainly advantageous, to propound ideas – about education, welfare, pensions and legal process and basic equality, for instance – which a generation ago would have seemed to most people not simply disputable but frankly *immoral* and to threaten the health and coherence of society as a whole. These anxieties have a poetic prehistory as well as a recent past, a literature as well as compliant media. They provoke complex and sometimes internally contradictory literary responses from left, right and centre. The Thatcherite 'unthinkable' can be felt a long way back – for instance in feelings of end-of-empire Englishness present in Larkin and Geoffrey Hill. The anxieties can function retrospectively, too, as in the weary, nostalgic regression of Ted Hughes's laureate poems. They are present in the treatment of class in Tony Harrison, nationhood in Douglas Dunn and homelessness in Ken Smith. They figure in the estranging practice of Roy Fisher, the dyspepsia of Peter Reading and the treatments of personal and social history of poets as various as Carol Ann Duffy, Carol Rumens and Kathleen Jamie. The confidence of Irish poetry in the last two generations is in part an oblique commentary on the exhaustion and anxiety of Englishness, and this may also be true of the new generation of Scots poets. It seems for the moment that poetically *anything* is possible, though not necessarily desirable, and that form is undergoing a radical inspection. At the same time the margin for political change is as tiny as the need is vast, though of course the critic should resist being tempted into the ringing formulations which are the leader-writer's stock-in-trade. For some readers the torsion between a decaying polity and a rich and protean phase of the poetic imagination might be summed up as a feature of the postmodernist condition and might best be treated in formal terms; but these essays are entangled – the word is used deliberately – with history.

There are numerous interesting poets who don't figure here, in some instances because I couldn't fit them in, in others because I couldn't find a suitable way to write about them. There are poets written about here to whose work I feel in various ways opposed: needless to say, to have taken the trouble to disagree with them is a mark of respect. There are also poets I haven't written about, because although readers I respect are enthusiastic about their work, I can't see their claims myself. Huge areas of contemporary poetry fall outside the limits of this already over-egged book. Neo-modernism, language poetry, performance poetry and the neo-conservative strain in English poetry are all for the most part absent. Perhaps an opportunity will arise to deal with them. A matter of greater urgency to me is the under-representation of women poets and of Black writing.

Given so many exclusions, I should suggest some of the reasons for the shape the book takes. These essays have their history in my own preoccupations as someone born in the early 1950s, marked by a particular background and education. I have written by and large about the poetry which has staked the strongest claim on me personally. The book begins with the earliest contemporary poets who mattered to me – Larkin and Hughes. Since the fact may not be apparent, I should mention that I hold them in high esteem, whatever my disagreements with their work or opinions. The book continues with a trio of poets – Tony Harrison, Douglas Dunn and Ken Smith – whose concerns with history, class and politics have been close to my own and from whose example I have tried to learn.

From here my attention shifts to Ireland. As a schoolboy in the late 1960s I had a conversation with an interested teacher about an anthology of Irish poetry I was trying to read in his biology lesson. Surely, he said, with the death of Joyce and the exile of Beckett, the heat had gone out of modern Irish writing. At the time it was hard to disagree, but what neither of us knew was that the first books of Heaney, Mahon and Longley were already upon us and the landscape was about to alter completely. Recognition of this fact was of course by no means uniform. As an undergraduate in the early 1970s when I applied to the Cambridge English Faculty Office for permission to write my Long Essay on Heaney I received a curt note to the effect that 'Seamus O'Heaney' was not considered a suitable subject for study. Such moments make it all worthwhile, in retrospect. My then tutor sympathetically suggested I tackle R.S. Thomas instead – 'who, though Welsh, is also a Celt', as he put it.

Equally significant, though not as heavily represented here, is the fact that during the years of reading, discussion and speculation which have resulted in this book, poetry by women has come into clearer focus, both as poetry and in terms of attempts to redress excessively masculine accounts of literature and its history: Fleur Adcock, Carol Rumens and Carol Ann Duffy and several other poets of stature have shed a good deal of light while getting on with the poet's main task, writing poems. At the same time, poetry as a whole has ramified. The section 'A Daft Place' acknowledges uncategorisable features of what might now seem the mainstream – poets as various as Roy Fisher, Peter Reading, Peter Porter and Peter Didsbury, all of them inextricably bound up with matters of England. An emergent generation of Scots and English poets is considered at the close of the book.

In writing about particular poets I have not felt obliged to provide an overall view of their bodies of work, but have been selective as my interests directed, and on odd occasions as much interested in a poet's critical writings as in his or her poems. Despite these warnings, this isn't a random aggregation of essays disguised as a coherent book, or a selection of reprinted reviews, though within some essays I have incorporated a small amount of material written for other purposes, for example about Ted Hughes, Tony Harrison and Craig Raine, because in these cases it says what I have to say. I have tried to give some account of the experience of reading and thinking about contemporary poetry over thirty years, from the viewpoint of a poet and critic for whom curiosity tends to outweigh certainty, and for whom many questions about meaning and value remain (fruitfully, I hope) open. The heat of history makes itself felt in poetry in many ways – with respect to subject matter, style, history and the demography of poetry. It straddles the poem as object and the climate of its production. Such interests can lead to some peculiar contradictions. They may also blind the critic to the virtues of those with whom he argues or about whom he is silent.

Although these essays may not bear it out, they are written in the conviction that criticism had better be readable. It is of limited use to me to read criticism written in the interior code of a class or professional cadre, and I suspect this is the case for most readers and poets. Much of my reading in recent years has been done in the context of working as a reviewer for magazines and newspapers. In newspapers, at any rate, writing about poetry doesn't on the whole carry the same claim to editorial attention as writing about fiction or biography, but it's clearly important for poetry to go on staking its claim in public, in a language both appropriate to its subject and available to the general reader, whoever he or she may be. What we also need is an expansion of space for more considered public discussion of poetry than the times seem to find convenient or necessary.

*

I am grateful to John Walsh, Harry Ritchie and Geordie Greig of the *Sunday Times*, and to Alan Jenkins and Mick Imlah of the *Times Literary Supplement* for giving me space as a reviewer. Thanks are also due to my editors, Andrew McAllister and Bill Swainson, who can have had no idea of what they were letting themselves in for; to Douglas Dunn, Ian Duhig, John Osborne, Michael Blackburn, Alan Ross, Peter Forbes, Don Paterson, Michael Donaghy, Giles Foden, Stephen Plaice, Nicholas Baumfield, Peter Sansom, Stan Smith, Rob Watt and Ken Newton; and above all, as ever, to Gerry Wardle.

Introduction: *Who's in Charge Here?*

If it is a fiction to recall a previous age of cultural coherence, when questions of literary meaning and value could be argued on more-or-less common ground, in more-or-less common language, it is nonetheless the case that present circumstances go some way to explain and perhaps prolong the appeal of that imaginary consensus, for all its baggage of class- and self-interest.

The contemporary general reader (another, though necessary, fiction), never mind the academic critic, can hardly fail to be aware that for more than a generation the discussion of literature has been complicated by the questions Literary Theory has raised about what reading involves; about the definition, interpretation and ownership of literature; and about how writing is to be valued, and by whom, and for what purpose. These developments have been one feature, perhaps the most potent, of the attempt to revise the world from within the academy rather than the public political sphere.

I say 'can hardly fail to be aware' and believe this to be so; yet in practice the review pages of the newspapers, through which readers for good or ill receive much of their sense of the contemporary, have scarcely been affected at the level of method and style (the case is clearly, if only superficially, different as regards pop music and other popular media). Indeed, it could be argued that a rearguard action against Theory was fought before Theory gained much access at all to the review pages. Common Sense, dread gift of English life, has been quick to avert such a threat.

It might also be considered an error to think of Grub Street reviewing as part of the same enterprise as academic criticism. Much public literary discussion continues to be carried on not by academics but by journalists and writers whose vocabularies may be barely be coloured by the terms of academic criticism. They work in a context where criticism and commentary shade with worrying ease into that profiling of personalities which is the subject of Roland Barthes's 1950s essay, 'The Writer on Holiday'.[1] People may be interested in books, but most of them are more interested in people.

In parallel with this concern with the glamour of personality, which is of course neither new nor confined to literary matters, there is a strain in academic thought which seeks to dismantle the hierarchy of literary worth and replace it with a frank admission that society is entitled to the culture it wants and gets and to value it as it sees fit. It becomes legitimate to refer to *Middlemarch* as 'a costume drama', to think *Pride and Prejudice* would be improved by the insertion of sex scenes, and, in the case of Professor Terence Hawkes, to find *The Bill* more appealing than Shakespeare.[2] Indeed, Hawkes goes further, arguing that in the light of Theory the depth of insight and verbal power long attributed to Shakespeare are actually qualities we put there for ourselves. To respond that this speaks highly of us, while at the same time noting that it would be hard to ascribe comparable qualities to *The Bill*, is unlikely to settle the matter for the troubled phenomenologists of cultural Theory, whose preoccupation with power leads them to throw the baby of value out with the bathwater of class.

There's no denying that the interior complexities of Theory are extensive and fascinating, but to engage with them in detail often means attending more to Theory than what were once the primary objects of literary criticism – poetry, fiction, drama. For some this would be a legitimate pursuit, but for a poet interested in understanding the poetry of the times it could seem like one more means of marginalising an art which, despite recent signs and assertions of public interest, has a life more notional than actual in the public mind.

I hope these essays manage to remain aware of the historical, social and economic forces which go to form poetry. At the same time, the following chapters presuppose that in the imaginative sphere poetry has powers at its disposal which lend particular poems particular authority. They also presuppose that some poems can be shown to be better than other poems, i.e. more interesting, intelligent, subtle, honest, musically alert and imaginatively startling, more attuned to past, present and future: more seriously felt, more memorable, with more to offer. These, I would suspect, are among the qualities most poets search for in the poetry they read. They are certainly open to scepticism, but the imagination in action nonetheless finds them useful and durable constructions on which to rejoice. It is surely interesting, that in a period of widespread scepticism about meaning and value, much of the best energy goes into poetry, an activity predicated, however uneasily, on the necessity of both.

In William Friedkin's film *Blue Chips* the basketball star Shaquille O'Neal appears as a young player acquired for a college team. With the other new arrivals he sits unhappily in a lecture (an orotund professorial performance) on *Sir Gawain and the Green Knight*. Eventually and against protocol he intervenes to ask the lecturer why the class are studying *Gawain* rather than African folktales. The lecturer replies, 'Well, because we are,' and points out that the course description was available in advance. It's a funny moment in a sentimental ragbag of a film, and O'Neal's character has the viewer's sympathy. It's also an unusual instance of argument about the canon finding its way into a Hollywood film. The conclusion is, basically, that the professors can go to hell, because the days of deference are over. The episode is an economically contrived, if thematically bolted-on instance of a commonplace contemporary phenomenon – the levelling tendency that says: my opinion is worth as much as yours because, well, because it's mine, and the inequality of my opinion would be a demonstration, not of the merits of your view in this instance, based on study and reflection, but of my personal inequality.

This opinionated condition, which is quite at home in the prevailing anti-intellectual climate of Britain, is paralleled in the sheer volume of poetry currently published. There is a well-trodden path from writers' workshop, to pamphlet publication, to first small press collection, so that an ISBN can seem like the inevitable consequence of setting pen to paper. This would be of little interest if it were not for the weird inverse relationship between the number of people who publish their poetry and the number who read that of others, which amounts to a structural reversal. There are an awful lot of amateur golfers, but it would not be true to say that most of them are interested only in their own performance, since if this were so the leading professional players would be travelling by bus rather than private jet. Of course, the universality of language and the relative brevity of much poetry give the form an obvious appeal as a means of self-expression, but, to introduce another comparison, the prospect of many thousands of composers clamouring for publication and performance of their symphonies would be absurd. Just as contemporary music needs listeners, what poetry needs is readers. But somebody intending to start reading poetry faces the problem of where to begin, and for this reason many either don't begin at all, or else regard poetry as an activity which ceased in 1914 or earlier. It's not, of course, that the cultural resource of the many has been mysteriously mislaid or removed. The audience that poetry wants, though composed in part of the descendants of the readers of *Georgian Poetry* (4 vols., 1911-22) or Yeats's *Oxford Book of Modern Verse* (1936), consists much more substantially of those who in other times would probably have had little access to the body of written poetry. At the same time, though, it is also the case that literary authority, however disagreeable its premisses, has declined to a point where the interested reader can no longer alight with confidence on the contents of an *Oxford Book*, for example. Philip Larkin's *Oxford Book of Twentieth Century Verse* (1973), widely derided when it was published, remains an inadequate account of its period, while D.J. Enright's *Oxford Book of Contemporary Poetry* (1980) is equally, though differently, skewed by its own eccentricity.

Scepticism is something these anthologies have in common, but so too is a failure to represent effectively the work that makes their chosen territories interesting. If there is no fundamental reason why an *Oxford Book* should be the embodiment of authority, there persists a degree of expectation that this should be the case, even though the function of anthologies has become less a matter of establishing a canon than of overt advocacy of certain kinds of work at the expense of others, as the recent history of notable anthologies demonstrates. *New Lines*, *The New Poetry*, the *Penguin Book of Contemporary British Poetry* and the more recent Bloodaxe selections, *Poetry with an Edge* and *The New Poetry* (the last of which deliberately usurps Alvarez's imperious title), have served a polemical purpose, with varying degrees of coherence. The same holds true, in more specialised ways, of a number of other well-known titles – the *Children* and *Grand-children of Albion* edited by Michael Horovitz, Paladin's *The New British Poetry*, edited by several hands, Fleur Adcock's *Faber Book of Twentieth Century Women's Poetry* and the anthologies of poetry by women published by Bloodaxe – Jeni Couzyn's *Contemporary Women Poets*, Carol Rumens's *New Women Poets*, Linda France's *Sixty Women Poets* and Maura Dooley's *Making for Planet Alice*.

Space forbids an exhaustive discussion of even those works listed above, but it is worth restating and adding to the sequence of significant anthologies appearing in England in the postwar period. These would be Robert Conquest's *New Lines* (1956 – a whole decade after the end of the Second World War); Alvarez's *The New Poetry*, in its 1962 and 1966 editions; *The Penguin Book of Contemporary British Poetry*, edited by Blake Morrison and Andrew Motion (1982); and, most recently, *The New Poetry*, edited by Michael Hulse, David Kennedy and David Morley (1993). To some degree, and necessarily imperfectly, each of these anthologies illustrates an argument. In the case of *New Lines*, common sense, reason and formal shape are offered as antidotes to the excesses of the 1940s (and, at any rate by implication, of modernism). The true variety of work produced by a number of significant poets represented in *New Lines* – including Larkin, Thom Gunn, Donald Davie and Elizabeth Jennings – can be seen as evidence either of the limitations of the editorial thesis, or of the enduring strengths of sound poetic practice.

A number of poets from *New Lines* survived into Alvarez's *The New Poetry*, only to be admonished by the editor, whose argument, while assuming formal competence and moral intelligence as the first principles for the poet, demanded something else – a greater readiness to meet the horrors, both exterior and (especially, it seems) interior, of the age of Auschwitz and the Bomb. Foreign poetry, in the agonised persons of the Americans Lowell, Berryman, Plath and Sexton, was brandished as an example of openness and scope. The self in the confessional was the embodiment of the artistic good.

Whilst one can find a considerable variety of social background among the poets in these anthologies, matters of class and domestic politics compel little interest on the part of the poets (in subject matter) or their editors (as components of the anthologies' aesthetics). Literature is implicitly viewed as a zone of free exchange, membership of which is conferred by skill and recognition. (By contrast, the role of class is a constant preoccupation in English novels of the 1950s and early 1960s.)

Both Conquest and Alvarez include work by poets who dispute, exceed or ignore the terms of the editors' arguments. The same holds true of Morrison and Motion's *Penguin Book of Contemporary British Poetry*. While Conquest's concern was with a poetic version of empiricism, and Alvarez's with the need to match the poem to the crisis of its time (both editors being therefore in some sense prescriptive of subject matter), Motion and Morrison noted an extension of 'the imaginative franchise' – that is to say, an enriched sense of what poetry could deal with, and how, and, by implication, a wider sense of who could write it. At the risk of excessive simplification, but in the interests of clarity, these developments, which Morrison and Motion (in a sense, like Conquest but unlike Alvarez) saw as confidently underway in the British context, could be thought of as threefold. Firstly, poets were exhibiting a phenomenological curiosity about the world – with marked stylistic effects – i.e. Martianism. Secondly, and to some degree consequently, the possibilities of play, fiction and narration were of increased interest to them. Thirdly, the expansion of the franchise also involved a preoccupation, in writers from working-class backgrounds, with class, history, language and politics.

The result is an anthology quite as uneasy as either of its predecessors, though like them it contains work by a number of those who continue to seem the most interesting poets of the period. To make sense of their chosen evidence, Morrison and Motion would really have needed to respect *the variety within the franchise*, and to have seen this as a set of related though differing responses to historical circumstances, rather than branding the franchise with the sign of one of its contributing minorities, namely postmodernism, which now seems usefully applicable only to the Martians and to James Fenton. The introduction works from Seamus Heaney and his Northern Irish peers, through Harrison and Douglas Dunn, then to Craig Raine and lastly to James Fenton. It is odd how the track leads back to Oxford, and it remains difficult to feel that, Fenton apart, these poets really punch the same weight as their Irish or 'provincial'[3] elders, even if chronology seems to grant them the last, or at any rate, the latest word.

If this discussion seems to be keeping its distance from actual poems, it is clear nonetheless that arguments about literature have as much to do with cultural power as with the words on the page that excited us in the first place. This certainly has to be borne in mind when examining the argument and principles of selection employed by the editorial trio who produced the 1993 Bloodaxe anthology *The New Poetry*, which asks continually to be seen in opposition to its Penguin predecessor.

One of the most interesting reviews of the anthology – actually more a review of the introduction – was written by Andrew Motion and appeared in *The Observer*,[4] reminding readers that at one time that paper had great authority in the discussion of poetry. From his opening sentence – 'I suppose the editors of this anthology think I'm bound to dislike it' – Motion moves smoothly on to the offensive, saying yes, above all, to 'poetry recovering its role as social criticism' while damning their writing:

> This introduction is irritating because it is boring.
>
> Instead of advocacy we get publicity department guff (they reckon their poetry is 'fresh in its attitudes, risk-taking in its address and plural in its forms and voices'). We get shibboleths where we want style ('Eighties Britain grieved observers'). We get assaults on paper tigers ('The post-Romantic tradition in the British Isles has perpetuated the belief that poetry and political concerns are incomparable [sic]').

It might be fair to say that while Motion is correct in objecting to the gruel of committee prose served up by the editors, his dismissal of their political observations is not quite honest. For example, with the odd exception, British poets were slow to respond to the climate of Thatcherism, and you would in particular have to look hard among Motion's metropolitan peers for any very vigorous response to it.

Having said this, the difficulty of accurate commentary is increased by the 1993 *The New Poetry* itself, which occupies the awkward position of commending size and variety while needing to read them as a kind of unity. What is really a list has to pretend to be an argument. Where Morrison and Motion ran aground by identifying Irish and Scots writers as British and some working-class writers as provincial, Hulse, Kennedy and Morley, with no interest in "Britishness", include work by poets from the Irish Republic as well as Northern Ireland, from Wales, Scotland, the Caribbean and India. *The New Poetry* certainly goes a greater distance than before to represent the diversity of poetry in English. But the rainbow coalition which results testifies more to the poets' simple contemporaneity with each other than it can (beyond a basic level) to common preoccupations, while the formal methods on display are so various as to forbid inclusive discussion. Matters are further complicated by the character of *The New Poetry*'s exclusions. An imaginary anthology, a *salon des refusés*, the parallel universe remix of *The New Poetry*, could include all the poets published in Morrison and Motion, plus others born before 1940 not included in Morrison and Motion. Ken Smith, U.A. Fanthorpe, Matt Simpson, Roy Fisher, James Berry, William Scammell, John Whitworth, John Mole and Alistair Elliot were among those mentioned by reviewers. There are also vast numbers of younger poets (names again drawn mainly from reviews of the anthology) who were also omitted, including Mick Imlah, Alan Jenkins, Lachlan Mackinnon, Wendy Cope, Tony Flynn, Douglas Houston, Peter Sansom, Julie O'Callaghan, John Hughes, Michael Gorman, Maura Dooley, Andrew Greig, Mimi Khalvati, John Agard, Sarah Maguire, Linda France, Don Paterson, Graham Mort, Oliver Reynolds, George Charlton, Mark Ford, Chris Greenhalgh, Stephen Smith, Susan Wicks, Adam Thorpe, Fiona Pitt-Kethley, Jeremy Reed, Harry Smart, James Lasdun, Alison Brackenbury and Neil Powell. By this stage it's raining names and the point of the exercise may no longer be clear – even though the list of others who might be mentioned, Black and Asian writers among them – could be multiplied several times over. The problem is not new. Twenty years ago, Anthony Thwaite wrote his comic catalogue-poem, 'On Consulting *Contemporary Poets of the English Language*', in which he harked back to the disquiet of a much older figure. This is only an extract:

> Hamburger, Stallworthy, Dickinson, Prynne,
> Jeremy Hooker, Bartholomew Quinn,
> Durrell, Gershon, Harwood, Mahon,
> Edmund Wright, Nathaniel Tarn,
> Sergeant, Snodgrass, C.K. Stead,
> William Shakespeare (no, he's dead),
> Cole and Mole and Lowell and Bly,
> Robert Nye and Atukwei Okai.
> Christopher Fry and George Mackay
> Brown, Wayne Brown, John Wain, K. Raine,
> Jenny Joseph, Jeni Couzyn,
> D.J. Enright, J.C. Hall,
> C.H. Sisson and all and all...
> What is it, you may ask, that Thwaite's
> Up to in this epic? Yeats'
> Remark in the Cheshire Cheese one night
> With poets so thick they blocked the light:

> 'No one can tell who has talent, if any.
> Only one thing is certain. We are too many.'[5]

It is a bit worrying that the ravages of time have so far let almost all these names survive in the critical memory. To the cultural conservative, more may simply mean worse, but while to others this may not seem self-evidently true, there remains the problem of how to get to grips with the sheer volume of work available. Anyone who has worked as a reviewer, an editor or a judge is likely to know the sinking feeling produced by the sight of the umpteenth massive batch of books, from which only a bare handful can be chosen for even the minutest mention in print. Publishers with small and not so small presses well know the difficulty of getting notice for their authors' work. The devolutionary energies of much contemporary writing, with its disavowal of a single presiding Oxbridge-London centre of taste and judgement, has undoubtedly helped to produce a more widespread sense of the sheer variety of work available. At the same time, though, there arises the question of what readerly competence in understanding our period might now consist of, given the varieties of English, of attitudes and approaches, which can now be encountered.

There are those who would argue that rage for order, or even unease about its absence, is the legacy of discredited attitudes – Anglocentricity, centralisation, the imposition of minority tastes, possessive academic obfuscation. For others though (and many of them are poets) the necessity of making sense persists, even if they might not want to start from here or with the equipment at their disposal. It persists because beyond the barest expression of approval or dislike, beyond the acknowledgement of "relevance" or political common cause, poetry deserves a complex response. Without this, it is, for example, legitimate to suspect that poetry's current beachhead in the attention of a wider public may be temporary. However well intended, the status of fashion accessory is necessarily fleeting, and it may require more than a long spoon to sup with the devil, if the fiend in question is no longer issuing invitations. Poetry in public is often invited, and sometimes willing, to turn into comedy, or performance, or political succour, or moral outcry, or emotional reassurance. It can, of course, be all these things, but it is also more, and it risks losing its essential nature if it does not maintain a vigilant regard for its own interests as an art made of language.

I

THE ENDS OF ENGLAND

1. Philip Larkin: *If Home Existed*

In 'Beyond the Gentility Principle', the famous introduction to his anthology *The New Poetry*, A. Alvarez paired Philip Larkin's 'At Grass' with Ted Hughes's 'A Dream of Horses'.[1] While Hughes's horses are elemental creatures, supernatural powers in the medieval world of the poem, Larkin's are retired racehorses. Noting that by Hughes's standards Hughes's poem was not his most successful, Alvarez none the less commended its vigorous account of a world beyond the safely domestic, at the expense of Larkin's sedate pastoral. At the time, Alvarez was advocating a poetry capable of dealing with extremes of experience, and thus facing up to the character of the age – to which the violent energy of the horses is related more by association than argument on his part – as against the polite English evasiveness he finds represented in Larkin. Alvarez's account contains an element of travesty, and it's not entirely clear how psychic strain (undergone by the American confessional poets he admires) and political barbarism (the Holocaust) are bound up with each other. At this distance in time they can seem like the properties of an urgent distress which has not fully identified itself. Not that the world is less barbarous, but at present it seems that rather than consider the relative psychic authenticity of Larkin's and Hughes's poems it may be more useful to consider the versions of England imagined by these two writers, who were in the 1960s and 70s the dominant figures of English poetry. To do this involves bearing in mind historical and political features which, because of his own direct line from the personal nightmare to the global crisis of the Atomic Age, didn't really engage Alvarez's interest. The Englands of Larkin and Hughes can now be seen in the process of vanishing. Their work provides signposts for terra incognita, the matter of England – or, to paraphrase Seamus Heaney – 'what is the matter with England'[2] – and for the strikingly different poetry which has succeeded them and attempted to fill the vacuum they leave.

There is an obvious and fundamental difference between these two poets. Hughes writes from within a still-discoverable natural world, and finds the city alien; Larkin, on the other hand, is, like nearly everyone else in England, a townee. The appeal of Hughes's early work, in *The Hawk in the Rain* (1957) and *Lupercal* (1960), has much to do with its exciting, consoling remoteness from the experience of most readers. It takes place just down the road, but it's *out there*, vivid and secret, a stranger, less cluttered, more ancient world – a Nature to set against city life, its authenticity unchallenged because most of us will never live in it.

Nature for Larkin, by contrast, is somewhere or something you visit for the afternoon. He imagines a neat, tended countryside rather than its feral residents. Hughes's Yorkshire people retain a gene of Viking psychosis; Larkin's Northumbrians make drop scones for Bellingham Show and behave themselves. His solitude – see the Holderness coast at the close of 'Here'[3] – is not the haunt of creatures, but an analogue of private consciousness. His rural England is inherently remote, embodying its separateness by virtue of its history – as in the brilliant 'Domesday lines/ Under wheat's restless silence' in 'MCMXIV'.[4] It can also, in the much inferior 'Going, Going', stand as a condition of pastness (apparently a strong form of validation in itself) under threat:

> And that will be England gone,
> The shadows, the meadows, the lanes,
> The guildhalls, the carved choirs.[5]

Purveyors of Heritage would have been quick to enlist Larkin: the invertebrate narcosis of these lines seems like an invitation. We are not all that far from the 'English lane' down which, according to Dame Vera Lynn, we shall walk together when we meet again. In his fine book *Literary Englands*, during a discussion of Orwell's *The Lion and the Unicorn*, David Gervais notes Orwell's insistence that 'Nothing ever stands still'[6] and comments: 'standing still is, more often than not, what most imaginary Englands are designed to do'.[7] Certainly, Larkin's desired England lacks flexibility in the face of change. The future, it seems, will be wrong by definition: more time, like more education and more equality, 'will mean worse'.[8] Larkin's historical sense, you might say, leaves the history out in favour of religiose pageantry. 'England', which lies 'beyond the town' seems like something Larkin has hardly had to think about beyond supposing that it would outlast his time (which is in itself a curious emphasis). 'Going, Going' is also the point at which Larkin comes closes to Betjeman, though obviously he doesn't have Betjeman's learned ruin-bibber's interest in things English. The poem's values are rigidified and conventional. Its reading of history means *not here, not now* – a townee's version of the countryside as the immemorial site of truth and virtue, somewhere far more literary than actual. The language of 'Going, Going' is the degenerate descendant of Gaunt's great patriotic speech in *Richard II*, producing the weakest (because most public?) expression of the conservative pessimism which seems in later life to have become a governing and arguably a poetically disabling feature of Larkin's sensibility. It comes as no surprise to find that 'Going, Going' was written in January 1972, when Larkin's productive life as a poet was nearing its end.

James Booth has pointed out the error of confusing the England of Larkin's work with that of Betjeman. Both writers may have favoured 'class distinction, / Democracy and proper drains',[9] but their methods are markedly different. Equally important, while Betjeman can repose on his version of the Matter of England, Larkin's is always in danger of escaping his grasp or coming to pieces in his hands – strong material for a poet but of a kind Larkin seems (at first sight surprisingly, given his sense of *private* decay) to have been temperamentally ill-equipped to deal with. Yet this very incapacity gives some of his poems their edge: England is the more urgent for him because he cannot be sure of its solidity. Perhaps Larkin's own advocacy of Betjeman has encouraged a kind of stylistic osmosis in the minds of some readers, whereby the imaginative *loci* of the two poets come to seem identical. As Booth points out, compared with Betjeman's nostalgic ' "Englishness" of car brand names, places and lifestyles...Larkin would not have so confidently appropriated "England" to his own imaginative province'.[10] Over against the namings of Betjeman's ultimately philistine imagination must be set the more costly and uncertain effort of imaginative possession made in some of Larkin's best poems. It seems that what Larkin called Betjeman's 'palpably greater interest in things other than himself'[11] provides a superficial ease of access, while Larkin's unease about both the self and the external world offered the more serious artistic challenge (hence perhaps the fact he rarely needs to assert or explain the poems' cultural allusiveness: consider what the 'extrovert sensitive'[12] Betjeman would have made of the materials of 'Essential Beauty').[13]

It's important, then, when dealing with Larkin's reading of "England", to register the anxiety which animates it and which may, for example, offer the reader a fruitful inconclusiveness. Otherwise we risk selling Larkin a bit short, as seems to have happened in Tom Paulin's controversial reading of 'Afternoons'.[14] Paulin deals with the poem in a bluntly historicist fashion, seeing its true subject as national and imperial decline. The leaves on the trees on the recreation ground, he writes, 'fall in ones and twos, rather like colonies dropping out of the empire'. Surely this is a bit *bald*? He goes on to describe the situation of the young women in the poem:

> 'something' is pushing them to the side of their own lives and this is a metaphor for a sense of diminished purpose and fading imperial power... The poem's lonely voice promises an exit from history into personal emotion, but that private space turns out to be social after all. This lyric poem is therefore a subtly disguised public poem, for it comments on a social experience.[15]

This seems inadvertently to presuppose the very division it seeks to deny – an indication, perhaps, of Paulin's own poetic anxiety to get things out in the open. He makes the poem sound rather like one of his own, where the function of privacy tends to be to cry its name and nature in public. While Paulin is an acute and often a brilliant reader, he treats 'Afternoons' as a kind of algebra whose outcome will always be 'history'. Yet it is not clear how the poem may be said to have 'disguised' its concerns, which, though of course open to political interpretation, begin a good deal closer to home than Paulin is inclined to allow.

The presence of class, for example, is important to the poem's effects. The women have husbands 'in skilled trades' and albums labelled '*Our Wedding*'. They are the upper stratum of the working class, with a margin for aspiration. At the same time as 'Afternoons' deals with motherhood and the traditional fate of women, the poem's sense of lack and of the women's incipient irrelevance to their own lives owes something to this placing identification. 'Afternoons' was written in 1959, the Macmillan high noon, and in it the day has not yet come when class/economic barriers blur sufficiently to enable the majority of the skilled working classes to buy their own homes. Neither has the urge to do so been politically propagated. The recreation ground, food on the table, the fading of youth – these are what life has to offer these women, Larkin thinks. They are hardly past youth, but 'Their beauty has thickened', in a phrase which seems to hark back to the observation in *1984* of the 'brief blossoming-period of beauty and sexual desire'[16] of the prole women before their exhausting descent into lifelong menial labour. The limits of political efficacy are implied in the poem's atmosphere of bareness and suspended purpose, which in turn recalls George Bowling's unease about the 'raw, mean look…the kind of chilliness' of new housing in *Coming Up For Air.*[17] It is difficult, though, to tell from 'Afternoons' whether Larkin is thinking of the perennial human fate – age and decay – or of the inadequacy of contemporary life to meet the (unexpressed and maybe inarticulate) wishes of the women. The poem's strong but understated sense of period suggests the latter, while Larkin's emergent Tory pessimism has its eye on eternity; but the poem provides no clear sense of which element is the tenor and which the vehicle. In this sense Paulin's reading may in a broad sense be correct: the missing element might be the sense of purpose, albeit vague, unexamined and dimly religiose, bestowed on the English by the fact of empire. Yet there may be greater illumination to be had from an acknowledgement of the poet's limited grasp of his own ideological position (not that Larkin could have tolerated such a phrase), since this actually works to the construction of a baffled and memorable poem. As Robert Pinsky comments, having observed Larkin's 'toughness and insularity' in his admiring but disgusted account of *Required Writing*, 'in poetry he puts to the service of vision the very qualities that sometimes cloud his judgement in prose'.[18] If the poet doesn't know what things are coming to, his inclination to look for precedent leads not to confident authority but a larger pessimism.

There is a chill, too, in the more ambitious and complicatedly compassionate 'Ambulances',[19] written a couple of years later. Here Larkin addresses the central horror of his work: death, which, as is well known, he was inclined to take personally. 'Ambulances', though, like much of his best work, transmits a personal force of feeling through a sense of communal witness. As the ambulance draws up, the 'children strewn on steps or road,/Or women coming from the shops/Past smells of different dinners' momentarily 'get it whole' – the knowledge of death's power to abolish. It is knowledge of a kind which, we are told ('They whisper at their own distress') can only be grasped through the sense of personal fate. The (literal) vehicle of fate's accomplishment is seen to undo the entire apparatus of ordinary life, making life in turn less convincing for the survivors. The transformation from ambulance to mobile coffin has an eeriness reaching, as it were, from out of the back of history's mind. Poems like this gave Larkin his authority.

Far
From the exchange of love to lie
Unreachable inside a room
The traffic parts to let go by
Brings closer what is left to come,
And dulls to distance all we are.

To the appropriately closed system of the *abcbca* stanza Larkin adds a tolling iambic gravitas which might be more readily associated with the pentameter. These lines are a good example of his ability to apply the braking power of a kind of rhetorical dignity in hitherto unexpected contexts, and to end with one of the half-epigrams for which he is so widely misremembered. 'Ambulances' doesn't seem to have attracted political readings, though there is a clear opportunity to travesty the poem as a Beveridgean passage from cradle to grave. The sense of nullity to be found in some provincial fiction of the postwar years could have been purpose-built for Larkin to settle into, but the objective tenderness he conveys in 'Ambulances' is hard to find equalled elsewhere. It's his equivalent of affirmation.

Our own retrospect, plus Larkin's gradual literary aggrandisement and his gradual souring into overt snobbery, may incline us to position him at a higher, far more remote point in the social scale than this poem occupies. Even as we note the class assumptions which unreflectively colour the work, there are poems from *The Whitsun Weddings* and *High Windows* which speak with an accurate sense of "ordinary", i.e. working-class lives; more, they speak from the same streets, with the same underlying preoccupations. To working-class people, with trace memories of the workhouse at the end of the street, hospitals have been places of fear, signifying death – a state of mind currently being reinforced. 'The Building', with its 'great sigh out of the last century',[20] is a notably classless poem, as, equally grimly, is 'The Old Fools'.[21] In relation to his fellow residents of Hull, Larkin resembles the cousin who having got on, is ill-at-ease in family company but at the same time inextricably (and sometimes generously) familiar with its doings and feelings. If, as Orwell proposed, England is a family with the wrong members in charge,[22] Larkin's England is a Sunday family tea, where embarrassment can sometimes be outdone by sympathy.

Something of the kind can also be sensed in the strange and at times exhilarating 'Here',[23] surely one of the oddest of Larkin's poems, with its journey towards, through and once more away from his adopted city of Hull, ending at the Holderness shore of the North Sea. This much-enjoyed poem is resistant to interpretation, since its completeness is formal rather than thematic: while 'Afternoons' comes to rest on its own imperfectly explained pessimism, 'Here' seems to gesture at some missing term for affirmation or acceptance or assumption into the non-human elements. If the poem's argument appears at most cursory, though, its modulation of mood is surely convincing. That the attitude of the poem's close resists an exact description is (and again this effect is comparable to 'Afternoons') an index of its success. Much has been made of the evident contrast between the teeming activity of the unexpected city, with the bulging list of props and characteristics, and the empty land beyond its 'mortgaged half-built edges'. The atmosphere produced by this contrast has much to do with the flatness of the land and the size of the sky, as any resident of Hull is likely to confirm. Solitary Holderness is a strange and come-hither elsewhere which, to quote 'The Importance of Elsewhere',[24] 'underwrites' the city's existence – and which may also be felt to underwrite much of Larkin's poetry. 'Here' is in a sense an atlas of his work, in which can be located his subjects, his anxieties, his enthusiasms and his sense of straddling a border between social realism and a less earthbound poetry. If some later poets have come to doubt that such a border exists, that may be part of his legacy.

Interestingly, Larkin seems never to have approached this amplitude again. When 'Here' leaves the city, the subsequent poems never quite come back, as though his intrigued affection and obvious appetite for Hull's rural shadow-partner turned out to be a leave-taking. The large remaining set-pieces in the canon, 'To the Sea' (October 1969), 'Livings' (October-December 1971), 'The Building' (February 1972), 'The Old Fools' (January 1973), 'Show Saturday' (December 1973) and 'Aubade' (November 1977),[25] all have somewhat different interests. All of them are poems of an approaching end – of life, material, art itself – not of the opening-up of imaginative territory or the enjoyment of residence in it. 'To the Sea', for instance, a valediction which doesn't speak its name, is banal in a way quite exceptional in Larkin. The effort to site the imagination in relation to the proverbial is afflicted by some dimming of the senses; a dimming too of the power of organisation: the split between observed detail and moral conclusion is wide, leaving Larkin sounding parsonical, like an off-form Crabbe. It may be that the heavily pre-mythologised Englishness of the seaside, which lives us before we ever go near it, has short-circuited Larkin's contribution to the subject. He is certainly at his best when, rather than relying on them, he *produces* mythologies – characters deep in litter bins, traveller families up lanes, the train journeys, ambulances and chain stores of everyday life – to which others then refer. Like it or not, he has been felt to contribute significantly to a collective sense of the post-war years: his observations serve as our archetypes.

The long gap between 'To the Sea' and its predecessor is made the more intriguing by the likelihood that its predecessor was the pre-senile couplet 'When the Russian tanks roll westward', the sour obverse of the little *Daily Telegraph* morality on which 'To the Sea' limps to its close:

> It may be that through habit these do best,
> Coming to water clumsily undressed
> Yearly; teaching their children by a sort
> Of clowning; helping the old, too, as they ought.[26]

This sounds half-distracted from its material, as if the poet has come out of role. It may be right to suspect that such uncertainty is an early indication of that loss of grip on the contemporary evident in the late work and in the agonised and dyspeptic letters. There is a partial recovery in 'Show Saturday',[27] another unspoken valediction (as 'To the Sea' puts it, 'Still going on, all of it, still going on!'). In a setting where Hardy would have discerned the decay of old ways, Larkin wants the shot frozen. Unlike 'To the Sea', though, 'Show Saturday' derives some benefit from the ritual circumscription of its subject: the event is itself a set piece, a performance. As Eric Homberger has remarked, 'We might say that civilisation *is* a country show for Larkin.'[28] At the same time, the poem's form derives a larger truth from an observed fact: hardly has the spectator arrived at the show when its dismantling begins: 'But now, in the background,/ Like shifting scenery, horse-boxes move'. Just as much as the show exemplifies the perennial, it testifies to the temporary, and there is a poignancy – which emphasises the *Merrie England* cardboard of 'Going, Going' – about the evocation with which Larkin follows this:

Back now to private addresses, gates and lamps
In high stone one-street villages, empty at dusk,
And side roads of small towns (sports finals stuck
In front doors, allotments reaching down to the railway)[29]

Cousin to, but more modest than, Orwell's famous evocation of England in *The Lion and the Unicorn* (the one bizarrely quoted by John Major),[30] the melancholy delight of these lines could almost make the reader patriotic. They are also what many readers of *The Whitsun Weddings* may have been looking for, without all that much success, in *High Windows* when it appeared in 1974: the generation of poetry from ordinary but eloquent detail. This identifying feature of Larkin's work is mostly sacrificed in a division of forces between the transcendental and the irritably and sometimes furiously sceptical. Yet the valedictory sense of 'something nearly at an end' but somehow 'still going on' can still be found – for instance in a poem apparently very different from 'Show Saturday', the haunting 'Friday Night in the Royal Station Hotel' (May 1966).[31] This sonnet's Chekhovian inactivity, at once frantic and serene – 'In shoeless corridors, the lights burn' – is accompanied by a twinning of country and city which recalls 'Here': '*Now/ Night comes on. Waves fold behind villages*'. A poem which seems obliquely influenced by this is Douglas Dunn's 'Nights of Sirius' from *The Happier Life*: 'High summer, and dog-star nights/ Are still and hot, accepting death'.[32] What is explicit in Dunn's poem, the awareness of death, is the unstated subject of Larkin's. Where Dunn imagines someone completing a 'privately published/ Volume of family history', Larkin uses the notion of writing as a means of aesthetically stabilising the idea of death. Dunn's rendering of solitude depends on acknowledging the presence of others; Larkin's virtually excludes them. The final line of Larkin's poem, italicised so that we suppose it to be an act of writing imagined inside the frame of the original, also recalls by extreme contrast Auden's poem of July 1935, 'August for the people and their favourite islands':

I smoke into the night, and watch reflections
Stretch in the harbour. In the houses
The little pianos are closed, and a clock strikes.

And all sway forward on the dangerous flood
Of history, that never sleeps or dies,
And, held one moment, burns the hand.[33]

Elsewhere, Larkin can manage something of the same inclusive authority. In 'Friday Night in the Royal Station Hotel', though, he lays out some properties quite like Auden's, an array of objects not in use; but while for Auden the very stillness and quiet bespeak the continuing world-historical drama for which the time and place provide mere punctuation, Larkin excludes the historical sense altogether: this place seems to be situated outside history or after it is finished. The poem is oddly erotic: in fact Andrew Swarbrick has described it as 'a love poem, a sonnet addressed to the merely contemplative imagination which broods on empty chairs and passing hours simply because they are there'.[34] Despite the temptation to insert 'not' in the last phrase, this is finely put. It makes Larkin sound a bit like a middle-aged Laforgue, left to walk the halls of a privileged gloom following desertion by the ladies of the court, and to remember his own lines from 1947:

Waiting for breakfast, while she brushed her hair,
I looked down at the empty hotel yard
Once meant for coaches. Cobblestones were wet,
But sent no light back to the loaded sky,
Sunk as it was with mist down to the roofs.
Drainpipes and fire-escape climbed up
Past rooms still burning their electric light:
I thought: Featureless morning, featureless night.[35]

Larkin spoke of his wish to be different not from other people but from himself (the identification of work with the self is interesting),[36] and the later poems suggest that the only means of achieving this was to extinguish the self in the effort to remove it from the historical context to a transcendent artistic plane. While the poems of transcendence have been very interesting to critics, it's worth remembering that in an already small canon they are few in number, evidence perhaps of a mind that does, in the words of 'The Winter Palace' (1 November 1978), 'fold into itself, like fields, like snow'[37] (or like the expanse of blank paper in the 1971 poem 'Forget What Did', where even the poet's diary is abandoned).[38] While Larkin regretted that poetry had given him up, it seems that he did also unwrite himself. That some of the late poems revisit the nakedly symbolic vocabulary of the early work – sky and snow, for example – suggests the closing of a circle even as the poems themselves gesture at release.

What might be entailed in 'release' is suggested by the odd and only partly successful 'Solar' (4 November 1964).[39] Written in a comparatively unproductive period following the completion of *The*

Whitsun Weddings, it does what we hardly expect of Larkin, addressing its cosmic subject by name, offering a hymn of praise (a method picked up again in 'Livings II').[40] As with 'To the Sea', Larkin's mind doesn't quite seem to be on the job. It is as if his interest is really held by something seen over the shoulder of his ostensible subject. This impression is partly a matter of the poet's evident unease with his chosen method. We note the unconvincing emphasis attempted by the isolation of the single word 'Gold' in the second stanza, as well as the flatness of the ending: 'You give for ever'; but the reader is also aware of Larkin's difficulty in dealing with the impersonal, inhuman, albeit life-giving force of the sun, which he leaves halfway to abstraction. The poem wears a corona of incipient horror, as though the poet realises he is trespassing on metaphysical terrain whose very scale is vertiginous to him. Another poem of the 1960s addressed to the sun, Thom Gunn's 'Sunlight', celebrates its lysergically-fuelled compliance by an exercise of intellectual passion which Larkin quite misses: 'Enable us, altering like you, to enter/ Your passionless love, impartial but intense,/ And kindle in acceptance round your centre,/ Petals of light lost in your innocence'.[41] Larkin, in contrast, appears to be in search of something beyond nature, to which the physical world and its traditional sacred symbols are only the threshhold. This aspiration can express itself partly as impatience with things-as-they-are to the middle-aged eye, for example in Larkin's observation of the apparent social and sexual freedom of the younger generation in the 1960s in 'High Windows':

> When I see a couple of kids
> And guess he's fucking her and she's
> Taking pills or wearing a diaphragm,
> I know this is paradise
> Everyone old has dreamed of all their lives –[42]

Larkin was careful in the arrangement of poems in his books, and in *High Windows* this poem follows the religiose 'Forget What Did', with its desire to observe 'Celestial recurrences,/ The day the flowers come,/ And when the birds go.' The juxtaposition is bleakly humorous: birds go with bees, and bees make honey, as 'High Windows' ruefully observes. The more urgent passion of the flesh is not yet spent, as the opening implies. Youth is discovered yet again to be wasted on the young, who have little grasp of the meaning of their freedom in the eyes of an older generation who must try in their turn to do the decent thing by settling carnality into wisdom. Envy, anger, excitement and a cruelty of tone matching the speaker's own injured sense of an exclusion which though inevitable is hateful, all compete in this self-consciously casual stanza. In the subsequent stanzas, there is an argument between the certainty that the paradisal '*long slide*' is itself an illusion and a desire (familiar to Yeats: 'But O that I were young again / and held her in my arms')[43] which is equally compelling. Discussion of the famous final stanza has revealed some interesting variations of emphasis. James Booth, for instance, finds in it 'a sublime emotional elevation out of negatives',[44] while Andrew Swarbrick argues that even at the close 'the poem notes that it is thwarted' and enlists the closing negations ('the deep blue air, that shows/ Nothing, and is nowhere') as evidence that the vision is confined to the literary plane and thus 'out of reach'. Swarbrick goes on to propose that 'Outside the poem true absence beckons: silence'.[45] His comments are provocative in that they use the poem's own imaginative authority against itself – an approach with which the poem's language seems at odds. To say, for example, that the blue air 'shows/ Nothing' is not the same thing as saying it does not show anything. The poem surely depends on paradox: just as the closing image seems to put the speaker's itchy sexual unease in perspective, so the twin negatives produce a compelling image of absence, not the absence of an image. If the procedure seems in some way pathological, it also recalls the work of another poet at times unwillingly resident on earth, the John Clare of 'I Am':

> I long for scenes where man has never trod;
>   A place where woman never smiled or wept;
> There to abide with my creator, GOD,
>   And sleep as I in childhood sweetly slept:
> Untroubling and untroubled where I lie;
> The grass below – above the vaulted sky.[46]

Clare may just about remain within the limits of religious orthodoxy here, but it is apparent that for him heaven equals the extinction of tormented consciousness, not its blissful renewal. Larkin avoids Clare's sweetness, but his imaginative destination seems the same; and just as Clare's wish for himself is somehow unselfish, so Larkin's 'thought' escapes the threat of exclusiveness by indicating that no one at all is there in this sky-blue no-place. Auden, who remained sociable far longer than Larkin, might well have disapproved of this as heresy, but would have understood the paradox, having after all himself remarked that 'nothing is lovely/ Not even in poetry, which is not the case'.[47] Larkin's imaginative progress from engagement with the world, towards symbolism and then into near-silent retirement, produces another paradox: here is a poet of the Movement whose career trajectory resembles the modernist Eliot rather than his own commonsensical peers – just the sort of thing you'd suppose he'd have been keen to avoid.

2. Ted Hughes: *Time Not History*

The poetic climate in which Ted Hughes published his first book, *The Hawk in the Rain* (1957),[1] did not encourage political engagement. Survivors from the 1930s had moved away from the political here-and-now, and while the Cold War produced new terrors, the biggest of which was nuclear war, to which Hughes refers in 'A Woman Asleep',[2] the major American poet of the period, Robert Lowell, observed the symptomatic narcosis of the Eisenhower era: 'Ice, ice. Our wheels no longer move;/[...] and the Republic summons Ike,/ the Mausoleum in her heart'.[3] The English poets of the Movement, meanwhile, seemed to deal for the most part with anxieties and paradoxes befitting the uncertainties of Britain confronted by the 1956 Suez Crisis. David Lodge has commented that the opinions of Kingsley Amis before his move Rightwards 'focused in a very precise way a number of attitudes which a great many lower-middle class intellectuals find useful for the purposes of self-definition'.[4] That Amis should figure so centrally may now seem odd, given that he can hardly be termed a thinker; that his importance should be construed in terms of the identity-crises of 'lower middle class intellectuals' is inadvertently eloquent of a collective lack of imagination attempting, in Jim Dixon's words, to throw 'pseudo-light...upon non-problems'.[5]

There were some bolder spirits. Thom Gunn also addressed issues of identity and action, often with a fictive Elizabethan-Jacobean context which matched Hughes's own Shakespearean colourings. Gunn's use of the language of threat and pose, it's now clear, was in part a metaphor of his gay concerns. But as well as Hughes's debut and Gunn's *The Sense of Movement*, 1957 saw the publication of Stevie Smith's *Not Waving But Drowning*, Louis MacNeice's *Visitations*, Donald Davie's *A Winter Talent*, Roy Fuller's *Brutus's Orchard* and Anthony Thwaite's *Home Truths* – a varied and distinguished selection, but by no means a transforming or even campaigning one. Such a bibliographical snapshot is necessarily a partial truth, but compared with the American publications of the same year – Denise Levertov, Frank O'Hara, Theodore Roethke, Richard Wilbur and James Wright, it seems clear that Britain was having a fairly quiet time, with the emphasis on a blend of formal scruple and modest ambitions.

Hughes set out and continued in a direction of his own. Not for him the hopes and fears of the Welfare State, its friends and incipient enemies. Instead he wrote poems from his native Yorkshire, from feral nature and at times from a highly specialised sense of history, which, like Gunn's, leapt between the sixteenth century and our own. The shock of his originality is hard to recreate when we feel we know him so well. His novelty was supported by a strong appeal to the widespread sense in England that nature and the countryside were poetry's home ground – the embodiment of a time before industrial time. The sceptical Ian Hamilton, looking back from the vantage-point of *Crow* (1970), described Hughes's early work as 'ripplingly muscular neo-Georgianism' and observed that 'in a period of tame, chatty, effortlessly rationalistic verse, it was easy to overestimate a poet who possessed even the beginnings of linguistic vigour'.[6] This is to belittle Hughes's substantial accomplishments; but Hamilton's sourness is an indication in the negative of what a central, commanding status Hughes achieved between 1957 and 1970.

If the sensual immediacy and relish of Hughes's early poems served to extend, albeit surprisingly, a familiar tradition from the point at which Lawrence left it, the endemic violence of his imaginative world seemed to make his modernity equally manifest. In the 1960s the savagery of the natural world as he conceived it was popularly twinned with Gunn's more urbanised and erotic interest in aggression, and (for reasons no longer clear, supposing they ever were) a set of associations grew up around the two poets' work: nature-violence-the Holocaust-psychic crisis – a kind of cultural shorthand of which the present will have its own equivalents. Alvarez's essay 'Beyond the Gentility Principle', with which he introduced *The New Poetry*, as well as some of the essays in *Beyond All This Fiddle* and parts of the later study of suicide, *The Savage God*,[7] are key documents in identifying the emotional style of the Fifties and Sixties – some features of which seem barely comprehensible at the moment. This problem has a parallel in the experience of poets emerging in the 1950s themselves, to whom the political interests of the Thirties had begun to seem remote and implausible. Donald Davie, discussing his poem 'Remembering the Thirties', commented:

> the [poem] is about the pathos of the fact that no generation, however brilliantly resourceful and persuasive, can convey wholly to any other generation its sense of the urgency of the issues which confront it. The poem says that this is nobody's fault, but is in the scheme of things.[8]

Davie's regret and melancholy, and his acceptance of imaginative defeat at the hands of 'the scheme of things' bespeaks the political quietism and neutrality which were not far from the surface of Movement thinking, and which would in time, for some Movement writers, in tandem with success and assumption into the literary establishment, show itself in the aggressive adoption of conservative attitudes. The exhaustion of ideology in Butskellism at home and retrenchment abroad was matched by a kind of moral miniaturism in literature, a hoarding of meagre resources in the absence of any compelling ideal or political project. Such anxious common sense would prove vulnerable to incursions of the irrational – one example of which might be Amis's novel of 1969, *The Green Man*, whose use of ghost and horror genres may now read as an enabling displacement of more everyday (though not the less terrifying) experiences. Something, at any rate, would have to fill the vacuum once occupied by political activity, and it could hardly be Jimmy Porter's lament at the lack of a cause, or Amis's saloon-bar-utilitarian reflection in his 1957 Fabian pamphlet *Socialism and the Intellectuals* that 'the best and most trustworthy political motive is self-interest' (a comment which, interestingly, would enable Amis to find a home in the Blairite Labour Party of today).[9]

In the absence of an explicitly political dimension through which the intimacy of private crisis and global threat could be disclosed, there was a risk of mannerism. In the early work of George MacBeth, for instance, a poet of real talent but one magnetised by the *zeitgeist* to a degree most would try to avoid, the Holocaust-Cold War properties which the Movement poets themselves tended to treat obliquely, are dwelt on like fetishes, sometimes in poems about fetishism. The combination of relative affluence and the stagnation of class politics in the Butskellite period seems to have helped to drive the imagination inwards, or out of town. Realpolitik was something practised under other regimes, and endured by, among others, poets accorded an importance denied their Western peers. There was neither the need nor the opportunity for the kind of historical commentary supplied by Zbigniew Herbert in his 1956 poem on the Hungarian Uprising:

> we stand at the border
> called reason
> and we look into the fire
> and admire death.[10]

It is striking that Ted Hughes, though he has little to say of domestic politics, has long been interested in writing from the Eastern Bloc, whose poets (such as Vasko Popa and János Pilinszky) knew that the least utterance, however carefully encoded, is political – and that, equally, there is a kind of power in the encoding. The vigilant and unadorned language of some poets from Eastern Europe can perhaps be heard to influence Hughes's work from around the period of *Wodwo* (1967), at the same time as his mythmaking ambitions begin to emerge clearly. The two interwoven factors, the natural world and its mythic function, have provided him with an apparently bottomless well of material, even if, as Tom Paulin argues, what he draws from the well can seem to be the same poem, endlessly.[11] For the most part Hughes's 'one story' leaves alone, or avoids, or is uninterested by the developing social and political reality of the British Isles in his adult lifetime – though as Paulin has shown, Hughes's discomfort makes itself felt. What might be called the argument from eternity will propose that he has set his sights higher, or deeper, on the core of experience, on the wheel of creation as a whole, on time rather than history. It would not require a fanatical advocate of Hughes's work to acknowledge the magnificence of some of his writing, but in the same breath the reader is likely to ask what his omissions mean. Are they the result of choice or incapacity? The scale of his work will of course encourage some readers to deny that there *are* any omissions, on the grounds that his mythmaking approaches a primal authority and capaciousness able to absorb any merely historical phenomena. This would be the burden of *Crow* and *Gaudete*[12] and the implication of the authorial comment in *Wodwo*:

> The stories and the play in this book may be read as notes, appendix and unversified episodes of the events behind the poems, or as chapters of a single adventure to which the poems are commentary and amplification. Either way, the verse and the prose are intended to be read together, as parts of a single work.[13]

Whatever the case, his poems are shadowed by what they exclude. Despite his wishes, Hughes's foundationalism requires a history. On the other hand, his fascination with process, the onrush of one thing after another – the movement of a jaguar or the relentlessness of weather, poem after brilliantly snatched poem – suggests the homelessness which Paulin also detects.[14] Paulin ascribes the unsettled, unstable element in Hughes to ancestral Protestantism,[15] but the poet's displaced and private revolt also recalls the more recent, largely gestural rebellion of the Teddy Boy, the biker or rocker who almost invariably turns out true blue in the end, his objectless energies put to service. To live outside the law in that sense, even rhetorically, is not a means of access to Nietzschean 'free powers' of the natural world but – even for what Paulin terms 'the solitary committed toughness and risky certainties of the self-employed' [16] – to the tradesmen's entrance of the Powers that Be.

It is very striking that Hughes's most nearly political work should arrive quite late in his career, in the form of honorific occasional poems written as Poet Laureate, and with a determinedly anti-political, mythopoeic thrust. Such is Hughes's imaginative vigour that even in bowing to convention his work in *Rain-Charm for the Duchy*,[17] though poetically unsuccessful, is not a simply interesting oddity but an important tool in the understanding of his work. It illustrates with some pathos the virtual absence of the public realm from his poetic imagination, while giving hints about why this is so. The collection followed hard on the heels of the generally hostile or scornful reception accorded to his large study of Shakespeare, *Shakespeare and the Goddess of Complete Being*,[18] as well as further episodes in the war of attrition between the estate of Sylvia Plath and her critics and biographers. The Royal Family, variously the dedicatees of the poems, have undergone divorces, disgraces and public absurdity, and seem locked in a war of attrition with the press and the still-inchoate Republican energies which bid to bring their future into question. Hard public times for the Laureate and his patrons alike.

Hughes can hardly have failed to consider his role. His response has been to take the task entirely seriously and write more directly, neither left-handed nor piecemeal, in honour of the institution of monarchy than might now be supposed possible. The epigraph to *Rain-Charm for the Duchy* states his case:

> A soul is a wheel.
> A Nation's a Soul
> With a Crown at the hub
> To keep it whole.

The source of Hughes's royalism appears to be the Queen Mother, the heroine of 'A Masque for Three Voices', whom he sees 'at the centre of Britain's experience of the drama by which the twentieth century will be remembered,' not least because 'for those who fought in the First World War...she was the generation of their wives, and for those who fought in the Second she was the generation of their mothers'.[19] Not only does she wear 'the symbol of 'the ring of the people',[20] but – perhaps most famously during the Blitz – 'became the incarnation of it'.[21] The notes on this poem amount to a short essay on identity and patriotism, which is actually more interesting than the verse. Hughes gives a sharp sense of the unmediated impact of the Great War on 'the tribal lands of the north' alongside a too-brief autobiographical passage in which his boyhood self scouts the Calder Valley for sniping positions in expectation of 'clouds of German parachutists'.[22] The poem itself revealingly tries to strike the public note:

Tragic drama gives its greatest
  Roles to royalty.
The groundling sees his crowned soul stalk
  The stage of history –
'I know,' he mutters, 'but not how,
  That majesty is me.' [23]

Setting aside firstly the success or failure of these rather Kipling-esque lines, and secondly Hughes's adoption of the careful plain-spokenness more usually found in his work for children, it is clear that the stage is not merely a convenient Elizabethan or Shakespearean figure, but a sign of one of Hughes's imaginative homes – the elsewhere of imagined history, in the Renaissance and before, in which action and meaning are seen to be unified, and where, insofar as the poet gives his mind to such things, the social order is justified by the fact of its existence. If the seventeenth century was the time in which Eliot, another Royalist, saw 'a dissociation of sensibility set in',[24] the graveyard of Hughes's unitary myth is the Great War. The central, impossible part of Hughes's task here is to resurrect it through a myth of consolation. Again, the book is most interesting when closest to home:

I died those million deaths. Yet each one bled
Back into me, who live on in their stead,
A dusty blossom of the British dead.

Still spellbound by that oath at Agincourt,
The palace jewel – the bullet Nelson bore.
But Passchendaele and Somme disturb me more.

Being British may be fact, faith, neither or both.
I only know what ghosts breathe in my breath –
The shiver of their battles my Shibboleth.[25]

(Interesting that Hughes reads patriotism as primitivism.) This, the poem's third voice, is at once representative and personal. It draws both on family history and the amplified speech of the common man who is heard in discussion with the King in *Henry V*, in innumerable war films, including the BBC's Falklands drama, *An Ungentlemanly Act*, where a Royal Marine, instructed by his OC to surrender to the Argentinian forces occupying Port Stanley, apologetically blurts out, 'Fuck off, sir!' It is as hard not to admire this obdurate bravery as it is to accept its basis.

Not without strain, Hughes transfers his attention to the larger theatre of mythology. In the notes to 'An Almost Thornless Crown', the second part of 'A Birthday Masque for Her Majesty Queen Elizabeth's Sixtieth Birthday', we learn that the Crown 'does not belong to historical time and the tabloid scrimmage of ideologies, but to natural time'.[26] The Crown 'is the reminder...of this mystery in life – that historical time comes second'.[27] Correspondingly, and presumably in line with protocol, the poems make little of the individuals involved. In 'The Song of the Honey Bee: For the Marriage of his Royal Highness Prince Andrew and Miss Sarah Ferguson', the couple are advised:

Dance as dancing Eve and Adam
    Kicked their worries off
In paradise, before they heard
    God politely cough.[28]

Events have of course made irony, and travesty, out of Hughes's jaunty lines, though the imperative form carries a kind of insurance. It is noticeable how small a part the future has to play in the book as a whole – which seems to dispute Hughes's anti-historical outlook. Yet the resolute pastness does, of course, accord with the rural conservatism (as of poacher turned gamekeeper) of Hughes's imagination, in which modernity features as a kind of infernal Argos catalogue with added politics. Despite the assurance of eternity, real time is a source of real anxiety, and the book's affirmations seems, despite themselves, unavoidably valedictory, its imagined personages phantoms from a world long vanished, and its contemporary sources a rich and vulgar family rowing in public. 'Gods make their own importance,' as Patrick Kavanagh said:[29] maybe, but that doesn't mean anyone's listening.

3. Geoffrey Hill: The England Where Nobody Lives

> If one writes lyrics of which nostalgia is an essential element, naive or malicious critics will say that the nostalgia must be one's own. There are, however, good political and sociological reasons for the floating of nostalgia: there has been an elegiac tinge to this country since the end of the Great War. To be accused of exhibiting a symptom when, to the best of my ability, I'm offering a diagnosis appears to be one of the numerous injustices which one must suffer with as much equanimity as possible.
>
> GEOFFREY HILL, interviewed by John Haffenden[1]

> Alas, what mountains of dead ashes, wreck and burnt bones, does assiduous pedantry dig up from the past time and label it History, and Philosophy of History; till, as we say, the human soul sinks wearied and bewildered; till the past time seems one infinite incredible gray void without sun, stars, hearth-fires or candle-light; dim offensive dust-whirlwinds filing universal Nature; and over your historical library, it is as if the Titans had written for themselves: DRY RUBBISH SHOT HERE!
>
> And yet these grim old walls are not a dilettantism and dubiety; they are an earnest fact. It was a most serious purpose they were built for! Yes, another world it was...
>
> THOMAS CARLYLE, *Past and Present*[2]

In her 1978 novel *The Virgin in the Garden*,[3] A.S. Byatt assembles her characters to watch the 1953 Coronation of Queen Elizabeth II broadcast on television. This is a significant event in the reinforcement, in the collective mind, of the national reputation for ceremonial brilliance. Byatt uses the episode to contrast various views of the event and its historical and cultural significance, and to carry a couple of characters, the verse dramatist Alexander Wedderburn and the schoolgirl actress Frederica Potter, onwards in time to reflect on the matter with a quarter of a century's hindsight. There is also a strong discursive element that seems to come directly from the author herself, fed at times (by no means unconvincingly) into the development of her characters:

> True paradise, Proust said, is always Paradise Lost. Only when Frederica was old enough to equate the tenuous pastel hopes of 1953 with her own almost-adult knowledge that everything was a new beginning, that reality for her was the future, did she come to feel nostalgia with what at the time she diagnosed boldly as a blear illusion. In a Proustian way too, as she acquired age, she came to associate her obsession with *Four Quartets* with the Coronation, with the Coronation's gestures towards England, history and continuity. It had tried and failed to be now and

> England. There had been other worse failures. In the sense in which all attempts are by definition not failures, since now *is* now, and the Queen was, whatever the People made of it, crowned, it *was* now. Then.
>
> As for the others, they had their thoughts. The Ellenbys [the snobbish vicar and his wife] were delighted and reassured, as though the whole world wore, briefly and significantly, a Sunday aspect. Felicity Wells [a spinster schoolteacher] was in a state of cultural ecstasy, seeing the vaults of the abbey, imitating the inhuman perspectives of the reaches of Heaven, and the Queen's little white human face over her emblematically embroidered robes, as a promise of renovation. Eliot had said, and she remembered, that the 'English unbeliever' conformed to the practices of Christianity on the occasions of birth, death, and the first venture in matrimony...' Now a whole Nation was conforming to an ancient national Christian rite. It was a true Renaissance.[4]

D.J. Taylor has commented that *The Virgin in the Garden* offers 'fictional background plucked from the textbooks, if you like',[5] but at the same time notes Byatt's confidence in generating a sense of the collective consciousness of a nation which, though wearied by austerity, is not unhopeful. The cultural and religious imaginings of Frederica, the Ellenbys and Felicity Wells offer us a glimpse of the final, exciting and momentary efflorescence of the national myth to which the characters are variously seen to contribute according to their imaginative lights – and to which Eliot's verse dramas and those of Christopher Fry may be added. This fleeting New Elizabethanism (itself an end-of-empire guise for the memory of Victorian imperial confidence) is interesting in direct proportion to its airy, unsustainable character. Byatt herself uses Frederica to summarise what rapidly displaced it – the attitudes of the satirist and the cynic. That Byatt draws on broadly social rather than baldly political history (satire rather than Suez) to substantiate the novel's world is both conventionally novelistic and of particular interest in shedding light on the path not taken (or taken only momentarily) by the national imagination. It helps to dramatise the wish of some of her characters for a world elsewhere. There is a place for Geoffrey Hill in pageantry of this kind – as a sullenly superior artistic malcontent for whose preoccupations the past provides as absorbent a medium and as satisfyingly reflective a surface as it does for Miss Wells. The references to *Four Quartets* in the quoted passage have pertinence for Hill, too. He has always aimed at a gravity equivalent to Eliot's and a sense of Englishness as intense as, if no more precise than, that of the American émigré. One of Hill's harshest critics, Tom Paulin, has gone so far as to state that 'Hill is a parasite upon Eliot's imagination, and any account of his work must face this frankly in order to argue the ultimate authenticity of the style'.[6]

Paulin, I think, overstates the case, but something comparable occurs in more neutral terms to Stephanie Potter as she looks around Miss Wells's room, which is full of 'stuffs' ready to be turned into costumes for the coming production of the verse play *Astraea* in the grounds of the local stately home:

> Stephanie saw it all double, with wide clarity and narrow sharpness. She saw what things meant to be, and missed no detail of how they, in fact, presented themselves. She saw...the layered glowing mystery, the gorgeous stuff Felicity Wells saw, and saw further the ambition to embody, here, now, in the present time and place, the vigour, the sense of form, the coherence lost, lost with the English Golden Age. She saw how the hanging stage cope on Miss Wells's wardrobe-rail, and the *Illustrated London News* photograph of the Dean of Westminster in a cope worn at the Coronation of Charles II, brought out for the coronation of Elizabeth II, and Daniel's [the curate's] dog-collared presence, brought to Felicity Wells a happy sense of coincidence, superimposition even, of past grandeur and present business.
>
> She saw, and did not share. She saw too the hammered milk-bottle tops on the cope, and Daniel's complete lack of interest in ceremony, Shakespearean or High Anglican. She saw the chips in the teacups and the holes in the stockings. It was not her business to fuse any of these into new wholes. She just saw.[7]

Hill, who came of age in 1953, is not, of course, a New Elizabethan in any simple sense; no age is Golden in his book, and his poems move back beyond the Tudor imperium to the Wars of the Roses and to the early kingdom of Mercia. Yet distance in time does lend a grim enchantment to the view, and Hill's medieval excursions are sometimes more indulgently Tennysonian than his sombre demeanour might seem to suggest. More importantly, the unease produced by some of Hill's work, in particular 'Funeral Music', is connected with the sort of gap noted by Stephanie Potter between apparent aim and actual effect. The disposition of enormous technical skill in the field of the poems is undeniably impressive (Paulin is barking up the wrong tree when he criticises Hill's ear)[8], but this proud display of heavy engineering seems somehow to miss its own point. Hill's particular laboriousness may be evidence that he suffers, as it were, a dissociation of sensibility of the kind described by Eliot.[9] Strenuous half-abstraction is occasionally forced to produce a sensuous, compelling shape, but (to switch metaphors) the disparity between the amount of seawater evaporated and the gold produced is impractically wide. More importantly, though, the successful instances seem more like the product of a kind of childhood fetishism than a mature historical vision.

...Recall the cold
Of Towton on Palm Sunday before dawn,
Wakefield, Tewkesbury: fastidious trumpets
Shrilling into the ruck; some trampled
Acres, parched, sodden, or blanched by sleet,
Stuck with strange-postured dead. Recall the wind's
Flurrying, darkness over the human mire.[10]

They bespoke doomsday and they meant it by
God, their curved metal rimming the low ridge.
But few appearances are like this. Once
Every five hundred years a comet's
Over-riding stillness might reveal men
In such array, livid and featureless,
With England crouched beastwise beneath it all.[11]

These extracts owe a good deal to the reveries of a bookish child playing at soldiers (he can be encountered again in *Mercian Hymns*). The question raised is not whether this is a proper source for poetry (which of course it is: take it where you find it) but what the grown man adds to the child's intensity of response. Critics anxious to assert Hill's complex moral awareness might care to note the element of indulgence here: the mannered, costumed diction – with its rhetorical imperatives ('Recall', 'Recall') and fustian precision ('such') and the relished consonants (the hard *c*s in particular) allows an aestheticisation of violence of a kind which is widespread by other means in our own intensely visual period (as witness for instance, in popular form, the 'strangely postured' yet strangely glamourised dead in the closing tableau of the Battle of Camlann in John Boorman's Arthurian film *Excalibur*). This was also something a slightly earlier poetic observer, Keith Douglas (whose reputation a famous essay by Hill did much to raise),[12] noted in himself in his poem 'How to Kill' [13] and in his prose account of the North African campaign, *Alamein to Zem Zem*.[14] In 'Funeral Music' the exact identity of the poems' speakers – Suffolk, Worcester, Rivers, Geoffrey Hill (or 'Geoffrey Hill') – seems less significant than the imaginative access created by poetry 'caught between dramatic monologue and lyric meditation',[15] as Neil Corcoran neatly puts it: a culture which the poet knows but does not entirely inhabit is, allegedly, the participant in and the producer of the work. The poems' moral ambiguity, produced by the meeting of an intense sensory relish with real and horrific historical events, produces a strange air of moral luxuriousness. The conscientiousness for whose exercise Hill is famous seems to become a displayed attribute of the aesthetic instead of its moral underpinning. The further dimension of the poet's own self-mistrust can also seem part of the repertoire. This must surely be quite contrary to Hill's wishes, given his recourse both when interviewed and in the essay 'Our Word Is Our Bond' to Pound's insistence that 'The poet's job is to *define* and yet again define till the detail of surface is in accord with the root in justice'.[16] The problem apparent both in 'Funeral Music' and more intrusively in the Holocaust poem 'September Song' has been discussed with some delicacy by John Bayley in his essay, 'The Tongue's Satisfactions', where he describes 'September Song' as a way of dealing with a difficulty overcome 'at the cost of writing a poem whose "problem" in being what it is seems more important to the poet than the poem itself'.[17] It can appear that the issue is not so much that justice be seen to be done as that Hill should be seen doing it, and that the result is a sort of moral dandyism. It seems to seek the reader's admiration in a context where the posture of the poet, for all the sincerity of his anxieties, should be secondary to the event in view. In 'Funeral Music' 4, the speaker reflects:

> ...Averroës, old heathen,
> If only you had been right, if Intellect
> Itself were absolute law, sufficient grace,
> Our lives could be a myth of captivity
> Which we might enter: an unpeopled region
> Of ever-fallen snow, a palace blazing
> With perpetual silence as with torches.[18]

Corcoran, a scrupulously even-handed critic, argues that the poems of 'Funeral Music' set in 'mutually undermining relationship dictions drawn from opposed and antagonistic areas of experience; barbarisms against civilities; mimetic abrasions against oracular eloquence...'[19] This is to paraphrase Hill's own description of 'Funeral Music' as 'a florid grim music broken by grunts and shrieks'.[20] Corcoran goes on:

> Hill's sequences are as remote from Donald Davie's neo-Augustan recipes for purity of diction as is conceivable; the mixed dictions and registers are an attempt to ensure that the poet does not shirk confrontation and explanation, but that at the same time he continuously undermines any propensity in himself to become a 'connoisseur of blood'.[21]

But doesn't the poet protest too much? The 'mixed diction' of the address to Averroës puts in the speaker's mouth a wincing familiarity ('old heathen') which the context makes more appropriate to the kind of belle-lettristic hearty whose remote but button-holeable acquaintance would also include 'Kit' Marlowe, 'Will' Shakespeare and Good Queen Bess. The note is false. What is really at stake here is the chance to deploy the brilliant and alarming closing image – a winter palace of art, where ethics gives place to aesthetics, somewhere morally inadmissible yet far more imaginatively compelling than the pasteboard of 'old, unhappy, far-off things' behind which it has been smuggled into the poem. Clive Wilmer, in a clear and judicious essay, has remarked of 'Funeral Music' that 'One is apparently left with the insight that, whether one lives in doubt or faith, the human condition remains the same, so that one's system of belief simply articulates the dis-ease of that condition.'[22] This would seem to be a clear if rather elevated description of a conservative temperament – a pessimism whose recognition of the need for endurance has turned almost to love of the predicament itself. Whatever the poet's intent, the result of 'Funeral Music' is something like history-as-pornography.

Given that Hill refers so frequently to the dead (the word 'dead' occurs twenty-three times in his 1961 debut *For the Unfallen* alone) it might be superfluous to wonder who actually lives in his version of England. Its ancient battlefields are understandably empty (though loud with remembered fury), but its other landscapes seem almost equally bare of the living. There are solitary individuals, and the poet's eerily fastidious voices, but rarely a crowd or a community and never a sense of *belonging* to anything beyond the rarefied 'platonic' and largely exclusive sense of England on which, for example, the sequence 'An Apology for the Revival of Christian Architecture in England' tends to dwell. Paradoxically, Hill, who has affirmed that he views poetry as sensuous art, seems to lack a sense of the particular both in 'Funeral Music' and elsewhere, such as in the 'Soliloquies' in *King Log*:

> Recall, now, the omens of childhood:
> the nettle-clump and the elder-tree;
> The stones waiting in the mason's yard:
>
> Half-recognised kingdom of the dead:
> A deeper landscape lit by distant
> Flashings from their journey...[23]

There is a swift movement here from an occasion of contemplation familiar in Edward Thomas into a 'deeper landscape' which Hill doesn't substantiate. Not to do so might be legitimate if the poet doesn't know what the landscape consists of, but the tone of the lines suggests that unlike us he's probably in the know. Perhaps the thinness suits him better. It is hard to agree with Andrew Waterman's contention that much of Hill's poetry offers 'sensuous intellection healing the "dissociation of sensibility" Eliot talked about';[24] particularly since nearby, discussing 'Te Lucis Ante Terminum', he refers to Hill's 'finding graphic sensuous imagery for

[an] abstract concept',[25] thus reinstating the very division he has credited Hill with overcoming. But Waterman's remarks raise a fundamental point about Hill, over which readers are always likely to divide. Some will find him a poet of achieved sensuousness, while others will think that his work has more to do with the image of sensuousness known to an powerful literary *will*, which must often make do with the idea rather than the enactment:

> What I lost was not a part of this.
> The dark-blistered foxgloves, wet berries
> Glinting from shadow, small ferns and stones,
>
> Seem fragments, in the observing mind,
> Of its ritual power.[26]

If the reader wonders why Hill's poems often read like synopses for more copious works, the question also arises of why, as Waterman says: 'The human content of Hill's poetry tends to be given elaborately remote contexts: King Offa's Mercia and other recesses of history; religious concepts abstruse or arcane; the cryptic love of a fictive poet, "Sebastian Arrurruz"...'[27] This is not to doubt the legitimacy of the poet's literary, historical and religious preoccupations, which are anyway only in part voluntary; nor the legitimacy of the various mediating devices of voice and period which have been so important in the modernist repertoire; but it can seem that only with the help of flickering torchlight do we avoid noticing the gaps where the people ought to be.

As Waterman puts it, *Mercian Hymns* is 'less intensively wrought, wider-ranging, more sportive'[28] than the rest of Hill's work, though you wouldn't call it frivolous exactly. It is also the book where the first person seems closest to the poet himself. Less a narrative than a set of emblems, the poem allows the solitary child to leak imaginatively into the figure of Offa, a legend whom the adult poet synthesises from the ruined fragments of his regal history. So perfectly does the child fit the familiar view of the poet as a sickly, gifted oddity that Hill forestalls satire by anticipating it:

> my rich and desolate childhood. Dreamy, smug-faced,
> sick on outings – I who was taken to be a king of
> some kind, a prodigy, a maimed one.[29]

The child-figure provides a commentary on history, on the myth that surmounts it and on the fictive nature of art: out of such banal details – 'sick on outings' – a legendary figure can be constructed. And looked at from a different perspective, the miniature but potent obsessions and rituals of the child are both banal and strange, absurd and eerie:

> After school he lured Ceolred, who was sniggering with fright, down to the old quarries, and flayed him. Then, leaving Ceolred, he journeyed for hours, calm and alone, in his private derelict sandlorry named *Albion*.[30]

Just as, in the space of the imagination, the child partakes of a past which shades into legend, so Offa is felt to emerge, fleetingly yet authoritatively, into the Midlands of the present. His is another version of the Matter of England, and since Hill's poem tends at once to relish pastness and to collapse chronological time, Offa is driven by combustion, an engineering-industrial 'overlord of the M5' (i). He is 'contractor to the desirable new estates' (i); a 'best-selling brand', 'a syndicate' (ii); a plumbing contractor (xii); buried by 'Merovingian car-dealers' (xxvii); leaving behind 'frail ironworks rusting in the thorn-thicket' (xxviii), plus 'coins for his lodging and traces of red mud' (xxx). In the thickets of the poem, with his child-poet-companion, he is also the means for a rhapsody on greatness and decay and the chance survival of resonant odds and ends – the coins, the shadow of the dyke in the earth, the 'red mud' of a sandstone landscape. These 'workings' of time as ever excite Hill's sense of the workings of the imagination, a faculty which must discover a sense of necessity in any pretext, affirming even as it denies. Waterman remarks: 'That the grandest worldly show is passing, is an awareness Hill utters incisively as Shelley's "Ozymandias".'[31] But the transitory is given an eternal aspect in *Mercian Hymns*. In it the note of history is heard in perpetual decay, done but not finished. All the evidence of Hill's work suggests that he would be more than averagely contemptuous of the Heritage industry, but his too is an intransitive world, as the poem's numerous lists suggest. It enlists our presence without permitting us to live there. Where Larkin finds it almost beyond him to substantiate an English past, and Hughes wants to disqualify history from 'real' time, Hill (in what is by far his best book), rather than evade the difficulty, brandishes the paradox of England. It won't lie down, but it seems to be dead.

II

DIFFERENT CLASS

4. Tony Harrison: *Showing the Working*

The apparent contradictions from which Tony Harrison's achievement springs, and by which it is driven, present themselves with emblematic neatness. He is a classicist from the working class; a writer of considerable scholarship seeking a mass audience in the theatre and, more spectacularly, on television; a poet of great technical accomplishment whose work insists that it is speech rather than page-bound silence; above all, perhaps, a poet continually troubled by the knowledge that the gift which enables him to speak for his class is what separates him from it. These shaping tensions have bred Harrison's conviction that poetry 'is not something I can take for granted';[1] hence, perhaps, the scale and ambition of his work.

Aside from his theatre writing, two features insist on being present in any discussion of Harrison's poetry. The first and most obvious is his examination and dramatisation of the relationships between language, class and power. The second is the kind of poem Harrison has produced increasingly in the last decade or so – the large, deliberately public poem. This may use personal resources to address a national and cultural crisis (*V.*), or the issue of artistic dissent (*The Blasphemers' Banquet*), or war (*The Gaze of the Gorgon*). These are only a small sample from the massive though welcoming Harrison canon, but they are perhaps the most prominent works. Like his *School of Eloquence* sonnets, these poems require the reader to give thought to language itself, and, more precisely, to consider what is entailed in a poet's embrace of a public role. Is there an artistic cost in going public?

Living in contemporary Britain produces a curious sense of double vision (and voice) where language is concerned. On the one hand enlightened educational practice has sought for over twenty years, with the support of the Bullock Report,[2] to emphasise the validity of so-called variations from so-called Standard English and Received Pronunciation. Yet in many parts of society a conviction (and sometimes an aggressive assertion) persists that some kinds of English are less equal than others and that the apparent supremacy of a particular class variant of spoken English reflects an inherent value-relationship. The present situation has, of course, a history – one dramatically apparent in the repression of working-class politics and publishing in the early nineteenth century, though the decisive identification of language with class needs to be sought as far back as the Middle Ages.

That such matters can go unacknowledged by advocates of the "standard" form is an indication that in this sphere as elsewhere, class advantage has been naturalised. Linguistic snobbery is not the problem of the UK alone, and wherever it occurs its economic origins can be uncovered. Just as money is both a form of exchange and of exclusion, so too is the prior universal medium of language. The linguistic have-nots, as Harrison records, are 'those/Shakespeare gives the comic bits to: prose!'[3] As is also well-known, Harrison's resistance to this exclusion order ends in paradox: the scholarship boy's revenge on his linguistic detractors seems to leave the revenger as remote from those he loves as from his opponents. It is also the case that "enemies" will form much of his audience – a subtextual point in 'O Moon of Mahagonny!',[4] which is set among radical chic habitués of the Broadway theatre.

Significantly, a large proportion of the best work in *The School of Eloquence* is taken up with the poet's relationship with his parents, especially his father. This is not so much vexed as baffled, muffled, silenced – an Oedipal conflict never properly waged. The power of speech; linguistic mastery, as recommended by Arthur Scargill's father and Harrison's dumb uncle Harry, tireless brandisher of *Funk and Wagnall's* dictionary; the son's studies and his making of many books: none of this is a means of reconciliation or mutual understanding in the protagonists' lifetimes, though Harrison's art images the wish for healing and binding powers and is marked by the effort to explain and to show the empathy and affection which could not be told. The wish should not be taken for the deed: it is not true that as Stephen Spender claims, 'oppositions are reconciled on the level of the imagination in the poetry'.[5] These are the lines he quotes from 'Illuminations' II,

> and some days ended up all holding hands
> gripping the pier machine that gave you shocks.
> The current would connect. We'd feel the buzz
> ravel our loosening ties to one tense grip,
> the family circle, one continuous US!
> That was the first year on my scholarship
> and I'd be the one who'd make that circuit short.[6]

Even since beginning the sonnet sequence, Harrison has in a sense become an historical figure. The classically-educated scholarship student, the working-class self-improver admitted to the sphere of bourgeois manners and expectations in the grammar school, is becoming rarer by the day, while class distinctions are made both more complex and more severe. The beliefs which promulgated and sustained the idea of a classical education may either die away or entrench themselves with the status of living fossils among the privileged classes. And what seemed set to supersede the classics, namely a more expansive and less philologically-inclined humanist approach, has itself been increasingly besieged by the multiple claims of Theory on the one hand and the balder and no less absolute demands of finance-led vocationalism on the other. This prospect lends poignancy to Harrison's dilemmas. To think of them historically is to emphasise both their personal and their representative status. This perspective may also, as another look at Harrison's language suggests, indicate the necessarily and consciously rhetorical character of his literary endeavour, since nowadays inert and unexamined versions of the linguistic dialectic which is so urgent for him have, for example, become part of the *lingua franca* of youth culture as sold into the media.

As Blake Morrison has remarked, Harrison's utterance often draws attention to itself as working against the 'smooth' grain of tradition:

> If the metre and syntax sometimes seem strained, this is precisely Harrison's point: his poems let us know they have come up the hard way; they are written with labour, and out of the labouring classes, and on behalf of Labour Party aspirations.[7]

This is evident in the crowded 'gob-full' character of some of the sonnets when read aloud, and also by the deliberately strenuous recasting of the iambic line. Elsewhere, Morrison states that Harrison 'never lets us forget what a contrived and artificial activity poetry is',[8] and quotes the lines:

> I strive to keep my lines direct and straight
> And try to make connections where I can.[9]

Yet at the same time as Harrison's practice here may also seem to signify an effort towards the directness and truthfulness we like to think of as "natural", his ear and speaking voice emphasise the effortful, constructed quality of the poems. Poetry is *work* and Harrison is at pains in all areas of his writing to *show the working*. Not so much *Look: me Tarzan*, as *Listen: me rigorous*. His indisputable accomplishment – would a poet from another background be rewarded so often with that compliment, which offers admission to a club he doesn't want to join? – is accompanied by signs of what it takes to achieve it. This deserves emphasis, in order to avoid confusing the strengths of Harrison's poems with a kind of higher authenticity which they cannot in fact possess. And just as it would not do to commend Harrison's "naturalness" against the artifice of tradition, so it is unsatisfactory to claim, as Morrison does, in a comment echoed by Stephen Spender, that *Continuous* 'repeatedly proves [the] effort to be worthwhile by discovering "connections" which transcend the labour and become love'.[10] To do this is to disarm the poems of the contradictions from which they earn their power. The term 'transcend' suggests an over-world, an elsewhere beyond the political, a marriage of art and 'the natural', to which the poems may be thought to aspire and in which their struggle finds fulfilment through liberation from or denial of its own causes. Even sympathetic readers like Morrison seem obliged to introduce such a substitute vocabulary. In her educational edition *Permanently Bard*, Carol Rutter, a markedly enthusiastic and well-informed advocate of Harrison's poems, employs one of Harrison's figures of speech against what appears to be the mood of the poems:

> ...it is useful to keep in mind the image Harrison invents in 'Wordlists I' of a gauge, one end marked 'words', the other "wordlessness" with an arm swinging between them going 'almost ga-ga'. Harrison's poetry isn't made up of contradictions. It is made up of points upon a gauge. It has a huge range and tolerance.[11]

But the gauge itself is an image of contradiction, strain, the competition of forces to which the poems are subject. (The gauge in 'Wordlists I' is also a half-buried phallic image,[12] as are the 'liana' and Labienus's 'flaming sword' in 'Me Tarzan').[13] That is to say, the contradictions are *experienced internally*. Rutter herself suffers something analogous when, elsewhere in *Permanently Bard*, she both condemns the division between high and low culture imposed 'by the mindlessness of teachers' and, while examining 'Thomas Campey and the Copernican System',[14] disposes of the work of popular novelists, such as Hall Caine, Marie Corelli and Ouida by means of a sneer of punctuation, as ' "literature" '. The point is not that you can't have things both ways – you can't avoid it – but that you need to acknowledge the strain involved in doing so, which is what the unified field approaches of Morrison and Rutter tend, knowingly or not, to avoid doing. The faith they imply in the liberating power of learning and literature seems comparable to the process of disempowerment, distraction and sublimation carried out in the grammar school: as Harrison points out in 'Wordlists III', 'society's not like the OED.'[16]

Stephen Spender goes further, almost beyond the scope of the Morrisonian transcendent. Lighting on the phrase 'Poetry's the speech of kings',[17] he offers an amazing piece of humbug by proposing that since Harrison has pointed out his own lack of literary ancestry it is interesting to think of him as a changeling, a royal Shakespearean child like Perdita, brought up among the peasants. Spender remarks:

> Despite his insistence on dialect, slang, obscenities and tags of abbreviations in his poetry, the tone is that of the aristocracy, of imagination and intellect.[18]

This is the English liberal intelligentsia at a loss to account for an equality it once claimed to encourage, and consequently falling back on fairy tale. As Luke Spencer has argued, Harrison's effort is between an attempt to 'fashion truly oppositional meanings out of fundamentally bourgeois establishment poetic forms'[19] – which are both to be found, and both potentially to be recreated, within the sphere of artifice. The multiple voices Harrison admits to the poems – the literary, the demotic, the vaudevillian, the quoted, the reported, the magisterial, the working-class, the young (*'Ah bloody can't ah've gorra Latin prose'*)[20] and the old, as well as those not heard, who occupy 'the silence round all poetry'[21] with the *'tusky tusky'*[22] of their pikes – all occur within literary (as well as social and political) history – specifically after Browning and Eliot, not in some phantom, resolving realm of The Imagination. The literariness (and the resulting discomfort) of Harrison's incorporation of his parents' language is emphasised when in 'The Queen's English'[23] his father picks out a book of dialect verse for him. Equally, Harrison may ruefully note the directness and sincerity of his father's verse epitaph for the poet's mother ('Book Ends', II)[24] but he also knows that it is 'stylistically appalling'. Harrison's own efforts at such truth to feeling produce brilliant successes like 'Continuous',[25] but this poem of memory, familiar in mode if not accomplishment, is just as literary and as "feigning" in its way as the highly complex opening sonnet from *The School of Eloquence*, 'On Not Being Milton', which seems deliberately to distance the reader with its anthology of voices, range of reference, vocabulary and method.

What about feeling? Rick Rylance has commented in a discussion of 'Marked with D.' that Harrison's writing

> is technically accomplished and verbally dextrous, but its primary impact is emotional...it bids for sentiment through its virtuosity, though the heart strings it plucks are familiar ones, and some find these poems clichéd. This is partly because the poem invites a response which professionally we are not accustomed to give. It is populist in cast, draws upon the sentimentality of popular entertainment, and wants to make us cry. This embarrasses the tough, conceptualised manner of much recent

> criticism, which has not wished to attend to such effects. Indeed, it has been suspicious of frank appeals to emotion...[26]

Apart from his appealingly condensed account of the affectively spavined condition he discerns in academic criticism, it is interesting that Rylance assumes that the readership for Harrison's poems, as for his own essay, will be a professional one. Were this true, it would make nonsense of Harrison's writing, which is compelled to walk a line between isolated literary (not academic) "professionalism" and at any rate the *idea* of a general audience. But the problem of the poem, if there is a problem, is something Harrison experiences, not an impersonal matter of the intersection of cultural energies: Harrison may not choose his material, but he certainly seeks to shape it to his dissatisfied will. In place of the studied mediation to be found in Gray's 'Elegy', which stands behind Harrison's epic revision of his own central themes in *V.*, there is an emotional glut in 'Marked With D.', a readiness to speak of feeling *as a non-speaker might*, i.e. valuing sincerity over respectability or decorum. When this gets written up, it can certainly resemble sentimentality:

> When the chilled dough of his flesh went in an oven
> not unlike those he fuelled all his life,
> I thought of his cataracts ablaze with Heaven
> and radiant with the sight of his dead wife,
> light streaming from his mouth to shape her name,
> 'not Florence and not Flo but always Florrie'.
> I thought how his cold tongue burst into flame
> but only literally, which makes me sorry,
> sorry for his sake there's no Heaven to reach.
> I get it all from Earth my daily bread
> but he hungered for release from mortal speech
> that kept him down, the tongue that weighed like lead.
>
> The baker's man that no one will see rise
> and England made to feel like some dull oaf
> is smoke, enough to sting one person's eyes
> and ash (not unlike flour) for one small loaf.[27]

The embarrassment and discomfort, the unease about the fitting of manner to matter, to which Harrison exposes us (an affordable risk, perhaps, in a sequence where various strategies are tried) has an obvious location in the disruption of the iambic end-stresses with the trochaic 'Florrie' and 'sorry', which reproduce the bathos resulting from an amateur versifier's good intentions. As well as this, though, Harrison inserts the grotesque, terrible and extremely artful image of the cataracts in order to embody the hopes of the hereafter alongside the destruction of the flesh. Bizarrely, Spender claims to detect here 'a certain literalness of imagination [which] may be where Tony Harrison is nearest to being a working-class artist'.[28] Spender finds affinities with Keats, though the poem harks back further, to Milton's sonnet 'Methought I saw My Late Espoused Saint', specifically 'I trust to have/Full sight of her in Heav'n without restraint'. Harrison refers to this poem elsewhere, in 'Confessional Poetry', a poem dedicated to Jeffrey Wainwright, in which he responds to his fellow poet's doubts about the truthfulness of his (Harrison's) methods, concluding: 'I'm guilty, and the way I make it up 's / in poetry, and that much I confess',[29] lines which clearly advertise their own necessary ambiguity. The structure of feeling in 'Marked with D.' is complicated by Harrison's role as intermediary between his parents and the audience, and by the gulf that opens up under the religious forms of his father's longings (the kind of belief recorded in *The Uses of Literacy*).[30] At the same time, as well as conveying the absoluteness of his own disbelief, Harrison lends a horrifying and somewhat Jacobean literalism to belief itself (see, for example, 'The Nuptial Torches').[31] Furthermore, he brings a combination of adult distance and of tenderness to the contemplation of his parents, who under his gaze seem somehow childlike and thus utterly separate from the poet, for all his respectful sympathy. These complications of attitude are sustained by the juxtaposition of the manifestly poetic – 'chilled dough', 'ablaze with Heaven', 'mortal speech', 'the tongue that weighed like lead' and all the Biblical overtones of prayer, Pentecostal tongues of fire, the bread of life and so on – with demotic verb forms like 'went in an oven', 'I get it all', 'made to feel'. There is also the abruptness of the switch to the quatrain with its offensively and offendedly 'finished' image of loaf, smoke and ash. (This echoes Wainwright's nearly contemporary poem, '1815',[32] with its description of the industrial dead as 'common as smoke' – which sounds like a rather Harrisonian pun: 'common as smoke/muck'.) By the close of the poem the earlier wrong note (the 'Florrie'/'sorry' rhyme) is accompanied by a sense of waste, but by anger and horror too. The poem's artfulness, and the artful departures from decorum, certainly do make an emotional appeal (it might be truer to say that they create an emotional climate from which the readers find it hard to extract themselves and in which the poet permanently resides), but the appeal is not to simple sadness or sympathy, nor the generalised assent of an unexamined populism. The clash of idioms, feelings and tones demonstrates both a fury with art itself and an understanding that art is the only articulation this fury can have, the alternative being silence. Harrison's 'ludding Morphemes'[33] cannot escape the claims of art or of history. Quite how Anthony Thwaite, another enthusiastic reader of Harrison, can refer to the sonnets as 'Harrison's central achievement on coming to terms with society, class and language'[34] remains unclear: 'coming to terms' suggests an accommodation, which is the last thing on the poet's mind.

This poem necessarily raises larger historical questions to accompany its personal grief. It is striking that of the two major features of working-class culture found hand in hand at the beginning of the industrial age – religious belief and political organisation – it should be religion that persists into the lives the poem recalls. Despite the warm maternal presence, family life, home and hearth – the original world of the sonnets – feels as cold as a room with an underfed fire. It is monochrome; without expectation. There's nothing there you could call beautiful – except, intermittently the cadences of the poems themselves, and the poems are inextricably linked to the very conditions which, in competition with 'litter-chewer',[35] continue to shape the poet's imagination. Class, lack of money, lack of education and lack of power, all go to produce the context in which Harrison was brought up and which he so insistently remembers (though of course these conditions produce particulars, not inert generalities marked 'Class' or 'Power'). There seems to be little in critical writing on Harrison to date which touches on its strain of desperate, unaffiliated sourness, which is the near-identical cousin of his tenderness and is just as important to its imaginative climate. The heat-exchange between love and alienation, and between understanding and distance, is matched by a dominant imagery of fire and cold (recurring in *The Gaze of the Gorgon*).[36] These extremes are brilliantly run together in the personal dialectic of 'Continuous' itself. Here Harrison assembles Cagney's *White Heat*, the chill of a choc-ice, the feel of his father's hands cupped around his own, the durability of a ring that has survived the fires of cremation, and the absurd resemblance of a cinema organist's lift to the moving platform which bears a coffin to the crematorium flames. This is spectacular work of the imagination, for it satisfies the longing for the consolations of closure while denying the residual sense of coherence and shape 'out there' on which the practice would seem to rely. 'Continuous', like 'Marked with D.', succeeds in the teeth of contradiction, rendering its materials coherent by responding to their enormous outward pressure with the counterbalancing and somehow icy grace of Harrison's combined lyric and dramatic skills.

Harrison's intently political scrutiny of his upbringing leads us to feel that his own home life (the speechless Uncle Harry aside) had little to say of politics. His own reference to E.P. Thompson's *The Making of the English Working Class*, the classic account of grassroots radicalism, insurrection, self-education and free-born Englishness, finds no equivalent in the poems' immediate prehistory, which is firmly located in the home, with some references to Harrison's education or to work, but rarely to the larger world, except the end of the Second World War. What we almost overhear in the surrounding silence is the fear of losing the not very much you have by asking for more – one of the roots of working-class small-'c' conservatism. This is the converse of class solidarity: an imprisonment whose victims seem barely aware of it. As Douglas Dunn wrote later of a deeply demoralised community, 'You hardly notice that you have grown too old to cry out for change.'[37] Some of what we do hear is reactive – the half-spoken racism of the poet's father as his home district sees an influx of Asian immigrants. Luke Spencer takes Harrison to task for not making his own opposition to racism plainer, but this seems unsubtle.[38] Having dedicated the opening poem of *The School of Eloquence* to two Frelimo activists, Harrison may feel able to rely on the reader to follow where the poems lead, including the contemplation of abhorrent and ignorant attitudes which should hardly require comment. Indeed, the silence around *this* subject may be a more eloquent indication of the pain that goes with filial love than any merely corrective statement could offer. The poems are not sermons.

The sense of exposure and anxiety which partly characterises the life from which the sonnets emerge tells us of a history "from below" which will be familiar to many observers of the present day. It reminds us that one of Beveridge's Five Giants to be overthrown by the welfare state was *Ignorance*, and that what has replaced it has not been *Knowledge*. There is an understandable wish among many readers to find a poet not just for "our times", but for "our side". It is his clear-eyed, unsparing approach which makes Harrison's sonnets of value in this regard: we see injustice visited on the spirit, and not the flesh only.

V. was the first and remains the most important of the poems in which Harrison has attempted to carry poetry into the awareness of a wide, non-specialist public. It succeeded both in attracting an audience when it was broadcast and in producing a vigorous and acrimonious debate of the sort reserved for sex, politics and the use of four-letter words, three of the great Anxieties around which England continues to conduct its cultural arguments.

Harrison himself expressed doubts about whether *V.*'s detractors had actually acquainted themselves properly with the work; much of the debate was conducted on the one hand by its literary advocates and on the other by its political critics. Whatever the quality of the discussion, the poem is now as nearly canonical as the contemporary can hope to be, and the result of the row might be described as the literary equivalent of an away draw.

To say that language is foregrounded in *V.* is an understatement. Indeed, during the controversy, all that was visible and audible to the poem's opponents was its emphasis on "bad" language – the 'fuck' and 'cunt' of 'inarticulate' spraycan discourse. The 'dreadful schism in the British nation'[39] could appear to be four letters wide. In this respect *V.* succeeded in using the issue of linguistic propriety to emphasise existing social divisions: there are strong feelings in Britain, partly about what may be said, and just as significantly about how and by whom the saying may be done. What the controversy to some extent obscured was *V.*'s readiness to plead for incorporation and unity, despite the antagonistic thrust of much of its language and energy.

The title itself gathers a set of contending meanings: the v-sign as insult; the v-sign as affirmation of solidarity in victory; the national unity embodied in wartime by the notoriously anti-working class Churchill and required in the collective "war socialist" struggle against Nazism – a matter of ready mythology then and since; the *v* of "versus", of being opposed, whether in a sporting fixture or in politics (which may in complex and fissiparous ways be the same thing); the Biblical and also general literary abbreviation for "verse"; or (again) Burke's 'dreadful schism in the British nation'. That so many significant social features and conflicts should congregate under the one-letter sign provides a thought-provoking example of the polysemantic scope of language, of which Harrison is so strongly and anxiously aware and which he so frequently explores. One might add that the meanings of the title *V.* are related as much by contiguity as by cause: they "add up" to a metaphorical unity which seems to point us back towards the dissolution of common cause. This contradiction is part of the poem as a whole, and in fact it resists the poem's own imagined conclusiveness (by exposing the fact that gestures at eternity are by habit conservative). The divisions of the title are as much suffered in as dramatised by the poem.

Harrison's armoury of formal disruptions, bringings-to-light and uncomfortable emphases is fully deployed from the outset. Luke Spencer has pointed out that as well providing semantic controversy, the poem assaults the iambic line.[40]

Next millennium you'll have to search quite hard
to find my slab behind the family dead,
butcher, publican, and baker, now me, bard,
adding poetry to their beef, beer and bread.[41]

The stress pattern marked above also has ambiguities. Are the last two syllables of 'millennium' and of 'family' to be elided, as seems likely in speech? If so, what about 'poetry', to which Harrison would give full articulation? Even though the home metre of *V.* is the iambic pentameter, a metrical analyst might argue that the third and fourth lines at least approach the limits of metrical acceptability at which, in Saintsbury's phrase 'the ear must decide'.[42] The third line is especially striking. As Spencer remarks, it 'is irregular to the point of a quantum difference from anything Gray would have countenanced or been capable of'.[43] It seems more nearly related to alliterative than post-Shakespearean verse. We may assume deliberation on Harrison's part: his metrical strenuousness is a strategic feature in the repertoire of a poet who assuredly knows his numbers. The effect is to insist that we read the lines aloud. Arguably, given 'the silence round all poetry', the lines *exist* to be spoken, just as much as Harrison's verse plays. Speaking them means trying Harrison's Leeds accent, feeling the crowding stresses and hearing the deliberate articulation of strongly consonantal, alliterative sounds.

From the outset, then, the poem exists in debate with its famous model. Gray's 'Elegy Written in a Country Churchyard' is the epitome both of the English anthology poem and of iambic control. Decorum is infringed by demotic as well as metrical means – the unpoetic 'search quite hard'; 'I'll not go short',[44] with its northern verb contraction and savour of commonsense Yorkshire materialism. The discomfort of the opening, for all its swaggering bluntness, indicates that there is also contention among the tones and idioms that constitute Harrison's poetic voice – a continuation of the dramatic practice of the sonnets.

The second stanza eases the metrical tension somewhat:

With Byron three graves on I'll not go short
of company, and Wordsworth's opposite.
That's two peers already, of a sort...[45]

By one of those marvellous coincidences of which Harrison's work and life seem full, his intended grave-neighbours on Beeston Hill are local tradesmen sharing the names of the great Romantic poets –

the aristocratic rebel, radical and exile, and his humbler compatriot, the youthful revolutionary who came home in the end to Toryism. The whole tradition of equality and similarity in death is raised for ironical consideration, from Shirley's assertion that 'Sceptre and Crown / Must tumble down /And in the dust be equal made/ with the poor crooked scythe and spade' [46] to Roger McGough's 'but all these divishns /arnt reely fair/ look at the cemtery/ no streemin there'.[47] There's something gleeful, a graveyard glee, in Harrison's writing at this point, and he plays an elaborate joke on Gray's vision of order and permanence. Where Gray writes,

> Each in his narrow cell forever laid,
> The rude forefathers of the hamlet sleep [48]

Harrison removes the false floor from under Beeston Hill:

> and we'll all be thrown together if the pit,
>
> whose galleries once ran beneath this plot,
> causes the distinguished dead to drop
> into the rabblement of bone and rot,
> shored slack, crushed shale, smashed prop.[49]

The qualifying clause, dropped as if it were merely information into its sentence and at the beginning of a stanza – run-ons across stanza-breaks are rare in Gray – parodies decorum by inflating it and departing from it. From here we move through a pun partly about euphemism ('distinguished') into a vivid bit of linguistic reclamation from the sixteenth century. According to *The Shorter Oxford English Dictionary*, 'rabblement' is encountered in 1545, meaning 'rabble...in various senses'; and also, more rarely, from 1590, 'riotous conduct'. To this mixture of sudden metrical elegance and wildly indecorous matter, the deftly conceived riotous assembly of the official dead and the pit's lost casualties, Harrison adds the spondaic piledriver-blows of the last line, which are as insistently physical a noise, and as bluntly concrete (as it were) a set of properties as could be mustered for the occasion: 'shored slack, crushed shale, smashed prop' – not the kind of thing Gray soils his hands on.

As Harrison reveals the "workings" underneath the graveyard, so he requires us to read the workings of his verse. His ingenuity is matched by his insistence on our noticing it. It's a kind of professional and political pride which is in part the product, at once anxious and self-delighting, of being one of those whom tradition 'gives the comic bits to... prose!' Ever alert to social gradation, Harrison builds a hierarchy into the strata of the poem, using rhyme to chart and unearth it:

The language of this graveyard ranges from
a bit of Latin for a former Mayor
or those who laid their lives down at the Somme,
the hymnal fragments and the gilded prayer,

how people 'fell asleep in the Good Lord',
brief chisellable bits from the good book
and rhymes, whatever length they could afford,
to CUNT, PISS, SHIT and (mostly) FUCK![50]

These lines seem to set out a unified field, where the worthy, along with those unnamed who died in battle, and those fondly recalled who died in bed, are all found together, and all similarly insulted by the spraypainted slogans. But the rhymes work against this grain. The Mayor is singled out by rhyming with 'prayer', while the war dead of West Yorkshire (which suffered as cruelly as Ulster in July 1916) are matched with an anonymous preposition, 'from', part of the poor bloody infantry of language without which nothing can happen but which is considered anonymous, as though en masse, like the dead (even when named) on war memorials. Further, 'Lord'/'afford' is hardly an accident, marking as it does the traditional association (in spite of Scriptural advice to the contrary) between wealth and access to Heaven. Altogether more blatant is the 'book'/'fuck' rhyme, whose interlocking joint of "good" and "bad" language looks forward to the arrival of the poet's skinhead doppelganger.

If the reader is unsettled by the detonations of the poem's beginning, this reflects the challenge the poem lays down to its author. On the one hand there is Harrison's aggressive pleasure in his skills, on the other the need for extreme alertness to the freight of historical and class associations carried by the material – in order to avoid accepting a social unity that doesn't exist. Noting that 'Harrison's dispirited political imagination...belongs to the 1980s', Terry Eagleton has suggested that what is at stake in *V.* is the choice 'between being pained primarily by oppression and being pained primarily by division and disunity – the difference, roughly, between radical and liberal'.[51] Eagleton awards wisdom in the case to the skinhead, who knows that 'the talk of "peace" and "unity" which so haunts his creator is in political terms an insulting mystification'. The distinctions Eagleton draws seem accurate. The humanist in Harrison is always likely to win out over the class warrior, especially in the context of a poem whose scale necessitates a kind of thematic carpentering by which the sonnets are untroubled. Faced with the challenge of scale, his love of form, point, epigram, shape and closure tend to the conservative. To say this may seem to insist on an over-simple connection between form and content, but Harrison's belief in direct mimesis is everywhere apparent in his work – from the local detail of its consonantal "concreteness" to its industrial remoulding of pentameter and sonnet form. To retain its radicalism, an epic might have to take more account of modernism and less of its audience. Even as we consider the multiple and often opposed meanings of the sign 'v', the poem is in the process of subordinating them to its own binding singularity. When the skinhead writes the poet's name on Harrison's parents' headstone, it is a means of dramatising both division and unity. The skinhead is the poet's other half – the irreconcilable member of the working-turned-underclass, the one who didn't get away, who can't tell Greek from French, whose fury rejects the evasions of poetry. Yet for all this ferocity, the poet remains the poem's primary speaker, with the last, resolving word. When he awakes, as it were, from political reverie, he assumes the competing voice into his own, making duality into unity. This procedure is reproduced throughout, on a universalising scale, so that a whole series of oppositions – white v. Asian, police v. pickets, man v. wife, Protestant v. Catholic, Communist v. Fascist, Left v. Right, soul v. body, heart v. mind – is gradually incorporated into a presiding awareness of time, with its 'vast, coal-creating forces'.[52]

This geophysical view is a source of awe and a sign of sure extinction, faced with which only love can offer a fleeting consolation, 'where opposites seem sometimes unified'.[53] Here the word-order itself suggests a rhetorical pressure away from "speech" towards "poetry", from the grinding here and now of politics (the skinhead's imagined epitaph is: *The cunts who lieth 'ere wor unemployed*)[54] towards secular humanist Wisdom. This, in closing, affirms, in the teeth of the skinhead's denial, that the poet really does still belong here in the graveyard and its community – 'if only', in the words of a poet with very different politics from Harrison's, 'that so many dead lie round'.[55]

5. Douglas Dunn: *Ideology and Pastoral*

I won't disfigure loveliness I see
With an avoidance of its politics.

DOUGLAS DUNN: 'Broughty Ferry'[1]

...by temperament I'm a quasi-mystical nature poet. I like nothing better than walking through the woods down by the shore thinking magical thoughts; yet here I am writing pamphlets about the poll tax, political verses and all the rest of it. You get a bit impatient with yourself: it feels like a kind of *trahison des clercs*, compromising the literary values to which you'd otherwise devote your life.[2]

DOUGLAS DUNN: 'Dimensions of the Sentient' (interview)[2]

'The only answer is to live quietly, miles away'[3] is one of Douglas Dunn's most striking lines. The truth of its proposal would of course depend on the question asked. The immediate context is the issue of how to live in the culture of commerce and/or mindless indolence which the younger, often bleakly moralistic Dunn saw as the residuum, and the ambition, of a degenerate materialism. Yet as Dunn or his persona, acknowledges elsewhere, by living in Hull he is already as far away as England will allow him to get, and the world persists in pursuing him even there. The result is a permanent standoff between private life and political engagement – a state of affairs which has become a strategic necessity for his poetry. Throughout Dunn's work the desire for privacy, peace and quiet, for liberty to address seemingly personal or local concerns (and through them, as 'life's accomplice'[4] to address life itself) is accompanied by an equally strong desire to publish his whereabouts and to see in this public retirement a response to more general conditions.

Having it both ways is one of the functions of pastoral. While the poet may be 'miles away', nursing his pessimism or his garden, his seclusion is indicated by the large tricolour brandished from an upstairs window. To 'plant the bergamot' in the Marvellian sense is, of course, an inextricably social act.[5] A witty and clear-sighted commentator on himself, Dunn has provided the image of his work as a train shuttling back and forth between the stations of 'Social Responsibility and Romantic Sleep'.[6] He is by no means alone on this route, though other travellers might get off somewhere. Few manage the round trip, but for Dunn the argument it embodies is fundamental and permanent. Like his poems, his criticism has often returned to what seems to him, as to others, the vexed relationship between art and politics.

Having written elsewhere about political vision in Dunn's work,[7] in this essay I want to look at some problems which politics pose to his imagination. It's clear that like Tony Harrison, though in a more expansive if less texturally dramatic way, Dunn has done much to make apparent the unavoidable centrality of political subjects – class, power, history – in contemporary poetry. Yet it is also the case that Dunn's formation and loyalties require him to inhabit imaginative tensions which his work does not resolve and which it may prove unable to reformulate. It should be emphasised that this is not so much a criticism as a means of identifying the situation of Dunn's work. In a recent essay, 'Back and Forth: Auden and Political Poetry',[8] Dunn writes with sometimes startling clarity about the productive torsion between political commitment and its private sources and limitations in Auden's early work, before going on to examine the way in which Auden's spectacular assertion of traditional formal mastery seems to have been a necessary accompaniment to a withdrawal from radicalism:

> Ingenious lightness of verse established itself with a special prestige in his priorities as if an aboriginal verse artistry were in itself a haven from some of the political subjects expected of him and to which he was drawn in any case.[9]

There are certainly comparisons to be made between this process as visible in Auden and in the course of Dunn's own work. Robert Crawford, in his essay 'Secret Villager',[10] has remarked in a Scottish context on what he reads as the conservatism of Dunn's aesthetic in comparison with the experimentalism of modern Scots poets from MacDiarmid, through W.S. Graham, Edwin Morgan and Ian Hamilton Finlay. To say so, of course, implies no disparagement of artistry: Dunn's concern with form has been important in his artistic growth and success – notably in some of his most strongly political work, the 'Barbarian Pastorals' [11] and the related Scottish-based poems in the subsequent *St Kilda's Parliament*.[12] Equally, however, Dunn himself makes the connection between formality and political retrenchment, and goes on to quote the lines from 'Letter to Lord Byron' where Auden's 'left wing friends' accusingly describe his political destiny:

> Your fate will be to linger on outcast,
> A selfish pink old Liberal to the last.[13]

It is well known which of the contenders – Marx, Freud and God – won out in Auden's case. Unlike Auden, Dunn has never had the option of Christianity. While his work does not ignore matters of the spirit – some of his finest poems patrol the border of imagination and belief – he is continually, and not merely notionally, delivered back into society. The problems of his situation can be illustrated by his treatment of pastoral.

The American poet and critic Dave Smith, characterising Dunn's work for the readership of the American edition of the *Selected Poems*, wrote:

> Dunn was raised in a rural parish adjacent to the industrial Clyde River area of Glasgow. His feeling for a labor heritage feeds a poetry which is at first fiercely opposed to and at last subsumed by mainstream British tradition... [14]

This holds a good deal in a couple of interestingly estranging sentences, which make an effective blurb. But to unpack them a little tells a story about Dunn which may seem more loaded to a reader in the British Isles than to its American author. We shall return to the matter of Dunn's being subsumed into tradition, but first consider the places involved. By Dunn's account, Inchinnan, his home village in Renfrewshire, was not simply a parish next door to the city, but somewhere he saw as under growing threat of absorption by Glasgow – a familiar tale of postwar development:

> You've got to remember that a good deal of the population in Scotland lives in small towns or villages. But attention is always drawn to Glasgow and Edinburgh. There are some people in Scotland, myself included, who don't associate themselves with either. I was born and brought up quite near Glasgow, but I was brought up loathing it, because we always knew at some point it was going to move west and take our land, and it did...I don't like Glasgow. Never have done, never will do.[15]

In another interview he has eloquently remarked about Inchinnan:

> ...because it was in sight of heavy industry and close to Glasgow, I sensed the vulnerability of the place – time past, time present, and time to come. I don't think it functions in my poetry so much as pervades it.[16]

The notion of existing 'quietly, miles away' was surely fostered by such a threat to Eden. Certainly, while his work shows a good deal of working-class solidarity, the Scotland he dreams of is not citified and industrial but the rural and small-town Scotland which dominates his short stories [17] and was the subject of his television play, *Ploughman's Share*.[18] This Scotland is perhaps embodied in north-east Fife, where he has lived for many years and whose apparently kindly pressure of authentication-through-habituation can be felt in his most recent collections of poems, *Northlight* and *Dante's Drum-*

kit.[19] While some might see Dunn's address as a sign that he chooses the provinces (in his previous home, Hull, he was notoriously called a provincial poet by Morrison and Motion),[20] he himself appears to detect an Horatian amplitude, a way of holding particular life up close for relish and inspection. In 'Preserve and Renovate', for instance, a neighbour is seen gardening with a truly Protestant fastidiousness:

...that blade-paddled, tended, watered lawn
Fit for a naked nymph to dance upon,
Though no nymph has, or would dare disoblige
The kirky vision of his husbandry,
        Or get away with it,
    When, with his watchful pedantry,
He guards each moment of his dusk-grey privet.[21]

Dunn's recognition of a certain narrowness is inseparable from affection for the comedy of propriety, while the love of the exact particular – 'an etched fragrance/From rubbed-down paint, glass paper and the smell' – is held in common. Further on we learn that the gardener looks like the poet's father:

                    I could gnaw
At that facsimile for ever more;
        But I know who I lack,
    Not him, but that dead, distant doer
Who looked like him, who leads me back and back.

It is hardly accidental that the poem carries reminders of two famous early poems by Seamus Heaney, 'Digging' and 'Follower'.[22] The first celebrates the discovery of the poetic vocation seemingly to grown naturally from the tradition of life on the land as embodied by the poet's father, while the second resents this very connectedness as what seemed like riches begins to feel like confinement. Dunn's poem, the work of middle age (in contrast to Heaney's youth), is more complex than either. He has neither the inheritance to renovate nor the obstruction to kick against. His writing, like Tony Harrison's is what separates him from his father. The gardener 'would not understand' the poet's work; 'nor could my father', Dunn admits, even as he tries to explain (to himself as much as to the gardener or his own dead father) what he's about:

            It's what I do,
This risk of feeling, that the sweet and true
Might be preserved, presented by my hand
Among the many others who do this
For the same sake that is obedience to
Time and experience, for what is due
To being, to be life's accomplice.

The idea of turning back, in order to contemplate what old but unforgotten manners and pieties might offer, is clearly urgent for Dunn. There is something half-apologetic, like belated acknowledgement, in the quoted lines, whose roomy form has become inadequate to the charge of feeling they have to carry to the edge of sentimentality and, in the phrase 'life's accomplice', back again. With its perspective of middle age, its preoccupation with belonging, and with belonging understood at a local scale, 'Preserve and Renovate' leads the reader 'back and back', to see how Dunn has arrived at this uneasy blend of celebration and elegy.

A clear point of departure might be Dunn's good wishes as his departing neighbour in 'A Removal from Terry Street' sets off with an as-yet unemployed lawnmower: 'That man, I wish him well. I wish him grass.' Elsewhere in Terry Street, green spaces are preyed on by rapists or grazed by 'sad and captured' horses.[23] But the urbanised pastoral has another mood, expressed in the elaborately utopian 'The Garden' a set-piece from *The Happier Life*. Here the cradle Calvinist Dunn attempts to proselytise on behalf of an 'oppositional horticulture', building a faith of sorts on a disinclination to do more than clear a space for a deckchair in the jungle at the back of the house. This shady erotic indolence

> ...upsets, the neighbours say, all their decent
> Trimmings. 'Why not *do* something?' But this,
> like the *hortus mentis*, is not so untended.
>
> Here we are perfect. Metaphysical greenbirds
> Perch over sunlit leaves; our feet converse
> With the refreshing grass. And here I am
> A very old man of twenty-eight, glad
>
> Of this random perfection, and you, so still
> We are as islands on an island, everything
> Ebbing into green around us; we know
> Though this might look neglected, it might grow.[24]

The charm of this lies partly in the nods to Marvell, which are at this early stage delivered without any attempt to take on a Marvellian form; partly in the easy movement between the demotic and something more traditionally and spiritedly rhetorical; but especially in the insouciant association of indolence with growth and fertility and – it seems implied – with an ampler seriousness than mere activity could hope to attain, thus echoing Fontenelle's proposition in his *Discours sur la nature de l'eglogue* (1688) that pastoral poetry should present 'a concurrence of the two strongest passions, laziness and love'.[25] The problem of living in 'Ted Heath's Britain', glanced at earlier in the poem, seems easily shelved in this climate of pleasure. For all Dunn's sombre engagement with *lachrimae rerum*, the contemplation and indulgence of pleasure provides a strong countervailing sweetness. Music, cookery, drink, sex, art and the delights of place are used to furnish what he calls 'the pleasant side of history'.[26] The mixture of sensuality and erudition with which he approaches these enjoyments testifies to a Francophilia seemingly at odds with the severer realm of 'liquid work'[27] and 'the Protestant clerks of northern Europe in Hell'[28] to which he is equally in thrall. In one of his most ingenious and lighthearted poems, 'Ratatouille',[29] which is actually a recipe, originally published in the Women's Page of the *Glasgow Herald*, he makes a lengthy and hyperbolic analogy between cookery and the virtues of pacifism. The poem's blend of practical instruction and outrageous commonsense is, Dunn says, 'a sort of dream, which coincides/ With the pacific relaxations called/Preferred reality'. It's an appeal to the court of its own civilised humour for time off from history for good behaviour.

The ritual elements of 'The Garden' and 'Ratatouille' have an obvious comic function, but custom and even ceremony are important to Dunn's search for tolerant order and basic decency. When he thinks about right behaviour, the terms he uses are not just highly specific but at times intensely local. An elderly resident in 'The Terry Street Fusiliers' produces a similar half-exasperated mixture of irony and respect to the gardener in 'Preserve and Renovate':

> If Terry Street was attacked, he would defend us
> With the breadknife, jumping out from doorways.[30]

Less certain in tone is the now-discarded title poem from *The Happier Life*:

> ...Moderate
> And better ways prosper only in private;
> Men find their own and disaffiliate
> From all repulsiveness that makes them hate,
> Or should, rather than fight what makes them sick
> With speeches of a stylised politic.
> Wise apathy's a proper stance, aspiring
> To wry complacencies of the retiring –
> To villas by a lake, a silent farm,
> Or any mortgaged hut away from harm.[31]

Dunn can be heard dismantling this unsteady scaffolding with one hand even as he erects it with the other. The unhappy mixture of Augustan and Audenesque shows the difficulty of finding a public mode and a middle voice (contrast Michael Longley's version of Tibullus, 'Peace').[32] It is a problem he has repeatedly sought to face. Here Dunn's urgent quietism is a response to a problem embedded in a couple of the poem's more striking phrases: 'Society's a sham' and 'Community's a myth' – which may go some way to explaining why Dunn's occasional vision of revolt is safely historical. The speakers of 'Gardeners'[33] in their Barbarian Pastoral may have hanged His Lordship in the shade of the garden of his great house in Loamshire, but they did so in 1789. The 'Barbarian Pastorals' were written from a prophetic sense of Thatcherism to come, and the way the poems put the clock back is richly suggestive, but Dunn's work has never found a political future to match his dramatic grasp of the past – a point which might be less pressingly apparent if his rendering of consciousness paid a smaller subscription to realist modes.

Another garden poem from the 'Barbarian Pastorals', 'In the Grounds (Yorkshire, 1975)', which actually precedes 'Gardeners' in the collection, is rather more accommodating towards the gentry. Innocently trespassing with some companions in the grounds of Nun Appleton House (subject of an important poem by Marvell), Dunn seems here to speak *in propria persona*: the hostility is all coming from the 'frightened mandarins' who own the place and 'when we speak proclaim us barbarous/ And say we have no business with the rose'.[34] He manages to make his voice itself register the residual power of class distinction to work 'downwards' to discomfit even those who don't believe in such things (a survival more typical of rural settings, perhaps). Interestingly, though, he responds with sorrow and regret, rather than fury. How, then does he read the garden?

> Gently the grass waves, and its green applauds
> The justice, not of progress, but of growth.
> We walk as people on the paths of gods
> And in our minds we harmonise them both.

(The suspicion of redundancy in the last line is rather Harrisonian.) If this stanza reads as deeply ambivalent about its image of order – yes, this is a "literary" experience for the trespassers, but its significance doesn't end there – it's typical of Dunn's honesty that his uncertainty as well as his attraction and anxiety is felt to be present. There is a comparable contradiction in 'The Come-On', the sequence's manifesto, which is partly an angry rejection of class distinction as embodied in proprietary Oxbridge culture, and partly a vision of true inclusiveness:

> One day we will leap down, into the garden,
>   And open the gate – *wide, wide.*
> We too shall be kings' sons and guardians,
>   And then there will be no wall:
> Our grudges will look quaint and terrible.[35]

The solution – meritocracy? – seems strangely pale compared to the problem, and to the lovely 'grudge' which fuels Dunn's political writing. At bottom we can be sure that Dunn lacks the ruthlessness which anger would require to gain its redress. As befits a pacifist ('In no war would I fight'),[36] his anger remains linguistic; in the words of a more recent poem, 'The Dark Crossroads', it is 'a defensive hate, bloodlust/ Soured into ink, a library carnage'.[37]

If the garden of these poems is the seat of both nature and culture, it can also be extended into the space where a fusion is proposed, and in 'The Harp of Renfrewshire' (*St Kilda's Parliament*) Dunn imagines (again, derived from retrospect) a resulting moral prosperity. Subtitled 'Contemplating a map', the poem reaches out to all cultivated ground:

> The patronymic miles of grass and weddings,
> Their festivals of gender, covenants,
> Poor pre-industrially scattered steadings,
> Ploughed-up davochs – old names, inhabitants.
>
> And on my map is neither wall or fence,
> But men and women and their revenue,
> As, watching them, I utter into silence
> A granary of whispers rinsed in dew.[37]

This optative present offers a lyric, though by no means blandly idyllic, equivalent of 'Ratatouille' – a world before enclosure, when people knew (or know?) what to do. Permission to dream will of course be granted the poet, though the fate of the Diggers, who saw the earth as 'a common treasury',[39] comes to mind. Dunn himself has counterbalanced lyricism with his odd thesaurus version of Shakespeare's 'pelting farms' and 'poor pelting villages',[40] just as the poem combines elegy and advocacy. There are several counter-versions of rural life in *St Kilda's Parliament*, but they all tend in the same direction as 'The Harp of Renfrewshire' – not so much towards impotent wisdom as towards the wisdom of impotence. The most oblique of these is 'Galloway Motor Farm', which, as is Dunn's habit, seems to offer itself in admiring competition with the achievement of a contemporary – in this instance Derek Mahon's:

> Scotland, come back
> From the lost ground of your dismantled lands.
> A carelessness has defaced even the bluebell.
>
> Tonight, by a steading, an iron reaper
> That once outscythed the scythe
> Is a silent cry of its materials,
> With all its blunt blades yearning for the stone.[41]

Dunn's inclination, evident as early as 'South Bank of the Humber' in *Terry Street*, to applaud the eventual triumph of the minerals, can be read as a riposte to materialism, and an insistence on a prior, more fundamental sense of scale. Yet it also argues against what he might have been expected to approve. This is also part of the burden of 'An Address on the Destitution of Scotland', with its imagined literal return to roots around the chilly campfires of the indigent itinerants. Even as national identity takes a clearer metaphoric shape, the return to this bleak but not unwelcoming setting involves an attempt at political divestment:

> My eyes are heavy now with alien perspectives,
> And I am sick of the decisions of philosophers –
> Dirty hands, dirty hands of turncoats and opinion-makers.
> It was a long road back to this undeclared Republic.
> I came by the bye-ways, empty of milestones,
> On the roads of old drovers, by disused workings.[42]

The closing quotation from Auden's 'Consider'[43] cannot be accidental: Dunn's poem moves, as it were, in the reverse historical direction, tipping its hat to an example whose political promise remained unfulfilled. While 'An Address on the Destitution of Scotland' ends with a kind of resigned relish, the adjacent 'The Apple Tree' attempts something more difficult, a form of affirmation through finding ground on which to stand and uphold loyalties that can bear some weight:

> Rather an ordinary joy – a girl with a basket,
> With apples under a linen cloth – than comfortless
> With windlestrae to eat. Forge no false links of man
> To land or creed, the true are good enough. Our lives
> Crave codes of courtesy, ways of describing love,
> And these, in a good-natured land, are ways to weep,
> True comfort as you wipe your eyes and try to live.[44]

This is another case where form doesn't impose sufficient pressure. We are close to uplift and sentimentality here, with the chains of alliteration almost too deftly attached. Where Dunn wrote in 'The Happier Life' that 'There are no pure',[45] here he wants to tell of a kind of purity of sentiment – and the excess of telling, though in this case we may put it down as a poetic failure, does also reveal the homelessness at the moral core of his work. It is this feeling that accompanies the poet during the fascinating 'A Snow-walk' from *Northlight*. The snowy landscape, intermittently whited out, then suddenly charged with detail, and haunted by the neutrality of its element, is at once a blank page for the mind's amusement and a site already saturated by contradictions between art and politics. Re-examined, the contradictions start to look like complicity. The mind domesticates the snowy woods –

Large tree-stumps, scattered through a chain-sawed wood,
Metamorphose to dust-cloth'd furniture,
Closed forest room, palatial solitude,
Iced armchairs and a branch-hung chandelier [46]

– only to find that the Zhivago-esque scene leads inescapably back from contemplation to consequences:

That fence again; a sign – *Guard Dogs Patrolling*.
Embedded in the snow, low huts appear,
A disused railway line, a shed for coaling,
A toppled goods van and a snow-filled brazier.

Home feels a life away and not an hour
Along the length of an industrial fence,
By friendly holdings and a water-tower
Robbed of simplicity and innocence.

The ending takes the same risk as 'The Apple Tree', of moving from an imaginative role into an explanatory one. The directness flaws the poem, perhaps, but is something Dunn clearly has to accommodate.

Dunn's left-leaning Scottish republicanism is predicated on a dream of social unity, an egalitarian reasonableness. The dream is an extrapolation from a state of mind which sees 'realism' as the acceptable face of pessimism. He has offered a wry description of the condition:

We could get independence in Scotland next week if enough people took two or three days off work in the middle of the week to go on the streets. But the idea of somebody in work in Scotland taking two or three days off, unpaid! There's something tremendously conventional and respectable in Scotland, which people from outside Scotland don't know about, mainly I think because intelligent people in Scotland are ashamed of it. They keep it quiet.[47]

If it's the case that thinking about Dunn's work leads uneasily towards the point where art has to leave off and action begin (as of course it won't), this seems a testimony to his conscientious readiness to expose the limits of his analysis. In the witty, severe, affectionate 'Remembering Lunch' [48] he pictures himself, a parody of the decent, staid Scottish dominie, walking energetically along the holiday shore, doing what comes 'naturally', only to be visited by an unanswerable enquiry:

Perhaps, after all, this not altogether satisfactory
Independence of mind and identity before larger notions
Is a better mess to be in, with a pocketful of bread and cheese,
My hipflask and the *Poésie* of Philippe Jaccottet,
Listening to the sea compose its urbane wilderness,

Although it is a cause for fear to notice that only my footprints
Litter this deserted beach with signs of human approach,
Each squelch of leather on mud complaining, *But where are you going?*[49]

It is no accident that the book taken along on the walk is Philippe Jaccottet, or that the poem terminates in a tone (deadpan mock-heroic) and setting (empty shore with sentient objects) strongly reminiscent of a number of poems by Derek Mahon. Mahon is the dedicatee of Dunn's poem 'Realisms',[48] which employs the Irish poet's patented triplet form, as well as the subject of an extremely appreciative essay which Dunn wrote in the late 1970s.[50] Mahon himself is one of Jaccottet's translators and clearly his anglophone poetic cousin.[51] Jaccottet's characteristic mode is a vestigial lyricism founded on minute observation of light, weather and other natural phenomena. His aesthetic is even more solitary and extreme than Mahon's, hard as that may be to imagine, producing a poetry which is always on the brink of ceasing to happen at all. In Mahon's case we witness a steady stripping-out of materials judged to be superfluous. As his poem 'Matthew V. 29-30'[52] foretells, these come to include virtually everything, as though Mahon is aiming to balance the scale of his despair with the fastidious delicacy of his renditions. Dunn's poetic range has always been wider than Mahon's: where Mahon's work is a refinement towards something bearing a suspicious similarity to silence, Dunn has always been able, and obliged, to re-nourish his poems with worldly detail. Yet Dunn too is drawn towards lyric purity, an emptying of the self into a world which, though it may be merely phenomenal rather than metaphysically supported, none the less evokes in him a quality of regard for which religious is as close a description as any. This is the case with some of the finest work in the romantic elegiac mode of *Elegies*, for instance 'The Clear Day' or 'Home Again', but the most accessible instance is a slightly earlier poem, 'Loch Music', from *St Kilda's Parliament*, which begins: 'I listen as recorded Bach/ Restates the rhythms of a loch' and moves through a Wordsworthian invocation of natural Presence towards a transcendent dissolution of the self:

Mist-moving trees proclaim a sense
Of sight without intelligence;
The intellects of water teach
A truth that's physical and rich.
I nourish nothing with the stars,
With minerals, as I disperse,
A scattering of quavered wash
As light against the wind as ash.[53]

The perfectly achieved music of these lines, pulsing on two main stresses in the tetrameter lines, may disguise the extremism (in his phrase, the 'personal extreme') of the attitude, which blends egotistical sublimity with a solo *Liebestod*. Given this sense of the neutral grandeur of the cosmos, and the poet's readiness for assumption into its impersonal processes, it would not be surprising if Dunn's politics began to show a more conservative tendency, like those English Romantic poets (in whom he is well-versed) who survived their youth. Dunn's love affair with the elements is a complex matter, however. He affirms and rhapsodises and, as it were, raises his foot to take the step which would let him claim that his instincts find a response in the natural world. One might see a sort of Taoism here, but Dunn's Calvinist inheritance seems to require him to place the template of a discarded theology over an experience which is ultimately solitary: 'daylight on Buddon Ness', he states in 'Daylight', another landscape hymn, is 'curative, clear and meaningless'[54] – a state which mirrors the anxiety which will always draw him back into society. Dunn's discontent is his perpetual companion on these rhapsodic outings. It has altered to accommodate the poet's own acquired stake in what he objects to – family, home, middle-aged responsibilities – but he continues to protest. *Dante's Drumkit* contains a number of bluntly condemnatory political pieces. As the debate continues, so we need to go back and consider Dave Smith's description of Dunn as a poet 'subsumed' into English tradition.

Generally speaking, Dunn's work has shown a gradual movement in the direction of standard metres, accompanied by an obvious pleasure in form – pentameter, quatrain, sonnet, tetrameter, *terza rima*, as well as Burns metre (Auden's adaptation of which he is quick to applaud). In earlier years he expressed some perplexity at the lack of an adequate prosodic account of free verse; nowadays he is more likely to speculate on the relationship between artistry and form, and the form is likely to be traditional. If *Love or Nothing*, with its handful of unpunctuated free verse poems and wealth of anxious technical enquiries, was his nearest approach to experimentalism, it is striking that in its successor, *Barbarians*, he chose to handle the complex and uncomfortable historical and political subjects of the 'Barbarian Pastorals' for the most part in manifestly, even volubly 'strict' forms. See, for example, 'In the Grounds', 'Gardeners', 'The Student', 'Here be Dragons' and 'An Artist Waiting in a Country House'. That the poems' impact and repute seems in a sense disproportionate to their number (though this vein continues in the poems from Scots history and literature in *St Kilda's Parliament*) is surely in part the result of their formal decidedness. This might in itself be read as an experimental choice. 'The Come-on' (an exception to the formal rule) stakes out a strategy superficially resembling Tony Harrison's decision to occupy the 'lousy leasehold' [55] of poetry by winning patrician form for oppositional meanings. I say 'superficially' because the Harrison of the sonnets has not so much embraced tradition as sought to bend it to his service, placing obvious and deliberate strains on metrical and musical norms. Dunn himself, though certainly an admirer of Harrison's work (and indeed one of its early advocates), has noted what he feels are 'flaws' in Harrison's 'sub-classical technique'; and in practice Dunn has construed 'occupation' as a matter of acquisition rather than transformation.[56] Thus the oppositional character of Dunn's work is far more evident in its content than in its form. There is an irony attached to this, in that Dunn's approach places him in that long tradition of gifted Scots on whom the English have had to rely to get their business done properly.

Furthermore, there is a complex linguistic and political issue behind the poems, too. Dunn writes in standard English – the form associated with Received Pronunciation – whereas Harrison continually offends this class-derived "norm". Scots words are not infrequent in Dunn's poems, but he couldn't be said to write in Scots – whether MacDiarmid's, or W.N. Herbert's, or the gleeful Glaswegian 'lang/wij a thi guhtr' [56] of Tom Leonard. (The military Scots of Dunn's television poem, 'Dressed to Kill' [58] has a deliberate air of pageantry rather than live speech about it.) A complex linguistic inheritance, in which class, race, education and questions of a national literature are inseparably bound up, necessarily gives the Scots poet, who feels the matter with an urgency unknown to many of his English peers, an angle of entry to traditional English verse forms which is different not only from the patrician but also from the English working-class dissident. It is a commonplace of the contemporary discussion of literature to suggest that power now resides in the old periphery of the vanished empire, in what were once the linguistic and political margins: the recognition accorded to Derek Walcott and Les Murray, as well as the achievements of numerous Irish poets, is evidence of this – and it may be best to try to see Dunn's achievement in *Barbarians* and *St Kilda's Parliament* in the same light – as a usurpation and renovation of the imaginative possibilities of English, though perhaps of a kind whose radical conservatism of form is difficult for an English audience to identify exactly.

I want to conclude on a note of uncertainty, by looking at poems Dunn has published since returning to public themes, in *Northlight* and *Dante's Drumkit*. *Northlight* includes some notable successes and shows Dunn's usual awareness of the way he is implicated in his own work. In the ambitious 'Here and There' he combines steeliness with good humour in rejecting a friend's suggestion that life in Tayport is provincial. The place, he says, is 'More like a world', affirming his alignment with the strain of modern Irish poetry which rejects the metropolitan/provincial pecking-order of seriousness. The Elsewhere of Tayport is not a place of evasion, merely 'miles away', but a threshhold. Yet Dunn's correspondent is allowed to name the anxieties of the situation (albeit more politely than Harrison's skinhead doppelganger):

> '...*You'll twist your art on the parochial lie.*'
> I loved the barbed hush in the holly tree.
> '*An inner émigré, you'll versify*
> *Not write. You'll turn your back on history.*[59]

The devil seems to be getting the best tunes. In Dunn's "own" parts of the poem there's a fissure between the instances ('the barbed hush in the holly tree') and what they are required to intimate. There are several brilliant moments, but 'Here and There' contains another, more dramatically embodied argument, which I think goes unacknowledged by the author – that is, between the general and the particular. It seems as if the details of place are being used to demonstrate, rather than substantiate, some of the very abstractions the poet may have come here to get away from. The attendant lushness of the verse – which does in places read as versifying – seems, correspondingly, like the naturalisation of traditional form. Perhaps it's true that you need a long spoon to sup with the devil.

Should the fiend assume the guise of urbanity, where better to locate him than in the supremely urbane person of W.H. Auden? 'Audenesques for 1960' is a wry homage, recalling the youthful Dunn's imagined colloquies with someone whom he only ever saw once, towards the end of Auden's life, across a room, and was too shy to talk to: 'Self-confident timidity got the better of me', as Dunn puts it. The poem is in part another way of dealing with the implications of Dunn's decision to live in Scotland and lay imaginative claim to the world from a position which some English readers incurably see as exile from the seat of artistic and political authority. Dunn reaches out to identify the common ground of art, and in doing so illuminates the Janus-faces of nationality/nationalism.

...it wasn't nice to have invented someone real.

It was our secret. I forgot to let you in on it.
Sorry. You were my more than useful friend.
Too often, the heartfelt is belated and shameful.
In this case some sort of national distrust –
Not mine, but others' – postponed it for years.

I was angered once by Glaswegians dismissing you as
'The Grand Panjandrum of the Homintern'.
Poetry has many enemies to contend with.
'A nancy poet, not a real one; and a fake socialist'.
One genius tends to use another as a doormat.

Nationality doesn't identify 'our side'.
Muses are international, and mine is a Lady
Who speaks all sorts of languages (in translation),
Collects guidebooks, maps, timetables, menus,
Wine lists and other hedonistic souvenirs.

So what if you were English? I speak that language,
But not its nationality; I love your poetry,
And our imaginary talks – I mean, remembering them –
Please me as proof of how imagination side-steps
Half-witted nagging about 'National Identity'.[60]

The poem gets its formal imprimatur from Auden's later, more unbuttoned and discursive practices, and might stand as a junior tailpiece to 'The Cave of Making',[61] Auden's elegy-cum-manifesto for Louis MacNeice. It deals, too, with a matter Auden touched on in the 'unwritten poem' of 1959, 'Dichtung und Wahrheit',[62] whose second section opens: 'Of any poem written by someone else, my first demand is that it be good (who wrote it is of secondary importance)...' Dunn's poem proposes an artistic freemasonry wiser than mere politics. But goodwill and enthusiasm are hardly an adequate basis for this proposed aesthetic liberty. There is something more than appropriately modest, something *flinching* in the attitude and texture of the poem. It has an air of always being about to ask, not just for Auden's but the reader's agreement, and to ask in such a way as to suggest that the poet is seeking a sort of reassurance he is uncertain that we can give or that he deserves. Dunn is riding the train towards Romantic Sleep, but sitting with his back to the engine, staring anxiously at the place he's just left, knowing that the noise and the people, however dislikeable (fellow citizens, like relatives, are given, not chosen) are not so easily renounced. And anyway, there are more serious challenges to artistic freedom than the dim ones he has been satirising. Given this argument, which takes place, as it were, in the administration of the poem, and which the reader can overhear, it's hard not to admire Dunn's readiness to expose the enduring presence in his work of the very division he has dreamed elsewhere of healing or abolishing. Using the diminuendo which also works to great effect in such different poems as 'Reading Pascal in the Lowlands' and 'The War in the Congo', he concludes his address to Auden:

> ...Day-dream tutorials,
> With teachers you never meet, end up as this –
> Whispers with the dead. It is greatly to be regretted.
>
> Pushing fifty, though, it won't be difficult
> To avoid it in future. I'm not sorry it happened.
> It's a Scottish night. I look at the still Firth.
> Avuncular and kindly wordless calm
> Shines on the aesthetically mooned water.[63]

Impossible, reading this, to resist adding to it, as to Larkin's 'Friday Night in the Royal Station Hotel', the close of Auden's 'Birthday Poem':

> And all sway forward on the dangerous flood
> Of history, that never sleeps or dies,
> And, held one moment, burns the hand.[64]

Impossible, too, to suppose that Dunn will really lower and fold away the tricolour at his window, however loudly he protests the contrary.

6. Ken Smith: *I Am Always Lost In It*

now the frontier is everywhere and everyone
on it a stranger

KEN SMITH, 'His epistle to the Tatars'[1]

Ken Smith seems to view himself as a journeyman, time-served, following his trade wherever the opportunity arises, a course which has led him to the USA, H.M. Prison Wormwood Scrubs (as writer in residence) and pre-1989 Berlin. The itinerary itself is striking, even in a period when mobility has become economically necessary as well as artistically desirable for poets. Still more interesting, though, is the atmosphere of exile which his work has carried from an early stage. This is partly a matter of theme: his poems are full of unsatisfied travellers, longings and memories of other places; but the estrangement is also a feature of his language itself. His writing indicates a marked lack of enthusiasm for the bulk of postwar English poetry. He looks back into the Romantic tradition, and beyond it to Milton, Chaucer and Anglo-Saxon – to pre-industrial England, though this is unlikely to be roses in Smith's imagination. Among American contemporaries he has admired Robert Bly, James Wright, John Haynes and W.S. Merwin, figures related by attachment to the 'deep image',[2] from whom the tide of British approval has receded since the 1970s and who have found comparatively few recent sympathisers. The same would probably hold true of Neruda. Modern English enthusiasms are D.H. Lawrence and Wilfred Owen, while the usually central figures of Eliot and Auden simply don't apply. This litany is necessary to suggest how Smith has distanced himself from the academy, metropolitan taste and what he terms 'the Rupert Bear School of Poetry'.[3] He has at once sought and been obliged to seek the margins.

At the time of its publication Smith's first collection, *The Pity* (1967)[4] seemed made for the ample compartment labelled Nature, opened up afresh in the wake of Ted Hughes by poets including David Wevill, Ted Walker and Jon Silkin. Its after-image remained with Smith for years, to his apparent discomfort. As he remarked, 'If I'm writing about my childhood, I'm writing about the country' – Yorkshire, where his father worked as an agricultural labourer.[5] The view is bare, wholly unromantic and quite unliterary. It is not Edward Thomas's England; nor is it a charming adjunct to a life spent elsewhere. The landscape may have the 'Domesday lines' of Larkin's 'MCMXIV' but in 'Family Group' it is also the Danelaw,[6] a peasant England, where the poet's father is seen

> ...stumping
> through pinewoods, hunched and small, feeling
> the weather on him. Work angled him.
> Fingers were crooked...[7]

There's no recourse to *An Englishman's Flora* in Smith's poems (though he had planned to write *The Backyard Herbal* in collaboration with his wife, the poet Judi Benson). In this exposed early landscape, he returns often to the figure of his father, a hard-working, frustrated, angry man, who comes to embody a life which seems inescapably limited and dissatisfied (a state which among his contemporaries can be paralleled in the figure of Tony Harrison's father and, less specifically, in the male population of the early work of Douglas Dunn). Throughout Smith's poetry figures move endlessly, haunted by the Good Place which is never to be found but at times rendingly glimpsed in the minds' eyes of his army of drifters.

Although industrialism is barely mentioned, the agricultural labouring life Smith refers to seems historically remote and vestigial even where it remains present. Yet the history recorded by books has to give place to a lingering sense of the proverbial, folksong world where remembered childhood meets up with dream. An unmapped Eden, somewhere 'in the north'[8] of the imagination, sometimes provides suggestions of simplicity and contentment sufficient in themselves, such as the 'tall green masts of the sunflowers' in 'The Bee Dance',[9] or the charm-like repetition of 'applemint',[10] but the permanent postponement of arrival weighs as heavily as the blues, for which Smith's work can seem an English equivalent.

The great social movements and energies to which Dunn and Harrison refer (particularly in their historical poems) can hardly figure in their own terms for Smith. As his work emphasises isolation and anonymity, so, correspondingly, large social events are experienced as rumour and hearsay – overheard fragments of bar-room conversation, the white noise of disenfranchised discourse. Whereas Harrison (emphatically) and Dunn (to some degree) are troubled by separation from their origins, Smith does not look back to a lost society, perhaps because there was none to lose. It is no paradox that his poems seem most at home among the homeless voices they record, with their litanies of names and aliases – Jack, Mother, Eli, Harry, Abel Baker and Charlie Delta, Stickincraw. The history Smith's poems hint at comes not simply 'from below' but from far beneath and even beyond the reach of the official record. Strikingly, *Burned Books* (1981),[11] Smith's ambitious reading of a political history through the fragments of the burnt library of President Perdu, installs a gapped, ambiguous and irrecoverable record as the operating basis of the book.

The subject-matter and stance which separate Smith from Dunn and Harrison can be matched in the method of his writing. In contrast to the local ingenuity in evocation, wordplay, narrative and description which marks some prominent strands in contemporary poetry (Dunn, Harrison, Muldoon, Raine, for instance), Smith's inclination is towards an exposed simplicity; or, more precisely, an emotional directness which guarantees the real seriousness of materials which may sometimes seem mysteriously complex. His practice is directed to persuading the poems to *perform* their subjects, to which end the concrete detail is subordinated to voice, in an effort to dramatise rather than gloss experience. In inferior hands this produces vatic inanity, and Smith's own failures have a willed, because-I-say-so quality. Yet over a distance the risks are rewarded. And consider the risks: a deliberately restrained vocabulary; refusal of abstraction; an extreme economy of metaphor, as if the imagination were still subject to wartime rationing and extravagance were a waste. Smith makes use of an ear which gives the plainest syllable its due, along with discreet parallelism and subtle pacing, for example, in 'Another Part of His Childhood':

> It was a life bound
> to the land, to silence
> of another kind, it was
> the other place.[12]

His strengths in the weighting of sound perhaps align him with another distinctively Northern poet, the Northumbrian modernist Basil Bunting. At his best, for example in some passages from 'Hawkwood',[13] the journal of a medieval mercenary, Smith achieves a kind of proverbial authority, as if writing from the viewpoint of Anonymous.

The pivotal work in Smith's career is *Fox Running* (1980).[14] With this poem he leaves the land for a nightmarish London where his wish for "language mobility" is fulfilled in spades. By contemporary standards the poem is an epic of sorts, but stripped of all leisure and stateliness, a headlong tour of a contemporary version of Hell, with the tube map as Virgil and no overarching theology to redeem the plight. The poem's hero, the eponymous Fox, is cut off from his own ground, pursuing an aimless but unstoppable course along the tube-lines and bus-routes of London, taking temporary shelter but unable to rest, to forget the lost love that threatens to destroy him, or to break the circle of his desperation:

> His single ticket to the city,
> a room, nights howling in the shower,
> sleeping drunk inside the wardrobe,
> dreamless, pissing in the sink.[15]

As the poem cuts between a narrative voice that acts out Fox's flight, and the comments of Fox himself, it claws in swathes of material. It stretches from the East End of 'Pakkibashers' Court' to the humiliations of the (then) DHSS ('standing at the cashier's window/hearing *oh we've written a book have we?*'),[16] from nuclear holocaust to the odds and ends of conversations, from Fox's dop-pelganger to the underlife of the city with its black economy of drugs and whisky. What lends the poem its alarming coherence is the energy and unsparing accuracy Smith brings to presenting the descent into the most harrowing of derelictions, the stage at which the original grievance is supplanted by the demeaning agonies of the present, a condition reproduced by the thousand in the ranks of the contemporary destitute. If a big London poem is bound to bring to mind *The Waste Land*, the most interesting comparisons are historical and cultural. Whatever the horrors of Eliot's ruined city and wrecked civilisation, his poem is able to call on implied knowledge of other, unfallen conditions. It is also to a significant degree a poem of commentary from outside or above: the author, however beleaguered, has somewhere else to go. Smith's poem, on the other hand, is written from below, at a point when cultural referents have lost even residual authority and the 'essential horror'[17] of things is not subject to the liberty of irony.

Whatever the sources of *Fox Running*, it opens a zone of Smith's imagination which he has frequently occupied since, so that his work, though very observant, is always more likely to be that of a participant in the traffic of anonymity than an observer privileged by position or linguistic distance. *Terra* (1986) turns its attention to the here-and-now of the Reaganite West, as it continually makes its entrance to the seconds prior to extinction. London is once again the setting, and to its bizarre injustice Smith applies his usual preoccupations – disorder, decay, things overheard, the marriage of technology and State terrorism. After 'Mr Mayhew's Visit',[18] 'the poor/ are pushing to the windows like the fog', while 'all the best words have moved to Surrey';[19] a bracing class enmity accompanies Smith's black humour. 'In Silvertown, chasing the dragon' speaks of a government

...known as *sh*,
they own the miles of wire, the acids
that devour forests and white words out
and they are listening in the telephone.[20]

The economy sonnets of these 'London Poems' and the manic, wildly funny aria 'Departure's speech' have an extraordinary suggestiveness, as if Smith has found a skeleton key to the Thatcher years. While some poets seek a match between private and public concerns at an argumentative level, Smith bypasses this stage. Instead he holds the language of dispossession, opposition and paranoia up to the light, and what he manages to disclose is the way in which fears, rumours and the back-street shooting gallery quarrels of '*uz*' with unanswerable Them have truths to tell about the times.

In one sense it is no surprise that Smith should have moved on from here to write about prison. It might be his perfect subject – a metaphor made actual. Even the non-prison poems in *Wormwood* (1987) have a claustral aspect, while the 'hulks' of Wormwood Scrubs enforce a community of solitaries, madmen, losers and unfortunates whose grief, fury and longing have much in common with (are perhaps the logical extreme of) the dispossession and longing that dog Smith's work. Imprisonment in the ultimate sense is prefigured in 'The meridian at Greenwich' from *Terra*:

No messages
passed late at night across borders, by hand,
by word of mouth, we who are lost together
telling tales the prisoner spins the jailer.[21]

This theme is cleverly developed in the framing of *Wormwood*. Smith's examination of the use of the word 'wormwood' via the Book of Revelations and Culpeper's *Herbal* confers on the Scrubs the force of a personification, like Bunyan's City of Destruction. Yet where some might use the opportunity to find man everywhere in chains, and thus mitigate imprisonment by locks and doors and razor wire, Smith moves inwards and downwards. Thus the speaker in the prose section 'Wormwood' goes

down the steps in chains and down the stairs in cuffs and backwards down the up escalator shackled to the jailer, and at last in a bodybag down the well under the cellar under the basement under the crypt under the undercroft and still some down to go.[22]

(The echo of the Blues is once more present: 'I've been down so long it looks like up to me.') The other freight of association carried by wormwood, as an hallucinogen, recalls Piranesi's *Carceri d'Invenzione*, the prison as inescapable and infinite, which exerted a powerful hold on the Romantic imagination. 'What the Righteous don't know' is that in Hell 'there's work painting the brick,/maintaining the fabric' and time to consider all the possibilities of the graffito 'time is what it is' in the 'failed university' of time.[23]

In his subsequent collection, *The heart, the border* (1990), alongside monologues by Ian Brady and the Hungerford gunman, Smith manages an imaginative unification of two of his major themes, in 'Writing in prison':

> Years ago I was a gardener.
> I grew the flowers of my childhood,
> lavender and wayside lilies
> and my first love the cornflower.
>
> The wind on the summer wheat.
> The blue glaze in the vanished woods.
> In the space of my yard I glimpsed again
> all the lost places of my life.
>
> I was remaking them. Here in a space
> smaller still I make them again.[24]

The reader may hesitate before this seemingly transparent poem. Certainly repetition, alliteration and internal rhyme lend memorability to a lyric almost bare of figurative elements. There is also something strongly appealing in the pitching of the speaking voice, which is both self-communing and oddly formal. But the slightly eerie quality of 'Writing in prison' has much to do with its apparent detachment in time: it is 'inside time', disenfranchised and set apart as a prisoner is. It is also oddly authoritative, as if speaking in the original voice from which our own voices are now hugely divergent. Its very strangeness makes it recognisable to us. The voice is ignored but not silent, discarded but enduring: it tells a story of the Fall, whether anyone is listening or not. It speaks from 'the other place', the impoverished countryside and the rat-runs of the city, and all the other places where England has been living in secret all this time with us inside it. If Smith's satire sees the contemporary world in exasperated and horrified close-up, his work as an elegist echoes across centuries.

III

ALL IRELAND (I)

7. Seamus Heaney: *The Space Made by Poetry*

Critical writing on the Nobel laureate is already industrial and may soon threaten the Tiger Economies of the Pacific Rim. One area in which there may still be some room for manoeuvre is in Heaney's own critical writing. What about this now-substantial body of work, which has progressed from an account of his own origins towards a definition of how, in what imagined space, poetry performs the work he has described as its redress? Among his leading contemporaries and younger colleagues from the North of Ireland only Tom Paulin has shown anything like Heaney's critical appetite. Paulin himself is a markedly contrasting critic, engaged to the point of fury in a strenuously political reading of literature of a kind Heaney has never gone in for. There are few English poets, aside from the late Donald Davie, a voracious and prolific essayist, who have shown Heaney's critical application and anything approaching his weight and substance. From Philip Larkin we have parts of *Required Writing*, from Ted Hughes *Winter Pollen*, from Thom Gunn *Shelf-Life*.[1] The people you might care to hear from, such as Tony Harrison or the Scot Douglas Dunn, have by and large kept their counsel – at any rate as far as critical books go. They have been otherwise engaged, though many of their American contemporaries, including for example Dana Gioia and Robert Pinsky, feel an obligation (for some perhaps a professional one) to have their critical say.[2] In England you might for a moment suspect that one reason poetry goes unread is that it also goes unwritten about. Heaney has stolen a march, anyway. More than that, he has sought to produce something definitive of his own convictions and practices, and although Heaney's essays are far more hospitable to mere humans than Eliot's graven judgements, his critical writing will prove as valuable for the interpretation of the poet and his times as Eliot's have been these many years.

Just as Heaney, despite the objurgations of the *Protestant Telegraph* when he moved with his family to the Republic of Ireland in the early 1970s,[3] and despite the pressure to produce 'something for us', i.e. the Republican cause,[4] has refused to be enlisted in support of anything but his own sense of right action and truthful writing, so his criticism has betrayed at most a local and restricted interest in the developments in literary theory which have been exerting such a marked effect on criticism in the last twenty-five years. In his essay 'Sounding Auden', Heaney records his gratitude to remarks by Geoffrey Grigson which helped him to understand a poet from whose work he had as an undergraduate felt excluded:

> Impressionistic and text-centred as such criticism may be, it still has a place in verifying the reality of poetry in the world. It may not be as up to date in its idiom as that found in some recent Auden commentators, such as Stan Smith, whose deconstructionist tools yield many excellent insights: Smith maintains that early Auden, for example, is both afflicted and inspired by his perception that he is the product rather than the producer of several world-shaping discourses. It may be that Grigson's way of talking about poems is not as strictly analytical as this, but the way it teases out the cultural implications and attachments which inhabit any poem's field of force is a critical activity not to be superseded, because it is so closely allied, as an act of reading, to what happens during the poet's act of writing.[5]

Leaving aside for a moment the circularity of the argument at the close of this extract, there is, notwithstanding his goodwill, a degree of strain apparent in Heaney's readiness to listen. It emerges in the nearly parodic phrasing of his reference to the vivid and ingenious writing of Stan Smith, and in the assertiveness of the subsequent return to first principles – poet, poem, reader, and their mutual interests, as though common sense could guarantee the innocence of these terms once history has got at them. Heaney, of course, is hardly short of ideas, but the tenor of his essays owes more to the tradition, born in the Renaissance, of the poet-critic, than to anything found in the academy proper, long though he was comfortably housed there. Wouldn't you expect, his poems seem genially and confidently to suggest, that the first people to look to for thinking about poetry would be poets? As Randall Jarrell points out in his essay 'The Age of Criticism', this would mean allowing the pig to judge the bacon competition.[6]

Such confidence in his own ground must owe a good deal to Heaney's early sense that 'verse, however humble, had a place in the life of the home [as] one of the ordinary rituals of life'.[7] This is not the sense of the domestic order of things which we receive, for instance, from Heaney's English contemporary Tony Harrison, whose relationship with home is an altogether more painful business than Heaney's, and whose interest in poetry is likewise unprecedented. The fact that Harrison's mother taught him his letters is seen as exceptional in a context where reading and writing were exceptional.[8] In the work of Douglas Dunn, who grew up on the cusp of country and city, the matter is never mentioned. As critics, neither Dunn nor Harrison is much given to Theory (which may be generational, though see their near-contemporary Terry Eagleton), but both have far greater and more explicit ideological preoccupations than Heaney, whose own concerns have more to do with sectarianism and, implicitly, with religion.

An important consequence of Heaney's ease about the place of poetry is that he stands to one side of a critical watershed. He feels able to write from the interior of the experience of poetic composition and what he presents as primary imaginative life, in the conviction that experiences and things in themselves have meaning and value, over and above those bestowed by institutional and class history, when made into poetry. The world, he proposes, is really lived in, and life in the world confers authority on the poet. While to the literary laity this is a statement of the obvious, its consequences for Heaney's understanding and advocacy of poetry are important. This is especially so as it bears on his evident sense of the power of poetry to transubstantiate language and claim a physical presence for its representations. What makes sense in the context of his own poems can look strange when applied elsewhere. Discussing a line from Auden's 'The Watershed'[9] – 'on the wet road between the chafing grass' – he remarks that part of the effect of 'chafing' is that 'it allows us to hear through its lingering vowel and caressing fricative the whisper and friction of wind along a hillside'.[10] Such a direct reading of mimesis is likely to have been part of the New Critical vocabulary with which Heaney grew up – as well as being naturally congenial to him. The same idea can be found in Ted Hughes.[11]

The relationship of words to things, in Heaney's book, is not the placing of counters on the unknowably Other. The world, though mysterious, speaks our language and is accessible to the senses. It can be made imaginatively present. More than once he refers to Eliot's idea of the 'auditory imagination',[12] a means of trawling the deepest reaches of memory and culture, in which form (sound) and content (meaning) are unified.[13] Something like this may constitute the inexplicit faith most readers bring to a poem, but it is quite at odds with the condition of much literary theory, which proceeds from a perceived fissure between signs and their objects. To such an understanding, the Fall is thus inscribed in the actions of language itself; but for Heaney, who was raised as a Catholic, language can exercise a redemptive power. Within Catholicism must also be considered the pagan dimension on which the church so successfully built – something seen in the 'gleam of the fabulous' residing as it were on the edge of modern consciousness.[14] By its light the habits of analogy and figurative language are not simply means of literary intensification but threshholds to a world-view which is still to a significant degree magical. The 'wet centre' of the bogland is 'bottomless'[15] according to the adults who said this to keep children away from dangerous places: on the poet's interpretation this also means that it is imaginatively inexhaustible and actual.

While Heaney has steeped himself delightedly in English poetic tradition – witness especially his love of Wordsworth and Hopkins – his firm sense of the poet's place in the scheme of things owes at least as much to Irish traditions, where even the modern poet may retain powerful tap-roots in the rural community. Heaney is quite aware of the view of history which sees Irish poetry as a history of dispossession, but despite English efforts to destroy Irish culture, despite the Penal Laws and the Famine, the emigrations and the status of subject people endured by Northern Catholics after Partition, he feels able to comment that 'one deracinates oneself'[16] – a view perhaps only sustainable by someone for whom rural life retains an actual rather than a nostalgic imaginative primacy; someone, moreover, whose attitude is not that of regret and defeat but of strength and endurance. Recording the youthful Heaney's reading of Daniel Corkery's *The Hidden Ireland*, where he learned of poets such as Aodagain Ó Rathaille, Eoghan Ruadh Ó Súilleabháin and Brian Merriman, the critic Michael Parker comments:

> it would have been surprising if Heaney had not identified with these poets, who treasure equally dialect and classical allusion, who attempted to create memorable phrases that 'touch the life of the folk intimately', who 'shared their people's life, and, indeed, their thoughts' and 'named' their parishes. The accessibility and popularity of Heaney's own writing bears witness to the assimilation of these traditional virtues of Irish poetry.[17]

There is of course nothing folksy about Heaney – none of the wishful ruralism which Dennis O'Driscoll has described as characterising much contemporary poetry,[18] the 'lifeless form' described by John Barrell and John Bull, the editors of *The Penguin Book of English Pastoral Verse*, 'of use only to decorate the shelves of tasteful cottages'.[19] It is, though, reasonable to suppose that a good deal of enthusiasm for Heaney is connected with notions of rural 'authenticity' which would draw the poet within the fold of English nature poetry – a point elaborated by Anthony Thwaite when describing the wide popularity of Heaney's early work:

> To the British (or perhaps more accurately one should say 'to the British and Northern Irish'), who have for many years been largely an

> urban people but who have keen yearnings for the country, Heaney's poems gave new impetus to nostalgias associated with Wordsworth, Hardy and Edward Thomas, and also seemed to relate to such works as Laurie Lee's best-selling evocation of his own rural Gloucestershire childhood, *Cider with Rosie.*[20]

Such an interpretation gains some assistance from Heaney's own fascination with the English tradition – part of the 'crossing' of native and imperial speech – though to be included as English in this sense is the kind of thing rejected by his mild avowal, 'My passport's green',[21] in response to another act of incorporation, by Blake Morrison and Andrew Motion, editors of the 1982 *Penguin Book of Contemporary British Verse.*[22] When Heaney politely takes issue with the editors of *English Pastoral Verse*, he is of course making an implicit case for his own practice. What intrigues him about the pastoral is its adaptability into the modern period, from Clare to Housman, Edward Thomas and Hugh MacDiarmid. He might nowadays add, among others, Derek Mahon, Michael Longley and Douglas Dunn to his list. A significant feature in contemporary poetry has been the desire to examine and renew the possibilities of pastoral convention, rather than, like Barrell and Bull, to declare its case closed. The views from exile (Mahon), or down a microscope (Longley) or in the light of history (Dunn) have all been enhanced by access to the pastoral. Which goes to show that on some important occasions poets will be found in the awkward squad – and in this instance it's because Heaney values the life of the pastoral mode above the neatness with which it can be laid to rest. If it's useful, then it can't be dead.

Heaney as a poet and critic is hardly alone in his interest in the ways in which poets seek to resolve conflicting needs and impulses in their work, to balance the claims of art and politics, art and nationality, world and spirit, and so on. Over his shoulder stands Yeats, the most audibly dialectical of poets. But his critical fascination with dualisms is clearly of special live importance for his own development as a poet. His summings-up and descriptions make great use of internal conflict. English poets such as Larkin, Hughes, Hill and Davie, he writes in 'Englands of the Mind', 'are being forced to explore not just the matter of England, but what is the matter with England'.[23] Later, when he writes about Larkin, he finds a way of making Larkin's symbolist excursions offset the great bulk of the other work – that art of depression to which Heaney is clearly temperamentally unhappy to give assent.[24] His second look at Kavanagh finds him a twofold poet – early on as a farmer, a dweller in County Monaghan, later as the invoker of 'a placeless heaven'.[25] The treatment of Hopkins in the early essay 'The Fire i' the Flint' is something like a negative of this approach – resisting, while admiring the poems, the essentially subordinate, servicing role he sees allowed to the imagination.[26] His review of Derek Walcott's *The Star-Apple Kingdom*[27] can perhaps serve to indicate the personal significance of this line of enquiry. 'Englands of the Mind' closes with the declaration: 'I have simply presumed to share in...exploration through the medium which England has, for better or worse, impressed upon us all, the English language itself'.[28] This seems, in Heaney's characteristically amiable way, a loaded remark – one remotely echoed in the quotation from 'The Schooner Flight' with which he closes his essay on Walcott: '...that's all them bastards have left us: words'.[29] If the imperially determined function of colonised peoples is to exit from history and become anecdotal, to cease to occupy their own present, it may be that the most effective form of resistance is to endear oneself to the occupying language and make it the subject people's own attribute. This is part of the burden of Heaney's discussion of Walcott, who, Heaney suggests, writes without bitterness out of the competing claims of the Caribbean and of British tradition:

> he has done for the Caribbean what Synge did for Ireland, found a language woven out of dialect and literature, neither folksy nor condescending, a singular idiom evolved out of one man's inherited divisions and obsessions, an idiom which allows an older life to exult in itself and yet at the same time keeps the cool of 'the new'.[30]

With appropriate adjustments this might be a description of Heaney himself. The best revenge is the discovery of a way forward, to become the inheritor, and then the lawgiver, of the imperial tongue, which is in turn enriched by its new subjection. The process is manifest in the essays themselves. At a phrasal level in Heaney's criticism the reader is continually struck by the capacity to make praise specific rather than notional, to move cleanly from instance to dictum. His discriminations are exact but robust. Ideas and qualities remain close cousins to the physical world, and – as the enterprise is governed by precise and dignified Latin: 'evolved', 'inherited', 'exult', terms as historically open to the claims of Irish culture as of British – his essays sound, as very little criticism does, as if intended to be spoken aloud, at once intensified and direct. This marks a form of mastery which has no need to assert itself except by pursuing its interests; and thus the argument, it may be felt, becomes the embodiment of its own justice.

When considering the relationship of poetry to the world, Heaney displays a deft insistence on having things both ways. Poetry, he proposes, should serve nothing but itself – 'crying', in the words he quotes from Hopkins, 'What I do is me: for that I came.'[31] Yet it is through insistence on this integrity that poetry is 'of present use',[32] of benefit to the world. It combines liberty and responsibility, fulfilling the latter by the exercise of the former. It is *about* the world but, crucially, not governed by it. By dint of conviction and rhetorical power, rather than by demonstrative argument, Heaney suggests a resolution of the ancient debate among the good, the beautiful and the useful. The attractions of the formulation are obvious: the untrammelled exercise of power which also turns out to be the exercise of responsibility is the poetic equivalent of the philosopher's stone. As Sidney gave poetry the advantage over history and philosophy, since it could escape the toils of the one and substantiate the proposals of the other,[33] so Heaney accords poetry the equivalent privilege in relation to contemporary preoccupations with politics and literary theory.

This declaration of imaginative liberty, this making of room, with its Shelleyan overtones, is not a secession from worldly concerns, any more than Shelley intended his *Defence* to be. It is accompanied by the conviction that poetry is a supremely adequate way of addressing the world – even if we might suppose that poetry's power to influence or become action stands in inverse relationship to its liberty of thought. Heaney quotes approvingly both Frost's description of poetry as 'a momentary stay against confusion' and the American poet's insistence that a poem, re-read, will hold in trust for the reader its initial sense of revelation.[34] The poem refreshes, we might say, the parts which theory cannot reach, while Heaney the critic refreshes those parts which to some other critics might seem illusory:

> When I thought of 'the government of the tongue' as a general title for these lectures, what I had in mind was [the] aspect of poetry as its own vindicating force. In this dispensation, the tongue (representing both a poet's personal gift of utterance and the common resources of language itself) has been granted the right to govern. The poetic art is credited with an authority of its own. As readers, we submit to the jurisdiction of achieved form, even though that form is achieved not by dint of the moral and ethical exercise of mind but by the self-validating operations of what we call inspiration…[35]

Or solipsism, as someone unpersuaded might object. Heaney can hardly be unaware of the teleological dimension here, as he urges us to believe in a point – or rather, speaks as though we already believe in a point – at which truth and 'achieved form' are blended. To a Catholic this may seem a rather Catholic means of argument. It awards the aesthetic impulse an authority analogous to Scripture. It carries us towards assent on a wave of controlled, judicial magniloquence. At the same time – and this is the most compelling feature of the passage – the form of his remarks ('in this dispensation') invokes a sense of the conditional, right here in the middle of the affirmation, because, presumably, this is not dogma being described, nor a finished act, but a state of permanent readiness, alertness and aspiration. However much we may dissent, it is a hugely attractive utterance – 'idea' is not quite the right word – which manages both to have and eat its cake, whether real or imaginary. It might be objected that this re-charged aestheticism is still dependent on an idea of validation drawn from the worldly disorder of history – the past, the tribal, cultural, conflict-ridden, word-and-object-fusing past – and is thus itself governed by history as a whole, not just the culturally preferred sample from which it draws nourishment. But that's another story. Whatever the truth of the matter, Heaney has tried to summon a more powerful artistic instrument than any English poet can muster.

8. Derek Mahon: *The World as Exile*

If Seamus Heaney has been the most written about of poets from this side of the Atlantic, Derek Mahon may prove to have been the most influential of Heaney's generation. The fierce affection his poems inspire is a sign both of Mahon's prowess – wit, economy, elegant music – and his sensibility, whose combination of romantic nihilism and idealism offers a riposte to the relativistic disorder which can seem to be the main selling-point of postmodernism. *There are indeed no grand narratives*, Mahon seems to say, *and I am here to describe them.* An afterlife of 'Gibbon and old comics'[1] entails both components of the phrase. The poet whose persona is 'through with history'[2] takes us repeatedly over its allegedly exhausted ground. After all, what else is there to do? Mahon's is the world conceived as *afterwards*.

In his brilliant essay 'Ulster Ovids', John Kerrigan concludes a discussion of Heaney, Paul Muldoon and Mahon by seeming to find in favour of Mahon. Of 'Ovid in Tomis', he declares:

> In the end the scope of the poem is larger than anything in Heaney (or Muldoon) because of its attention to the 'infinity' which inheres in changeable things – 'The cry at the heart/of the artichoke,/the gaiety of atoms.' Perhaps Mahon provides a view of poetry which, for all his indirection, tells us more than bardic gesturing about the tacit fertility of that estrangement from language which is the burden of so much recent verse.[3]

This is a large claim, to which many of Mahon's readers might assent with one half of themselves while resisting with the other. 'Ovid in Tomis' is surely not the best example through which to commend his achievement (as distinct from enjoying his imagination). For one thing it is a poem where the Mahon triplet, which has been a significant part of his equipment since *Lives*, has ceased to earn its keep, lending itself too readily to the cosmetically epigrammatic note which has dogged him since he made his first series of revisions for *Poems 1962-78* and which, as has been observed, has at times threatened to turn him from an ironist into a sentimentalist. Despite its undoubted scope, the poem is marked by another characteristic which Kerrigan superbly formulates elsewhere in his essay as 'the impression of faintly misplaced sophistication, of a stylist underemployed by his material though not his theme'.[4] Between the poles of copiously fulfilled ambition and the inertia of underemployment the true story of Mahon's work is to be sought. The search produces an uncanny match between cultural exile and a language and style apt for the 'terminal' themes of that exile – the latter pursued at considerable artistic cost.

If it sounds unflattering to describe a poet in terms of features absent from his or her poems, Mahon survives such scrutiny intact. His poems have few colours, often seeming to take place in an intensified monochrome which brings to mind Robert Flaherty's film *Man of Aran*, a work which seems strongly present to his imagination. Mahon's work tends to be hard-edged, a place of solids – hubcaps, oildrums, hatboxes, crabs, stony landscapes and shores, their consonantal quiddity relished with grim mock-heroic amusement. This is not to say that created things endure: extinction and transformation are continually at work here, and the great effacing powers of the elements, exemplified by the sea or snow, are usually to hand. Though he has tried, Mahon scarcely seems at home in a softer climate: the semi-rural life of 'Ford Manor' and 'Surrey Poems'[5] can be felt slipping from his grasp even as he attempts to relish it. 'Dry Hill', fourth and last of the 'Surrey Poems', opens:

> The grass goes silent and the trees cease
> when my shoes go swishing there.
> Vetch, thyme, cowslip,
> whatever your names are,
> there is no need for fear –
> I am only looking. Perhaps
> this is what you are afraid of?

Might the flora not reply that the bland simplicity of the language is the real cause for anxiety here? A contemporary sequence, 'Light Music',[6] which attempts celebration, is for the most part similarly inert, as though Mahon has missed part of the point – the extent to which his poetic gift is invested in crackling, right-angled, redemptively sardonic-affectionate music (the note of 'Whiskery pikemen and their spiky dogs/Preserved in woodcuts and card-catalogues').[7] At any rate, yielding surfaces and warm interiors – properties in which Heaney's work is by contrast extremely rich, the means by which he brings the world inside – are usually conspicuous by their absence in Mahon. The blending of elements is seen as peremptory, not mutual – and, despite its evident importance, domestic love, the human equivalent of such blending, is hard to grasp, something that melts in the telling. Like the tramps' boots in *Waiting for Godot*, the man-made objects Mahon sets before us – the artefacts and bits of junk – serve to emphasise the habitual exposure of his settings. For the most part Mahon's world exists outdoors. Anybody found inside may simply be waiting for the building to decay, or watching the growth of a pile of scrap in the garden, and seeing in this an ironic kinship with the ever-exiled gypsies in 'Gypsies Revisited'.[8]

The wide-open spaces are, naturally enough, rather thinly populated, but even when Mahon writes about the city – Derry, Belfast,

London – it is somewhere whose population is hardly to be seen. Belfast, for example, in 'Ecclesiastes', is 'the/dank churches, the empty streets,/the shipyard silence, the tied-up swings' of an endless Sunday.[9] If this seems apt for the period of political and military crisis which began afresh in 1968, as well as for the psychic economy of Ulster Protestantism, it also seems necessary to Mahon's sense of things. 'Teaching in Belfast', another occasion where people might be found, begins in the schoolroom but has much more to do with the poet longing for the weekend than with children, who enter the poem neither as individuals nor a living crowd.[10] One of the most telling images connected with Mahon's work comes not from a poem but the marvellous cover of *Lives*. The photograph of a crowd of workers leaving a shipyard becomes a metaphor for the poet's practice: we see the realist photograph treated until it begins to turn into an emblem, so that the crowd at the point of effacement recalls Mahon's favourite element, snow. This in turn looks forward to the title poem of *The Snow Party* (1974): 'Elsewhere they are burning/witches and heretics/in the boiling squares',[11] but in the poem's foreground is imponderable snow, which both distances the suffering and sharpens the poem's apprehension of it. There is no political succour to be had from Mahon's work: its solidarity is informal, even fleeting, and his individualism stakes everything on an accurate depiction of unaccommodated man. At the point of parody, one might say that this world is crowded with solitaries – wanderers, observers, commentators, mutes, interjectors ('Nobody comes here now but me', as the occupant of the rock in 'A Stone Age Figure Far Below' remarks)[12] – some of whom have retained the imaginative authority, if not the self-importance, of their romantic progenitors.

Mahon's pessimism might seem merely conventional – the *alas* of the amateur poet – were it not that his best work is punctilious in what it chooses to show us. The objects under contemplation are, as though by definition, somewhat distant from him by the time he comes to look at them. His imagination is at once epic in intent and miniaturist in execution. Seamus Heaney's reference to 'the large number of poems in which the Northern Irish writer views the world from a great spatial or temporal distance'[13] is especially applicable to Mahon, in contrast to Heaney's own actual-scale renderings, and to the poems of Michael Longley, whose work at times seems to propose a movement beyond mere intimacy with its objects towards a blissful merger. Mahon's perspective is not simply an immobile stylistic frame, though: it has brought into view, as it were, successively emptier and less sustaining scenes, even where the poems seem to attest the contrary. In consequence his work has become an extended valediction – for a world lost and glimpsed, for the world lived in, and the one aspired to: 'Meanwhile the given life goes on;/There is nothing new under the sun.'[14]

This uncompromising sense of things is the source both of the power of Mahon's writing and what we now see as the threat of premature exhaustion of its resources. Exiled by temperament from Ulster Protestantism, absent from Ireland itself for long periods, Mahon has also faced, for perhaps twenty years, the possibility of being finally cast out from poetry itself by the extremity of his own understanding. For all their brilliant successes, *The Hunt by Night* and *Antarctica*[15] are works of respite, not plenitude. The crisis is directly addressed in the first poem in the title sequence of his recent collection, *The Hudson Letter*, which finds him newly housed in New York, ready to write but needing to petition the Muse:

> ...but there's something missing here
> in this autistic slammer, some restorative
> laid like a magic wand on everything –
> on bed, chair, desk and air-conditioner.
> Oh, show me how to recover my lost nerve![16]

The plea is partly about being able to write at all, a matter of permanent anxiety for many poets, but it is inextricably bound up with the margin of operation Mahon's attitude to the world has left him with. (The New World itself, as advertised by the Big Apple, is novel only in the intensity with which it spends its energies, and in the deafening volume of its commodities.) The dilemma can have a damaging effect on Mahon's tone. It's not a new problem in his work. The quoted lines might be the kind of thing which at a much earlier date incurred the displeasure of Tom Paulin. In an essay published in 1980 about *Poems 1962-78*, he declared that with a few exceptions, 'Mahon's new poems are very disappointing – they tend to whine without much distinction.'[17] Paulin then commends an earlier, previously uncollected poem, 'A Mythological Figure', concluding that 'Only a rare and extraordinary imagination could invent such a figure.' He is surely correct.

> There ought to have been a mythological figure
> Condemned always to sing whenever
> She opened her mouth to speak. The gods,
> Perhaps, had frowned upon
> A too familiar attitude in her,
> An implied inkling of their random methods,
> But let her live because she was a woman.
> Then she began to sing, and her gestures
> flowed like a mountain stream;

But her songs were without words,
Or the words without meaning –
Like the cries of love or the cries of mourning.[18]

'A Mythological figure' is very suggestive about the course of Mahon's work. Whilst the problems of writing have long been an adequate subject for the poet, and the supreme fiction might be the poet's recreation of the world as the effect, rather than the purpose, of perfecting the aesthetic, Mahon is in the interesting position of finding a closing-down of the poetic faculty to be the apparently logical consequence of an aesthetic which reaches out for a post-industrial and post-linguistic world in which duration replaces progress. There, though 'wisdom is a five-minute silence at moonrise',[19] perfection is a world without witnesses. The predicament of the mythological figure is analogous to the one Mahon's imagination sets before him. Her condition is at once perfect and beyond the reach of human understanding, rather as if poetry had *become* the world it once described and invoked, and having done so has lost the capacity, if not the need, to speak for it. If it would be wrong to say that this difficulty could have been predicted, the potential is present from an early stage in the work of a poet whose imagination seeks, or is driven, to the margins of the social and the human. 'Bird Sanctuary', from Mahon's first book *Night Crossing* (1968),[20] raises the possibility, using the natural world, rather than mythology, to imagine a similar condition. The poem seems to owe something to Hitchcock's film *The Birds*, where the director's increasingly inhuman vision is given full play, and the story, instead of ending, simply stops, as if human understanding has been expelled from the world:

Will come a time
When they sit on the housetops
Shouting, thousands of them,
This is their own, their favourite dream
Beyond reason, beyond rhyme
So that the heart stops.[21]

The problem is that even after poetry has imagined its own extinction, the need to write does persist, however redundant the product, as can be illustrated in 'Last Night', the second section of *The Hudson Letter*. It describes a series of noisy interruptions as the poet sits marking students' essays in the city that never sleeps. For a time Mahon's interest seems aroused by the materials:

Around five a hand, with Gershwin nonchalance,
shook up the empties in the recycling bin
at the corner, shivering for a drop of gin,

its movements brisk, fastidious and, all at once,
successful... Dawn; the kick-start as some heroine
draws on her gloves for the Harley-Davidson dream trip
to Provincetown, Key West or Sunset Strip...[22]

The epistolary form seems nowadays to be assumed to allow a bit of slack, so that notation may gesture at the complete object waiting behind the roughcast surface. Mahon, at any rate, seems to take shelter in this possibility, as the brilliant evocation of a phrase of bottle-music ('Gershwin nonchalance') gives way to the vague and talky lines about the motorcyclist. The reader turns the page in hope of a unifying figure or a deepening of perspective, only to come away baffled:

To each his haste, to each his dreamt occasion.
Nor snow, nor rain, nor sleet, not gloom of night
stays these swift couriers from their appointed flight.[23]

The adaptation of the motto of the US Mail seems both humorously intended and inadequate for the occasion. The attempted irony seems arch, and the whole effect is weirdly sanctimonious. We see in what proximity success and bathos live. What divides them may be the capacity for thinking in images. Mahon's disquiet is more pronounced in the subsequent poem, 'Global Village', where he describes himself

exposed in thunderstorms, as once before,
and hoping to draw some voltage one more time
or at least not die of spiritual cowardice.

'After so many deaths I live and write'
cried, once, Geo. Herbert in his Wiltshire plot:
does lightning ever strike in the same place twice?[24]

There are several pointed self-borrowings in *The Hudson Letter*, and here Mahon's far from optimistic search for illumination recalls the mushrooms, startled by a camera's flash-bulb, in 'A Disused Shed in Co. Wexford':

They are begging us, you see, in their wordless way,
To do something, to speak on their behalf
Or at least not to close the door again.[25]

The earlier poem does 'speak on their behalf'. It takes weary facts – death, decay, fear, solitude – and reanimates them for the reader's contemplation. But when the poet retires into the first person, this margin of liberty sustained by the use of the correlative is eroded: it is harder for the imagination to acquire any momentum and thus harder to convert personal anxiety into imaginative generosity. Rather than wait for assistance which may be a long time coming, section IV, 'Waterfront', the most impressive poem in *The Hudson*

Letter, attempts total immersion in characteristic material – a recension of ocean liners, snow, ice, remote shores and polluted landscapes, all done with that dizzying combination of brevity and detail which has made Mahon's poetry so intensely loved. This approach has seemed to be less interesting or available to him in recent years. It is as if he has assumed that the discursive-epigrammatic elements of his work are sufficiently compelling in themselves; as if he taken to preferring later Yeats to MacNeice without noticing that his own music has grown more comfortably mellifluous and shown less of that capacity for apt surprise which would better suit a poetry more drawn to statement. Here, though – and it's a relief – detail provokes and even displaces commentary rather than vice versa. For all his purity of intent, Mahon cannot actually function in a world without objects:

Where once the waters spun to your fierce screws
– *Nieuw Amsterdam, Caronia, Île de France!* –
ice inches seaward in a formal dance
where now, adrift with trash and refuse barges,
the photo-realist estuary 'discharges
its footage' into the blind Atlantic snow.
Smoky and crepitant, glacier-spiky, slow
in its white logic, it is a linotype
from *The Ancient Mariner*, from *Scott's Last Voyage*
or *The Narrative of Arthur Gordon Poe*;
and Heraclitus might have walked here too.[26]

The gaze is firmly and inventively on the object; rather than prodding it with disconsolate urgency, the poet is *interested* in his material. If Mahon's view of the world offers no way out and 'nothing new' there are perhaps ways back in. Behind 'Waterfront', for all the sombreness of its closing line of graffiti – 'QUESTION REALITY. DEATH IS BACK. MIGUEL 141.' – can be heard the brilliant early poem 'April on Toronto Island', where a romantic vocation is seen as endlessly renewable:

Slowly, in ones and twos, the people are coming back
To stand on the thin beach among the
Washed-up flotsam of the winter,

Watching the long grainers move down to the seaway.
Their faces dream of other islands,
Clear cliffs and salt water,

Fields brighter than paradise in the first week of creation –
Grace caught in a wind or a tide, our
Lives in infinite preparation.[27]

9. Paul Durcan: *Look At It This Way*

Should there be anyone in the world who has not got mixed feelings?

PAUL DURCAN, 'The Woman with the Keys to Stalin's House'[1]

Readers outside Ireland, considering the work of Paul Durcan with a mixture of delight, confusion and irritation, may have to remind themselves of something so obvious as to have become invisible: culturally, if not in his precise beliefs, Durcan is an Irish Catholic. This is a much intenser matter than it might seem to the non-Catholic or even the lapsed Catholic of Irish descent living in Britain. Durcan may have presented himself in published work since 1967 as a hippie-bohemian, a belated romantic legislator, a satirist, an anarchist, a lover, an exile and so on, but even as he excoriates the Church, Catholicism remains the mediating fact of his imaginative life. His *non serviam* depends on what it opposes: there is no means of simply leaving it behind. Whether the speaker of 'The Repentant Peter' is the actual Durcan or one of the voices he enters is immaterial to the cultural force (and the authority of the dead father the poem addresses) acknowledged in its account of a forty-five year old man kneeling to pray:

> I do it
> Because that is what you taught me to do.
> I could not
> Not do it.
> You taught me that like you
> I am destitute animal,
> Frailer
> Than plump lamb under candlelit chestnut,
> Frailer
> Than mother cat wheezing in cartwheel,
> Frailer
> Than galaxies of geese,
> And that behind all my sanctimonious lechery,
> It is all night, with only daylight above it.[2]

The very form of this, one of Durcan's baldest, least subversive poems, depends on liturgy, sermon and the presence of both in the everyday vernacular wisdoms and terrors which guided an unbringing. Catholic Ireland shadows and tethers both his subject matter and his style – and while his passion speaks far beyond Ireland, there is a significant part of his work whose language must seem strange to those not thus governed. The power of his technique, with its redeployment of a Catholic rhetoric as satire and protest, may affect the reader without him or her quite being able to identify it, which may account for the feeling occasionally encountered that despite the manifest power of his writing Durcan *has no* technique. Uncertainty as to how to handle Durcan's work may be increased by the powerful, contrasting familiarity, from a rather earlier date, of poets from Northern Ireland, especially Mahon and Longley, whose frequent formalism is both inviting and explicable in terms of English verse traditions. While both Mahon and Longley are poets of the ear as well as the eye, Durcan's sense of the poetic depends in a much more public way on the co-presence of language as writing and as oratory, as well as on the traffic between haphazard talk and more deliberate public address. In a slightly more rarefied and estranged fashion than Brendan Kennelly's, Durcan's poems also speak in the awareness of what the older poet has called 'the relentless, pitiless anecdotalism of Irish life, the air swarming with nutty little sexual parables, the platitudinous bonhomie sustained by venomous undercurrents, the casual ferocious gossip'.[3] (The 'performance' poet in England, with fewer such resources, is a much more suspect species than Durcan.) Even in revolt, then – as in 'The Divorce Referendum, Ireland 1986' – Durcan is much more firmly the occupant of his native culture than any of his English contemporaries could be. When the priest at Mass states that the teaching of Christ and that of the Church are one and the same, and that marriage is indissoluble, Durcan, or his persona (does the difference *matter* in the case of such a protean imagination?) declares:

> I have come into this temple today to pray
> And be healed by, and joined with, the Spirit of Life,
> Not to be invaded by ideology.
> I say unto you, preachers and orators of the Hierarchy,
> Do not bring ideology into my house of prayer.[4]

The condition of being culturally indoors, if not entirely at home there, has consequences for the kind of social criticism Durcan delivers. Edna Longley has summarised a significant part of Durcan's endeavour:

> Durcan's furious fantasies assail verbal pieties which mask materialism, sexism, the commodification of relationships and of art, authoritarianism in the Church, and the violent subtext of Nationalism.[5]

Longley is surely correct, except that her terms are part of a vocabulary, and draw on a tone, somewhat remote from the poems' own practice: to speak of the poems in this way is, in a sense, to *translate* them and risk losing the very peculiarity which makes Durcan's work so compelling. In the case of 'The Divorce Referendum, Ireland, 1986', it might seem rather late in the day for an educated person to be so outraged by the presence of 'ideology' in a place of worship, or to be setting aside the fact that a Catholic Church on Sunday is no place to go for a value-free meeting with 'the Spirit of Life'. The oddity of Durcan's situation is emphasised by an earlier and definitively satirical headline poem, 'Wife Who Smashed Television Gets Jail'. It may be that the poet *understands* the insane complicity of authority and commerce perfectly well:

> Justice O'Brádaigh said wives who preferred bar-billiards to family television
> Were a threat to the family which was the basic unit of society
> As indeed the television itself could be said to be the basic unit of the family
> And when as in this case wives expressed their preference in forms of violence
> Jail was the only place for them. Leave to appeal was refused.[6]

Yet no English poet could undertake such a stark poem and hope to be taken seriously. It would be to state the merely obvious. The nearest approach would be the hit and miss soft-left satire of Adrian Mitchell. For Durcan's poem, collected in 1976, though, as for Ireland itself, television and the world of consumer objects retained a certain (to Durcan, stark and alarming) novelty. What keeps the poem from inadequacy is the picture it flashes in the back of its cave, showing the absence from the poem – and the nation – of any sense of secular civil reality, even during the relative decline of the power of the Church. Church, state and business interlock, all of them feeding in various ways, as well as feeding *on*, the notion of the family. But it is important to note that Durcan's understanding of materialism is not itself materialist: in place of economics he has morality, and in place of politics he has hope, and when that fails he shows an alarming emotional frankness. In his most recent book, *Christmas Day* (1996), he declares in the title poem that 'Poetry's another word/For losing everything/ Except purity of heart.' To the English reader these terms may seem impossibly flimsy (as well as weirdly redolent of 'Me and Bobby McGhee'),[7] and help to confirm that we are a good deal less interested in what Durcan thinks than in how he sees and experiences the world, which is a point implicit in Bernard O'Donoghue's astute summary of another part of Durcan's practice: 'his vivid narratives are more atmospheric than metaphysical'.[8] The tendency towards boneless spirituality and abstraction in some recent poetry from the Republic of Ireland, which can create difficulties for the uncommitted reader, can sometimes be seen surfacing in Durcan's work. It is a relief when he plunges back into the scalding, punishing element in which he was reared in order to wield his individual conscience against the pressures of conformity.

He is engaged in a bitter struggle with Irish Nationalism. The link suggested by proximity in Edna Longley's list between 'authoritarianism in the Church, and the violent subtext of Nationalism' is nightmarishly clear in 'Poem Not Beginning With a Line By Pindar', where the murder of Protestant workmen, echoing of the slaughter of the Miami Showband, is imagined provoking the following response from the poet's father, a judge and President of the Circuit Court. He

> Does not dissemble as he curls his lip,
> Does not prevaricate as he gazes through me:
> 'Teach the Protestants a lesson,'
> And, when I fail to reciprocate,
> 'The law is the law and the law must take its course.'[9]

A crux of this kind enables Durcan to feel that absenting himself from politics is a possible and legitimate course. Edna Longley remarks that the 'hypocrisy, cruelty, indifference and evasion diagnosed by Durcan's socially explicit poems, condition the schizophrenia in his strange dark visions'.[10] In fact he also discerns the same disorder in the Irish state and society itself. The judge's two remarks can be read as belonging to different categories (sectarian prejudice and legal objectivity), but the first serves and is validated by the second. If this is a version of a tendency present in all states, Durcan clearly wants to call attention to the readiness of Irish Nationalism to resemble Fascism. This is the burden of 'Fjord', which again recalls the poet's father, this time in teaching mode, handing over a piece of vocabulary for the son's use – 'As if you'd invented Norway and the Norwegian language/ Especially for me', only to pollute its geographical innocence with other associations:

> You'd confide that we had fjords of our own in Ireland
> And the noblest of all our fjords was in County Mayo,
> The Killary fjord in the safe waters of whose deep, dark thighs
> German submarines had lain sheltering in the war.
>
> Look into your Irish heart, you will find a German U-boat,
> A periscope in the rain and a swastika in the sky.
> You were no more neutral, Daddy, than Ireland was,
> Proud and defiant to boast of the safe fjord.[11]

This is an eloquent example of Durcan's limitations as a poet resistant to politics yet convinced of the authority of his own testimony in the field. The complexities of history are not Durcan's concern:

what interests him is the dramatic conflation of the 'Irish heart' of the poet's father with Ireland itself, for a purpose contrary to the usual sentimental identification of place with person; and the result of its use in the subversion of the romantic aura of opposition is indeed striking and chilling. Yet it is also, as a matter of record, unjust to the many Irish participants on the Allied side of the conflict, as well as to those neutrals for whom a hatred of Britain did not entail an enthusiasm for Nazi Germany. A dislike of misty-eyed nationalism issues here in a matching simplification, which in turn makes Durcan's exclusion of himself from 'ideology' more comprehensible and perhaps something of a relief as well – although his lack of political engagement may have more in common with the political neutrality of De Valera's Ireland than he likes to think. As R.F. Foster comments at the close of his description of the country's wartime position: 'Eire had not accepted the values of the warring nations and did not intend to do so in the future.' [12]

The most significant expression of Durcan's rejection of politics can be found in his love poems and poems about women generally, in which there persists a glimmer of worldly redemption, a utopian margin. Here too, though, Ireland and the Church have been before him. However contemporary in their sexual liberty ('Teresa's Bar', 'Sister Agnes Writes to Her Beloved Mother', 'The Woman Who Keeps Her Breasts in the Back Garden', 'Hommage à Cézanne') [13] however unmaternal in their conduct, the women in Durcan's poems are, as Longley suggests, inversions of Catherine ní Houlihan.[14] They also have a fairly close kinship with the Virgin Mary. Durcan seems perfectly aware of this, as he attempts to parlay his own idealism into feminism. Yet whilst he gives many of the best lines to women, the poems rest, a bit unsteadily, on a traditional frame of reference, as can be seen in 'The Divorce Referendum, Ireland 1986', where the poet sees a child taking communion:

> Curtseying, she smiled eagerly, and flew back down the aisle,
> Carrying in her breast the Eucharist of her innocence:
> May she have children of her own
> And as many husbands as will praise her –
> For what are husbands for, but to praise their wives? [15]

This courtliness is an extension of the franchise, not a revision of the theology. If Longley seems rather stern in her suggestion that Durcan's poems to his estranged wife in *The Berlin Wall Café* 'might be seen as exploitative',[15] it is worth asking if the repentance they serve is not itself a form of self-interest defined by the terms of Catholicism. 'Hymn to a Broken Marriage' seems to un-invert the uses of formal religious address in pursuit of a proper tone:

> For, even you – in spite of your patience and your innocence
> (Strange characteristics in an age such as our own) –
> Even you require to shake off the addiction of romantic love
> And seek, instead, the herbal remedy of a sane affection
> In which are mixed in profuse and fair proportion
> Loverliness, brotherliness, fatherliness:
> A sane man could not espouse a more intimate friend than you.[17]

It might be harsh, but it would be understandable, if the recipient of such a poem punched its author in the nose, partly for the belatedness of its generosity, partly for the way its acquisition of wisdom seems to bring with it a peculiar assumption of authority. Durcan approaches the problem from a different direction in 'The Pietà's Over', which, speaking in the woman's voice, can be read as the poet's own riposte to his presumption:

> By all means look around you, but stop looking back.
> I would not give you shelter if you were homeless in the streets
> For you must make a home in yourself, not in a woman.
> Keep going out the road for it is only out there –
> Out where the river achieves its riverlessness –
> That you and I can become at last strangers to one another,
> Ready to join up again on Resurrection Day.[18]

It is hard to decide whether this is a sentimental poem or a poem about sentimentality. At any rate, the mother figure cannot ultimately refuse consolation by saying 'never', and this fact prolongs the narrative even in closing it.

The 'riverlessness' towards which the woman urges the poet to aspire might perhaps be located at the less rigorous end of utopia. Richard Kearney, in his essay 'Myth and Modernity in Irish Poetry', where he discusses utopian elements in Durcan's work, provides a handy distinction between the terms *ideology* and *utopia*:

> ideology refers to that complex of myths and images which serve to maintain the *status quo*; and *utopia* refers to the use of myths and images to challenge and transform the *status quo*. Utopia can accordingly be equated with that unconquered power of imagination, that surplus of symbolic desire, which resists the closure of ideology. Utopia has of course to remain *critical*, lest it degenerate into a new ideology...[19]

Kearney goes on to read *Going Home to Russia* (1987) in the light of this description:

> If the Russian nation is a utopia betrayed and the Irish nation a utopia delayed (until the reunification of North and South), then, Durcan is saying, we must have done with ideologies of nations. Durcan feels a foreigner in his native land and a native in a foreign land. His utopian images stem from a basic ambiguity towards homelands. As he puts it in one poem of the Russian sequence, 'Should there be anyone in the world who has not got mixed feelings?[20]

Both in itself and as a formulation of Durcan's sense of things, doesn't this seem rather too neat and easy? The enlightened utopian 'no-place' doesn't seem to exert or invoke enough imaginative or critical pressure, and surely in this sense it risks lapsing into ideology. As to what that ideology might be, in Durcan's work it looks like a cult of human relationships, of paired-off passions and intimacies in which individual fulfilment validates a flight from the political. It's an interesting coincidence that Durcan's first book appeared in 1967. The high summer of hippiedom sought a suspension of history. Such freedom offered no significant threat to the *status quo* because it never considered the enduring connection between high romance and vulgar finance. Durcan, of course is at some points a much finer poet than this sceptical account might suggest. To take a single example: a monologue such as 'The Haulier's Wife Meets Jesus on the Road Near Moone'[21] succeeds precisely because of its attention to the particulars of an individual life, and reveals the sense of the dignity of others in which Durcan's work is so rich. Within such a frame, Durcan is able to reverse the polarities of moral convention and social expectation, to reveal, with great pathos, a chink of the possible. But it would do him a disservice to expect the vivid, powerful and generous feelings of a fundamentally lyric poet, whom the times have forced into satire and dream-exile, to offer a sustainable (as distinct from a passionate) critique of his society.

IV

A DAFT PLACE

10. Roy Fisher: A Polytheism with No Gods

Realism is a difficult word –
RAYMOND WILLIAMS: *Keywords*[1]

…that force without which life flows away unheard –
THEODOR ADORNO and MAX HORKHEIMER:
The Culture Industry: Enlightenment as Mass Deception[2]

The peculiarity of Roy Fisher's relationship to the English poetic mainstream is appropriate to his intensely paradoxical work. 'I get used as a between-worlds counter in reviewers' debates,' he has remarked.[3] He is the modernist (and postmodernist) the non-modernists enjoy and to some extent understand; the acceptable face of what is still seen, by detractors and some supporters alike, as *avant-gardisme*. This doesn't mean Fisher writes modernist-*lite:* another way of characterising him would be to say that he has the artfulness to support the radicalism of his aesthetics and to invite readers into the complicated landscape of his work.

'Birmingham's what I think with' is the Bakhtinian declaration which opens 'Talking to Cameras', the first of the 'Six Texts for Film' in the 1994 collection *Birmingham River*.[4] While seeming to hark back to Louis Zukofsky's injunction to 'Think with things as they exist',[5] Fisher applies a wry English humour to its implications:

It's not made for that sort of job,
but it's what they gave me.[6]

The city at the centre of Fisher's universe, of which he writes with compelling passion and fascination, is both an analogue of consciousness and a feature of it. His awareness of the twinning of the mind and its objects, and of the play of memory over both, means that there is always more to say than he can include or bring into view. He can constantly be overheard in negotiation with all the rest of what might be said. The effect on the poems across more than thirty years is both bracing and destabilising. As Ian Gregson has commented,

> Fisher's poems are…indeterminate in their form and meaning – they never present themselves as definitive or conclusive, but as provisional statements leading to other provisional statements…Fisher comes closest to making definitive statements at those points in his work where he stresses the impossibility of being definitive.[7]

In the English context, Fisher is a markedly anti-foundationalist poet: we might say that his *modus operandi* depends on rejecting the idea of ends and purposes. Yet his work also reveals the mind's hankering after teleology – the gritty ghost in the machine, put there by language, which implies closure as well as ramification. No origin is available, but the mind is paradoxically engaged in a continual search. The master narrative of Birmingham is both dreamed and denied by the fragmentary and continually revised map of this endeavour. In 'Talking to Cameras' Fisher states:

> you can be sure, if it's Birmingham,
> that everything'll be altered
> by the time you'd have wanted it again.[8]

There is no secure history of the 'thinking'; it must continually start up where it was left last time, amid a landscape which has changed, or been changed, around it. Fisher states this starkly in 'Handsworth Liberties': 'Nothing has a history. The most/ gnarled things are all new...'.[9] Yet the poet is also a historian of the normatively invisible details and corners of the epically ordinary. In a prose section of *City* (1961), Fisher describes an old inner-city residential district:

> ...These streets are not worth lighting. The houses have not been turned into shops – they are not villas either that might have become offices, but simply tall dwellings, opening straight off the street, with cavernous entries leading into back courts.
>
> The people who live in them are mostly very old. Some have lived through three wars, some through only one; wars of newspapers, of mysterious sciences, of coercion, of disappearance. Wars that have come down the streets from the unknown city and the unknown world, like rainwater floods in the gutters. There are small shops at street corners, with blank rows of houses between them; and taverns carved only shallowly into the massive walls. When these people go into the town, the buses they travel in stop just before they reach it, in the sombre back streets behind the Town Hall and the great insurance offices.[10]

This compelling but rigorously underplayed passage, which has none of the Dickensian flourish the subject might seem to invite, makes the reader pause to ask if this can really be England. It sounds almost more like nineteenth-century Europe – for instance, like the 'manufactured' Polish city of Lodz, 'the Polish Manchester' – while its massiveness has something of the dismaying anonymity of Edward Hopper's *The City* (1927). It has the salutary effect of making the seemingly familiar mental category 'English industrial city' look like a work of fiction.

The sense of scale both large and small, of the relation of the detail to the whole, and the apprehension of secrecy and mystery, lead towards the point at which, for another writer in another period (Eliot, for instance) religious belief might emerge. Although we can hardly avoid imagining that invisible template in the author's mind, Fisher's search leads instead into further districts and details, to dead ends which can seem like ends in themselves. It runs, as it were literally, into the brick walls which are the objects of fascinated attention (Fisher's repeated reference to urine-soaked brick, for example, has been pointed out by Donald Davie).[11] There may be nothing 'behind' the surfaces, but this too must be tracked down. The unattainable city is the object of an almost courtly passion:

> Brick-dust in sunlight. That is what I see now in the city, a dry epic flavour, whose air is human breath. A place of walls made straight with plumbline and trowel, to dessicate and crumble in the sun and smoke. Blistered paint on cisterns and girders, cracking to show the priming. Old men spit on the paving slabs, little boys urinate; and the sun dries it as it dries out patches of damp on plaster facings to leave misshapen stains. I look for things here that make old men and dead men seem young. Things which have escaped, the landscapes of many childhoods.
>
> Wharves, the oldest parts of factories, tarred gable ends rearing to take the sun over lower roofs. Soot, sunlight, brick-dust; and the breath that tastes of them.[12]

There is a scriptural subtext here. Behind the third sentence seems to stand Isaiah 40.4: 'and the crooked shall be made straight and the rough places plain', though the fascinated calm pessimism recalls 1.15: 'That which is crooked cannot be made straight: and that which is wanting cannot be numbered'. It's striking that in the thoroughly secular context of Fisher's work these traces should show up: for this son of Nonconformist industry, belief is a grammatical inheritance rather than a philosophical position, recalling Nietzsche's declaration in *The Twilight of the Idols* that 'I fear we are not getting rid of God because we still believe in grammar'.[13] Fisher also shares with Ecclesiastes 1.8 a sense of the potential endlessness of perception: 'All things are full of labour; man cannot utter it: the eye is not satisfied with seeing, nor the ear filled with hearing' – though we note the dominant (and, as it were, visible) silence of Fisher's world, where the present seems at times the phantasmal and diminished re-enactment of a past which is not to be regained. Yet although the past is crucial to the poems, it is not an ideal from which we have strayed or been expelled: there is no Golden Age in Fisher's work any more than there is in Geoffrey Hill's. A version of objectification evidently influenced by Charles Olson thus meets a thoroughly English pessimism.

The place described seems at once charged and emptied, concrete but constantly sliding into the typical. It is minutely detailed but somehow hard to contextualise – spatial rather than thoroughly pictorial, again harking back to Olson, specifically his comments on description: 'The descriptive functions generally have to be watched, every second, because of their easiness, and thus their drain on the energy which composition by field allows into a poem.'[14] Whether readers agree that description is 'easy' (can Olson prove it by doing it himself?), or indeed whether or not they accept the brew of aesthetic passion and hearty scoutmaster-ish guff found in Olson's essays, Fisher, most place-obsessed of poets, does by and large refuse the transcendent option offered by figurative language, and this befits a poet of process rather than outcome. Rather than helping the poet to establish a total picture, the detail forbids it. The visual trespasses on the discursive, while the effort of inclusion suggests but does not provide a revelation. This unsettling employment of metonymy works to dramatise the observing and participating consciousness, which is always abroad in its own work. Fisher's view is haunted by idealism (as Neil Corcoran has observed, his resistance to Romanticism is surely a sign of his attraction to it),[15] but the full view can never be obtained. Over against the questing spirit is a relentless, unstable sense of the city as, in Thom Gunn's phrase, 'extreme, material, and the work of man'.[16] Fisher has a sense second to none of the friction between mind and material, and of their seeming interpenetration. 'I'm obsessed,' he writes in 'Wonders of Obligation', 'with cambered tarmacs, concretes,/the washings of rain'.[17]

Reading Fisher may at first be a disorienting and thereafter at times a perplexing experience, and readers may resist a strain of dry deliberation in some of the poems from *The Thing About Joe Sullivan* (1978) onwards; but in *City* (1961) as a whole (as also in 'Handsworth Liberties' and *A Furnace*),[18] the combination of meticulous notation, scepticism and insistent enquiry creates a climate which may be far more familiar from the common lived experience of English cities than from much of what other English poetry has had to say about them. This point has not always been taken by critics. Dealing dismissively with Fisher among other English experimentalists, Anthony Thwaite comments that Fisher employs 'cinematic techniques of scanning movement and close-up to present an urban landscape: the device is at least as old as the 1920s – a remark one could make with asperity of much of the work considered experimental today – but there are greyly atmospheric moments'.[19] Thwaite begs a number of questions here, revealing that undertow in English poetic thought which reads the anti-modernist reaction from the 1930s on as a return to mature standards of artistry. Fisher has in fact characterised himself as 'a 1920s Russian modernist',[20] which indicates a sense of humour as well as of history. Why should modernism *not* exhibit durability and a sense of its own traditions? Is its concern with live rather than academic tradition felt to exclude it? The underlying point is that in English poetry the implications of modernist practice as a register of consciousness have not been fully examined. From this perspective, Fisher's particular reading of estrangement is surely of considerable use and value in dealing with ordinary English life in the industrial and post-industrial landscape. As the preface to *A Furnace* states: 'Some of the substances fed in are very solid indeed; precipitates, not only topographical, of industrial culture in its rapid and heavy onset, when it bred a new kind of city whose images dominated people's intelligences in ways previously unknown'.[21]

Because of Fisher's inclusion of consciousness itself in his poems, the poetic imagination has, as it were, no back wall to rest against. The mind itself is continually becoming part of the picture. While this has become a commonplace of contemporary thought, few notable English poets have sought to live by its implications as Fisher has. The witty opening passage of 'Talking to Cameras' approaches the matter through a descant on the theme of the bad workman who blames his tools. Here is a craftsman who explains the impossibility of his task even as he performs it. The poet/workman is always *in medias res*, in a world of perpetual bodging, having to get the job done without knowing why or even what the job is, or whether it is completed. This could be history-from-below's version of Eliot's desiccated lament in 'Ash Wednesday' about inadequate equipment, with a levelling addition of humour. The mind at work is both protean and mechanical, and there's a great relish in Fisher's adaptation of Brechtian 'crude thinking' in order to run dramatic and discursive currents through the world of objects.

The intensity of Fisher's approach has important consequences for the moral and political character of his work. As he has resisted the sense of closure by which English poets are commonly governed (and which often subordinates matter to manner), so he has tended to avoid the expression of consensus humanism, preferring, it would seem, to begin his reflections as though at a prior point. To say this might make Fisher's writing sound cold, which finally it isn't, but his fascination with materialism seems to precede, and then displace, some familiar mental habits. People, for example, are not usually "characterised" or presented in terms of a familiar set of humane assurances. Love, family, ancestry and the actual processes of work – these hardly figure in Fisher's poems. The early poem 'Toyland' (originally part of *City*), for example, establishes an elegant but baffled sense of estrangement:

> I might by exception see an ambulance or the fire brigade
> Or even, if the chance came round, street musicians (singing and playing).

For the people I've seen, this seems the operation of life:
I need the paint of stillness and sunshine to see it that way.

The secret laugh of the world picks them up and shakes them like peas
    boiling;
They behave as if nothing happened; maybe they no longer notice.

I notice. I laugh with the laugh, cultivate it, make much of it,
But still I don't know what the joke is, to tell them.[22]

An interesting comparison could be made between this seeming plain style and the exuberant inventiveness of Craig Raine's 'A Martian Sends a Postcard Home'.[23] We might, for example, note that Raine is as good as his word, making his estrangements somehow neutral and, despite the good-humoured curiosity, slightly inhuman, interesting in themselves but yielding no structural principle except the endless reflex of likeness/difference. Fisher, on the other hand, makes a crisis out of his little neutrally-rendered drama: he assumes the world's indifferent gaze in order to ask what ordinary public behaviour means; having done this, he cannot simply reassume a "normal" viewpoint. It is plain which poem is the less cosy. Fisher holds detachment, distress and curiosity in tension, as if a refusal to be absorbed into the scene should provide a clue to understanding what in fact is unavailable to understanding – i.e. the interpretative sum/surplus of all these moving parts. For an English reader, this method may go some way to make sense of Projective Verse. Fisher in effect 'projects' projectivism against the screen of English historical and social anxieties. The effect is to interrogate, though not to break, the familiar frame of English poetic reference.

There are other comparisons to be made. Louis MacNeice, himself fascinated with Birmingham, is famously the poet of the patterns of contingency and transience, but the state of flux serves to reinforce his classically-inspired humanism. Fisher, on the other hand, is not content (nor, arguably, is he equipped) for estrangement to function as a figure in a discourse whose ends are already known to rhetoric. The effects of this stubbornness are sharply revealed in another poem which invites comparison with modern English city-poetry. The markedly Audenesque 'The Hospital in Winter', unusual in the Fisher corpus for its rhymes, noticeably stops short of the decisive reading of a lesson, though it places itself within reach of traditional resonances:

On benches squat the afraid and cold
    hour after hour.
Chains of windows snarl with gold.

Far off, beyond the engine-sheds,
    motionless trucks
grow ponderous, their rotting reds

deepening towards night; from windows
  bathrobed men
watch the horizon flare as the light goes.

Smoke whispers across the town,
  high panes are bleak;
pink of coral sinks to brown;
a dark bell brings the dark down.[24]

An unfavourably-disposed reader might declare this poem simply a list. What, this reader, might ask, does the poem *make* of its circumstances and properties, beyond the remote closing reference to Gray's 'Elegy Written in a Country Churchyard'? One way to address this question is to set Fisher's lines alongside a passage they unexpectedly recall. It comes from 'The Age of Anxiety', where Auden, another Birmingham poet, writes:

In a vacant lot
We built a bonfire and burned alive
Some stolen tires. How good and strong one
Felt at first, coming home through
The urban evening. It was supper time.
In hot houses helpless babies and
Telephones gabbled untidy cries,
And on embankments black with burnt grass
Shambling freight-trains were shunted away
Past crimson clouds.[25]

John Bayley comments on these lines:

> Auden delights in turning into poetry – in 'nullifying' into the poetic as Sartre might call it – the most ragged and viscous aspects and experiences of life. He seems to find its randomness and essential absurdity a challenge to his skill...The brilliancy of description does not lead anywhere ...But it conveys a sense of the occasion at once and with vivid accuracy, and gives the reader the unpursuing satisfaction of contemplating a formal triumph. It is difficult for the most conscientious reader – if he enjoys the passage at all – not to repose upon the event described, upon its sense of the particular...[26]

Bayley goes on to draw the obvious comparison with the Eliot of 'Preludes', with his 'careful evocations of the shabby and incomplete urban moment'.[27] Implicit, I think, in Bayley's acute comment is the assumption that more serious claims will be staked elsewhere in the poet's work, where the operation of the imagination is made to answer to moral concerns. And this is true of Auden; but the impression given by Fisher's writing is that such inconsequent, unfinished places are the ground where moral concerns must stand or sink, since they are where (and to a great extent how and why) people live and die. The hospital and its patients in Fisher's 'The Hospital in Winter' are not the object of *style*. We could read the whole of Fisher's work as a flight from the stylish set-piece. He has in fact characterised style, in order to exempt himself from it, in an eponymous poem:

> That marriage (like a supple glove
> that won't suffer me to breathe)
> to the language of one's time
> and class. The languages
> of my times and classes.[28]

The pathos and near-horror of 'The Hospital in Winter' in fact arise from the eschewal of a rhetorical conclusion. If, after religion, humanism must serve as the heart of the heartless world, Fisher will not deny the heartlessness, and thus in the poem the consoling, conjuring properties of music are damped, just as the image of the bell is foreclosed. From such work we can learn what Fisher means when he calls himself 'by temper, realist':[29] what he presents is a domestic world, the homeworld of streets, work, weather and time, in its undomesticated form. Sobering as this is, the practice can also issue in an impulse at least partly celebratory, though of a kind perhaps unfamiliar to liberal convention. The famous 'For Realism' is a case in point, where the brutally mundane, which poetry might normally reserve for pity, satire or condemnation, is seen living according to its own lights:

> there presses in
> – and not as conscience –
> what concentrates down in the warm hollow:
>
> plenty of life there still,
> the foodshops open late, and people
> going about constantly, but not far;
>
> there's a man in a blue suit
> facing into a corner,
> straddling to keep his shoes dry;
> women step, talking, over the stream,
> and when the men going by call out, he answers.
>
> Above, dignity. A new precinct
> comes over the scraped hill,
> flats on the ridge get the last light.
>
> Down Wheeler Street, the lamps
> already gone, the windows have
> lake stretches of silver
> gashed out of tea green shadows,
> the after-images of brickwork.
>
> A conscience
> builds, late, on the ridge. A realism
> tries to record, before they're gone,
> what silver filth these drains have run.[30]

If in the unsettlingly neutral description we have a foretaste of parts of Douglas Dunn's *Terry Street*, we also have an imaginative critique of two key terms, realism and conscience, conducted with urgent literalism and concreteness and on ground to which in an English social context the words might be felt particularly to refer – the demolition and rebuilding of the industrial city in the post-war period. This was perhaps the final great endeavour of 1945 socialism – though much of the urban transformation was carried out under the Conservative administrations of 1951-64, including the period of so-called Butskellite consensus. As we now know, the results were extremely mixed, though the history of the re-housed working class remains to be written. Historical information of this kind has an ambiguous status in the poem: you need to know something of the mixture of good intentions and expedient fudging involved in the rebuilding in order to see how conscience and realism are being inspected and satirised; but at the same time the meaning of narrative history and the political rhetoric of the period concerned are part of what the poem refuses, the better to re-imagine the subject. Fisher goes further than this, though. Not only are documentary and journalistic methods discarded, much of the time here Fisher seems to step back from the poetic, from the rhetorical elevation present in much apparently realistic urban writing. Instead, he writes like a painter, obliged to discern and recreate a moral shape (supposing there is one) in the visual field. *Ut pictura poesis* is put rigorously to the test.

Thus an enquiry is instituted into the true weight, and the striking ambiguity, of the two terms in question. If conscience here seems feeble and belated in the face of the life it ought to represent or redeem, both words are exploited to sharpen the sense of the substance, and the diminution, of that life. The political and the phenomenal can be seen to fuse in realism – a term found in art (as a style); in politics (ditto?); in everyday making-do; and as a means of discarding what has become (economically, politically, ethically, historically) difficult or inconvenient to maintain. Meanwhile the inadequacy and self-interest of reformism are both felt in conscience. The word cannot carry over the Hoggartian closeness and familiarity of community into the new high-rise estate – because there is something neither good nor bad but simply inimitable about what is discarded (the 'silver filth') in the process of rebuilding. Readers interested in linking Fisher to Bakhtinian ideas may care to consider that 'silver filth' might be a condign example of carnival at work in the visual (and thus, for this poem's purposes, in the moral) field. Groping for an account of what the poem does, and wanting to avoid banal workerism, the critic may be struck, anyway, by the appropriateness of Fisher's method. It never has to fall back on morality, since this is embodied in the process of enquiry and meditation, which serve to refresh the reader's sense of both the physical world and moral problems it holds. Fisher himself has voiced objections to readings by critics

> who will very characteristically go at my work from the representational end or the end which appears to have morality and might be what you could call comforting in that the poetry might be left and the concepts which it gives rise to might then be discussed away from the poetry.'[31]

One can go along with Fisher's dislike of reductive readings and yet feel that he's being a bit disingenuous, since in practice his work, with its concern for the processes of perception, representation and interpretation, does invite (and arguably necessitate) discussion in conceptual and abstract terms, even as those terms themselves come under inspection. (One of Fisher's strengths, surely, is that his poems make abstractions poetically thinkable.) In such a discussion morality may figure rather nakedly. Short of a metacritical re-writing of 'the poetry' its hard to see how discussion could proceed otherwise, except through obfuscation. Fisher is certainly enough of a pragmatist to accommodate these facts in his own writing, even at its most concrete, for example in this passage from the 'Introit' to *A Furnace*, which recalls a trolley-bus ride:

> ...the road
> from Bilston to Ettingshall begins
> beating in. Whatever
> approaches my passive taking-in,
> then surrounds me and goes by
> will have itself understood only
> phase upon phase
> by separate involuntary
> strokes of my mind, dark
> swings of a fan-blade
> that keeps a time of its own,
> made up from the long
> discrete moments
> of the stages of the street,
> each bred off the last as if by
> causality.
> Because
> of the brick theatre stuck next to the roadside
> the shops in the next
> street run in a curve, and
> because of that there is raised up
> with red lead on its girders
> a gasworks
> close beyond the roofs...'[32]

Fisher's mechanical rendering of perception here, and his pointing to the (as it were) ghost of causality bred (as it were) mechanically out of place by the need of mind and memory for reason, purpose and order, are distinctly 'moral' procedures. They reveal the effort of the mind to make sense of its surroundings and to discover how to live among them. This is an examined life. Realism of temperament produces an appropriate method: Fisher's awareness that temperament and method are sited *in time* helps him to produce a recreation of urban consciousness which is both exhilarating and sombre, and which is drawn always on to the next thing, in the unadmitted hope that it might be the last, explanatory thing. Fisher's importance for English poetry – an importance few other seemingly experimental poets can claim – is twofold. Firstly, he maintains a dialogue of sorts with the habits he's trying to break – closure, epigram, consolation, 'realism' – which is of course rather an English way of proceeding. Secondly, we benefit from its corollary: that Fisher is able to make us foreign to ourselves – not at the level of theoretical assertion, but through discomfiting practice.

11. Peter Reading: *The Poet as Thatcherite?*

> ...Reading has made himself the unofficial laureate of a decaying nation. He writes with a journalistic commitment to the present social moment and scorns an aesthetic idea that prizes the lapidary and the fixed.
>
> TOM PAULIN[1]

> ...sotted
> No-God and Species Decline stuff...
>
> PETER READING, 'Thanksgiving'[2]

Adducing Peter Reading's absence from (and his likely indifference to his absence from) anthologies published during the 1980s, Dennis O'Driscoll characterised Reading in an essay written in 1991[3] as 'a natural outsider' in contemporary English poetry. One sees what O'Driscoll means: Reading didn't belong to those tendencies which were publicised in that decade, such as Martianism or New/Secret Narrative, and thus didn't receive the kind of attention largely reserved for Oxbridge/London poet-journalists who were quite often involved in the editing of the papers and magazines where publicity was created. This is an old story. Yet as O'Driscoll points out, Reading for many years had London publishers (Secker, Chatto) and was frequently published in the *TLS*, whose one-time poetry editor, Alan Jenkins, went on to edit and introduce Reading's selected poems, *Essential Reading.*[4] Without wanting to engage in theologically nice distinctions, it would be fair to say that there are less happy states of outsiderdom to occupy, as many under-read poets would presumably attest.

If the role of outsider is relative, what about the relative outsider's themes? Here O'Driscoll seems to be on firmer ground. Noting the widespread poetic avoidance of such avowedly contemporary matters as 'the revelations of science, the disseminations of the mass media, the destruction of the natural environment', he offers Reading as a poet prepared to engage with such subjects, and to do so on a scale appropriate to their gravity. Most contemporary poetry, O'Driscoll seems to suggest, is characterised by an evasive miniaturism – 'Elegies, childhood reminiscences, ironic anecdotes and holiday-cottage nature poems typify the contents of the average slim volume'.[5] This Peterloorycism is another old story, a sign of decay observed long since in Charles Tomlinson's contemptuous description of the 'suburban mental ratio' of English poetry.[6] The persistence of this theme begs the question of why anyway we would spend much time on the 'average', having once discovered it to be so – especially when a good deal of the far-from-average, thematically and in terms of ambition (at least) has become available during the period O'Driscoll refers to.

More seriously, in the good cause of lively provocation, O'Driscoll begs the question of the authority poetry bears in relation to the urgencies of its period. This seems a more complicated matter than can be dealt with according to a prescription along the lines of 'science good, holiday cottage bad', which seems implicit in O'Driscoll's view. As O'Driscoll is undoubtedly aware, Patrick Kavanagh, a founding father of modern Irish poetry, made the famous declaration in the person of Homer, in 'Epic': 'Gods make their own importance'[7] – Gods, be it noted, having traditionally at least as large a stake as the literary critic in matters poetic. Subject-matter and contemporaneity in themselves cannot supply gravity to poetry: it is the manner of a thing's doing which will determine its status. The comically disastrous consequences of whoring after "relevance" are illustrated by the success of *Whale Nation*,[8] a book so attuned to the sentiments of the times that in some quarters to question its literary value was to invite the accusation of wanting the extinction of the whale.

This is, I admit, a little unfair to O'Driscoll. It is not, he makes clear, just that Reading engages with scientific subjects – archaeology, for example – but that he seeks to inhabit their languages and attitudes imaginatively:

> The palaeontological, medical and astronomical experts who inhabit his poems are fully realised creations speaking a professional patois and not some simplified poetical version of it...Reading's world is large not only because of the largeness of his linguistic resources (as Randall Jarrell said of Wallace Stevens) but because he knows – or is prepared to learn – more about the world than most poets.[9]

The reference to Stevens here looks bizarre, to say the least, since his transcendent imaginative language seems to live at the other end of the (if not in a quite different) universe from Reading's relentlessly anti-symbolist, de-resonated approach. The impression given by Reading's sense of the world is of extent without variety or grandeur, an epic of size but not apprehension, done in black and white. We might characterise Reading as a poet of the Coleridgean Fancy (meaning aggregation) rather than Imagination (meaning transformation). He may be one of our first genuinely post-romantic poets – and, on his prognosis, probably one of the last poets of any complexion. His literary enthusiasms – Swift and the eighteenth-century novel, for instance – seem to support such a view. To most understandings – and this is not to discredit Reading simply for being different – such a sensibility will offer a diminished sense of the world's possibilities. Presumably, however, Reading would suggest that his view is the case, not just for poetry but for the world as a whole, which is wrecked, doomed, occupied by a species staring, for the most part indifferently, at extinction. The problem, at any rate for this reader, is the feeling that poetry of necessity preserves something of itself from the general wreck – not optimism or hope, necessarily, but the power of imaginative production which can depict the visit to the underworld in *Aeneid* VI, or the fate of Paolo and Francesca in the fifth canto of the *Inferno*, or the 'unreal city' of *The Waste Land*. This power seems to live in a kind of useful disinterestedness, in Keats's negative capability. It is also part of the ethical peculiarity which attracted Plato's suspicion to poetry but which also enabled Aristotle to characterise poetry as more philosophical and serious than history.[10] This is a rather grandiose list of instances and witnesses: Reading has enquired in *C*, 'Where is the European cultural significance of tubes stuck up the nose, into the veins, up the arse?'[11] Presumably it depends, as Professor Joad might have said, what you mean by significance. But these examples can at any rate imply much that is no longer present to Reading's imagination. It is not that his gloom and despair are objectionable (Reading himself has neatly parodied critics who take this view) but that his imaginative power seems, whether coincidentally or consequently, limited by his attitudes.

But where is Reading situated? Poets perhaps deserve better than to be known by the critics they attract (or repel), but some of the commentary on Reading helps to illustrate the polar opposition his work can provoke. The notably sour Martin Seymour-Smith, for example, representing Reading to the world in *The Oxford Companion to Twentieth Century Poetry*, argues that 'the manner of his verse... has worn somewhat thin. *C* (London, 1984), 100 prose poems of 100 words each, displays him at his least effective: the pieces are supposed to be composed by a man dying of cancer, and are no more horrible or interesting than clinical notes would be: it works to no point. Such writing, not in verse, seems to operate as an oblique defence of the writer's own sensibility, which the reader now inevitably begins to suspect may be commonplace or sentimental'.[12] Seymour-Smith has praise to offer as well – of Reading's humour, for instance – but in the context this seems like the offer of a final cigarette before the firing squad takes aim. On the other hand, Isabel Martin, introducing Reading's *Collected Poems*, can find nothing whatsoever to complain about. In her view Reading presents a body of work of remarkable, orchestrated unity and unswerving purpose, deploying an extraordinary range of verbal and metrical effects, which combine with a matchless breadth of reference to extend the reach of poetry itself – all in the cause of unsparing truthfulness. This is praise indeed. Can she and Seymour-Smith be reading the same poet? The reader ill-at-ease with the size of Martin's claims may pause interestedly over the following remark:

> ...while Reading may cover a lot of ground, he has no time for spiritual speculation. His no-nonsense outlook never leaves the realm of secular common sense, thus also appealing to those readers who tend to favour the normally less ethereal world of prose fiction.[13]

This alarming declaration may simply be badly formulated, but it suggests a limited familiarity with prose fiction, and maybe with poetry as well. Even supposing we can construe fiction as a single 'world', it contains a good deal more than Martin seems to have dreamed of. The really troubling feature, though, is the matching assumption that poetry can be characterised as trading in the 'ethereal'. This is a strikingly anachronistic term to employ at the far end of the twentieth century – even, or especially, when it's applied to a subject about which the public, when it thinks of it at all, is markedly ignorant. It's peculiar to find a critic seeming to disclose, or not to question, an assumption which has no place in the serious discussion of poetry. Yet the other implication, that poetry would do well to learn from this example and adapt itself to the supposed tastes of putative novel-readers, is still more bizarre. It would be comprehensible coming from Auberon Waugh; and on that note the case against Martin might satisfactorily rest – were there not a suspicion of anxiety in her peculiarly botched statement. It's the anxiety of looking for a clinching remark, which perhaps accounts for the grotesque result. The claim on the attentions of the supposedly prosaically minded novel-reader seems made to insure against the objection that Reading is not doing what poetry has to do, i.e. refresh the texture of language. On a dissenting reading, his immense ingenuity disguises a hollowness at the core, an absence of verbal life, for which no amount of patterning or interior allusion or incorporation of found, borrowed or adapted materials can compensate. It could be a small, dry irony of Reading's apprehension of 'Species Decline' that such decline should also manifest itself thus, in diminished poetic potency.

Martin views Reading as an inheritor of the tradition of English pessimism and as a humanist who knows that humanism will fail, one who foresees the extinction of human life, followed by the reign of 'arthropods'.[14] A Swiftian contempt is accompanied by an agonised sense of waste. Part of the humanistic repertoire to which Reading aligns himself is an attachment to the explanatory power of reason. Yet it has been suggested that this is the source from which the very downfall of humanism and thus of humanity may arise, in the form of reason's political and economic debasement as the provider of justifications for the expediencies of realpolitik and the exploitation of resources to the point of exhaustion. To be here at all, on this interpretation, is to be compromised: the Fall is re-written by the printing press. Reading's anti-romantic stance entails some obligations to this view; indeed, he can seem to relish the darkening perspective – to enjoy with part of himself, as Auden proposed all poets do, the scene of disaster. Faced with such signs of catastrophe, though, there remains the less extreme perspective from below the salt, as it were, with its interest in the doings and muddlings-through of people 'going on' with their lives in the teeth of the dreadful evidence – 'well you has to *LIVE* don't you?' as Viv puts it in *Ukulele Music*.[15] Louis MacNeice, another student of the classics, declared: 'There will always be people',[16] which Reading would seem likely to dispute; but people are much of Reading's subject (and much of prose fiction's), so what does he make of them?

To provide a context for Reading's writing about people, it is worth mentioning some other common features of poetry largely absent from his work, such as metaphor and the visual and loco-descriptive components, which are the staple of much English verse. We do not often ask Reading about the appearance of the world, either literally or figuratively. 'Here is perpetual smoke of a city unpierced by sunlight/where ye Cimmerians dwell, unvisible from above'[17] – an Ovidian moment in *Ukulele Music* – is about as specific as he gets. This might seem surprising in the work of one who trained as a visual artist (then again, it might not: horses for courses). The auditory and to some extent the tactile sense, and the voice, occupy positions of rather greater privilege. That this should be so has much to do with Reading's own poetic preferences, of course, but it also indicates the weight placed on speakers and on their speech, which they must bear if the poems are to succeed.

Reading's first full collection, *For the Municipality's Elderly* (1974),[18] was the work of a manifestly decided sensibility, a much clearer and more organised book than most debuts. Its restrained, eloquent gloom contains virtually all of the poet's subject-matter: what it awaits is the full ventriloquial polyphony of its successors. But the tenor will not change: the book provides an index of despairing summings-up. It's even grimmer than Larkin:

I hope I haven't given the impression
that married life is not my cup of tea;[19]

May we then, in the event of our general
annihilation, regard as our forte
our once existing unknown to any,
our permanence and achievement a matter
of individual conscience – our handful
of plastic curlers and rubber-goods transience
lost to remain unwitnessed after
a deeper already gathering maelstrom.[20]

The scarcely living are more numerous than the dead.

...everything worthwhile is already closed.[21]

A speaker
crackles that history is that
which remains. This assumes historians.[22]

...but I was not there, just a cardboard copy.[23]

But having found love I am left with nothing to say.
And I find, in place of Socialist leanings
a ninety per cent misanthropy
which once expressed gains nothing by repetition.[24]

The last remark seems like a hostage to fortune, since, having declared his hand, Reading has had to go on playing it. Faced with the extreme negations offered by this admittedly very impressive book, it's possible to see the attraction of psychiatric versions of poetry and poets. The severity, relish and hinted arrogance of Reading's stance recall the condition of pathological narcissism sometimes ascribed to Sylvia Plath. This may be no more than melancholia writ large, yet it also resembles the increasingly sclerotic posture of the later work of Kingsley Amis. There, as in Reading, boredom and amazed contempt are backlit by occasional intervals of the nice as opposed to the nasty – wine, food, fleeting but self-validating pleasures – in a context of residual pastoralism. The repressed Housman was the repressed Amis's favourite poet – able to give vent to lyric emotion in a way quite inaccessible to Amis. Reading's own poetic enthusiasms include an earthy, debunking comic poet – Gavin Ewart – and the slightly remote Roy Fuller, whose work is as fond of statement and as intrusively opinionated as Reading's own. For Reading the world has gone to the dogs and its people do not pass muster, being ignorant, trivial and brutal. The abandonment of a 'socialist leanings'[25] strands the poet between Middle England and its rural periphery, where he inherits the tones and prejudices of the apolitical small-c conservative. This emerges offensively in 'Luncheon',[26] whose rendering of a waiter's speech – 'a Mediterranean type' – places the man in the line of comic foreigners which runs in prose writing through Amis and Malcolm Bradbury, a form of Little Englandism whose more popular expression is found in Richard Ingrams and Peter Simple. It would not be necessary to disagree completely with such a view of things in order to sense also on the poet's part a rush to judgement is accompanied by a narrowing of scope – and a powerful projection of self-loathing onto the general public; a projection moreover emphasised by the curious inaccessibility of the poet's own personality to his work.

The latter might go some way to account for the heroic scale of Reading's endeavour as conventional collections give way to through-composed books. Reading's love poems, whether fictive or in propria persona, particularly in *The Prison Cell and Barrel Mystery* (1976),[27] often concern the reappraisal of a love affair after a gap of several years, as in the title poem:

I have not seen you
for so long now that
you count as a corpse.

Already you dress
put black on your eyes
to cross the river
again for the city.[28]

If the chill at the heart of this seems in any doubt, compare it with leavetaking pieces by other Liverpool poets. This founding experience of adulthood comes to seem the point at which the world for Reading is robbed of its plenitude. After this, the imagination must seek elsewhere for echoes of vitality – in the banal or silly or earthbound voices which the poet irritatedly or (we seem meant to infer) compassionately overhears. The vein of appalling comedy is opened up, for instance in the musings of the several speakers in the black-pastoral 'Duologues'; tales of love and loss which hark back to Housman, Hardy and Wordsworth but also partake of Stella Gibbons:

'...Then I sid im again, one Pig Day it were in the Arms,
and e says as e loves me and would I get wed to im
(only would I answer im quick or eed af to wed er).
Well, I never says "ar" nor "no" for days, till e thinks
as it's no and e weds this other out Clungunford way
and they moves down Tenbury country – Glebe Farm an summat.
An e dunna get on with er, an just now e writes me
as e loves me, an I writes back as I loves im an all.
Just now all is stock dies – that Foot and Mouth year afore last –
and they says as e got debts an that's why e shot isself.'[29]

The tale resists interpretation, seeming at once to demand and deny dignity for its nameless protagonist. Given Reading's fondness for orchestration, it can hardly be accidental that this poem precedes the stoically nasty 'Soiree', a vignette of unwanted social life endured for the sake of the poet's wife:

> ...their damn fool questions 'tell me Peter,
> what do you write *about*?' (cunts like you, mate).
> 'Peter, you interested in history?'
> (Mate, I ain't even interested in
> the present.)[30]

To discriminate between the value of the remarks recorded in these two passages is 'a matter of individual conscience', as Reading says in another context,[31] since there is no adequate scale against which to measure them. At the same time, the reader is aware that the vocal arrangements are having to assume the role of supplying overtones and resonances which another poet might seek in other parts of the repertoire. The effect is like a shadow play, throwing silhouettes on a flat canvas and claiming it as an entire world. Having emptied the human sphere, he moves from the saloon bar view to that of eternity, in which human time (the Holocene) is a mere eye-blink. Yet his subject, wherever he travels, is actually England – the incoherent, complacent, presumptuous, witless, feral, snobbish, kindly, illiterate saloon-bar England Reading tells us he has overheard. It is a nightmare of decay and disaffection:

> This is the age of the Greatly Bewildered Granny & Grandad,
> shitlessly scared by the bad, mindless and jobless and young;
>
> also the Age Of The Dispossessed Young, with nothing to lose by
> horribly hurting their sires, babies and cripples, and whose
>
> governments, freely elected and otherwise, function by mores
> not altogether removed from their own bestial codes –
>
> those sort of policies, that sort of hardware do not imply much
> kindly respect for *H.sap*, mindless and jobless and young...'[32]

Reading's political exhaustion can produce a desperate eloquence, but it leaves a huge hole where causality ought to be. This is as far as analysis takes him – hardly to the doorstep of the discussion: he is more interested in the comparison with childhood seen through his own then-innocent eyes, a gently ironised age of the last genuine British achievement – the first ascent of Everest, which was in fact accomplished by the New Zealander Edmund Hillary and the Nepalese Tenzing Norgay. Reading's major device is juxtaposition, which might, for instance, encourage us not to enquire too closely into the weight accorded to nostalgia. In *Stet* (1986),[33] a passage in which an astrophysicist is interviewed includes the statement: 'Oh yes. Quite happy to accept Reasonless causal physics.'[34] This clanging irony is made to resound, in and beyond *Stet*, through all Reading's gruesome accounts of cruelty and unreason. In the absence of any intention behind the cosmos, why reason out the activities of muggers and wife-beaters? Why move beyond the point of assertion that these people are 'pongoid' or 'morlocks'? One reason for doing so might be that this path of least intellectual and moral resistance delivers the poet and his poems up to the cruelly Manichean "rationalisation" which lies behind Thatcherism, and thus to the use of effect (brutalisation) to justify cause (impoverishment). You don't, surely, have to approve of violence to want to know why it happens and to seek solutions by eliminating its causes, do you? – though it might make despair less easy to achieve. The poetry of 'Junk Britain',[35] in Tom Paulin's phrase, is not written in the expectation of being an Horatian monument more enduring than bronze, and has a nervy journalistic authenticity; but like much journalism it shrinks its subjects to fit the requirements of its rhetoric. The 'ordinary people' who can be heard speaking in *Ukulele Music*, for instance – the cleaner, Viv, and the unnamed barroom philosopher – are proletarian stereotypes whose origins lie closer to depictions of the lower classes in pre-New Wave British films than to life itself. Viv comments on the author at one point, 'He don't *invent* it, you know.'[36] Yes and no, Viv, yes and no; and sometimes it seems to be *invent*ing him.

12. Peter Porter: *A Planet in the Mind*

Of all the poets discussed in these pages, the one who has most to say about London is himself a foreigner. Peter Porter was born in Brisbane in 1929. He came to England in 1951 and has lived in London ever since. He was part of the great postwar tide of young Australians curious about Europe, and England in particular. His adopted city has been one of his most important subjects – the centre of a world, a point of crisis both personal and general, with historical perspectives leading back through the city as lived in by Pope, Rochester, the Jacobeans and Shakespeare. With some proving exceptions, London is England for Porter. Given his achievement, this is probably forgivable.

His early work is full of references to the capital – Harrods, the Kings Road, Bond Street, South Kensington, Lyons Corner House, Cheapside and the Marshalsea, Chelsea, Piccadilly, Gloucester Road, Paddington Library, the Natural History Museum, the ABC in Westbourne Grove, Highgate Cemetery, the departures board at Waterloo, a small South London park, St James's Park, Frognal, Queensway and the ICA. From a certain point of view, Porter has "done" London. In the meantime it has also "done" him: the place viewed by Douglas Dunn's young men in the provinces as 'a sea of restaurants' is in Porter's work also a reservoir of other pleasures to which the novice must struggle for access and in doing so learn to suffer and survive.

While his predecessors in the nineteenth-century novel might have tried to conquer Paris, Porter's personae are simply looking for a way in. His anxious tyros get a rapid education in the workings of the capital – at any rate, of the part to which they are drawn and to which they will not ultimately be admitted. Sex, money and power exert a single magnetic force. In 'Beast and the Beauty'[1] the hero has 'this great piece of luck' – acquiring (so he thinks) an attractive upper middle-class girlfriend, who teaches him about sex and introduces him into her fascinating and 'stylish' family before dumping him and moving back into her proper echelon: 'In the loft there waited trunks / Of heirlooms to be taken seriously.'

Porter's sourly observant reading of the workings of this world of 'barristers and wine-wise drunks' may be something only an outsider could manage: his English equivalent would probably have seen this lot coming and had less to say, or complicated the matter with the exception-making irony on which the class system partly depends for its survival. The Porter-tyro may never belong, but he has an excited understanding of the world beyond the breathed-on glass – the Establishment, which acquired that now-familiar and time-worn name even as he wrote. In his depiction of London at the end of the 1950s in 'John Marston Advises Anger', the poet-malcontent is as aroused and energised by the pertinence of the drama as he is angry at its real-life performers:

> The colonel's daughter in black stockings, hair
> Like sash cords, face iced white, studies art,
> Goes home once a month. She won't marry the men
> She sleeps with – she'll revert to type – it's part
> Of the side-show: Mummy and Daddy in the wings,
> The bongos fading on the road to Haslemere
> Where the inheritors are inheriting still.[2]

Bruce Bennett, in *Spirit in Exile*,[3] his critical biography of Porter, records that this poem was written after seeing Marston's *The Dutch Courtesan* with a then girlfriend, Diana Watson-Taylor, who later remarked of Porter that 'although she enjoyed his company very much she never intended to marry him'.[4] The point is not so much the autobiographical source of these poems as the transition from raw experience to the shapeliness of fiction, with no loss of energy: Terry Eagleton has remarked interestedly of Porter that 'the more depressed he gets, the more poetically inventive he becomes',[5] perhaps because of the evident dramatic opportunities of the material:

> It's a Condé Nast world and so Marston's was.
> His had a real gibbet – our death's out of sight.
> The same thin richness of these worlds remains –
> The flesh-packed jeans, the car-stung appetite
> Volley on his stage, the cage of discontent.[6]

A. Alvarez, who included Porter's early work in his influential anthology *The New Poetry*,[7] had pertinent things to say about one of Porter's masters, Auden. In an essay in *The Shaping Spirit* he complains that Auden 'has never written, by the standards of his own best work, a good personal poem'.[8] Alvarez goes on to complain in particular about a famous example. Of 'Lay Your Sleeping Head',[9] he states that 'there is a kind of vague, generalised feeling to the verse, as though Auden were writing a love poem to someone he had never properly been introduced to'.[10] The latter may inadvertently be true of Auden's gay experience, and while the overall complaint may seem just or not to the reader, it helps to identify a way in which Porter, the poetic disciple (he has written numerous essays, lectures and reviews on the subject of Auden), differs from his teacher. Auden makes a strength from detachment and Olympian clarity. Porter aims at the same inclusiveness and authority, as 'historical' monologues such as 'Soliloquy at Potsdam' (spoken by Frederick the Great)[11] or 'Septimius Severus at the Vienna Gate'[12] or the late-Audenesque history lesson, 'Vienna'[13] seem to indicate. But this is not a position he can occupy easily for long. History – his, England's, the world's – is *personal* for Porter. Part of the younger man seems always to be fighting it out inside the whale of his own work and experience.

The engine of the poet's youth is sexual; he sees hypocrisy and unfairness but makes no particular claims to rectitude himself. As Thom Gunn put it in another context, 'Whatever is here, it is / material for my art',[14] which for Porter can in turn convert the blended repulsion and attraction into a sombre, red-lit comedy. London for Porter holds little explicit topographical interest: his landscapes are always *moralisé*, and the city's real site is in the imagination of its beholder (Porter has always been at home with the social construction of reality). Upper-class fiction is one of the imagination's districts, as Porter shows in the precise, energetic but ultimately sombre improvisation on the work of the novelist Simon Raven, suggested by *Close of Play* (1962):[15]

> Meanwhile sturgeon from Odessa packed
> For *Black's* and *Tan's*, renowned St James's clubs,
> Laced with Spanish Fly, cause randy scenes
> At Ascot, a bishop's face is smacked;
> Debs and guardsmen break up Chelsea pubs,
> Blackmailers send snaps to dons at Queens.[16]

Alms for Oblivion (1965-76), Raven's sequence of ten novels about postwar upper middle-class life, is prefaced by an authorial note: 'If there is one theme that dominates the series it is that human effort and goodwill are persistently vulnerable to the malice of time, chance, and the rest of the human race.'[17] Goodwill is in fact a rare commodity in Raven's work. His world is a much grimmer, more lurid and downright filthy place than Anthony Powell's comparable creation in his (at one time) more widely acclaimed sequence, *A Dance to the Music of Time*.[18] But Raven, like Powell, is a classicist, and the sense of horror and implacably approaching destiny in his work adds to his determined vulgarity a perhaps unexpected resonance, a sense of waste, scale and frailty from which his bully-boys and tarts are permanently on the run. The proximity between the mean trivialities of fashionable power and the underlying and abiding horrors of life fascinates Porter, too. His London could be Rome, and his readings of Martial in his book of versions *After Martial* (1972)[19] relishes the grubby venality of the Latin poet's world ('men are pharisaical, / They're always whoring after the classical'),[20] in particular the task described by Bruce Bennett of 'finding equivalents for Martial's argot of lustful sexual activity'.[21] The classical antecedents of the powerful homoerotic dimension of Raven's work (see, for example, *Fielding Grey*, 1967)[22] also find a place in Porter's Martial. IV XVIII tells of the bizarre and terrible death of a boy impaled by an icicle falling from an aqueduct, 'and as in a murder in a paperback the clever / weapon melted away in its own hole'[23] – a grotesquerie worthy of Raven (for whom at a metaphorical level the destruction of innocence is a sexual act – a sign of the appetites of the gods or fate reproduced at a human level).

Porter's detractors may complain about his allusiveness, his desire to include his reading in his work (as though reading were not a proper activity for a writer). It's true that the range of reference can be forbidding: but this is not the showing-off of the academic poet, designed to exclude the less learned. Porter's reading enters his imagination and arrives on the page with a life of its own: the poems refer not so much to books, music and paintings as to the crowded imaginative life to which these things are thresholds. In one poem we learn about the misfortune of following a poisonously flatulent 'Metternich of the party-going world' upstairs;[24] in another Madame de Meurteil reflects on her enduring viciousness of temperament and action;[25] in a third the momentary names of fashionable clubs London clubs – 'Sa Tortuga, Grisbi, Bongi-Bo' – pass across the screen of the imagination.[26] Anthony Thwaite, an admirer of Porter, remarks that some of his non-artistic references 'will need footnotes before long',[27] but the scope and omnivorous detail of Porter's work seem both compelling in themselves and to be means of keeping faith with a world from which he does not feel that poetry should withdraw. His fascinated presence in the mire is part of what enables him to live up to Thwaite's approving description of his poems as 'not... documentaries but fictions' and his further comment that 'sometimes they read like discontinuous parts of a whole verse novel, a *roman fleuve* of our time'.[28] Certainly they remain more readable than such period novels as Andrew Sinclair's *The Breaking of Bumbo* or Derek Raymond's *The Crust On Its Uppers*.[29]

If Thwaite's description is just – and I think it is – it makes it the more regrettable that in some places Porter's work seems to be viewed as merely forbidding: the novelist's *vademecum* is there to be heard. The multiplicity of life which the novel grew to include is also a means for Porter to map his own contradictions. ('A public worthy of its/ artists would consist of whores and monsters.')[30] The satirist, for example, is also an aesthete, to whom music has an artistic supremacy which stands at the door of belief, capable of redeeming the poisoned life of everyday. In 'Walking Home on

St Cecilia's Day', it is a power felt in the silence of the speaker's mind. It is

...useless, impartial as rain on a desert –

And conjures the listener for a time to be happy,
Making from this love of limits what he can,
Saddled with Eden's gift, living in the reins
Of music's huge light irresponsibility.[31]

Such experience, Porter's poems about music continually suggest, is remarkable but not exceptional. The very ordinariness of life – music included – is what amazes. Perhaps this is what enables him to sustain what he has called his 'Janus-faced'[32] attitude, veering between celebration and despair without seeming simply at the mercy of his occasions. It offers no moral guarantee: as Frederick the Great comments from the extreme end of the spectrum, 'Who would be loved / If he could be feared and hated, yet still/ Enjoy his lust, eat well and play the flute?'[33] This sense of complication also lends persuasiveness to the sombre, visionary mode, the oracular authority and the scale which many of Porter's poems attempt, as here in 'The Historians Call Up Pain':

We cannot know what John of Leyden felt
Under the Bishop's tongs – we can only
Walk in temperate London, our educated city,
Wishing to cry as freely as they did who died
In the age of Faith. We have our loneliness
And our regret with which to build an eschatology.[34]

The frankness is cunningly organised so that the denials seem to fall away under the pressure of the scrutiny from which the poet does not allow his own gift of eloquent finality to distract him. 'Europe: An Ode' goes further, attempting an entire history, only to upend its own ironies with its chilling final stanza, where we – the Europeans, the West, the empires, are

Launched in the wake of our stormy mother
  To end up on a tideless shore
    Which this is the dream of, a place
    Of skulls, looking history in the face.[35]

This idiom is elsewhere made to run up against the corruptions of advertising copy ('Love goes as the MG goes'; 'An American machine is coming / with Hot Gothic printed on its brow').[36] The exemplar of such contrasts may be Eliot in 'A Game of Chess',[37] but Porter is genuinely curious rather than merely repelled, too absorbed to make a principle of misanthropy. At a formal level, his manipulations of tone and register, evident from the beginning of his published career, show him to be a poet for whom some features of postmodernism were an extension of existing practice rather than paradigm-breaking novelties. His excursions into 'experimental' poetic fiction – see 'Short Story'[38] – can be paralleled in the work of his contemporaries and members of The Group, George MacBeth and Alan Brownjohn (whose impressive recent poem 'Sea Pictures'[39] may be a last word on this topic). The sense of historical and linguistic discontinuity on which some postmodernist poetry seems to depend, and which some of its advocates find suspiciously convenient, is not apparent in Porter. He lacks the bad faith which might tempt someone born to the role of cultural insider and in Bruce Bennett's words, 'He had not come to the literary capital to be cultural fringe-dweller'.[40] His restlessness and confidence produce juxtapositions of poems about George Herbert and churchyards on the one hand, and bizarre and hectic 'The Sanitised Sonnets' on the other:

> Somebody must have been telling lies about Porter
> for they took away his sense of pitch
> and they wouldn't let him scratch his itch
> and they put a strain on his aorta
>
> and they said he suffered from Porter's complaint
> i.e. inability to feel anything when feeling[41]

The title poem of his pivotal collection *The Last of England* (1970)[42] undertakes to bind and resolve some contradictory senses of 'England', insisting that the meaning of the place is above all its language, its 'haunted tenses':

> Sailing away from ourselves, we feel
> The gentle tug of water at the quay –
> Language of the liberal dead speaks
> From the soil of Highgate, tears
> Show a great water-table is intact.
> You cannot leave England, it turns
> A planet majestically in the mind.[43]

Managing to be both elegiac and celebratory, this stanza obviously makes a different case from Eliot's, which it obviously has in mind, being neither Royalist, conservative nor classicist, nor even especially patriotic, but instead awed and moved by the language's durable world-imagining endeavour. The poem is not a historical but a trans-historical work. This may also be the place to note that Porter's phrase-making powers, which are deliberately underplayed here, are sometimes seen as superior to his musicality. Alan Jenkins, for example, finds Porter's 'customary, controlled eloquence' to be 'a matter of phrasing rather than formal or musical properties',[44] but in 'The Last of England' the quiet insistence of the trochaic openings to the first, third and fifth lines helps to underwrite the authority of several metrical variations in the stanza, which is in turn not an assembly of lines but a working-out of a complete musical theme – the kind of artistic tact which gives the lie to the idea that Porter is merely a snappy journalistic observer.

It would be very difficult for younger poets to essay this subject (and perhaps the method as well) nowadays. The basically guileless liberal affirmation which underlies the poem, with all it implies about Porter's un-doctrinaire inclination to the left, may seem to have been put under historical arrest in the years since its composition – and to be vulnerable to the attention of the numerous cultural and political enemies of disinterested enlightenment. Porter himself has certainly grown grimmer and more circumspect, sceptical about art and the artist, though still quick to celebrate when the opportunity arises. His more recent work is a subject for another essay, but it should be added that Porter's generosity as a critic may have disguised the extent of his own poetic influence – as a poet of the dramatic monologue and lyric, as a sceptical yet passionate investigator of language, as one who has contributed to the blending of the formal and the demotic. He has, in short, done much to map the territory which the middle and younger poetic generations take as their own. If Porter is not an epochal poet he is certainly an important one, showing how we might usefully proceed under present conditions. What might have been merely eclectic, a gesture at the fleeting contemporary, turns out, often, to be salutary. His current slightly occluded place in the firmament can be read as a sign of the times' own problems. His seriousness and copiousness, his unembarrassed allusiveness and frequent difficulty do not – at the moment – play well with an audience which is almost unknowingly growing accustomed to reading the limits of its own immediate knowledge and concerns as the Pale of reasonableness. More fool us.

13: Peter Didsbury: *Getting Some Things Down*

The title of this section, 'A Daft Place', is the title of a poem in Peter Didsbury's first book, *The Butchers of Hull* (1982). The poem is an amused but not unaffectionate journey from the outskirts to the centre of Hull, the estuarine northern city where he has lived, with intervals of absence for study and work, since childhood:

> A daft place this.
> Going south from here to the river
> is to follow a daft line of questioning.
> First the estate with its daft new names,
> then the suburbs with their daft front doors,
> then the ruined Town with its sweet daft secrets.
> Everywhere the domestic architecture
> is either daft or missing.
> Daft to start with, ruined by daftness, daft in being gone.
> Even the river mud is dafter than we care to own.
> There are more gulls on the dustbins than on the estuary now.
> All gone daft. All eating daft food, like us.[1]

Investigation would reveal that the daft names on Orchard Park council estate are cod-Viking; that the city has made a good deal of its past without (until recently, when its past has become its only attribute) doing much about it; that there are more gulls on the dustbins than the estuary now because the fishing industry, Hull's economic mainspring, is almost defunct following the Cod Wars of the 1970s. It's not a flattering portrait, but the poem is only marginally a work of social criticism. The ubiquity of 'daft' (to be given a flat northern *a* suggests that if these were not the problems and irritations and ignorances, there would be no shortage of others: it's that kind of place, a city of bodging, cack and making-do, known to the author from the inside as it never quite was to Larkin.

With this poem, which seems very English in its wryness, and very much *echt* Hull in its permanent air of tolerant, wearied, unsurprisable exasperation, Didsbury domesticates a device, the obsessive, mantra-like repetition which he may first have noticed in the New York poet Kenneth Koch's 'Sleeping with Women',[2] and which he also uses in 'In Belgium' and 'In Britain'.[3] These poems bring together, almost in cartoon form, two of the most striking features of Didsbury's work – his powerful sense that his medium must be part of his subject, and an equally powerful grasp of the particular (especially of place) which gives equal attention to the mundane and the numinous. Another early poem, 'The Pub Yard at Skidby', reads a semi-rural landscape in order to align these forces in a slightly different way:

> ...The gulch of cow parsley and marvellous docks
> is a place where the sun has always westered
> and I say I think I drink here
> on the borders of somewhere 'very large'.
> If there are holes in the sky
> then this spins directly under one of them.
> Significance floods in, and someone
> is 'doing up a caravan' in it now.
> To get those pagan discs and clusters right
> (the hedgehog singing against the silver)
> has taken him a year – and all his knowledge,
> and all his lies. Just like it did theirs...[4]

For language here we can read imagination. The light-heartedness, the comic spirit, of the poem, which sits as it were at speculative ease in the evening, allows what appear to be potential contradictions to occupy the same space. On the one hand, there is the numinous setting, at the border of somewhere humorously 'very large', perhaps with access to the transcendent ('holes in the sky'). It is flooded with a 'significance' which the poem's task is to note rather than define. On the other hand, a place 'where the sun has always westered' depends on a human, rhetorical contribution, a conversion of place into metaphor. And the decorations freshly painted on the caravan are in some sense 'lies' – human approximations of the governing powers of such sites, perhaps; or acts of homage or worship which, not knowing their object, must imagine it. 'The Pub Yard at Skidby', we might say, is a poem about the happiness of the anticipatory present tense, which springs from a sense of the place's – the world's – potential, rather than the completion of its meaning.

At the close, the pattern of 'lies' is imagined reproducing itself on a larger scale, to include the speaker and his companions; they figure in a kind of heraldic pastoral whose 'significance' appears to be its shape. Painted or written into the landscape the poet has evoked, they are seen as part of it rather than its interpreters: as a later poem, 'The Globe', comments: 'Men are not gods. They just hold the same things in common.'[5] Art, whether it be the decoration on a caravan or a sophisticated poem, is always adjacent to an urge to worship in Didsbury's work.

The expansion of the mundane here-and-now into something rich with possibility is characteristic. The streets of Hull are always on the brink of elsewhere, and Didsbury's imagination carries him from Hull's remote province far and wide in time and space. In 'The Autumn', 'A grainy autumn day' in a windy street is visited by 'real devils from China' and the poet comments, 'I can see why the dead would want/ to get back to a set-up like this',[6] the exotic mediated by a relaxed vernacular. 'The Hailstone', one of his finest poems, makes a large imaginative journey out of a trip to the local shops. The rest of England is translated by the same terms. Equally beguiling, the world of 'The Experts'[7] – two men fishing in the River Kennet during the eighteenth century – celebrates a fantastic ordinariness in an eighteenth-century language that is neither pastiche nor lifeless reproduction. The poem's ironic calm is stuffed with details of food, husbandry, property ownership and local legend; but its supreme achievement is to be a place where the men can fall asleep after lunch. For there, as in the imagined Byzantium of 'Scenes from a Long Sleep', 'The light and heat are from a sun in his splendour./ It is, and will continue, the middle of the day.'[8] Didsbury's rendering of duration takes on a supernatural cast, as if its mere fact might be evidence of the Creator's existence, his presence, his gaze and unbending intent. In 'Venery', an extraordinary depiction of a mundane medieval scene around a royal hunting lodge, 'It is high hot noon, as every thing declares'; further, 'The day stays at noon'.[9] In the winter world of 'Mappa Mundi' the fact of existence itself is made awesome without the intervention of anything deserving to be called an event; history, it seems, may consist largely of intent, loaded intervals:

> still many hours away, for example, a grandee in furs
> alights from his carriage at a crossroads in the hills
> and knows he is regarded, as he bends
> to fill the carcass of a fowl with snow,
> as well as who regards him...[10]

If it is sometimes apparent that the work of John Ashbery has interested Didsbury,[11] it is clear that he cannot simply be read under the aegis of Ashbery's digressive style. Didsbury's interests and rhetorical skills equip him for kinds of memorability and closure (and occasionally grandeur) to which Ashbery does not seem to aspire – see the end of 'The Globe', as well as 'The Hailstone', 'Glimpsed Among Trees', 'The Classical Farm', 'Eikon Basilike', 'The Shore' and 'Part of the Bridge'.[12] Didsbury's interest in Ashbery, and before that in English experimentalists such as Christopher Middleton and Roy Fisher,[13] in whom the work of modernism is continued and transmuted into the postmodern, is a sign of his restless search in the 1970s for an imaginative locus in which to work, one that would bypass the well-made (and not so well-made) poem of the day and privilege what Middleton called the 'mineral, frisky'[14] properties of language itself. Enthusiastic critics of Didsbury, including John Osborne, Ian Gregson and David Kennedy,[15] have tried to map a place for Peter Didsbury's poetry among the post-modernists, and while Didsbury has his doubts, it would be hard to disagree entirely with these critics. But it would be a mistake to impose too neat a development on a poet whose peculiarity is as much innate as acquired, a poet who changes his mind, feels differently at different times and has less of an aesthetic programme than an inclination to write poems. It would be especially mistaken to try, as John Osborne appears to, to disarm the religious dimension of Didsbury's work. Here, Osborne states:

> All religions are adjudged to be of equal value, in the sense that they are fictions designed to facilitate the living of life in accord with our small aptitude for the spiritual. The distinctions between religion and myth, canonical and apocryphal texts, orthodox and heretical beliefs cease to apply, all being narratives whose reification of life stems, not from their empirical veracity, but from their allowing the concept of the sacramental a controlled, and therefore utile, entry into consciousness. The world's great myths and religions provide an inexhaustible storehouse of images, archetypes and tall tales for deployment in poems whose commitment is to no religious denomination, but to all that is peaceable, humorous and tolerant...Aware that our present atheism estranges us from any truth left in these archaic symbolisms, Didsbury's poems seek to retrieve that truth by secularising, dislocating and on occasion parodying the rejected theological lexis.[16]

Osborne's most powerful inclination as a critic is to discover order in the works he examines. Nothing will be left to chance. His formulations can be so neat as to seem paranoid, while the works themselves can appear to have been waiting all along for their translation into the gleaming, clean-lined filing system of his commodious critical imagination. It can all be made to *make sense*. But when he comes up against the element of belief in Didsbury's work, his linguistic materialism runs out of steam: how feeble it sounds, this post-religious enlightenment, compared with the grandeur and terror of what it seeks to replace. And it simply cannot account for the bombardment of religious references which occurs in Didsbury's work, which has much more to do with unfinished business than with 'our present atheism'. Osborne understands the speculative dimension of Didsbury's poetry, which includes his capacity to entertain possibility and to hold language itself up for inspection; but he is altogether uncertain in the area where 'fiction' (as in the Sterne fantasia 'A Winter's Fancy')[17] encounters and crosses over into belief, as in the unredeemed world of 'A Shop'.[18] The first does not preclude the second: to expose the workings of the machine does not presuppose the absence of a ghost.

That is to say, while Didsbury might be seen, as Osborne sees him, as having constructed 'a poetics which stands in relation to Realism as linguistics does to language',[19] his understanding of meaning and value does not confine them to the sphere of human production: they exist in relation to an order or power – the universe beyond them – which language celebrates rather than invents. As Didsbury expressed it when writing about his most recent book, *That Old-Time Religion* (1994):

> For me, the excitement of language itself, with its literally infinite possibilities, and the conviction that in writing a poem one is exemplifying, in however small a measure, the creative processes and hunger at the heart of the universe, are the *sine qua non*. These are premisses which do nothing to constrain. They also, incidentally, help me to formulate my distaste at being described as a post-modernist. To make no other objection, I believe I'm engaged in tasks and duties and pleasures which are nothing if not ancient.[20]

If the power 'at the heart of the universe', which a poem 'exemplifies', does not lend itself to precise definition, the poet is hardly alone with the problem, since that is its nature. Whether the reader shares the religious disposition or not, the poems require it to be entertained if they are to be fully experienced. Osborne's resistance to this approach produces a brilliant but contorted reading of 'Eikon Basilike',[21] a poem subtitled 'for the soul of William Cowper'. This dream-vision of exclusion from God's love springs from the harrowing fact that the poet Cowper (1731-1800), author of 'The Castaway' and 'God Moves in a Mysterious Way', a devout and gentle Christian, was afflicted with the certainty that he was damned beyond redemption. One can read the poem's narrative as a displacement of Cowper's own psychic odyssey. Osborne has mined it for references of all kinds, and offers a psychoanalytic reading, but the atmosphere of damnation refuses to go away. This is partly because the poem, deranged as its 'reasoning' must seem, is so palpably embedded in its setting. The landscape is clearly that of Holderness in East Yorkshire – a marshy, inhospitable plain bordered by 'the German Ocean' and crossed by 'a drain', like the identical frozen landscape of an earlier poem of damnation, 'The Drainage'.[22] This is Hull, nor is the poem out of it: until the 1960s much of the city stood on a network of broad, open drains, a 'bricky and entrenched landscape' whose now-buried watercourses are still quick to reveal themselves in wet weather. The presence of this place – the chill obverse of the 'daft' place – in Didsbury's poetry is not simply a linguistic construction. The freezing landscape is certainly symbolic, and beyond its particular local significance we sense the same powerful (though now implacably averted) presence as in the poems of heat and ease – but the persuasiveness of these features of the poem depends on the realisation of the setting. It may be the fact that this fusion of the supernatural with the local, or the empirical with the transcendental, is not to be *explained* is what unsettles a critic such as Osborne. His work reveals a paradox within post-modernist criticism: if the old Big Picture myths and explanations have given way to uncertainty, what grounds has uncertainty to be so peculiarly sure of itself?

It is as a celebrant, too, that Didsbury should be celebrated. He sustains a peculiarly northern sense of cultural continuity while encompassing a powerful sense of a civilian England – seashores, minsters, nouns of congregation, butcher's shops, public libraries, salty parks, dead sailors and rain which falls as a blessing 'adding to thousands of feet through clandestine air/ another thirty through the centre of my house'.[23] It's an identity which seems to require none of the internal glibness or external abrasiveness of conventional patriotism. Didsbury has the advantage over Larkin, it would seem, in actually knowing his way around the sites of England. He returns often to the shores of the Humber, turning over archaeological remains, dreaming up a 'complex lodge for a free and scholarly people',[24] as entranced as Peter Porter is by the image of England as an imaginative possibility, something capable of outliving the nonsense done in its name. He marks with as keen an eye as Roy Fisher the vestigial survivals of the day before yesterday:

Rose red rubble constitutes the evening.
A man with a worn and shiny billhook.
The coloured marble forecourts
Of shops that vanished in wartime.[25]

Those forecourts in the shopping streets of Hull seem as eloquent as much older sites: this history is through-composed. At the same time, Didsbury can also be as energetically contemptuous as Peter Reading, for example when contemporary fraudulence intrudes on something that matters to him:

Next is a porcelain plaque,
fixed by a nail
to the trunk of a churchyard yew.
There's a supercilious pillock in a trench-coat
standing next to it, holding a clip-board,
and talking straight to camera.
Yeah, right first time.[26]

One of the ways in which Didsbury differs from Reading, though, is in having substantial and sustainable positives to set against the dismal, de-historicised character of contemporary life. For the anti-Romantic Reading, for example, what is remembered seems by definition *lost*, a sign of mortality sweeping up at our heels. In Didsbury's case, memory is a gift, the granary of the imagination. A hailstorm, for example, provokes a Lockean association of ideas, its fervent detail a little reminiscent of Peter Redgrove:

> We ran by the post office I thought, 'It is all still true,
> a wooden drawer is full of postal orders, it is raining,
> mothers and children are standing in their windows,
> I am running through the rain past a shop which sells wool,
> you take home fruit and veg in bags of brown paper,
> we are getting wet, it is raining.'
>   It was like being back
> in the reign of George the Sixth, the kind of small town
> which still lies stacked in the roofs of old storerooms in schools,
> where plural roof and elf expect to get very wet
> and the beasts deserve their nouns of congregation
> as much as the postmistress, spinster, her title.
> I imagine those boroughs as intimate with rain,
> their ability to call on sentient functional downpours
> for any picnic or trip to the German Butcher's
> one sign of a usable language getting used,
> make of this what you will. The rain has moved on,
> and half a moon in a darkening blue sky
> silvers the shrinking puddles in the road:
> moon that emptied the post office and the grocer's,
> moon old kettle of rain and ideolect,
> the moon the sump of the aproned pluvial towns,
> cut moon as half a hailstone in the hair.[27]

Running home through the rain provokes a momentary experience of the uncanny, as if the mind wakes up to its own presence and contents, refreshed and restored to the original vividness of relations with local and domestic culture. Stirred by the fact of identity, the poet then relishes its detail: 'It was like being back', and the past tense is quickly exchanged for the present, and the authoritative once-and-for-all world of early schooling is shown in apple-pie order. The feeling is more complex and more energetic than mere nostalgia – partly because the world the poem recreates has to be past in order to achieve this pencil-shaving freshness for the imagination; it is seen as something held in store. When the wave which has carried the poem to this point begins to fall back, we wonder how, in closing, the imagination will fuse the moon with the hailstone. Invocation accompanies diminuendo, as if the moment of clearest knowledge and intensest pleasure is also a leavetaking, an acknowledgement of a necessary but not a bitter transience in the confirmation of wholeness. Moon and hailstone are shown as parts of the same local/universal 'usable language', or as emblems of a language grasped for a moment in its entirety, to be revered and celebrated, no matter the terrors that must also take their turn. This extremely literary poet tries to show us a world before literature gets at it.

V

REDRESSING THE BALANCE

14. Fleur Adcock: *All the Things Men Do*

> I think I was a very late developer as a feminist. It took me a long time to realise I wasn't just a man in some basic sense. The poets I modelled myself on were men and I earned my living and I got a mortgage and I did all the things men do. And then it leaked through almost accidentally.
>
> FLEUR ADCOCK, interviewed by Clive Wilmer[1]

Although the New Zealander Fleur Adcock (*b.* 1934) has lived in England so long as to have acquired honorary Brit status, she published her first book, *The Eye of the Hurricane* in New Zealand in 1964,[2] and its successor, *Tigers*, in Britain in 1967.[3] The poems from these collections which survive into her 1983 *Selected Poems* reveal a poet already sure of her stylistic ground. If in response to Clive Wilmer's description of her early work as 'slightly Movementish', she has commented: 'I was into Larkin and all those people',[5] this characterisation, in terms of the commonly understood sense of the Movement as downbeat, empirical, undemonstrative, does not seem wholly adequate. For one thing there is a strong erotic and hedonistic strain in the poems – see for example 'Note on Propertius':

> ...Onto her bed
> He rolled the round fruit, and adorned her head;
> He gently roused her sleeping mouth to curses.
> Here the conventions reassert their power:[6]

An amused formality, of tone as much as method, is used to distance and clarify, and at the same time to emphasise pleasure – in the act imagined, in its rendition, in the power to render it. The poet exults in competence. This surely has much to do with Adcock's training in Classics, where entry to an alien medium has to be earned, and the student is aware both of absorption and detachment.

The most startling and peremptory of the early poems is 'Instructions to Vampires', an *odi et odi* piece which imagines with gruesome coolness the literal inscription of female power on the male on whom revenge is being taken. Calling in the vampires, the poet/woman asks not that the man be drained of blood, as is traditional, or driven mad, which is likely. Rather, she says:

> use acid or flame,
> Secretly, to brand or cauterise,
> And on the soft globes of his mortal eyes
> Etch my name.[7]

This is alarming and funny and perversely sexy – hardly the response of a victim, one might think. While Adcock has written a good deal about the give-and-take, the pleasures and pains of the erotic life, and has assumed recognisable roles as injured party and avenger, her work is most strongly charged when it enters the apparently amoral territory in which erotic encounter begins. The game has rules which, somehow, everyone already knows, which is part of what makes it interesting:

Beauty inclines a modest ear,
Hears what she has decided she should hear.[8]

There are times when the imagination is merely trying out its apparatus, for example in 'Advice to a Discarded Lover',[9] aptly described by Alan Robinson as 'Grand Guignol' and 'rather belated Romantic agony'.[10] But the fusion of impulse with form in the best work, and the resulting coolness for which it has often been noted (a description, incidentally, to which Adcock objects)[11] seems to align her with American formalists who came to prominence in the 1950s, such as Richard Wilbur and Anthony Hecht, rather than with Larkin or for that matter Elizabeth Jennings.

While Adcock sees clearly some apparently unchanging patterns in love, she is not opposed to intervention in their workings. She has declared (in one of her most political poems): 'I do not write political poems',[12] and one of her most celebrated pieces, the very funny 'Against Coupling' is – in our time at any rate – intensely political by its very subject, which is the efficient pleasure of masturbation as contrasted with the mess, distraction, and, as it were, crowdedness of sexual intercourse:

There is much to be said for abandoning
this no longer novel exercise –
for not 'participating in
a total experience' – when
one feels like the lady in Leeds who
had seen *The Sound of Music* eighty-six times;

or more, perhaps, like the school drama mistress
producing *A Midsummer Night's Dream*
for the seventh year running, with
yet another cast from 5B.
Pyramus and Thisbe are dead, but
the hole in the wall can still be troublesome.[13]

To anyone who wasn't there, it's tempting to ascribe the poem's weariness to the 1960s' religiose elevation of sexual experience as the be-all and end-all. Certainly to opt out is to turn as certain largely male conception of things upside down. But what lends subversiveness to the poem is the sense that the speaker's attitude has been confidently and matter-of-factly in place for some time. The laconic voice does not so much reject argument as seem bored by it in advance. The poem makes its declaration from a position of (at the very least) equality with the rejected suitor. Yet the liberty affirmed by 'Against

Coupling' exists alongside forces which brook no denial, as is shown by the immediately succeeding poem, 'Mornings After' one of Adcock's several poems about dream life, in this instance apparently a rather gruesome experience, since the poem concludes: 'I do not care to know. Replace the cover.'[14] But the later 'Dreaming' insists on venturing an interpretation of a dream, in the context of a relationship with a man who says 'I never dream':

> It was obscure; but glancing towards the end
> she guessed that killer and lover and doctor were the same;
> proving that things are ultimately what they seem.[15]

'What they seem', presumably, to an unsettled but unsparing imagination, which knows that life's civilities are made and not born. As elsewhere, the adjacent poems – the chilling 'Street Song'[16] and the understated 'Across the Moor' – shed light on their neighbours.[17] 'Across the Moor' is so discreet (and brief) that it would be easy to ignore its narrative skill. A man, seemingly a potential rapist or murderer, follows a woman across what sounds, from the nearby evidence of 'Street Song', like the Town Moor in Newcastle in the days after the Hoppings, the big annual summer funfair. He has almost caught up with her when a third part interrupts his stalking:

> ...he saw
> that she was not the one, and let her go.
>
> There had been something. It was
> not quite clear yet, he thought.
> So he loitered on the bridge,
> idle now, the wind in his hair,
> gazing over into the stream
> of traffic; and for a moment
> it seemed to him he saw it there.

Adcock can deliver blows to the male ego with the best of them, but in the case, where outrage would seem especially appropriate, she concentrates on an imaginative recreation of the stalker's state of mind, insofar, she implies, as any outsider is able to do this. She construes him as a pronoun, driven through an empty landscape by a compulsion which rewrites the world in the cause of its own fulfilment. His vestigial personality – strangely delicate in some way – is part of the poem's set-up, but also what it's about. How, the poem asks, can you know this Other, in the sense of seeing, for a moment, as he sees? He makes his surroundings and their occupants ghostly, and he himself is ghostly too, like 'the quiet shape you'll meet/on the cobbles in Back Stowell Street' in 'Street Song'. The effort of imaginative empathy casts on him the light he casts on the world; and we leave him *in medias res.* The poem is characteristic in the way that Adcock maintains equanimity by keeping the gaze firmly on the subject. Part of her unfussy authority is earned by her readiness for imaginative boldness.

Her own slightly hawkish quality is something Adcock has fun with elsewhere, in the more light-hearted context of 'Declensions', part of the series of poem from *Below Loughrigg* (1979), arising from a year spent in the Lake District. Observing and relishing the famous landscape, its light and birdlife, she states:

> I am not at all sure that this is the real world
>   but I am looking at it very closely.
> Is landscape serious? Are birds?...[18]

What, she seems to ask, can the urban moralist make of this apparent holiday from history? It is the kind of question that might also be found in the work of Peter Porter. While Adcock's work is rarely as laden with cultural impedimenta as Porter's, the two poets share what might be termed a visionary scepticism. In Porter's words, 'Life is a dream, or very nearly'.[19] In Adcock's work the disposition figures as the lightness of touch with which she holds language up as though to compare it to the world. She finds both equally strange and equally, though unfathomably, persuasive. The poet turns back to a renewed study of Greek:

>   quaint thorny symbols, pecked with accents:
> as I turn the antique model sentences:
>   The vines are praised by the husbandmen.
> The citizens delight in strife and faction.
>   The harbour has a difficult entrance.

In terms of the English poetic mainstream, these lines – funny, elegiac, wistful, baffled – are postmodernist *avant la lettre*.

The classical world imagined in 'Declensions' is also an influence on the mood of one of Adcock's best-known and most powerful poems, 'The Ex-Queen Among the Astronomers',[20] though no actual historical period is specified. Alan Robinson, an appreciative reader of Adcock, sees this as a poem against patriarchy, and it would be hard to disagree; but the term is of limited helpfulness – like saying a poem disapproves of evil or rotten weather:

> The ex-queen represents all women, socialised into conformity with male erotic expectations (lines 18-19) and then abandoned when her novelty has been outgrown. The male astronomers as satirised as self-important rationalists, whose scientific pursuit of knowledge is, it is suggested, a quest for materialistic possession; their exploitative desire to reduce the world to ordered control is the counterpart to their patriarchal oppression of women. Both are objectified sadistically by the male's scopophilic drive, manifest in their obsessional voyeurism...[21]

Were this all, were the poem a sort of moral jigsaw, it would hardly have been worth writing. It's interesting that Robinson's analysis of the astronomers' patriarchal behaviour actually reproduces the reductive rationalism of which he accuses them. Not unnaturally, Adcock's own remarks about the poem seem to keep faith with it rather better, by allowing for the irreducible oddity implied in the poem's starting-point:

> Of course, you don't have much control. You don't sit down and say: 'I am now going to write a poem about somebody who is this and represents that.' It just comes and you find you're writing it. Afterwards you get the rational explanations to give to the people who ask you things – the students who write to me and say: 'What does the ex-queen represent?' She doesn't represent anything – she represents a certain type of person who is brought up to please men, but at the time I was just seduced by the oddity of the phrase, 'The Ex-Queen Among the Astronomers'.[22]

To quote this is not to deny the basic accuracy of Robinson's account, but it's like comparing an index with the atlas it refers to, or with the globe itself. The poem's interest, which is certainly compelling, resides in the ambiguous and part-dramatised world it generates. Adcock's own self-contradiction ('She doesn't represent anything... She represents...') may be prompted partly by exasperation at those who read poems like algebra, but also by her own sense of the poem's unique situation, its rendering of a world that precedes and is more copious than interpretation.

The poem occupies a dualism which many nowadays want to question – between the rational, scientific, abstract, impersonal view held by the male astronomers, and the earthbound, emotional, physical life of the ex-queen. It would be hard to find a set of more traditional (or male-derived) gender descriptions. The power relations they embody are reproduced in the poem's own sentence structure, by which the queen, stripped of her powers, is shown as a reactive figure. The first three stanzas, describing the scientists, all open with bald, direct, subject-verb-object constructions, whereas the queen enters the poem in an antithesis. What she does thereafter is belated, or on sufferance, or, at best temporarily subversive. The *mise en scène* is strong enough to carry us past simple objection and into interrogation. Why doesn't she act differently? Why does she give over the external universe to men? And so on. If the answer is that she lives according to male descriptions, what are we to make of her sexuality ('she seeks terrestrial bodies to bestride')? Are her encounters involuntary, conditioned acts, or does what she seeks have an element of the active, or even the wilful? And in the close of the poem, during the lovemaking (which is, as it were, generic – the partner being no one in particular, just one 'he' from the many) is the momentary conflation of her appearance with the powers and properties of the far skies a sign of her residual power? Or of its reduction to an occasion? Or something awarded by the more powerful male's momentary gratification? Or another world entirely, of which the astronomer is unaware, since all stars are equal and equally remote in his 'dreamy abstract gaze'? If the poem has to be said to have purpose, it is surely to invite us to ask these questions, rather than to transmit an answer. The blend of the general and the circumstantial seems to give the poem the status of a myth, in which we can recognise, though not resolve, our own conditions – except into art.

15. Carol Rumens: *The Room You Are in Is Also History*

If Fleur Adcock feels that she was slow to arrive at feminism, Carol Rumens's work has long been concerned with sexual politics. In 'A Marriage', an impressive poem from her 1981 second book, *Unplayed Music*[1] (a collection sternly pruned for *Thinking of Skins*, her Selected Poems, which appeared in 1993),[2] she looks back across a growing cultural division at those who 'have kept their places,/ trusting the old rules', for whom marriage is 'a small civilisation', rich in children, ritual and courtesy, where 'his wife sits by the window,//one hand planting tapestry daisies'.[3] The ambivalences are carefully balanced. The couple's marriage, rendered as though in tableaux, has its attractions. It's a world which has already been mapped, free of uncertainty; its confinement can be read as security. Yet the condition is unthinkable for the speaker, something seen across a gulf, part of a world whose powers reside in the male teller, not in the conjugal tale:

> I listen while he tells me about her sewing,
> as if I were the square of dull cloth
> and his voice the leaping needle
> chasing its tail in a dazzle of wonderment.
>
> He places an apple in my hand;
> then, for a moment, I must become his child.
> To look at him as a woman
> would turn me cold with shame.[4]

When the poet contemplates her parents' marriage in 'Before These Wars' she is again concerned to credit the strengths of a relationship now ended, as they appeal to her regretful imagination:

> In the early days of marriage
> my parents go swimming in an empty sea
> – cold as an echo, but somehow *theirs*,
> for all its restless size.[5]

The poet's sense of the necessity of freedom is amplified by knowledge of what must be lost when 'the possible happens/eventually'. Liberation, equality and choice are not garments to be easily donned or discarded, but signs of a transformation which can seem as ruthless as any process of change or decay found in the natural world. A later poem, 'A Woman of a Certain Age', from the earlier 1987 *Selected Poems*,[6] can be read as a companion piece to these earlier works. It closes with the character's declaration:

> 'It's simple, isn't it?
> Never say the yes

you don't mean, but the no
you always meant, say that,
even if it's too late,
even if it kills you.'[7]

Where some might move to a position of extreme scepticism about relations between the sexes, Rumens's work has a utopian dimension: 'we must' she says, 're-imagine one another across all the barriers of gender and nationality'.[8] Though Rumens is as entangled with history as any one, her view of the task of poetry, it would seem, is that it should imagine the possibility of *becoming*. The alternative, she adds, is destruction, but her work continually holds out for reconciliation, a state blissfully imagined at the close of 'A New Song', her poem on the Arab-Israeli conflict:

A slow psalm of two nations
Mourning a common pain

– Hebrew and Arabic mingling
Their single-rooted vine;
Olives and roses falling
To sweeten Palestine.[9]

Although Rumens was a new voice in British poetry, her work appeared to require no great leap of understanding. Like Anne Stevenson's, her manifestly well-made poems could be seen to refine a particular version of tradition, rather than to break with it. The context for her work seems to have became clearer with the belated recognition of other members of older generations of women poets, including U.A. Fanthorpe, Elizabeth Bartlett, Jenny Joseph and Elma Mitchell. These are all highly individual and wide-ranging poets, but they have common ground in the study of life as it is lived, and suffered, in the everyday world. Their ultimate concern is with people. Furthermore – and here Rumens sometimes parts company with them – they can all be described as formal pragmatists. They do not seem especially curious about form, voice, perspective or the status of language, a fact which may account for their 'friendliness' to readers uneasy with much modern poetry. Like them, Rumens seemed at home, formally if not ideologically, with the extended afterlife of the Movement, and also, as Neil Corcoran has noted, with the 'Auden line'.[10] It is perhaps the latter which accounts for the reader's sense of a lyrical and socially observant talent working hard to extend itself in order to disclose a relationship between the lyrical particular and the larger political realm. A somewhat uncharacteristic poem, the melancholy satire 'In the Craft Museum', with a rather Adcockian tone to its hexameter couplets, takes a tart stab at the condition of 'Eng. Lit':

Some nations lock up their poets. Ours have the key
to a high, clean room labelled sensibility.[11]

As Rumens suggests, and is far from alone in thinking, this inertia, the decayed institutional aspic of Arnoldian 'culture', transmitted via school, university and all the other apparatus of Englishness, can be as effective in its way as any organised regime of censorship. She might have added that the regime works on readers as well as poets: it kills their interest. 'Ballad of the Morning After' goes further:

This is a free country
The jails are for the bad
The only British dissidents
Are either poor or mad.[12]

These not especially radical observation would have been difficult for an English poet to make twenty years earlier, when poetry's transactions were made primarily with a sense of itself in the tradition, and while the political nature of that state of affairs was largely occluded by the context of poetic production – white, academic, middle-class, often shadowed by a sense of postwar retrenchment.

In her search for an ample, charged, authoritative language in which to counter the deadening, domesticating gravity of Englishness, Rumens has sought examples in Russian literature. This has produced a kind of Russianness in some of her own writing – for instance in the title poem of *Star Whisper* (1983),[13] where extremes of climate and sensibility meet in the Arctic landscape:

It's what the stars confess when all is silence
– Not to the telescopes but to the snow.
It hangs upon the trees like silver berries
  – Iced human dew.[14]

In the same collection there appears one of her best poems, 'The Hebrew Class', which works to fuse the here-and-now of Jewish studies in prewar Europe with anticipation of the peremptory approach of totalitarian politics. The lesson

...is the golden honey of approval,
the slow, grainy tear saved for the bread

of a child newly broken
on the barbs of his Aleph-Bet,
to show him that knowledge is sweet
and obedience, by the same token.[15]

The envelope quatrain, with its delayed, understated closure, is suited to our sense of the fusion of pleasure and obligation, as well as emphasising an enduring conviction about the truth of both. Rumens's lingering recreation of the integrity of the occasion also renews the reader's feeling of oncoming danger:

Oh smiling children, dangerously gifted ones,
take care that you learn to ask why,
for the room you are in is also history.
Consider your sweet compliance

in the light of that day when the book
is torn from your hand;
when, to answer correctly the teacher's command,
you must speak for this ice, this dark.[16]

Ice and dark are an ur-language for those oppressed by Hitler and Stalin, and Rumens often reaches for these moving out of the confines of the first person as she does so. When Fleur Adcock says she does not write political poems,[17] she may, like most poets, have in mind the problem of integrity: the political poem is proverbially held to be threatened by obligations not in themselves loyal to language. Resisting the danger of allowing poems to illustrate rather than constitute meaning, Rumens's practice tends to an intense particularity and lyricism even in the most dismayingly 'political' context, as in 'Outside Oswiecim':

The hardest hope to lose is the last and smallest.
Those words on the gate, some dreamed of them, and loved
To walk in their shade, suck out the iron of their promise.[18]

Arbeit macht frei (Work makes you free), the words inscribed over the gate of Auschwitz, are alluded to with gentle downcast yearning, sounded in the double caesura of the second line. The dramatic play of sound and pause seeks to affirm the possibility of poetry even in this terrible context. The existence of barbarism is not a reason for poetry to renounce its own resources. The poem poignantly includes a respectful sense of the ordinary human scale of wishing, as well as implying the massive and absolute denial of the Nazi military state ranged against it. Rumens goes some way to allay the suspicion that to write of this is to ventriloquise or to appropriate suffering. Like Douglas Dunn in his homage to the holocaust victim Robert Desnos, 'The Deserter',[19] and Michael Longley in 'Ghetto',[20] she manages a kind of supra-personal, polyphonic mode.

Rumens's imaginative engagement with international history, politics and art has also had marked effects on her writing about Britain, which she is able to present as a foreign country. In 'Surrey', place has become property, a private England, 'a place of signs,/ White-lettered threats'[21] – a rural version of Mrs Thatcher's Dulwich retreat. 'A Lawn for the English Family' imagines,[22] and as quickly renounces, an unofficial pastoral, on a site not very far from that of Douglas Dunn's poem of trespass, 'In the Grounds':

I did not invent this garden
though I put the children in it.
I was not its ruler. I wanted
only pity and beauty to rule it.[23]

The anti-pastoral is completed in 'Our Early Days in Graveldene'.[24] The monologue of a woman remembering young adult life in a council maisonette, it can be read in terms of change and decay with a background of larger historical decline (Tom Paulin's reading of Larkin's 'Afternoons' could also have applied to this poem),[25] but the dismantling that takes place requires a larger acknowledgement than simple regret. The accumulation of details, showing how a beginning and a meantime turn into a life, takes on its own dismaying rhythm, revealing a terrible, compliant reasonableness where politics ought to be:

Houses eat money, even council houses.
Ours was officially a *maisonette*.
It was first in a block of twelve, its shiplap coat
Still neat and almost white. We were 49.
Not far from a pub, The Bunker's Knob

– Named for some veteran's clopping wooden leg.
Each cul-de-sac spoke rustic legends: Foxwood,
Broombank, The Grove. I worked on the inside
Where everything could change. I glossed the stairs
Orange. Orange for hope and happy children.

I had two friends in Graveldene, both *Elaines*.
Big Elaine moaned about her hips and her husbands.
As we queued for the bus, she'd shift their weight with sighs.
I used to sit in the summer with little Elaine,
Drinking Coke on her rust-streaked balcony.

She looked too young to have children, too small.
I was scared sick when her toddler swung the kitten.
He's killing it, I cried. She wasn't bothered.
She smiled with her own kitten-face, creamy, cruel.
I thought of battered babies, I couldn't help it.

There was Stell the single mother, Rose the widow
– Women who worked and were always dashing out
For cod and chips. There was the Rasta, Cyril,
Who slashed his throat that time the bailiffs came.
When they came to us we hid behind the door.

They pushed through a folded paper, promising us
Distraint of Property. Oh boy, we simply
Had to laugh. One mattress, several prams,
A high-chair for the eldest, a rush-mat
Halfway to Shredded Wheat, and the transistor.

'All you need is love,' sang the druggy Liverpool voices.
We knew by then they weren't singing for us
And that love ate money, just as houses did.
The sixties were dying, starved for LSD
In the mines and factories, on estates like ours.

We split up in the end. We've done all right.
Sometimes we meet. The other day he said,
'I drove round Graveldene just for a look,
And the door of 49 was off its hinges.
I went inside. I saw your orange stairs.'[26]

Here Rumens muffles her lyric ground-note with a seemingly flat narration – a strategy also employed by Carol Ann Duffy. Flatness is part of the poem's real subject: in one sense the speaker's voice hardly echoes beyond her own immediate confines. She may have 'done all right', but she looks back in exhaustion at the way what looked like chance observations have come to exemplify lives spent barely getting by. The weary solidarity of working-class women and the absence of men (the speaker's partner only becomes 'he' in the context of eventual separation) are familiar from a thousand newspaper features, but the poem is not the journalistic piece it might appear to be: its task is to exceed its apparent means, to produce something almost supernaturally mundane. It scores by its quiet indication of the humiliatingly exact match between person and category, life and stereotype. We have read about the teenage mother Little Elaine. We know why she's not up the task of child-rearing, just as we know that her infant son will grow up as a problem, with problems, in the vanguard of the re-invented under-class, as economic decline takes hold and the 'white hot' energy of the 1960s is spent. We also suspect that such lives are merely personal and not to do with us, and thus that they are not "personal" at all. A further skewing of cliché occurs in the use Rumens makes of the soundtrack of the period: the poem notices the fissure which appeared in the 1960s between seeming cultural vitality and those who must overhear its excitement distantly through a radio and then, later, be described in terms of the mythology of a period in which they could claim no stake. 'Our Early Days in Graveldene' is a desolatingly effective creation; a voice for someone who both is and is not "representative", whom history shapes and imprisons and then ignores. An apparently "documentary" realism is turned against itself. Without a single angry note, the poem condemns a failure from which we have yet to recover.

16. Carol Ann Duffy: *A Stranger Here Myself*

All childhood is an emigration. Some are slow,
leaving you standing, resigned, up an avenue
where no one you know stays. Others are sudden.
You accent wrong. Corners, which seem familiar,
leading to unimagined, pebble-dashed estates, big boys
eating worms and shouting words you don't understand.
My parents' anxiety stirred like a loose tooth
in my head. *I want our own country*, I said.

CAROL ANN DUFFY, 'Originally'[1]

Like several of the most striking poets now at work in England, Carol Ann Duffy has Celtic ancestry and a Catholic background. The latter is the subject of the furiously dissident 'Ash Wednesday, 1984' and of the study of old age, 'Words of Absolution' from *Standing Female Nude* (1985).[2] The great emigrant cities of Glasgow (her birthplace) and Liverpool (where she studied) stand behind her work, and she has written of her childhood as 'an emigration' – part of that series of interior economic diasporae which led the Scots south (to Stafford in the case of Duffy's family) in search of work. Such displacements, as many would testify, make for a complicated unease in those fallen among the English:

...Now, *Where do you come from?*
strangers ask. *Originally?* And I hesitate.[3]

That familiar question, though often harmlessly (or meaninglessly) intended, is always unsettling. Neither uprooted or rootless, but not having taken root, Duffy can stand as an emigrant in the country of which she is technically a citizen. This state of affairs may matter less to the increasingly mobile and often indifferently deracinated English, on the move in much (though not all) of England, than to the immigrant from the militarily (if not imaginatively) conquered periphery. The edge of estrangement is usually somewhere to hand in Duffy's work: it is part of what enables her to dramatise the experience of a wide variety of other strangers, many of them born here, who find themselves abroad in contemporary England.

What must soon strike the reader is that while Duffy's poems suggest a good deal of background and show a fascination with the past (it is *The Other Country*) they do not contain much *history*. Her sense of the past is particular and anecdotal, proceeding from a personal or familial or local account of things. In it the shaping energies of the age can be felt (sorrowfully, for instance, in poems about Liverpool, where drink, drugs, economic decline and death are all entangled), but she rarely steps back for a direct attempt on the long perspective by which numerous male poets, including Larkin, Hughes, Hill, Harrison and Dunn, have been in the various ways concerned – and to which, as we have seen, they are all in thrall. This is not an adverse criticism of Duffy: her poems' comparative lack of interest in the world before 1945, and the resulting sense that history has 'gone missing', contribute to the subtle representation of fragility and exposure which recurs in the poems. They also testify that until recently women have largely had to go without history in the official record. That history might now best be written from the ground up.

In Duffy's poems of contemporary life, not only has social and political consensus collapsed, it is difficult to identify where it began, or how or even whether it existed, though an emotional investment in it continues to be felt. There is considerable art in her treatment of this: it is in part by the sophisticated exploitation of her speakers' and other characters' limited, vernacular understanding that Duffy directs us to the larger picture, which is made the more chilling by virtue of a scale and peremptoriness against which the poems can hardly offer to arm us.

The condition of being in but not entirely of England is certainly useful for the poet who in early adulthood will witness the dismantling of the nation's hitherto (at any rate apparently) broad consensual understanding of itself. To poetry's knowledge of the proverbial evanescence of all things (Duffy is a powerful elegist) is added the salt particularity of real times and places undergoing cultural and political dissolution. She achieves an unusually sensitive realisation of the incursions of larger change and decay into 'ordinary' life:

> I dreamed I was not with you. Wandering in a city
> where you did not live, I stared at strangers, searching
> for a word to make them you.[4]

This is both an archetypal and – in its bareness – a very modern-seeming predicament. The wedding of public and private (or, perhaps more precisely, the subjection of the private to the apparently public) is managed with great force and simplicity here. This narrative moment recurs more elaborately in 'I Remember Me':

> Despair stares out from tube-trains at itself
> running on the platform for the closing door. Everyone
> you meet is telling wordless barefaced truths.
>
> Sometimes the crowd yields one you put a name to,
> snapping fiction into fact. Mostly your lover passes
> in the rain and does not know you when you speak.[5]

These are not Duffy's most successful lines, but they reveal a strategy. If 'despair' seems, like the rest of this weirdly denatured experience, part of a familiar but desolating urban homogeneity, the flatly declarative sentences work paradoxically to sound the alarm. This ground bass enables her to raise the stakes elsewhere, so that a powerful emotional charge can be suddenly and up-endingly felt at large in the poems.

While the quoted lines could have occurred at any time in Eliot's century, and would not have been thematically out of place in Baudelaire's, Duffy's work also includes knowledge (in the sense described above) of a specifically modern road not taken. Socialism, as one of her poems states, is 'the bird that never flew',[6] and the humane anger which can often be felt in her work arises from a sense of the diminished or vanished expectations of the community and its members.

This is especially apparent in her writing about school and education, which offer a micro-history of recent times – from the relatively emancipated Arnoldian spinsters of 'The Good Teachers'[7] via two readings of knowledge in 'In Mrs Tilscher's Class'[8] and 'The Captain of the 1964 Top of the Form Team',[9] to the utter exhaustion of 'Like Earning a Living'.[10] 'In Mrs Tilscher's Class' invokes an idyll, the prelapsarian acquisition of General Knowledge:

> You could travel up the Blue Nile
> with your finger, tracing the route
> while Mrs Tilscher chanted the scenery.
> Tana, Ethiopia. Khartoum. Aswân.
> That for an hour, then a skittle of milk
> and the chalky pyramids rubbed into dust.
> A window opened with a long pole.
> The laugh of a bell swung by a running child.

Duffy's use of verbless sentences or passive forms evokes the receptivity of the child delightedly absorbed by both the curriculum and the routines of school; at the same time, by framing the memories as stills, the device helps to set the limits towards which the poem is working – the end of early childhood, the beginning of the end of innocence, where sex and death, in the shadow of the Moors Murderers, make themselves felt. The poem is not nostalgic in the unthinking sense, because it knows the cost, and the value, of its affections. Mrs Tilscher, a figure half-mythological, as teachers tend to become, is last seen in the role of a folktale gatekeeper:

> That feverish July, the air tasted of electricity.
> A tangible alarm made you always untidy, hot,
> fractious under the heavy, sexy sky. You asked her
> how you were born and Mrs Tilscher smiled,

then turned away. Reports were handed out.
You ran through the gates, impatient to be grown,
as the sky split open into a thunderstorm.

General Knowledge, which crops up in fragments several times in Duffy's poems, is what the child 'knows' of imperial ideology and its world-picture. It hardly seems accidental that a quarter of a century or so later, the man who was formerly 'Captain of the 1964 Top of the Form Team' also finds the Nile the most prominent feature on the map of his memory: 'The Nile rises in April. Blue and White.' He is, in the cliché, a mine of useless information, though the poem is coloured by the unasked question of when 'information', the sort of thing you were praised for knowing simply for its own sake, became subject to the judgements of utility. (Back in 1964, he recalls, he looked 'so brainy you'd think I'd just had a bath' – a historically perfect conflation of education and class aspiration.) Even Gradgrind, M'Choakumchild and Bitzer were keen on sheer *information* – though they would have agreed (as Sissy Jupe uncomfortably learns) that there are proper and improper kinds. When, in about 1964, a member of the Hull Grammar School *Top of the Form* team revealed during the broadcast quiz that he didn't know who the Beatles' drummer was, he was praised in the local press and given an award – something inconceivable nowadays. Duffy's speaker can name six Dusty Springfield songs and has a good deal of other improper information, but his childhood world was still all of a piece, from his Pathfinder shoes to pre-decimal currency: 'My country.//I want it back.' As they endure his recital of the name of Ian Smith, a line by Yeats and much else, he bitterly adds: 'My thick kids wince.' It's a remark which Duffy has ensured is so ambiguous as to be undecidable. He's a bore, but the kids don't seem to know anything. He has ended up as uselessly middle-aged as anyone else but some phantasmal possibility still nags at him. And so on, indefinitely. Knowledge, which for him consists of the offcuts of a grand imperial narrative of which he seems to remain unaware, turns out not to be power, but an index of powerlessness. The fabrication of the poem is so satisfyingly detailed as to seem able to make a crossing from fiction into history. Duffy is unusual in being able to present both continuity and individual disjunction in time, so that the individual peculiarities of her speakers' predicaments, which are sometimes extreme, acquire a representative role by default of any larger sustaining structure of sense in society at large.

Contradiction within continuity is also one of the concerns of 'The Good Teachers'.[11] The reader may be struck by how often Duffy goes straight at a subject which many poets might think too naked a part of common knowledge to provide any imaginative purchase. The spinster schoolteacher would be a strong contender in this field – someone 'everybody' unreflectively 'knows about', though maybe it needs to be recalled that this social role owes much to the slaughter of the Great War, and to the insistence of the authorities, until the Second World War, that women teachers should leave the profession if they married. A shortage of teachers to meet the needs of the rise in the birth-rate beginning in 1945 led to the encouragement of married women to return to or enter the teaching force, but this politically expedient recognition of necessity did not simply uncreate the spinster schoolmistress role: hence the staff of the school in Duffy's poem, which takes place in the 1960s. The good teachers are 'virtuous women'. They 'swish down the corridor in long brown skirts,/snobbish and proud and clean and qualified'. They are the embodiment of their own aspirations, educated, independent professional women, exemplars of emancipation. And yet, for all these strengths,

> You roll the waistband
> of your skirt over and over, all leg, all
> dumb insolence, smoke-rings. You won't pass.
> You could do better. But there's the wall you climb
> into dancing, lovebites, marriage, the Cheltenham
> and Gloucester, today. The day you'll be sorry one day.

Duffy's use of the second person is both a way of addressing the reader, particularly the female reader, and of intensifying the recognition the poem provokes in its audience. At the same time, the pronoun (a democratic equivalent of 'one') *introduces* the reader into the poem. This may have been *your* life, the poem suggests – an adolescent revolt into sexuality as against the "pure" pursuit of a vocation. The starkness of the alternatives may make the contemporary reader pause, but it's not inaccurate, since much of the energy of feminism has gone into trying to alter the collective understanding so that sexual identity and working life cease to be cases of either/or and are seen as equal and simultaneous possibilities. It's a story pursued, for instance, in enormous and scalding detail by Frederica Potter as a Cambridge student in Byatt's *Still Life*,[12] the sequel to *The Virgin in the Garden*[13] and in the character of Cassandra, the enraged and frustrated don, in her earlier novel, *The Game*.[14] Duffy's sense of contradiction and seeming impasse are the equal of Byatt's.

There are dangers in expecting the poet to work as a social historian – dangers to which the realistic novelist writing in the third person seems less vulnerable; but Duffy has the advantage of being able to suggest all that is *not there* in the social fabric – the kinds of consciousness, for instance, which have yet to discover themselves. This is part of the strength of 'Litany', where an earlier generation – that of the poet's mother – is seen 'being sorry' without admitting or maybe even recognising the fact. 'Litany' is a poem of horror, a Pooter-world with no jokes, in which a group of female neighbours assemble to pick items from a mail-order catalogue.

...Language embarrassed them.

The terrible marriages crackled, cellophane
round polyester shirts, and then The Lounge
would seem to bristle with eyes, hard
as the bright stones in engagement rings,
and sharp hands poised over biscuits as a word
was spelled out. An embarrassing word, broken

to bits, which tensed the air like an accident.
This was the code I learnt at my mother's knee, pretending
to read, where no one had cancer, or sex, or debts,
and certainly not leukaemia, which no one could spell.[15]

We might know about this from Alan Bennett or the films of Mike Leigh, but the laughter Duffy provokes is the sort that comes when you don't know what else to do. The poem presents rigidity bordering on paralysis, women who have become almost Jonsonian embodiments of their own inhibition, occupying a bored, inarticulate hell of middle age, into which marriage and childbirth have automatically and immediately consigned them. They are the end of a class development – the pursuit of 'respectability' – begun in the nineteenth century, and like 'The Good Teachers', though more ignorantly, they have outlived their occasion without having the liberty to notice the fact. Duffy's rendering of the perceived marriage of words and things, and the women's tribal fear of invoking something by naming it, carries the poem beyond the notation found in a thousand post-Movement Slices of Life and into something close to expressionism – an English cousin, perhaps, to the sharp-fingered near-hysteria of the figures in some of Kirchner's paintings. What the women fear – chance, disorder, self-revelation, loss of face – is seen writ large in the room's atmosphere, in their gestures and appearance, their sharpness, brittleness and the guilty excitement unsuccessfully contained by the effort to rigidify the body and its wants. The sleep of reason breeds monsters, the poem implies, and here they are with the Littlewoods catalogue. What is 'not there', in the poem's chosen period, is any sense of why this should be so, any process of creation leading them to complicity in such extinction of the spirit. The women are trapped in this little room in history, and the very absence of political analysis argues the urgent need for it; but understanding will come too late to help these people. The horror arises from this sense of secular damnation.

'Litany' is not without a strong charge of authorial dislike for its characters. Just as the poem doesn't *explain*, neither does it overtly sympathise. The anger of the poem, and its objectivity, seem akin to requisites for survival. The assertion of freedom entails acceptance of responsibility, and responsibility seems also to be imposed retrospectively on the women. One could argue that Duffy has no need to spell the matter out more explicitly, but a certain deliberate detachment is often important to her work. This is more obviously a *device* in the monologues, whether spoken by the mad ('Education for Leisure', 'How Are We Today?', 'Psychopath')[16] or the seemingly powerless ('Dear Norman', 'Warming Her Pearls'),[17] where the chosen register seems slightly and unsettlingly too formal for what we think we know about the characters. Ian Gregson has shown how a linguistic privilege at odds with the marginal status of such speakers serves a dialogic purpose. He quotes Bakhtin's description of 'a hybrid construction':

> an utterance that belongs by its grammatical (syntactic) and compositional markers to a single speaker, but that actually contains within it two utterances, two speech manners, two styles, two 'languages', two semantic and axiological belief systems.[18]

Duffy's readiness to reveal her own means of representation in the process of exposing her speakers and characters as prisoners of socially acquired representations of themselves leads us back to the sense of homelessness and exposure she so powerfully conveys. Where is the ground of identity to be sought? What is its bedrock? The answer takes a negative form: the place to look is in the historical void on to which the poems, especially those about women's lives, seem to open. The women will be what they are described as being. As Alan Robinson has neatly phrased it in a discussion of 'A Provincial Party, 1956',[19] the woman forced to watch a pornographic home movie will reveal 'ingenuousness and circumscribed linguistic register (befitting one who customarily is spoken about rather than speaks the dominant discourses)'. She is, he adds, therefore allowed 'no satisfactory subject position'.[20] But this disillusionment offers, if not liberty, a certain room for manoeuvre, more tentative and patchy and imaginatively contradictory, perhaps, than the language of formalist criticism could easily allow.

This kind of incomplete and contradictory testing of limits is explored in 'Warming Her Pearls'. This is one of Duffy's most popular poems, a fact which may have something to do with the assurance of the speaker, who is both mild and obdurately observant and imaginative – a familiar dual female role; and also with the poem's oblique treatment of the genre of historical romance, a widely despised form of 'women's book': 'Warming Her Pearls' is as open to the reader of Catherine Cookson as to the educated student of the Brontës. Ian Gregson is surely correct to comment that 'what constitutes the most reliable source of value in [Duffy's] work...is an appreciation, respect and understanding for otherness especially of the spontaneous and vivid kind that occurs in love'.[21] However, his reading of 'Warming Her Pearls' tells only one side of the story:

> ...the identification is of the sympathetic kind which is analogous to the writer entering the minds of characters – it allows the maid to understand the life of her mistress, whose routine is mediated for the reader through the maid...She thinks of her all day...The bodies of the mistress and the maid mingle via the pearls – the 'faint, persistent scent' of the maid is imagined by her puzzling the tall dancing partners of the mistress. In this way love is shown tentatively negotiating otherness, enjoying its difference, influencing it (as the maid does both by her scent and, at least for the reader, by her personal interpretation of how the mistress lives) but not attempting to annex it, not resenting its freedoms.[22]

But this optimistic, even utopian reading is one-sided. It neglects the very tensions – of class and power, and between desire and its dreamed fulfilment – that make the poem so memorable. We 'understand' and sympathise with the maid's feelings, which she can never declare, but the emotion in question is not – inwardly, at any rate – of a gentle or simply admiring kind: it is *desire* and to feel it is to burn, all night, insatiably, without hope of alteration. Whether it is better to desire than not is a matter left unraised: for all the poem's apparent calm, it is the inward, lyric utterance of a passion which cannot be spoken in the hearing of the world. The mistress is as physically unknowable to the maid as she is in terms of personality to us. What we are witness to is the tremendous but – to the world of privilege – inaudible pressure of longing. If the maid does not resent her mistress's freedom, only in part can we read this as showing the infinitely accommodating nature of a love glad to exist; there is also no way out, and we, at any rate, must see the burning in its cruel disproportion to the gentleness of the maid's utterance. The reader will of course have noted that this is, in a sense, a poem about history, set unspecifically but in a time to which the constraints briskly described by Hans Magnus Enzensberger in his essay 'The Industrialisation of the Mind' certainly apply:

> No illusion is more stubbornly upheld than the sovereignty of the mind, It is a good example of the impact of philosophy on people who ignore

> it; for the idea that man can 'make up their minds' individually and by themselves is essentially derived from the tenets of bourgeois philosophy: second-hand Descartes, run-down Husserl, armchair idealism; and all it amounts to is a sort of metaphysical do-it-yourself.
>
> We might do worse, I think, than dust off the admirably laconic statement which one of our classics made more than a century ago: 'What is going on in our minds has always been, and will always be, a product of society.' This is a comparatively recent insight. Though it is valid for all human history ever since the division of labour came into being, it could not be formulated before the time of Karl Marx. In a society where communication was largely oral, the dependence of the pupil on the teacher, the disciple on the master, the flock on the priest was taken for granted. That the few thought and judged and decided for the many was a matter of course and not a matter for investigation... Only when the processes which shape our minds became opaque, enigmatic, inscrutable for the common man, only with the advent of industrialisation, did the question of how our minds are shaped arise in earnest.[23]

The maid has a *margin* of liberty of thought and feeling, but there is no reason to suppose that this is the prelude to emancipation. She has no guilt about her desire, or the intimacy of her fantasies, but she is isolated with them. We cannot assume that love stands in for liberty: this is not to deride it, rather to note that it must be its own (in this case, imaginary, or at best one-sided) reward. Yet as Gregson says, it is in the theme of meetings with otherness, in the expression of affection and desire, that Duffy locates her sense of the positive. The private life might mean nothing to the passage of history, but as it finds expression it has a strength which can only be understood in its own terms. Duffy, as we know, is a fine love poet. It is a tribute to her that the pursuit of the true voice of feeling, and her feeling for the individual life, are so thought-provoking.

VI

ALL IRELAND (II)

17. Paul Muldoon: *The Advanced Muldoon*

> I myself of course don't think the poems are quite as difficult as some people might suggest.[1]
>
> That things do make sense is very important to me.[2]
>
> PAUL MULDOON, interview with Sean O'Brien

Contrasting the responses of Seamus Heaney and Paul Muldoon to bombs and the threat of bombs in Belfast, Tim Kendall finds Muldoon's poem 'A Trifle'[3] 'less self-important' than Heaney's account of a cancelled recording at BBC Belfast.[4] If this remark by a privileged observer sets the teeth on edge, Kendall's discussion of the poem makes matters worse by missing much of the point:

> When a bomb explodes in Belfast, Heaney worries whether he ought to abandon his recording; some years later he writes an essay about his decision, and the anecdote leads into a lofty discussion of Art and Life. As its title suggests, 'A Trifle' is less self-important. Muldoon presents himself as an aesthete, contemplating a trifle (with its obvious double meaning) even while his office block is hurriedly evacuated. Yet this is merely '*another* bomb alert' (my italics) – implicitly a commonplace in inner-city Belfast, inconvenient for those trying to work through lunch or to finish their trifle. It takes 'four or five minutes' to run down 'the thirty-odd flights of steps'; the approximations suggest a routine mindless and monotonous, enlivened this time only by the wonderful absurdity of the 'blue-pink' and vaguely mammary dessert. Muldoon's trifling unrhymed sonnet captures the extent of the real 'Suffering' in Belfast, where a bomb alert itself is no more than another trifle: paradoxically, only a dilettante would labour the event. The poem suggests that those who go about their everyday lives amidst the ever-present threat of violence cannot afford the indulgence of Heaney's artful scruples.[5]

This seems vulgar, more like name-calling than criticism – not least since Heaney did a good deal to create the possibility of Muldoon's work. (And the sonnet, incidentally, is not unrhymed.) For Kendall the 'obvious double meaning' of the 'blue-pink trifle' with its dollop of cream appears to be the pun on the dish and the grim but familiar experience of the bombscare. Either the resemblance of the trifle to the colours of the Union Jack doesn't claim his attention, or he counts it as so 'obvious' as not to merit mention, even though Muldoon places it squarely (or rather, roundly) before us. Kendall appears to be so concerned with Muldoon's disinclination to make a drama out a crisis that he himself neglects the crisis altogether; yet the poem would be merely a stylish display of *sang-froid* without the historical and political dimension. To quarrel over a flag is a 'trifling' act in one sense; but it is costly in terms of lives. To quarrel over a territorial claim is equally 'trifling', but equally expensive. While complaining that the Irish are obsessed with ancient history, at the same time the British defend the expensive fruits of imperial and intermittently genocidal conquest. The British also complain about the cost of paying for Northern Ireland while offering the province the sustaining or (according to taste) unwanted tit of imperial subsidy parodically sketched in the poem. Further colours of the union flag are also those of the main British political parties, but their differences are melting away in the 'trifle' so that the British state continues to seem its old inimical, monolithic and perfidious self. These features are as much present in the poem as the stiff upper lip. They may be 'obvious', but the meaning of the obvious, as Shklovsky famously explained, is what life steals from us[6] – and the 'obvious' is what the civilians in the poem are learning to endure.

Not content, then, with having abused Heaney, Kendall has simplified Muldoon, even though every page of his detailed (and, to be fair, very informative) study is at pains to show us how very Advanced Muldoon is – a poet designed for (and perhaps *by*) academics. For most of his book Kendall does not convince us that he has been excited or moved by Muldoon's poems, though surely he must have been in order to take such pains. He also presents (again, to be fair, this may be the result of his elaborate task as explicator) a rather limited version of what poetry consists of: Kendall's Muldoon is an intellectual, a pattern-maker worthy of his interpreter, but he reveals little grasp of drama, sensuousness, gesture or voice, or of music beyond a rather mechanical level. His most ambitious work, *Madoc: A Mystery*, is a spelling into verse of ideas already resident elsewhere. He sounds rather like a poet influenced by 'Paul Muldoon' but with more limited gifts than his platonic original. And he would rather drink hemlock than acknowledge the weight of the political making itself felt in the poems.

There is apparent warrant for this in Muldoon's own comments. Interviewed by Michael Donaghy, he responded to a question about his politics:

> I don't think it matters. I don't think it's of any interest...It doesn't matter where I stand politically with a small 'p' in terms of Irish politics. My opinion about what should happen in Northern Ireland is no more valuable than yours.[7]

This is a sane response, in that it allows the poems to deal with the matter without being held to ransom by what would inevitably be a simplified response to an interview question. But given Muldoon's practice as a poet – 'we mustn't take anything at face value, not even the man who is presenting things at face value'[8] – and elsewhere in interview, it would be unwise to take his remarks as a simple or even accurate statement of conviction. All we may fairly suppose is that Muldoon feels his beliefs or lack of them can best be expressed in his poems; and given the endemic and vertiginous ambiguity of the poems, this must seem like common sense. But over against common sense is the horror of a poem such as 'Gathering Mushrooms', where the airiest hedonism finds itself imaginatively in thrall to history and martyrology as they take a new form in the time of the hunger strikes: Muldoon may not like the instructing republican voice of the poem's close, but in his way he understands it as inescapably as Heaney understands 'the exact, tribal, intimate revenge' in 'Punishment'.[9] Kendall's anxious reminders that Muldoon sees the errors of extremism are hardly the point.

If we never live to see the day we leap
into our true domain,
lie down with us now and wrap
yourself in the soiled grey blanket of Irish rain
that will, one day, bleach itself white.
Lie down with us and wait.[10]

A more useful area of contrast between Muldoon and Heaney lies in their contrasting treatment of origins. If Heaney's poems return often to the theme of having somewhere to come from, Muldoon's have a much more unstable, complex sense of the past and of identity. Heaney often earths himself imaginatively in the family farm and its surroundings, while Muldoon's home ground is always already an elsewhere. The Moy is as exotic as it is familiar: the early 'Dancers at the Moy' seems to show the familiar *is* the exotic.[11] If Heaney belongs to a tribe, Muldoon wonders what a tribe is, and comes up with the answer 'Mohawk'.

Clearly the differences, large or small, between the poets have much to do with the generations from which they come, and with the flattening-out of certain cultural hierarchies in the years between Heaney's youth and Muldoon's. Indeed, Muldoon, by the chances of upbringing, the promptings of temperament and the imaginative working-through of certain ideas about language and perception, does much to create his readers' sense of this levelling. His comments in the *Chicago Review* interview with Michael Donaghy express both relationship and difference:

[Northern Ireland] is a very small place...You tend to be brought up much the same kind of way and have the same kind of experience. My

> experience was very much like Heaney's – brought up in the country, going to the same university, and pretty much following the same kind of tack – though he's fifteen years older (and I think those are a significant fifteen years). It's true that a lot of things I write about are similar to things Seamus Heaney writes about, and early on I found comparisons a bit galling...[12]

The 'same', that is, for a Northern rural Catholic. Religious background may not be very directly or insistently felt in Heaney's poems (though there is a Marian dimension in the idealisation of the feminine), but the social and political position of the Northern Catholic can be felt as a powerful influence (see 'The Other Side').[13] Muldoon's 'The Sightseers'[14] is scaldingly anecdotal and 'open' in comparison. Religion is the object of satire ('Duffy's Circus', 'Cuba')[15] in Muldoon, who handles the social context much more sceptically and with less harking back to inherited circumspection ('The Boundary Commission'),[16] as befits someone growing up in the 1960s (there is also some concern with class in Muldoon). If the family is a sustaining and unifying principle in Heaney, for Muldoon it is a matter of anxious curiosity, and he admits to it a sexual element alien to Heaney's treatment of the subject (see 'October 1950')[17] which allies him more closely to the grim claustrophobia of the early novels of John McGahern[18] than anything in Heaney. Rural life, for Heaney, offers a basis for the interpretation of all life, whereas for Muldoon it is less a birthright than a past from which, with mixed feelings, he is carried away by opportunity and experience. Muldoon, in the end, differs from Heaney in being able to dissent from a condition of social freedom which Heaney's generation was just beginning to explore.

As to words, there is a major difference between the two men's understandings. Heaney's world is full of objects: Muldoon's is full of language. Heaney himself said as much in giving his *imprimatur* to Muldoon's early books, finding that his poetry 'insisted on its proper life as words before it conceded the claims of that other life we all live before and after words'[19] – though the distinction drawn in the latter half of the statement would seem disputable, at any rate in the context of Muldoon. While Heaney's language is sensuous, visual and tactile, Muldoon's is more inclined to be dictionary-driven, myopic and, though it does not offer a world without objects, it is less at ease among, less convinced by, solidities than Heaney's. Physical facts in Heaney's poetry seem mutually sustaining: they contribute to the sense of a complete three-dimensional world, whereas Muldoon's poetry often lacks a sense of the fore-, middle- and background: the perspective of realism is displaced by sudden attention to objects adrift from their ordinarily defining context. Heaney's words are cousins to their objects, his placenames betrothed to their places: Muldoon's are signs leading into a labyrinth of further signs. Heaney's language pursues order and underlying truth, whereas Muldoon's treats the formal order of a poem as a way of holding disorder in perspective: he lends the psychiatric conditions of echolalia and flight of ideas an aesthetic form: 'Gallogly, or Gollogly,/otherwise known as Golightly,/otherwise known as Ingoldsby,/otherwise known as English,/gives forth one low cry of anguish...'[20] Heaney's King Sweeney is a madman in a poem, while Muldoon's voices are not so clearly confined. Here, too, in clear contradiction of the poems' evidence, Muldoon is fond of disclaiming their peculiarity. It's a strategy as sensible for the art as for the politics. The deadpan of his interview manner is a public means of control equivalent to the privately run lightness, the speed over the ground, of much of his poetry. His alleged narratives get you to turn the page. They keep the reader moving onwards, because to stop might be to acknowledge that there is no clear direction.

Wondering at the variety within Irish poetry, which could produce such vastly different writers as Muldoon and Brendan Kennelly, Edna Longley memorably described *Quoof* as 'implosive'.[21] Muldoon's is indeed an imploded view. Insistence on 'proper life...as words' opens a rhyming dictionary, where all the possibilities of meaning are simultaneously available, so that language is 'encyclopaedic' in the sense described by Roland Barthes in *Writing Degree Zero*[22] and applied to Muldoon by Clair Wills, one of his most committed readers:

> the characteristic 'hermeticism' of Muldoon's poetry is partly based on its polysemousness, the instability of meaning and reference encouraged by the loose structures of the poems, and the 'encyclopaedic' nature of words divorced from the single and particular meanings they are required to carry in 'relational' discourse.[23]

An ancient, urgent but unanswerable question is raised here about authorial control. Is the poet the 'author' of the rhyming dictionary, having its resources at his disposal as part of his rhetorical equipment, or is he its inhabitant, victim and exponent? Neither? Both? Muldoon has in fact claimed, at first sight implausibly, that the author must exert final control.[24] Perhaps the way in which this might be so can be sought in the most obsessive and prominent feature of his work, its use of rhyme. Two points from T.V.F Brogan's survey of rhyme in *The Princeton Encyclopedia of Poetry and Poetics* may be useful here. Firstly Brogan summarises the view of de Cornulier:

> rhyme does not exactly reside at line end: its positioning shapes the entire structure of the line, so that we should more accurately say that the rhyme resides in the entire line. Removing rhymes from lines does not merely render them rhymeless; it alters their lexical-semantic structure altogether. End rhyme is no mere ornament.[25]

Secondly, he describes Bolinger's affirmation of what every child knows:

> in every language, words which begin or end alike come to be perceived as related even when they have no etymological connection at all. This sort of paradigmatic or synchronic associativity is even stronger than the historical kinship of words...[26]

In the *Chicago Review* interview, Michael Donaghy remarks to Muldoon, 'I'm always wondering how you're going to complete or default on a rhyme'.[27] This is more than professional curiosity: we are *meant* to wonder about this, since rhyme is the spinal column of Muldoon's work, linking the noises in the poems' heads to their rhythmic fleetness and swerving passage. If for a mediocre formalist poet the function of rhyme is largely to staple meaning together, in Muldoon's case rhymes can also, as Ian Gregson suggests, 'not so much clinch ideas as force a double-take that reassesses them'.[28] Bolinger's view provides a description of this vertiginous tendency in Muldoon. At its theoretical extreme the use of rhyme as a form of overt or covert comparison would be so far extended that the distinction between likeness and difference is collapsed, and all that would remain in operation would be the system itself, not the meanings we are accustomed to seek in it. This philosopher's antistone remains, of course, part of the promise of Muldoon's rhetoric, not a possibility to be fulfilled, though we might occasionally feel its breath, as Baudelaire felt himself to be brushed by the wing of madness.[29] What saves Muldoon is that he has subject matter, even though from one point of view it may in fact be his subject matter – family, love and sex, politics, history, perception, and language – which has so far estranged his language.

If rhyme is the presiding, driving feature of Muldoon's poems, its reach can also be felt to extend beyond its apparent boundaries. As has been pointed out, for instance by Tim Kendall, Muldoon works largely by analogy.[30] The process is relentless. It can seem at odds with the narrative impetus until the reader notices with puzzlement that it *is* much of the impetus of 'Immram', 'The More a Man Has, The More a Man Wants', 'Madoc' and 'The Annals of Chile'[31] – which among other things accounts for the Chinese-food feel of these poems: they're more-ish but afterwards you wonder what or whether you've eaten. Full of local life, they have no *localities*: the force is only passing through. It is as if, faced with Forster's injunction 'Only connect', Muldoon has taken him literally and indiscriminately. It's a tendency of which he makes ironic use in 'Something Else', which responds with habitual plain-spoken obliquity to Heaney's 'Away From It All'.[32] 'Something Else' is a critique, it seems, of a kind of aesthetic positioning of which Muldoon is suspicious. Heaney's poem moves between the luxury of good talk over a long dinner and a nagging anxiety about the lobster (the creature itself and in its half-absurd role as one embattled in the murk of history). The poem's reservations, Muldoon manages to suggest, are to a significant degree rhetorical: it is the poet himself, and his companion, who are the significant emblems here, as they might be in a poem by Lowell, or Auden, or Mahon, or Walcott. All of these poets attempt the public note against which Muldoon is temperamentally armed – in this case by enlisting the services of the completely unemployable figure of Nerval with his pet lobster, after whom Muldoon's speaker declares he thinks 'of something else, then something else again'. Kendall reads this as a method of trying not to think about death.[33] Yet perhaps death is not just accorded the respect of evasion here, but simultaneously sidelined by the poem's surplus of analogies: 'and then...and then' is at one glance sinister ('now that's something else again, an altogether other, graver matter') and at the same time an inconsequential link that merely links other links. This poem is an example of the 'done with mirrors' aspect of Muldoon's work. Analogy is the pararhyme of ideas.

Louis Simpson's enthralling and shocking poem 'To the Western World'[34] evokes in miniature the course and cost of European exploration of the Americas and, implicitly, of America's subsequent 'exploration' of the world, concluding: 'And grave by grave we civilise the ground.' This is part of the subject of *Madoc*, as well as of 'Meeting the British' (with its 'blankets embroidered with smallpox'),[35] but while Simpson works in a clear public light and is himself an agent, albeit a melancholy one, of enlightenment, Muldoon's imagination has no pioneer spirit. It does not clear or civilise the ground. Instead it flits like a rapparee down paths through a forest which to the gaze of others may seem trackless. It declines to translate itself into the public discourse which would make it accessible to a large audience. With *Madoc* the poem's own frame of reference has become part of its subject, so that narrative cul-de-sacs are evidence of power and limitation equally. There are many precedents for this, and if 'difficulty' was a defining feature of modernism, it is the source code itself of postmodernist writing, the condition of its integrity. The discomfort of some of the poem's readers may have more to do with their expectations of poetry, the poetry of Northern Ireland in particular, than with the poem's originality.

But can the same be said of 'Yarrow',[36] Muldoon's elegy for his mother, which is in some ways more vexatious than 'Madoc'? Kendall points out the gradual division in Muldoon's books between a major concluding poem and a selection of other more or less directly related pieces.[37] By the time of *Madoc* the long poem is by far the greater part of the book. In *The Annals of Chile* the balance shifts, with 'Incantata' staking a major claim for itself, both in its scale and the directness of its address, to balance the epic 'Yarrow'. 'Incantata' is a lament for and a celebration of Muldoon's former lover, the painter Mary Farl Powers, who died of cancer in 1992. The poem has a full-throated openness rare in Muldoon's work but apt for the occasion. The cajoling, mystifying low voice in your ear which has typified this most coolly circumspect poet to this point is replaced by something shouted from the rooftops:

> I thought again of how art may be made, as it was by André Derain,
> of nothing more than a turn
> in the road where a swallow dips into the mire
> or plucks a strand of bloody wool from a strand of barbed wire
> in the aftermath of Chickamauga or Culloden
> and builds from pain, from misery, from a deep-seated hurt,
> a monument to the human heart
> that shines like a golden dome among roofs rain-glazed and leaden.[38]

Here 'art' itself is an object of passion, not simply an attribute of the poet's curious and self-delighting imagination. The flaw in the stanza, the closing inversion, is an uncannily apt illustration of the poem's primary contention, that art is an essential, and even ennobling expression of humanity rather than an end for which life is simply material (the latter being an attitude whose presence could occasionally be suspected in some of the grimmer poems of sex and violence in *Quoof*). It is difficult not to see 'Incantata' and 'Yarrow' as engaged in mutual commentary on the issues of the public and the private, the memorable and the arcane. It is interesting that it should be another notoriously difficult poet, Peter Porter, who has wondered about the method, status and success of 'Yarrow'. Porter has also written a famous and much-admired poem of grief, 'An Exequy',[39] an elegy for his first wife, expressing the same frank tenderness as 'Incantata'. Just as Muldoon draws on Cowley and Yeats, Porter makes use of an earlier poem, Henry King's 'Exequy'.[40] Porter, moved to admiration by 'Incantata', provides the rationale for both poets when he comments:

> We may be miles from knowing what Muldoon knows, and almost as far from instinctively sympathising with his particulars, yet there is a public mode which leads us into the entire verbal edifice. The general is seen to prop up the private, as it must in grief...[41]

For Porter, then, 'Incantata' is an island of emotional clarity at the edge of the continental shelf, beyond which lies the unplumbed sea of difficulty represented by 'Yarrow'. Unsurprisingly, given his enthusiasms, Porter looks for a comparison in Auden, and comes up with Auden's most mysterious work, *The Orators*:

> Auden's creation is, for all its forensic detail, *en plain air* compared with Muldoon's. His is murky and lit by a kind of lyrical hellfire glow: its dramatis personae seem barely to know each other and to have no valency among themselves or in the poet's mind. If Muldoon's poetry were not obviously powerful and his tropes commanding in themselves, the critic would have no reason to worry that a reading of 'Yarrow' evokes such a sense of frustration. Hard work will yield up the pertinence of most of the difficulties of reference and allusion in Auden...Such hard labour will not be so effective with Muldoon. Yet he doesn't use *non sequitur* as a deliberate technique as John Ashbery does: he is simply unconcerned with any need for emotional logic. The connectives in the course of this long poem are as mysterious as crop circles...Everything is subordinated to the lyrical impulse, the pavane-like procession of heroes and the summoning of numerous ghosts. Authority is assumed, not even claimed. Readers who are not clansmen are expected to recognise the sound of command, even though they could not hope to be initiates.[42]

It could be argued that the distinction Porter draws between the approaches of the two poets is really one of degree rather than kind, but the disinclination of 'Yarrow' to provide a helpful perspective on its own workings (or, as Porter puts it, to indicate its 'valency') suggests a slightly different sense of audience from Auden's. Yet while Porter's frustrated reaction is representative of the strain the poem puts on the goodwill of some readers towards Muldoon, the assiduous Tim Kendall sets out the organising principle of the work. It is a series of interlinked sestinas, in which twelve sets of end-sounds are repeated fifteen times through the poem.[43] Kendall argues:

> Muldoon's imagination is liberated by the elaborate form of 'Yarrow' which ... has replaced literary sources as the poem's template or scaffolding; the mythical method in recent volumes has been superseded by a formal method. No matter how complex or seemingly arbitrary, Muldoon's chosen form is always integral to his subject...form and function are one. The scattered sestinas of 'Yarrow', for example, correspond to the poem's 'intercut, exploded' time-schemes and locations.[44]

The reader might blink at this. It sounds like an effort to make what is merely *the case* sound like the product of *necessity*, which leads us back, in conclusion, to the theme of analogy. To the unpersuaded reader it might appear from Kendall's account that Muldoon has sought to reach an ultimate analogical stance, a point at which form is meaning. If so, it would be worth hearing more of this; but 'Incantata' remains more powerfully attractive than 'Yarrow' – perhaps because in that poem the reader feels like a sympathiser with a common grief rather than, as with 'Yarrow', an intruder on someone's privacy, superfluous to its requirements.

18. Tom Paulin: *The Critic Who Is Truly a Critic*

Tom Paulin is as close as Britain comes nowadays to having a public literary critic devoted to poetry and able to speak authoritatively to the scholar and the general reader alike. Other prominent contenders for the position are all in some way less suitable. John Bayley is too comfortably patrician; John Carey too accommodating to populism; Germaine Greer too little interested in literature; Terry Eagleton too clearly divided between the roles of academic analyst and public commentator. The list can be extended, but the point holds. Paulin seems almost alone in *believing* that (rather than acting as if) a continuum exists between 'academic' literary interpretation and the public journalistic sphere, and both the strengths and the weaknesses of his essays and reviews derive from this conviction:

> Ideally, journalism and theory should support or challenge each other, but instead they go their separate ways and don't communicate. Even so, it's clear to most contemporary critics that literary theory has effected a huge sea change in the way criticism is now written. I know it has changed my own critical practice, though I still find it impossible to offer theoretical readings of literary texts. Brushed – scratched even – by theory, I'm unable to theorise or apply many of the highly sophisticated concepts and technical terms that have evolved from this type of critical practice.[1]

This is both modest and slightly misleading. The reader senses (without all that much in the way of explicit evidence) that while Paulin has digested a good deal of political criticism, much of formalism and deconstruction remain in an important way foreign to him. Alan Robinson has noted Paulin's belated exploration of some aspects of poststructuralist thought,[2] but what will always stand between him and theory is the fundamental reason that he is a critic: he believes in making, and his work *depends* on making, value judgements of a kind about whose legitimacy many theorists have necessarily been sceptical.

Although younger than a number of prominent critics engaged with Theory, including David Lodge, Terry Eagleton and Stan Smith, Paulin's thinking reveals a Leavisite, almost Puritan, cast, which places considerable weight and authority on personal conviction. It also inclines him to the close reading of texts, whereas some of his contemporaries have preferred more purely theoretical argument. At the same time as he is a close reader he is always manifestly a *social* critic. To all areas of his work he brings a powerful interest in history, which sets him apart from the purely text-centred New Criticism of the 1940s and 50s. This is formidable ordnance for the conduct of interpretation and judgement. What is also striking is that Paulin's rigorous desire (which he seems to feel as an obligation) to judge, to praise and dismiss, has not closed his mind to the strengths of popular culture and the vernacular: the presence of the human voice, speaking or singing, is vital to his sense of things. Hence blues and performance poems find their way into his *Faber Book of Political Verse* on their own terms, not by populist default.[3] Yet equally, it's worth wondering how he would respond to a comment such as the following, from Andrew Ross's 'Poetry and Motion: Madonna and Public Enemy':

> On the page, the lyrics of Madonna's songs are almost as trite and vapid as anything Tin Pan Alley ever produced...[but in] providing a useful ordinary language with which people can express and make sense of their experience of a whole range of problems and desires encountered in every day life, Madonna is exemplary of what pop music does best...[4]

Aside from patronising such popular artists as Lieber and Stoller and Chuck Berry, this, surely, is needlessly hospitable to what is, on any reasonable assessment, garbage. At the other extreme, an example of the rococo decay of theory, by Paul H. Fry, from his book *A Defence of Poetry,* seems equally unhelpful:

> To say that poetry concretises philosophy and idealises history is to impose shape in advance...on any hermeneutic of suspicion in the wake of Kant: thus one is permitted now only to say that poetry desublimates (or refiguralises) philosophy and sublimates (or dis-figures) history...[5]

This is the critical equivalent of the Latin Mass, an exclusive code whose initiates, whether by preference or default, speak only to each other – though it should be added, since despite his title it won't be apparent from this extract, that Fry *likes* poetry and wants to make it a special case of language. Paulin, maintaining a space between the extremes that might be termed culturalism on the one hand and elite code on the other, attempts to go on talking and writing a language of a kind in ordinary use. The line he talks also travels between the various excesses of the academy and the corrupt, homogenising tendency of the public prints. In the newspapers and weeklies, lack of space might serve in mitigation of the lack of all but the sketchiest account of how and why 'literary' judgements are made, but the sceptical reader knows that much of what he or she reads there is bankrupt, in cultural receivership and not even really *about* its ostensible subject, having much more to do with career and position than any literary interest. Hence the deadly dominance of the frequent implicit appeals to moribund common sense. Paulin, in contrast, is both openly partisan and willing and able to account for his opinions. His work is an act of secular faith, in which dissent is the sign of seriousness:

> With the advent of theory, there returned that polemic and argument which real criticism thrives on, because the critic who is truly a critic is almost never consensual, never balanced or judicious, but always trying to break away from the orthodox and the accepted. Like Prometheus, the critic steals fire from heaven and brings it to humans on this earth...[6]

This does of course bear the marks of the world after Leavis, whose efforts to place the study of literature at the centre of culture, and to assert a tradition of great literature, have been rejected by his successors as an attempt, albeit inadvertent and well-intentioned, to institutionalise and thus nullify the radicalism of literature, thus reintroducing by other means, as liberal humanism, the literary conservatism he had worked to displace. For Paulin, the power of the critical imagination exists at the margin and in the vanguard of literary activity rather than at the centre of its establishment. (While an English readership has been hospitable to Irish poetry for a generation, Paulin has succeeded remarkably in persuading the audience to pay attention to the kind of political and historical detail of which the English are habitually rather shy.) What is more apparent from his poems than his criticism is the extent to which he is a writer of the future tense, dreaming ahead, sometimes from an historical starting-point, into the possible. 'Trotsky in Finland', for example, uses an imagined present to reclaim a sense not simply of what might have been, but of a time before the revolution took on definition:

> He is completely alone. At nightfall
> The postman carries a storm in his satchel:
> The St Petersburg papers, the strike is spreading.
> He asks the thin boy for his bill.
> He calls for horses. Thinking,
> 'If this were a fiction, it would be Byron
> Riding out of the Tivoli Gardens, his rank
> And name set aside. Forced by more than himself.'
>
> He crosses the frontier and speaks
> To a massed force at the Institute,
>
> Plunging from stillness into history.[7]

Paulin brings the same excitement to bear on his various accounts of Protestantism in history. It is as if a faith in the immediate presence of the Word could transgress historical time and deliver its potential to the present. This is particularly apparent in his

1991 essay 'The Fuse and the Fire: Northern Protestant Oratory and Writing'. Even as Paulin acknowledges the theatrical, rhetorical dimension of what he describes, it is clear that what grips him is the hope that lies beyond the merely *written* condition of the language. Criticism of this type might almost be dreaming its own abolition or redundancy, even though he himself can write with Orwellian point and clarity:

> The Puritan aesthetic that shapes vernacular discourse is founded on an anti-aesthetic of 'truth' or immediate divine inspiration. On the surface there is usually an appearance of directness and information, but it is a carefully calculated illusion which can make the preacher resemble a method actor in his urgent authenticity and professions of personal sincerity. The church becomes a theatre where we witness the intense drama of consciousness and where a powerful sense of the absolute importance of the present moment – the urgent *now* of utterance – springs from the fusion of audience attention with the preacher's voice and gestures. The frequent dashes and exclamation marks that appear in printed texts signal an impatience with the fixity of print and a liberating ambition to make a primal reality of the spoken word. Like Emily Dickinson, the puritan writer wishes to substitute a series of exclamatory speech moments for the codified formality of print.[8]

Paulin points out that the material he is considering consists of 'forms of writing that are often dismissed as ephemeral or non-canonical – familiar letters, political speeches, oaths and toasts, sermons, pieces of journalism, overtured addresses, the minutes of synodical and other meetings'.[9] This is not quite true: the non-canonical feature of these writings is not their form or content but their provenance; but this is less important than the way Paulin seeks to erase the mental boundary between literature and history. From the excitement with which he describes the republican thought of the United Irishmen in the period of the 1798 rising you might almost suppose they won, whereas internal divisions of class and religion helped to weaken them at a crucial time and the rebellion was, as is customary, brutally put down.[10] This historical fact, though, seems less important than the eternal *now* of possibility, which carries a charge so powerful that it competes with the actual – something well caught in Neil Corcoran's description of 'a place possible at present only in the poem, not the *polis*: not the historically identified and constructed "Ireland" but the imaginary, renewable potential of a still unconstructed "someplace"'.[11] This description might be contrasted with the sour response of Edna Longley:

> The projection on to 'history' of contemporary aspirations accords with the Republican viewpoint from which history stands still: an attitude

> that refuses to accept the internal Northern vendetta as at least a variation on the old colonial theme, that writes Northern Protestants out of history unless prepared to go back and start again in 1798.[12]

Yet as Bernard O'Donoghue has pointed out:

> Longley has tended to assume two things about [Paulin]...first, that he is a radical literary theorist like his friend and Field Day colleague, Seamus Deane...The second wrong assumption...about Paulin is that he is well-disposed to the Irish Republic or to the possibility of its subsuming Ulster as a political unity centred on the Dail...[13]

Paulin's republicanism is of a much more radical kind than Irish republicanism is inclined to offer: it proposes, for instance, a resolution of conflict, not a victory, and this possibility – the 'free equal republic' of 'Liberty Tree' – necessarily makes its first home in the imagination. Such a view may owe less to theory than the language Paulin has overheard while growing up. It is something he understands in the writings of Ian Paisley, whose account of his father's river-baptism Paulin quotes in another essay:

> My father tells when he went under the waters of that river he identified himself with is Lord in death, in burial and in resurrection. When he came out that day he had lost many of his friends, he had lost many of the people that once associated themselves with him in the gospel. He realised that there was a reproach with the gospel. My father as I told you, was uncompromising in his character. He did not care. The more he was opposed the more he preached and the more he was persecuted the more he excelled in evangelism. God blessed him and eventually he went to Armagh to business.[14]

There is of course an element of the ludicrous here: quite what 'persecution' one Protestant sect could really offer another at the turn of the century, even in Ulster, is hard to imagine. Absurd, too, is the overt identification of the father with Christ and (by implication) of father and son with God the Father and God the Son. If this egotistical messianism comes as no surprise to those who've had to listen to Paisley's particular ravings for the last quarter of a century, it is nonetheless hard not to be struck by the simple cleanliness with which the baptism story spells itself into a condition of biblical permanence and timelessness. This is the corollary of the furious immediacy Paulin has described elsewhere: the here and now lives by virtue of its matching-up to the larger ur-story of scripture. Although Paulin has noted in an angry essay on Geoffrey Hill that 'the buried Anglican' in him 'has a soft spot for [Hill's] visionary mustiness',[15] he really likes his meat stronger, and while his own view is secular it is charged by the continuous creation of certainty he senses in the fires of Ulster Protestantism. It is this, perhaps, that fuels his contempt for the Unionist establishment, with its weary orthodoxies and permanent nay-saying. The wilder reaches of Protestantism may house the murderers, but they may also be open to change, perhaps through the recognition that class and not theology needs to be the subject: it is the paramilitaries, not the official Unionists, who have shown an interest in breaking the deadlock in the last few years.

The consequences for Paulin's view of poetic language are important. 'Desertmartin', the most powerful of Paulin's early poems, applies the notion of revealed truth to the physical appearance of a small Protestant settlement. Everything here bespeaks the rigidified posture of Unionist culture; the village is as much an advertisement for Unionism as any gable-end mural. This is the point: the depiction of an exhausted, paralysed, physically externalised attitude:

> At noon, in the dead centre of a faith,
> Between Draperstown and Magherafelt,
> This bitter village shows the flag
> In a baked absolute September light.
> Here the Word has withered to a few
> Parched certainties, and the charred stubble
> Tightens like a black belt, a crop of Bibles.[16]

The poem strains towards a kind of critically imitative form, stretching its sounds on the rack of a psychic discomfort felt by the poet and displayed, as a sort of negative aesthetic, by Desertmartin itself. This attempted embodiment of a form of zealotry which has become an end in itself, a geologically immoveable posture of defiance, gave marked offence to Edna Longley, who tried to see the poem off in a couple of sentences in her essay 'Poetry and Politics in Northern Ireland'. Paulin, she asserted, 'cannot temper the extremist techniques of satire for the purposes of inward dissection'. Further, 'That clichéd, external impression of the Protestant community exposes Paulin's own "parched certainty".'[17] The placing of the term 'extremist' seems both deliberate and wanton, belonging more properly to the right-wing British press than to literary criticism. Poet and critic are perhaps condemned simply to disagree, but it's worth noting that while for good or ill the poet has done his job, the critic has merely answered with a denial. Ulster says no? Paulin has a further linguistic turn to offer.

As Bernard O'Donoghue suggests, the co-presence in Paulin of a strongly political cast of mind and equally strong belief in artistic liberty provides a fruitful conflict.[18] What serves to enrich this is the emergence of a markedly un-theoretical view of language. Such a view is not conditional on a background like Paulin's (something not dissimilar can be found in Heaney), but Paulin's attraction to urgent, frank testimony makes his a particularly vivid case. To the stern, unyielding, at times nearly melodramatic diction of some early poems – 'Something made a fuck of things', a 'hemp noose over a greased trap', a 'rain of turds' [19] – which in themselves could startle the foreigner with Ulster in-your-faceness – Paulin has added the vivid, snarling, vinegary resources of Ulster speech. In the 1983 collection *Liberty Tree*, for example, can be found 'glooby', 'boke', 'choggy', 'humpy', 'clabbery', 'sheugh', 'screggy', 'geg', '*weebits*', 'blups', 'yawp', 'slob'.[20] The origins may be multiple ('boke' is familiar in Scots, for example), but they have a location; they also have features in common, being non-latinate, insistently concrete and physical, notionally onomatopoeic and stressing their intimacy by a liking for the diminutive. All this is apparent before any consideration of meaning. Anthony Thwaite has fastidiously described Paulin's practice as 'a free and sometimes freakish use of Ulster dialect, aggressively challenging supposed "English" decorum and creating 'scathing, laconic, sometimes obscure annotations of Ireland'.[21] This is clearly not the same as Douglas Dunn's less dramatic incorporation of Scots words into some poems from *St Kilda's Parliament* onwards, which he says is done 'for affection's sake'.[22] Affection is obviously part of Paulin's feeling, but he makes Thwaite uneasy as Dunn would not, exposing the housemaster badly concealed in Thwaite's liberalism. At the same time, in his summing up Thwaite calls Paulin's 'a vexed, gritty, impatient, sometimes choked and incoherent talent, arresting but frustrated'.[23] If there is incoherence (Thwaite lacks space to demonstrate it) it links Paulin with the tendency described in the essay on Ulster oratory:

> That enduring Presbyterian preference for the direct testimony of consciousness over formal argument creates a solipsistic universe gnawed at its edges by anger and incoherence.[24]

'Incoherence' might be one way of describing a furious desire to communicate a truth preceding or displaced by the established forms of order and decorum. It might also be a way of describing the effort of something to bring itself into being, a kind of utopian dictionary that seeks to make public what has previously lived in the unofficial dimension of common speech – the spirit, as it were, that precedes the letter. This is what excites Paulin in the work of John Clare or in Hopkins. As is usually the case with Paulin, the idea lives in the light struck off its own contradictions. Even as he seeks out a densely physical language, and produces savagely undeluded poems about *realpolitik*, he also remarks that the Protestant imagination is 'never quite at home in this world'.[25] The quiddity

Paulin seeks in the language seems like something only truly available in the prelapsarian state, the prehistory before 'the thing deserts the word', in Derek Mahon's phrase,[26] or when Adam named the contents of Eden. Finally staking everything on conviction, this is the thinking of a theologian rather than a literary theorist. Paulin also succeeds in requiring the same quality of attention for his prose ('political speeches', 'sermons', 'pieces of journalism') as for the poems, and in insisting on this continuum he does for the good of the commonwealth what the theorist might do only for the institution.

19. Ciaran Carson: *These Things Are What We Are*

> ...These things are what we are
>
> CIARAN CARSON, 'Two to Tango'[1]

Considering the effort of accurate remembrance in 'Queen's Gambit' from *Belfast Confetti* (1990), Ciaran Carson writes: 'With so many foldings and unfoldings, whole segments of the map have fallen off.'[2] Memory is a task described by Walter Benjamin as 'the capability for endlessly interpolating' into what has been,[3] and Benjamin's 'A Berlin Childhood Around the Turn of the Century' is quoted in the epigraph to Carson's *Belfast Confetti*. Declan Kiberd has suggested that these poems 'brilliantly mapped [Benjamin's] European architectonics...on to that very place' while also noting the poems' 'conclusive tenderness'.[4] This is well put. Although Neil Corcoran has pointed out the depth of 'quite unironised'[5] and linguistically vengeful anger Belfast's history provokes in the poet in 'Slate Street School' from the earlier volume *The Irish for No* (1987),[6] much of Carson's work is a love poem addressed to his native city. It is a passion the city may be said to requite in the form of change ('love is not love/ Which alters when it alteration finds'),[7] so that the digressive habit of Carson's poems might be something learned at the city's knee as well as from the traditions of the *seanachie*. The city grows in the telling, as memory and imagination play across the web of associations which opens and shifts from moment to moment. Digression, or divagation, is Benjamin's habit, too, as though to be astray (and preferably lost) in the city might be the means to most nearly encompassing it: 'A Berlin Chronicle',[8] for instance, reads as a perpetual preparation for description, rather than the thing itself.

The antidote, if one were needed, might be an accurate map. But the map, in Carson's work, is not a static depiction. He refers to maps containing features that were never built, and he illustrates the gap between his own interior map and the streetplan of the present. He also uses the map as a way of illustrating and elegising what is lost:

> ...on this 1986 reprint of the 1920 Ordnance plan of North Belfast, for instance, where *the interesting panopticon shape of the gaol is not shown here for security reasons*, though it is *a sad reflection that apart from one surviving farm* (which in any case is now a barracks) *the only spaces on this map are the prison exercise yard and the parade ground of the military*

> *barracks* (which is half a barracks now, and half a high-rise urban complex, only the prison remains inviolate) – a sad reflection on what, on this ubiquitous dense graffiti of public houses, churches, urinals, bonding stores, graving docks, monuments, Sunday schools and Orange halls...[9]

The litany continues in a single unresolved sentence for another page, a rhapsody of loss and a demonstration of both the fascination and the insufficiency of cartography. The military presence, and the sense that the civil and the military have fused, leads ironically back to Benjamin's observations on the idea of charting his life in map form:

> First I envisaged an ordinary map, but now I would incline to a general staff's map of a city centre, if such a thing existed. Doubtless it does not, because of ignorance of the theater of future wars.[10]

In the case of Belfast, a city on a seemingly permanent war footing, such a map is one means among many for the surveillance of the population. Carson's discussion of maps is preceded by a passage drawing heavily on Jeremy Bentham's idea for the panoptic prison, in which the occupants could be observed at all times and at all angles while their keepers retained the status of privacy: '*hence the sentiment of a sort of invisible omnipresence*'.[11] The mingling in this context in the poet's imagination of the forces of military and legal compulsion remind us both that the present conflict in Northern Ireland is a continuation of others, and that Carson himself has a civilian imagination.

Carson's Belfast is under occupation: as Neil Corcoran puts it, 'people's lives are taken out of their hands by the alien mapmakers and mapreaders of their destinies' [12] – something we don't sense much in Paul Muldoon, the native of what Corcoran calls deciduous Armagh,[13] a poet for whom the authority of Belfast is exterior rather than imaginative. There may be many reasons for this difference in emphasis, but one of them is surely the poets' differing attitudes to place. In Muldoon's poems, place is scarcely present on its own account. It is somewhere for poems to start from – see, notably, 'Yarrow',[14] where the family home is a jumping off point for imaginings which tend to efface the terrain itself. Place gives rise to language, but the reverse does not seem to be true – whereas for Carson the experiences of language and place are mutually productive, and he is thus writing history of a kind Muldoon rarely touches on. For instance, in Carson's study of the local etymology of the word 'Brick' in the essay-poem of that name,[15] it is hard to say from one moment to the next whether the object of study is a word or a place: the effect is to produce, QED, a proof of the mixed natures of solid *brick*, cloth containing flaws (*brack*) and discardable waste (*brock*), all of which rise from and fall back into the 'alluvial and tidal muck' (*sleech*)[16] on which the city is built:

> As the tall chimneys and catacomb-like kilns of the brickworks crumbled back into the earth, the very city recycled itself and disassembled buildings – churches, air-raid shelters, haberdashers, pawnshops – were poured into the sleech of the shore to make new land; vast armies of binmen or waste-disposal experts laboured through the years transforming countless tons of brock into *terra firma*; the dredged-up sludge of the Lagan became Queen's Island, that emblem of solid work and Titanic endeavour.[17]

Carson's approach tends to forbid a taxonomy of equivalences between 'thing' and 'idea': the field of his imagination is unified at birth. This seems to be the burden on the second part of 'Brick', where the poet recalls the epic of 'feats of miniature engineering'[18] played out with a friend on the banks of a stream on a new estate in Andersonstown: 'a series of dams, canals, harbours, breakwaters, run-offs, cul-de-sacs and overspills' in which 'We built and sank navies.'[19]

This makes clear the appeal of the idea of 'the second Venice, dreamed by George Macartney, Sovereign of Belfast in the late 1600s'.[20] Although the reader must wonder at a comparison between the mercantile thalassocracy of Venice and the 'barbarous nook'[21] of Belfast, both have been dependent on violent acquisitiveness and commercial ingenuity, and both provoke depths of affection not immediately commensurate with or answerable to the historical facts. To make sense of Carson's Belfast we need to read it as a world, as somewhere whose variety and complexity exceed explanation and whose energy can rebuff any ready-made moral objection – though Carson is, implicitly, a moralist at every turn. These are characteristics which might make more obvious sense in the context of an English industrial city, where the absence of military and sectarian (though not racial) conflict makes the passionate mixed feelings and possessiveness of the inhabitants somewhat more readily understandable.

As with place, so it is with objects: an intense apprehension of the material world drives Carson's work, particularly from *The Irish for No* onwards. This is not a matter of the easy nostalgic recital of brand names and defunct commodities deployed as a means of evading the present: rather, it seems to arise from a sense of the way the self reaches into and identifies itself, wholeheartedly if never quite with a finished coherence, in concrete realities, from the building-bricks of the city to what is eaten, drunk and smoked there. It is an appetite well caught in Tom Paulin's description of 'the intense linguistic hedonism which many Belfast people share', from which 'they emerge as lovers of junk food, children, white lemonade, lashings of tea, cigarettes, alcohol, history, song and an entity called "people" – i.e. themselves'.[22] This would not be a bad start to an inventory of Carsoniana, and it has a partial equivalent in 'Loaf', where the speaker remembers a summer job in McWatters' bakery, and there is a discussion of the merits of various whiskeys:

> ...Joe reckoned that Jameson's *Three Swallows* was hard to beat.
> Though you could make a case for their *Robin Redbreast* or Power's *Gold Label.*
> One had the edge the others didn't, though you couldn't quite describe it.
> Like Gallaher's *Greens*: dry, smoky, biting.[23]

This isn't a set-piece evocation, but a way of signalling the young men's absorption in their time-passing chat in the workplace. It displays an intense everyday aestheticism, a relish of the thing, whatever it might be, and an awareness, even in casual circumstances, of the wish to get behind mere seeming and 'describe it'. *This is where we live and what we live in*, the poem suggests, and the characteristic multiple strands seen and heard vanishing and re-emerging in Carson's poems do honour to their acrid, smoky setting in the lived mystery of city life. He is a secular mystic, the Symbolist poet of Paulin's 'people'. Few poets have rendered the olfactory with such relish: smell and taste seem like the guarantees of the unified field of Carson's world, even as they resist definition. (By a sort of historical pun, Baudelaire's 'Correspondences', Carson's version of which appears in *First Language*, includes among its scents 'le benjoin', gum benzoin or benjamin: had this been Muldoon's poem he would certainly have made something of the coincidence.)[24]

This loving regard for the material world, I have suggested, sets Carson apart from Muldoon: it also contributes to the evocative power of his work, which is hardly rivalled among his contemporaries, and it makes his a postmodernism of a particularly valuable, exemplary kind, for in it a broad democratic humanism has retained its place while the poet's scepticism has been constructively applied to the rhetorical structures of poetry itself. If Muldoon's approach involves a view of metaphor as process rather than product, the Symbolist Carson may (in a sense) have gone a stage further: his work consists of metonymies for an unstated (and, we infer, unstatable) whole. The object of the search would make an imaginative equivalent of the Real Presence at the Communion service – a comparison intriguingly implied in the more recent poem 'Eesti', from *Opera Et Cetera*, in the Estonian city of Talinn.[25] In *The Irish for No* and *Belfast Confetti* a palpable, sensual, finite but unbounded world survives, and thrives on, the poet's interrogation.

In contrast, it is difficult to resist reading *First Language* as a book invaded by crisis, where the poet is thrown back on himself and the balance between things and words falls more heavily on the latter. The book *speaks* more volubly than most. The poems seem to want to be off the page and back in the mouth, to declare, like W.R. Rodgers in 'Epilogue' (though Rodgers is speaking of Protestant Ulster),

> I am Ulster, my people an abrupt people
> Who like the spiky consonants in speech.[26]

But plain declaration is not, by and large, an option. The poems function as crossroads where language and power intersect. They seem to ring and shudder and at times to suffer cartoon-like distortions under the impact of competing discourses. The effect is urgent but by no means solemn: comedy and horror are continuous with each other. The sense that Carson is writing English as if it were Irish is especially strong in this book. And as is usual in Carson, the speakers may not be exactly authorities in their own texts – see, for instance, 'Grass' and 'Two to Tango'.[27] In the first, a group is betrayed by an informer, a 'fact' elicited from a glut of doubletalk and euphemism which sounds at least as hellbent on perpetuating itself as the speaker is on exacting revenge. The poem provokes the question of how anything anyone involved in whatever this lot are up to could possibly be a secret for longer than five minutes, given their inherent mouthiness – which returns us to the absurdist figures of earlier narrative poems, such as Young Flynn in 'Dresden'.[28] 'Two to Tango' replaces the blathery (and alleged) solidarity of the group for the solitary life of someone who sounds like an agent under deep cover. Trained in a minute alertness to every tic and gesture, the speaker finds him(?)self becoming his own performance:

> And then you think, not to repeat yourself is not real life. And so you do.
> You develop mannerisms. Tics and tags, without any of them looking
> like they're pseudo.[29]

The assumption of the speaker into his assumed identity is paralleled by the slippage of language between contexts:

> For when you stop saying *never*, that's when you'll get dead. You'll
> put your sweet lips
> A little too close to the phone and talk of *always* in a fatal momentary
> lapse.[30]

There's a quotation here from Jim Reeves's Country and Western song 'He'll Have to Go'. This famous love song about a triangular affair is conducted down the telephone and sung with aching, melancholy sweetness, as though the singer recognises his own guilt and knows that he could be next: 'Put your sweet lips a little closer / to the phone / and let's pretend / that we're together / all alone.../ And you can tell your friend there with you / he'll have to go.'[31] Country is a genre whose appeal to the white working class crosses sectarian and national borders. In Country and Western music perhaps more than any other popular form, sentimentality and truth to feeling, the inauthentic and the real, are dependent on each other, perhaps because the basis of the Country and Western song is an extreme of disappointed passion which has become an everyday condition. There is an obvious parallel with the position of the undercover soldier. And there is a comparable complication for the poem's audience in the fact of a poem firstly referring to this despised form *at all* and at the same time seeming to invite readers to lose themselves in an analysis of a kind for which white-trash music was certainly not designed. Carson's inclusion of this fragment of Nashville lyricism is more direct and convincing than the Chandlerian presence in Muldoon: the latter is (albeit inevitably) studied, but the former sounds like something ordinarily to hand.

One commonplace response to such strain and confusion is to take to drink, to dwell awhile within its zone of unhistorical success, and this is the strategy of several of the poems in *First Language*, not least the version of Rimbaud's 'Le Bateau Ivre', 'Drunk Boat'. The effect is not so much to offer the reader a glimpse of hallucinatory power, though the poem is extraordinarily vivid in Carson's version, as to show in English (which itself is made to sound like a foreign language) what it might be like for language to dream its own incarnation:

> Through the tug and zip of tides, more brain-deaf than an embryo,
>   I bobbled;
> Peninsulas, unmoored and islanded, were envious of my Babel-babble.
>
> Storms presided at my maritime awakening. Like a cork I waltzed
>   across the waves,
> Which some call sailors' graveyards; but I despised their far-off,
>   lighted enclaves.
>
> As children think sour apples to be sweet, so the green sap swamped
>   the planks
> And washed away the rotgut and the puke, the rudder and the
>   anchor-hanks.[32]

This, we might imagine, is what the now-forgotten poets of the Romantic recrudescence of the 1940s might have wanted to do.

The complete ship's orchestra is playing simultaneously. Uttering thunderous consonants, vertiginously skating vowels, rhymes so frankly *present* that they might be by Robert Service, the whole sound-system exuberantly seeks to snatch out the cloth between itself and the table of the line, to break its own bounds and become what it utters. Rimbaud doesn't hold many fears for Carson, and in the context of Northern Ireland this version of his famous poem is a notable affirmation, though its close is naturally sombre, like that of the equally riotous 'Ballad of HMS *Belfast*', which despite its jovial crew of 'Catestants and Protholics' ends with a bitter awakening:

> I lay bound in iron chains, alone, my *aisling* gone, my sentence passed.
> Grey Belfast dawn illuminated me, aboard the prisonship *Belfast*.[33]

Carson's work continues to defy the times by its regard for language. In *Opera Et Cetera*, with a boldness which has become characteristic since his re-emergence in 1987, his blend of nervy, feverish aestheticism and warm, minutely detailed ordinariness is at times subjected to a classicising coolness, with further startling effects. Carson's line and stanza-forms have long drawn attention to themselves. The long line has attracted comparison with C.K. Williams and Louis MacNeice, and Carson himself has sought to clarify its principles. Yet even as many of the poems seem triumphantly successful and innovative, it's hard to find a convincing description of how the forms work. With *Opera Et Cetera*, the reader may, perhaps, have grounds for slightly greater confidence. Without crunching the numbers, it does sound as if rhyme, already an important presence in *First Language*, has become several degrees fuller; and, as for example in 'Opus 14',[34] it is often syntactically as well as aurally conclusive. At the same time, form is to some degree, clarified, albeit tangentially, and rhythm emboldened. 'Opus 14' assembles fourteen couplets; from the same volume, 'Opus Operandi' dances attendance on this magic number, too, as its three sections contain successively six, seven and eight couplets.[35] To pursue this to the point of absurdity, these of course add up to a total of twenty-one, which, multiplied by the lines of a couplet makes forty two, which, divided by the number of sections in the poem makes… fourteen. It would be interesting to know if a Muldoonologist could make anything of this. It seems like the kind of thing which if deliberate is designed for the poet's amusement and if not is the kind of happy accident whose neatness no one would be inclined to discard. At the same time it seems to blend overtones of parody with those of serious enquiry, like the variations on the consonantal pattern 'rgn' in Paul Muldoon's *Meeting the British* noted by Mick Imlah,[36] a series from which the excluded term is 'origin', where what seems to be under examination is not so much the alchemy of the word as its snake-oil. Given these deliberately 'external' and amusingly factitious-sounding formalisms in both poets, it is at any rate hard not to feel that Carson's recent work stands in an enquiring relationship to Muldoon's. This possibility might be examined in relation to the two poets' handling of the sonnet and their employment of rhyme in relation to line-length.

The sonnet is one of Muldoon's formal passions. Among contemporaries he has signed it as clearly as Tony Harrison or Les Murray, from as far back as 'Ma', through 'Immrama' and 'Why Brownlee Left' and its employment as a stanza in 'Anseo' and 'Promises, Promises', until its fullest exploitation in single and multiple form in *Quoof.*[37] Arguably the sonnet has ceased to be 'simply' a significant form in Muldoon's work and has become a motif in itself, a figure whose shape he continually shifts, to which he will always return. It is his tick-over, warm-up exercise as well as the site of his most impressive work: in *The Prince of the Quotidian* (1994),[38] a minor interchapter in Muldoon's work, thirteen of the thirty poems are sonnets (magic number time again). The ten-line rhyming couplet form which Carson employs in the sequences 'Letters from the Alphabet' and 'Opera'[39] in *Opera Et Cetera* seems to be his latest approach to the sonnet and to comprise a peremptory statement about form as a whole, by means of the stanza's bareness and immobility of rhyme.

Over the years, Muldoon's line has become subservient to rhyme, while rhyme has become more recherché and been more subtly offered to the ear: as indulged in *The Prince of the Quotidian* it has become its own justification. In Carson, for whom it is a more recent preoccupation, rhyme is not only loudly emphatic (as was suggested above) but in a sense more isolated and isolating: it will never osmotically become the lines' texture. This can be baldly apparent, as in the mannered, quizzical urgency of 'I' from 'Letters from the Alphabet':

> *I* is the vertical, the virtual reality. I tell it slant.
> I am leaning into you to nudge you. I am Immanuel, and you are
>   Kant.
>
> I have been around so long, I have the memory of an elephant;
> Although, I think that I deserve some praise, I hope you're not a
>   sycophant.[40]

If Muldoon feels obliged to rhyme so variously as to defeat expectation, Carson operates in quite a contrary way. At times he keeps us waiting, like Ogden Nash reborn into a parallel universe. It is as though, at least in part, he is indicating a discomfort with the airiness which is always in the offing of Muldoon's work. For the reader troubled by the low value placed on objects and sensations – as opposed to amusing glances at them – in Muldoon, it is striking how often Carson crowds his lines to the point of synaesthesia with the things of this world and the feelings they startle into life, including a joy in the poem's onward momentum which is foreign to Muldoon:

> O porcelain metropolis, inlaid with palaces of majuscule Baroque
> And Trojan *equus* statues; fountains, spices, frozen music, gardens,
> oranges from Maroc! [41]

Perhaps the ultimate difference between the two poets lies in their susceptibility to irony. If Muldoon has it like an accent or a badge of rank and can sometimes seem delicately muffled by it, Carson will not let the habit of literature shut him off from life or the humane moral energy which fuels his love of the world.

20. Matthew Sweeney: *A Separate Peace*

Recent Irish poetry has acknowledged American example and influence in various ways. There is, for instance, Heaney's elegiac poem about Lowell;[1] or, less obviously, the formalist perfection of some of Mahon's work; or, more boldly, Carson's redeployment of C.K. Williams's Whitmanesque long line. The Irish poet, like the Irish citizen in general, often feels a readier access to the United States than his or her English counterpart. With the youngest of the Irish poets under discussion here, this becomes almost casually apparent.

Matthew Sweeney (born 1952) admires a wide range of American poets – among them Frost, Plath, Charles Simic and Thomas Lynch, with the influence of Frost and Simic perhaps strongest, though Sweeney has gone a long way to establish his own ground, taking in the work of Kafka and Peter Huchel on the way (Sweeney is a fluent German-speaker). Yet whilst his own voice is occasionally imitated, Sweeney rarely sounds like anyone else. The early resemblance to Paul Muldoon has long been refined away, and it could now be argued that in one sense his practice is diametrically opposed to Muldoon's. Whereas Muldoon's poems are a continual striptease, Sweeney's purport to be naked as nature intended and seem to lay their emphasis wholly and even baldly on subject-matter, though this approach is of course by no means guileless.

Several features make Sweeney's work increasingly recognisable through five collections since 1981. There is his approach to narrative, with sinister or (though less often) comic elements to the fore. There is also his view of figurative language: he is a poet of statement and hint, of talk rather than rhetoric or image – hence the appeal for him of elements of such very different poets as Frost and Simic. The decidedness of Sweeney's approach to vocabulary and diction (and frame of reference) can be indicated by contrast with his near-contemporaries, the American Irish Michael Donaghy and the London Irish Ian Duhig, whose appetites for the baroque are as distinctive as Sweeney's austerity. The difference may also indicate that Sweeney's own education was not the standard poet's study of literature but began in engineering and progressed through a German-language study of literature at the University of Freiburg. Of similar importance is Sweeney's choice of a tensile stress-metre rather than the iambics to which many of his contemporaries have been drawn.

The effort to place Sweeney quickly reveals his highly selective, personalised sense of the contemporary world: in some sense his poems, even including 'No Answer',[3] which features Reagan and Thatcher on the telephone, take place in private. There is a corresponding lack of the kind of forcible interest in history which is so apparent in other living Irish poets from Thomas Kinsella to Muldoon. His rendering of his home landscape in coastal Donegal is geologically and geographically impressive but historically bare. In place of the discourses of history and politics Sweeney suffers (and often employs) the paranoia of someone from a far province uprooted and cast adrift in the city. The poems are full of doubles – other selves, other lives. This is especially striking in poems of love and parenthood such as 'A Daydream Ahead', 'Calais' and 'The Shadow Home',[4] as well as in the more light-hearted children's poem 'The Burglar'.[5] The sense of unease and threat are both the subject of many of his poems and part of Sweeney's imaginative means.

What is often most initially striking in Sweeney's poems is the sense of something withheld – an explanation, a cause, a link between events, a perspective which would ensure the meaning of what is described. If Beckett and Kafka come to mind, they are not simply influences but kindred imaginations. This is not quite the same thing as the power of suggestion required of any competent poet. Sweeney's language dances around the missing terms, gesturing at them but rarely naming them, as though subject to a constraint which has converted itself into a style of the imagination.

One way to illustrate this is by examining one of Sweeney's less characteristic (because most nearly public) poems. 'A Couple Waiting', from the 1989 collection *Blue Shoes*, is about terrorism, but it leaves out all the apparatus by which guerrilla warfare is ordinarily described and judged, in order to look afresh at the participants before the onset of demonisation. These are particular people in a particular place:

> He calls the woman over and feels her stomach,
> then asks why she thinks the boat is late.
> Like him, she's harassed by an image –
> the boat, searchlit, in French or Spanish waters,
> guns pointed, a mouth at a megaphone.
> Like him, she does not voice her mind,
> instead sends him to the hill once more
> in the dying light, to watch the red sun
> sink in the water that's otherwise bare,
> while she sits in the dark room, thinking
> of the country their child will grow up in.[6]

The poem's success lies in its disinterested sense of what is at stake in such conflict – for the couple that is – 'the country their child will grow up in', with the clear hint that the conflict will be perpetual. Sweeney's language carries, without brandishing it, a critique of the day-to-day discourse of power. The narrative, with its barely described coastal setting, generates an unsettling sense of isolation (from the seat of power, for example) and also emphasises that for all their anonymity, this civilian couple with their bare domestic situation are carriers of history, the servants of an epic whose bare essentials – sunset, dark room, empty sea – at once dwarf and sustain their vestigial identity. The effect is not to approve the intended deeds but to question the interpretative framework we as readers may bring with us, to deny us moorings in the familiar. This is one of several of Sweeney's poems that might be described as written simultaneously in English and another language.

Alternatively, the unknown factor can seem implicit in the donnée of the poem – a constituent element experienced, as it were, before the poet can choose to manipulate it. The lyrical 'Dog on a Chain',[7] also from *Blue Shoes*, celebrates the dog who comes to replace a dog which has died. For the imagination the new dog is the reincarnation of its predecessor; but the poem makes the dog at once intensely familiar and wholly other – the 'same' dog, except that the condition of dogness is itself made strange to us. 'Making strange' has of course become one of the crutches of contemporary poetry – nothing strange about it, in fact – just like nature or confessionalism in previous decades. Yet in Sweeney's case the process is far more than the habit of the times. It is a primary determinant of sensibility, and only thereafter a strategy, though one which he can employ very subtly.

The poems' air of obsession and the author's readiness to discern or create ritual suggest a complex relationship with Catholicism. Sweeney's is a world, you might say, with a metaphysic but no God. We may suspect that it is only by strategies of fiction and distancing that it remains imaginatively supportable. The speaker in 'On My Own'[8] has dropped out of a school cross-country race in order to abscond. He pauses at the railway track to listen for an approaching train, remembering 'last week, and McArdle/ headless when the train had gone.' The monks of a boarding-school education appear to patrol the work's uneasy corridors, which tend continually, if sometimes humorously, in the direction of death. At times (for instance in the monastery tale 'Pink Milk'[9]) the humour can be grinding. It hints in little at the same insane *thoroughness* as Patrick McCabe's flawed but powerful novel of the decline of Irish Catholicism, *The Dead School*, which attends with a kind of anti-hagiographical minuteness to the downward progress of two protagonists we know to be doomed as soon as they enter the stage of the book.[10]

This frame of mind, already deeply estranged, has effects ranging from the tedious, such as 'The Man with the Budgie on His Back',[11] to the troubling and haunting, such as 'The Women'. Here Sweeney presents a familiar situation – a drunken domestic party where a skirmish in the sex war is being waged with the weapons of inertia by the men and mockery by the women:

The women are lighting fires
and snapping drunks –
their own drunks, men
whose eyes will be closed
on the prints that come back
from the chemist; men
seen past a whisky bottle
on a table, drinking
from delft eggcups
beneath pictures of the dead.

The women are drinking too,
off-camera – till a child
grabs the camera
and snaps them, their laughs,
their glasses raised,
their mock dances to music
on the wireless; and the men
with their eggcups still,
deep in chairs, watching.
And the child wondering.[12]

This manages to be both contemporary and archetypal. The situation has a worrying ugliness; half-understood antagonisms act themselves out in play or immobility. At bottom, perhaps, these people do not like each other: they are merely *with* each other, irredeemably entwined. The child's 'wondering' at these dim events is made to arise not as a sentimental abstraction but in response to the ambiguity of the men's state – eyes open, eyes closed. A whole cargo of unfinished business is waiting to tilt and burst. The quiet intensity with which the end arrives is managed in the absence of all but the plainest narration. (The facts can do it for you, we are told, but what exactly are the facts here?) The women's 'mock dances' are a brilliant observation. What is happening in the poem seems to be doing so by other means, as if elsewhere. There's no denying the acuity or dramatic persuasiveness, or the economy which marks a poet in control of his/her material. What makes 'The Women' especially interesting, though, is the resolute ordinariness of its vocabulary, the preference for statement over image, and the weight placed on the evenness of the imagined voice of the poem as it carries us inexorably through the four 'takes' of which the piece consists. It moves across two unrelenting sentences, opened with main verbs and then sustained by emphasis, by repetition and placing of vocabulary ('drunks', 'men') and grammatical forms (the possessive) before reaching a conclusion whose implication is that this is how things will remain.

If 'The Women' reads as the product of insatiable anxiety carefully contemplated, Sweeney can also produce a more leisurely and fantastical sort of poem. 'The U-Boat', for example, deals with a man who spends his leisure basking on a raft and occasionally swimming down to enter the hull of a sunken submarine, passing his 'friend/the skeleton, until my breath runs low,/then I hit the surface he saw long ago/but never quite saw in the end.'[13] The poem seems to drowse in its own midday heat, while sustaining a perilous balance between the worlds of air and water – a balance the swimmer threatens by the pathological whimsy of his repeated demonstration of secret knowledge of both worlds. While 'The U-Boat' plants discreet symmetries in the mind, Sweeney goes further with 'Symmetry' itself.[14] The *reductio ad absurdum* of his own sometimes wanton pattern-making tendencies, the poem recalls films and television drama of the 1960s, such as *Modesty Blaise*, *The Avengers* or *The Prisoner*. Just as their visual style worked to displace narrative meaning in favour of repetitive gesture, so 'Symmetry' proposes a setting where obsessive design has anticipated and excluded the moral significance of the speaker's desires and commands – much as prayer by rote might deafen the supplicant to his own moral urgency. As in much of Sweeney's work, the sense of derangement is complemented by a sombre and slightly mechanical humour. This is the whole subject of the *tour de force* 'A Postcard of the Hanging',[15] whose evident accomplishment seems warranted only by its own grim momentum. This slightly metallic quality can be traced as much to the kind of pretended narrative in which Sweeney deals as to language and tone. A poem which begins in the midst of things is likely to end there, too, for all the uncluttered economy with which Sweeney moves his non-events along. It would be only partly apt to think of Sweeney's narratives as dreamlike, since they have cleaner and ostensibly simpler lines than most dreams; but they can seem, as dreamers often feel themselves to be, rooted to the spot. This may account for the power of two of his finest and plainest poems, 'Where Fisherman Can't Swim' and 'Tube Ride to Martha's'.[16] Both are accounts of terrible accidental death, the one of a victim of the King's Cross fire, the other of a fisherman drowning off the coast of Donegal. Frost's "'Out, Out–'" is in the background:

> The youngest in the crew leapt out
> onto a rock to push the boat away,
> then laughed when he couldn't jump back.
> But exactly when did he realise
> that the boat would float no nearer;
> that all those pulls on the engine cord
> would yield no shudders; that no rope
> or lifebelt existed to be thrown;
> that those flares were lost in cloud;
> that the radio would bring a copter
> an hour later?

Sweeney's 1992 collection, *Cacti*, proved harder to assess at first. At some points it seemed as if the appetite for the strange and sinister had set into a mannerism. 'Monkey', for example, could be a little anthology of the Sweeneyesque:

> Even when the monkey died
> they never invited us round
> to eat green banana curry
> and play braille scrabble
> in that room underground...[19]

But if the reader suspects that oddity is being pursued for its own sake towards a *Python*-like demonstration of the law of diminishing returns, there is a remarkable certainty and rhythmic zest in the speaking voice, like somebody shouting a joke across a noisy pub. These energies recur in the slightly more 'ordinary' context of 'Asleep in a Chair', where domestic anger goes nuclear while the poem's voice takes up a position somewhere weirdly between the judge and the condemned man:

> Asleep in a chair for three hours?
> Take that man away. Bind him
> and bundle him into a mini-cab,
> drive through the Southern English night
> till you see the lights of Brighton,
> then throw him out on the South Downs.
>
> Hopefully it will be sub zero
> and wet as Ireland. (*Drunk* and
> asleep in a chair for three hours,
> with the TV and the gas fire on?)
> Pick a field with cattle in it,
> or better still, a nervy horse...

Sweeney's emphasis on dramatic voice and bizarre properties rather than figurative ingenuity would seem difficult to sustain. You might be able to fight with one hand tied behind your back, but having demonstrated your prowess, would you want to do so permanently? Yet a powerful effect of his method is to present an indisputably solid material world, however peculiar the behaviour of its inhabitants. One might speculate that debates about poetry and politics would be unlikely to engage Sweeney, whose work can seem both wilfully and necessarily myopic. But then it's is also clear that his loyalty is to stories, folktales, fable, hearsay and all that is suggestively local and timeless, rather than to the sophisticated city cousin called History. Alone among Irish poets of the period he has succeeded in establishing a separate (if uneasy) peace with the forces which demand his attention.

VII

POSTMODERNIST, MOI ?

21. John Fuller and James Fenton

'Vers libre could come to nothing in England,' Thomas Hardy remarked to Robert Graves. 'All we can do is write on the old themes in the old styles, but try to do a little better than those that went before us.' His view was quoted by A. Alvarez in 'Beyond the Gentility Principle', the introduction to *The New Poetry*,[1] as an example of the inhibiting and complacent attitudes which, Alvarez felt, had promoted a series of 'negative feedbacks' in English poetry during the twentieth century. One result was the weighting of Alvarez's approval towards the American poets – Lowell, Berryman, Plath and Sexton – whom he included in his anthology. Alvarez suggests an antithesis: on the one hand is the American capacity to build on the formal and historical curiosity and rigour of modernism, adapting it to deal with the crises of contemporary life; on the other is a reactionary, 'genteel' retirement of English poets into an inertly notional tradition. Half a lifetime later this distinction may seem so burdened with exceptions and contradictions as to be unhelpful, but its terms function like an ancient family row in the background of recent poetry. The business may not be explicitly referred to very often, but everyone knows it's there, and its echoes are heard from generation to generation. Even when the current subject of concern appears to be rather different (and sometimes the polarity can seem nearly reversed), the antithesis reproduces itself – modernity versus tradition, avant-garde versus mainstream, establishment versus rebels – sometimes with allegedly identical positions taken up by people who given the chance, would go back and run each other over twice be to certain. The contributors to Iain Sinclair's anthology *Conductors of Chaos*[2] might as well be writing a different language from the poets included in *The Penguin Book of Contemporary British Poetry* or even the vast majority of those in Bloodaxe's *The New Poetry*.[3] Yet many of them could be – have been – described as postmodernist poets. If that term is not simply a marker of chronology (if it is, many people have wasted their lives seeking a more elaborate definition for it), how should it be used? Perhaps the answer is: as a means of conflict rather than its resolution. So we might infer from the exasperated observations of the L=A=N=G=U=A=G=E poet and critic, Charles Bernstein:

> prominent proponents and opponents of postmodernism suggest that the term designates the whole arena of contemporary sociohistorical cultural developments corresponding to, for some, the

> period Ernest Mandel defines as Late Capitalism and, for others, simply that same period of time without reference to economic determinants; still others see postmodernism as a condition or epistemological perspective, unbounded by historical period or objective economic correlatives, that reaches back to Laurence Sterne or Gertrude Stein while excluding (indeed, being in opposition to) most present cultural production. There is no agreement on whether postmodernism is a period, a tendency within a period, an aesthetico-philosophical category transcending indeed deploring, periodisation, much less exactly who or what would constitute the definition of the term even if one of these options were elected... Moreover, the intensifying discussions of postmodernism bring into sharper view the fact that there is no single definition of modernism, which is seen by some commentators as beginning with Augustine (though perhaps Plato's late dialogues should really be added)...[4]

The term, then, seems to offer room for most, if not necessarily enlightenment for many. Even as he satirises the profligacy and contradictoriness of Theory, Bernstein's summary can highlight the inadequacy of a comment such as that offered by Peter Forbes, the editor of *Poetry Review*, on the condition of poetry in England: 'the use of postmodernism in poetry is a relatively trivial sideshow'.[5] Apart from the peculiar choice of the word 'use' here, as if postmodernism were something as straightforward as a typographical affectation, Forbes is simply mistaken: postmodernism is a notable though various presence in a good deal of contemporary poetry, from the avowedly experimental to the seemingly mainstream (and 'mainstream' is another term where the balance of economic and aesthetic components could bear examination), whether as a conscious principle or a received idea. The very problem of definition may indicate the ubiquity of postmodernism, as well as the way the term has grown in the telling, expanding its range of application from the context of literary criticism to encompass the entire character of experience. As Patricia Waugh puts it,

> by the early eighties the term has shifted from a description of a range of aesthetic practices involving playful irony, parody, parataxis, self-consciousness, fragmentation, to a use which encompasses a more general shift in thought and seems to register a pervasive loss of faith in the progressivist and speculative discourses of modernity. Postmodernism is now used to express the sense of a new cultural epoch in which distinctions between critical and functional knowledge break down as capitalism, in its latest consumerist phase, invades everything including the aesthetic, the post-colonial world and the unconscious, leaving no remaining oppositional space.[6]

It might be objected that when a term which begins as a figure becomes the ground in this way, it loses its usefulness; but the apparently all-consuming character of postmodernism may be, paradoxically, its distinguishing feature. At the same time, the 'aesthetic practices' continue in use in the work of a wide variety of poets, and can help to illuminate both their powers and their limitations. In the mainstream of English poetry, postmodernism entails a deliberate awareness of and curiosity about poetic devices, often allied to the redeployment of familiar kinds of poem, particularly narrative. The concern is less with immutable truth than with the means we employ, and by which we are led, to construct ideas of it or to question the possibility of doing so. Some poets will only acquire the habits of the time, of which scepticism is one; others will use this in order to enquire further.

If the poet exhibits a rage for order, it is a modest fury in comparison with that of the critic, who, like the speaker in Peter Porter's 'Tending to the Condition', insists that 'there is a shape to the world, more real/ than time, more absolute than music'.[7] There is likely to be part of any poet, however theoretically inclined he or she may be, which acknowledges the fruitfulness of uncertainty, and relishes flying blind across the page. Contrary to what some critics might claim, theory is always belated – a point implied in Frank O'Hara's famous non-manifesto, 'Personism'.[8] The unwritten moment-to-moment history of poetry accommodates mess and disorder, chance and distraction, just as much has the determination to make it new and see the picture whole. Poetry is fuelled by contradiction, as Yeats reminds us, and as any attempt to retrace the emergence of postmodernism in poetry written in Britain will indicate. It may lead as far in the direction of Auden as of Olson and Ashbery. It may owe as much to the apparent failures and the aesthetic waste-products of predecessor poets as to what is prized in them. What Randall Jarrell saw as the corruption of Auden's style by facility[9] is echoed, and converted into something like an operating principle, in Ashbery himself, in John Ash and Frank Kuppner. The most acclaimed English postmodernist poet, James Fenton (though that is not why he is acclaimed), is part of the succession of Oxford-educated poets for whom John Fuller has been a tutelary spirit, and Fuller's lord and master (like that of his father, the seemingly antimodernist Roy) is clearly Auden, whose entire career can be read as a journey away from modernism – on which he was followed by at least two generations of poets. What these very different contemporary poets – Fenton, John Fuller, Ash, Kuppner – have in common is a curiosity about the poem's status and the workings of language which makes the frame of reference and the means of construction into part of the subject. If this tendency appears in John Fuller as a kind of cultural stylishness, something that might at first seem only superstructural, in Ash and Kuppner, as for a time in Fenton, it becomes inseparable from the entire poetic endeavour.

Among Fuller's early published poems is 'A Footnote to Ovid', a donnish title for an epigrammatic reading of the story of Daphne and Apollo (from the first book of *Metamorphoses*) in which the nymph is turned into a laurel tree when she rejects the amorous advances of the pursuing god. The title itself will sound like a closing door to many readers, suggesting enclosed academic smugness, but rather than supplying a commentary the poem is a chilling little drama, which the god concludes:

> The tree stirs, seems to be saying yes:
> Art is appeased. The slim girl running still.[10]

Keats's 'Ode on a Grecian Urn' is part of the field of reference here, but the poles of that poem are seen in reverse: the issue is not the enshrining of life *sub specie aeternitatis* but the 'appeasement' of art (in the person of Apollo, the god of art). The word 'appease' has grim overtones in the twentieth century. The reputation of Neville Chamberlain is entirely coloured by his role of appeaser to Hitler, for whom the only ultimately satisfactory 'appeasement' (calming, bringing to peace, pacification by satisfying demands, propitiation, assuagement) would be surrender. In the poem, Daphne does not surrender: she is conquered by the transforming will of the god. Fuller's poem also harks back to Browning's 'My Last Duchess', where the duke is both murderer and connoisseur – a combination which has become a cliché in the discussion of Nazism. And Fuller's mingling of eroticism and violence looks sideways to Tony Harrison's horrifying 'The Nuptial Torches', which deals with Spanish atrocities during the Dutch wars of the sixteenth century and which closes (in the voice of the King): '*Come, Isabella.* God *is satisfied*'[11] – a line where the identification of King and God is alarmingly clear. The intimacy of art and atrocity is not a matter Fuller *resolves* (neither does he brandish it as Geoffrey Hill does), but what emerges repeatedly in his work is a wariness about assuming that poetry has a secure ethical ground. This can take a practical form, for example in various deformations of the readerly norm which occur in poems apparently remote in theme from 'Footnote to Ovid', among the strange little half-narrations which comprise some of Fuller's earliest published work. 'Girl With Coffee Tray'[12] recounts in slow motion someone tripping up and bursting into tears. It excludes (deliberately, it would seem) the emotional subtext which would enable us to "place" the event securely. At the same time as the poem dwells with peculiar attentiveness on an isolated event, it records the girl's distress with the nearly neutral amusement of someone watching a golf match in which they have no more than idle interest. 'Band Music' describes rural domesticity in ur-Martian terms (where cows have 'ears like mouths of telephones').[13] 'Edwardian Christmas' discovers a Freudian family romance at work amid the celebrations, whilst sustaining a dry archness of tone.[14] The disturbing 'In a Railway Compartment' likewise uses childhood games and puzzles to show power in action, in this case seemingly in a sexual assault.[15] Here too, though the horror of the event is hardly in doubt, there is a sense in which the poem does not *intervene* in what it recounts. The reader's disquiet here finds later counterpart in the work of a younger poet associated with Fuller's circle, Alan Jenkins. His poem 'Politics' narrates a harrowing rape, with a degree of neutrality which (surely contrary to the author's intention) begins to sound like complicity of a kind familiar in the hard-boiled thriller.[16] The tone is complicated and unbalanced by a further and more glaring influence, that of Paul Muldoon: mishandle those rhyme-driven cadences and you can end up sounding facetious. It is a misjudgment which Jenkins has been at pains not to repeat. His more recent work, in particular the collection *Harm*,[17] has shown a much firmer emotional engagement.

Fuller's interest in the idea that the rules and rituals of games and children's play are symbolic forms of appeasement to the unbiddable forces of will and desire takes a further turn in 'Alex's Game'. A boy playing with model figures in an improvised tabletop landscape finds that his carefully reasoned empire strikes back. He places a cowboy to guard a girl: 'But look what she does: up she swings/ Her one stiff arm and belts the cowboy hard./ Now that was not in his imaginings.'[18] Except that of course it was, albeit unknown to Alex. Subtly or blatantly, all these early Fuller poems subject themselves and the reader to enquiries – about expectations, tone and the precise allegiance of form. While doing this, and maybe in order to do it, they exploit a talent for description and evocation of a kind which Charles Olson – whose writing produced early discussion of postmodernism in poetry[19] – would have felt compelled to reject. Yet it is undeniable that however bourgeois their mental climate, Fuller's poems apply to the beliefs and assumptions (the cultural narratives) from which they are born the troubling scepticism we have learned to think of as postmodern. A poet clearly extremely well-versed in convention examines the nature of convention.

Having said this, there is also a problematic dimension to Fuller's writing which cannot really be accounted for by an exposition of his themes and methods. For some readers a degree of assent may have to be withheld on the grounds that we never encounter particular poems by which Fuller must stand or fall: it is as if his great skill and ingenuity have always moved on to the next thing – the mark, perhaps, of the supremely professional English amateur at work. Anthony Thwaite, in a brief but appreciative discussion, seeks to make the opposite case, citing 'In the Corridor' as a poem of 'real and piercing feeling',[20] but perhaps this is to conflate the reader's knowledge that feeling has been present with the poet's capacity to engage the feelings of the reader. Encountering a dead friend, Fuller writes:

> Like an over-insistent host,
> 'Francis, what *happened*? Tell me. Tell me how you escaped,'
> I silently mouthed and gaped,
> Eager and simple for a startling truth. I was so compelled
> To what seemed to be withheld
> That I moved along the corridor towards your stillness
> As doctors deal with illness,
> Reckless of answers that the only cure requires,
> Immune to its desires.
> But of course the darkness shielded you from inquisition
> And I froze in the position
> Of one whom the dead night's noiseprint has suddenly caught awake
> Like one frog in a lake
> When all else is slow mist rising to meet the moon
> And the first light all too soon
> Shocks us to a reappraisal of that brief deep
> And self-satisfied sleep
> Which is our charmed life...[21]

The use of the intelligence as a means of control and clarification can hardly be objectionable in itself. Here, though, something in Fuller's meticulousness serves to muffle the event. The effort of precision, signalled by the delays of the syntax and by the surprising deployment of contrasted images drawn from the human and the natural realms, seems intended to indicate the insubstantial nature of the speaker himself and thus to make dramatic what is ostensibly rather discursive. But there are contradictory signals. All the learned skill, the alertness to nuance, and the anxiety to be as accurate as possible, come to seem the signs of an impotence which it may seem proper for the poem to admit, but which also function as means of not having to test the imagination at its fullest extension. There is a lack of perspective among the local details. It seems – paradoxically – to indicate a degree of authorial reserve which is surely not proper in this context, since it asks the reader to locate the author/speaker both in and outside his own creation; and in the poem's supernatural context this reads as a strange, scrupulous form of bad faith. It is certainly odd to blame a poet for under-inflation.

If the reader of Fuller is made uneasy by an apparent division between feeling and superabundant intelligence, what compels approval in the work of James Fenton is a combination of direct feeling and an ability to develop themes suggested by Fuller, to ironise and reveal apparently academic habits of mind in order to unearth the feelings they might otherwise not release, and to engage his readers' anxiety as well as their curiosity. The mad-professorial strain is prominent in Fenton, in the service of something more than cultural assurance. See, for example, 'The Pitt-Rivers Museum', from his first collection, *Terminal Moraine* (1972).[22] This is an early example of Fenton's interest in interfering with, or removing, the interpretative frame through which readers may at first believe themselves to be viewing a poem. The result is a poetic reverse *trompe l'oeil*, somewhat akin to the workings of a Borges story such as 'The Lottery in Babylon'.[23] The poem is a 'museum-piece', whose random inventory gradually ushers us towards the realisation that to excerpt and categorise items from the world and encase them in a building does not enable us to stand outside the world from which we have removed them. The poem in fact makes an elaborate fetish of the museum, in order to view this place of learning or idle contemplation as the embodied unconscious of a culture, a place where child and adult, wish and knowledge, are simultaneously engaged:

> ...For teachers the thesis is salutary
> And simple, a progress culminating
> In the Entrance Hall, but children are naturally
> Unaware of and unimpressed by this.[24]

A possible ur-poem for Fenton is William Empson's 'Homage to the British Museum', with its 'supreme god in the ethnological section' and its dry observation that 'People are continually asking one the way out'. But Fenton is a far more narratively and dramatically-inclined poet than Empson, and while seeming to share Empson's view that 'we have no road',[25] he moves further into the interior, using a characteristic (and residually Audenesque) novel-fragment to insist on the poem's mythopoeic attraction:

> All day,
> Watching the groundsman breaking the ice

From the stone trough,
The sun slanting across the lawns, the grass
Thawing, the stable-boy blowing on his fingers,
He had known what tortures the savages had prepared
For him there, as he calmly pushed the gate
And entered the wood near the placard. 'TAKE NOTICE
MEN-TRAPS AND SPRING-GUNS ARE SET ON THESE PREMISES.'
For his father had protected his good estate.

Neil Corcoran detects the influence of John Fuller behind Fenton's 'development of a mode of poetic representation more interested in the possibilities for poetry of novelistic fiction than those of psychoanalytic therapy'.[26] It's not necessary to disagree with Corcoran to want to add that matters of the psyche are also at the centre of Fenton's work, as they were of Auden's, and that Fenton follows Auden into the production of psychically charged landscapes. Fenton clearly gains in the relative indirectness of his approach, which enables the psychic strains of amnesia ('A German Requiem'),[27] displacement and class/cultural exhaustion ('A Vacant Possession', 'Nest of Vampires')[28] to become matter for poems rather than rhapsodies on themselves, as they might in the hands of inferior writers in the confessional mode against whose leading advocate, Alvarez, Fenton directs some of his satire in 'Letter to John Fuller':

He knows what makes the poet tick.
  He knows society is sick.
Gentility just gets his wick –
  It makes him scowl
With rage. His hide is tough and thick
  As a boiled owl.

He tells you, in the sombrest notes,
If poets want to get their oats
The first step is to slit their throats.
  The way to divide
The sheep of poetry from the goats
  Is suicide.[29]

In contrast to the impression sometimes created by Robert Lowell, the exemplary confessional poet, that the tragic task of history has been to arrive at Robert Lowell, who will then record the process, Fenton, in what remains a small body of work, has little time for notions of heroic or tragic individualism. Rather, as befits the work of a one-time Marxist, his poems seem to read history not as a backdrop but as the animating or destroying element among whose oceanic pressures the individual sinks or swims. It is the function of the groundless voices of Fenton's handful of major poems to gesture at, and to invite us to imaginatively enact, conditions that seem both monolithic and incoherent, to prove, in Ian Gregson's phrase, 'the impossibility of a fully comprehending vision'.[30] Fenton deals with an historical phase which has been exhausted but not replaced. The vampires of 'Nest of Vampires' will be remembered by a mirror in which, according to tradition, by their very nature they cannot be seen. Their absence comes to testify to their enduring but unproductive power.

This inertia is reflected in the uncertainty about the precise period at which some of the poems take place and in the fact that while the country house poems are weirdly underpopulated they offer room to no one. Such uncertainties and blockages are also reflected and contested at a syntactical level. What seems at first like a factitious decisiveness in the language (the Audenesque manipulation of articles, the suggestion of common ground between reader and text which may well not exist) is a means of gaining some purchase, and acquiring some mobility, in otherwise monolithic contexts. Alan Robinson has drawn an illuminating parallel between Fenton's work and later modernist poems such as *The Cantos* from *Section: Rock-Drill* onwards and *Paterson*, where

> the implicit structure of coherence is lacking, or alternatively is impotent to contain the seemingly arbitrary indeterminacy of the work with its accumulation of ready-made material. The result is a poetry that is resistant to efforts to reduce it to the kind of readily assimilable pattern which could be inferred from High Modernist long poems. This recalcitrant fragmentation is...characteristic of an emergent tendency in Postmodernist writing which parallels the deconstructive preoccupations of much contemporary literary theory, albeit in a dismissively jocular guise.[31]

In one instance Fenton carries the process of exploration a stage further. 'A Staffordshire Murderer'[32] creates a kind of political negative, where murder, the ultimate transgression, is considered against a historical and geographical background to which its extremity might seem irrelevant. The 'political negative' develops from the conversion of incompatibilities of theme and language, stylistic figure and moral ground, into an assertion of authority in which can be distortedly mirrored the actual incoherences of the society at which the poem gestures. The continual inappropriateness of the language interferes with the ordinary courses of understanding, asserting that these, and not the poem, are under the sway of illusion.

The approach in 'A Staffordshire Murderer', as Alan Robinson has suggested, is in part a wild exaggeration of the scene-setting characteristic of the detective story[33] or, more recently, the crime novel – the establishment of an idyllic or pleasantly dull provincial surface from which the grave-clothes will be removed to show violence at the heart. By coincidence, an interesting recent example of the form, Frank Kippax's *Fear of Night and Darkness* (1993), is also set in the Midlands:

> In the heart of middle England, there are still places that most people who have never seen them might not believe exist. A quirk of planning, the downgrading of a major road, the building of a motorway to siphon off the traffic, and they are bypassed, isolated, lost. In the empty midland plains there are roads that still have cattle gates across them, there are pubs where passing trade is virtually unknown, in villages that are essentially forgotten. Rowsley is such a place, a lost oasis in a featureless green flat landscape, whose peace is shattered only by the intermittent crashing screams of US and Nato fighters as they train to keep the peace. On a blazing day in early summer, Rowsley can be so tranquil as to seem improbable.[34]

Kippax seems to be trying for the kind of authoritative sketch at which Orwell excelled. His theme is disorder: a well-to-do family is brutally murdered and mutilated by a trio of robbers, borderline psychopaths from the excluded underclass. *Fear of Night and Darkness* is, seemingly despite itself, a reactionary novel, baffled by its own horrors but with ambitions to diagnose the condition of England in the long dry spell of conservative rule after 1979. It marks an upper limit to the kind of populist realism which has dominated drama output on television, and the reader comes away harrowed, aware of Kippax's entire seriousness but probably none the wiser.

By contrast, in Fenton's poem the usually unreflective devices of such storytelling become part of the process and part of the subject of investigation. They are as it were are called in to help the poet with his enquiries. At length the reader may wonder what the investigation actually concerns and whether, like 'The Pitt-Rivers Museum' the poem's subject isn't in fact an entire society. This seems part of the implication of the use of place and history, the local, the familiar, the proverbial, the contents of what used to be 'general knowledge'. The one thing 'A Staffordshire Murderer' doesn't supply is a narrative. Its cubism offers a series of menacing digressions into history and local conditions but no sense of novelistic 'real time'. What happens to the generic second person repeatedly addressed has to do with 'your' murder, but the chronology is confused and 'you' may well be dead already. The real interest is in neither whodunit nor why it was done, but in the frame of reference (in both its visible and unconsidered aspects) in which the 'event' occurs. This involves a sort of *locus classicus* of homicide – the 'quiet spot' which is by tradition at once definitive of peace and safety and especially helpful to the murderer:

> ...Today it is hot.
> The cowparsley is so high that the van cannot be seen
> From the road. The bubbles rise in the warm canal.
> Below the lock-gates you can hear mallards.[35]

At the same time as Fenton appears to satirise clichés of crime fiction, such as the intelligent, rhetorically-inclined murderer, whose Moriartian vauntings are (again, subversively) suggested in indirect speech, the poem offers none of the expected 'placing' of this material. There is no firmer ground given to the killer's 'scientific' approach than there is in Conan Doyle:

> You are flattered as never before. He appreciates
> So much, the little things – your willingness for instance
> To bequeath your body at once to his experiments.
> He sees the point of you as no one else does.[36]

Further, the 'voice' of the poem operates in a kind of complicity with the murderer. The reader feels trapped and dislocated, assailed by language which continually shifts its stance to reveal that there is no 'home ground' from whose safe retirement the audience may observe the poem's doings. The sense that the whole thing may involve a gruesome joke is strengthened by Fenton's incorporation elsewhere, in 'A German Requiem', of the surnames 'Sargnagel' ('coffin nail') and Gliedschirm ('condom') in a passage about gravestones which, as Gregson points out, seems intended to resemble 'found' material.[37]

It is another cliché of the crime genre that the detective feels a degree of exposure to underlying horror from which the public is ordinarily (and sometimes contemptibly) protected. Formally this is a framing device, which allows exposure to be mimed at a remove. It is a ritual element in the larger ritual which Auden, for example, felt the detective story to be. Fenton has chosen to exclude this device as he has sought to exaggerate others: where are we meant to be in relation to the events and tones and insinuations of this poem? Its presentation of the 'other side', of 'another England', places us comfortlessly at home there, where we began. If Ian Gregson is correct to find in Fenton's poetry a place where 'the linguistic representation of "otherness" encounters an experiential otherness so extreme that it subverts representation itself',[38] it remains true that the "underlying" issues of place, identity, cultural genre and the "familiar" have not gone away, for Fenton has political and moral interests at heart. It is as if he has trained under hothouse conditions a type of poem that might have been glimpsed in Auden's 'Bucolics',[39] to the point where it brings in question our capacity to grasp its internal contradictions, and where the only evidence of its own coherence and relevance to itself lies in the poem's insinuating tone.

Less alarming but in its way equally searching is John Fuller's recent poem 'England', which mounts a sustained evocation of 'the heart of England' while, like Fenton, stealing the ground from beneath the reader's feet:

> At the heart of England we are pursuer and pursued,
> Where frozen footprints are the history of that hunt
> And towns we think we never visited are like
>   Both past and future,
> Tremendously distinguished in the willed notation
>   Of our imagination.
>
> ...time itself is like this, an elder dimension
> Whose fondness for a particular country may turn
> At a stroke to a sly or bullying disregard,
>   Who knows that place is never
> The involving predicate that something meant,
>   Simply an accident.[40]

In one light this rich and sombre poem is about 'our' reliance on that necessarily unvisited elsewhere which is a phantasmal embodiment of meaning, purpose, hope, futurity and the unstable but powerful notion of England – in short, what sustains 'English' identity. Paradoxically, the reader is also driven to conclude that the title 'England' could be replaced by 'Death'. Such an 'unwriting' of England as Fenton, and latterly Fuller, undertake may be the most truly radical and is surely the most impressive of the varieties of English postmodernism to date. At the same time, it draws on a powerful sense of tradition which would recognise, even if it must also view with a scepticism bordering on travesty, the feeling expressed by the poet Hugh Pink in A.S. Byatt's *Babel Tower* (1996):

> They climb the stile, and cross into the afternoon fields, where a heavy white horse is grazing, where a bird is singing in a thorn bush, where Hugh trips on a molehill and rights himself. He has a feeling he can't find words for, although it is to do with his poetry. It is a feeling he simply thinks of as the *English* feeling, though in fact it may simply be a human feeling about death.[41]

22. Raine, Reid, Morrison, Motion, Hofmann: *Middlemen*

> Every day, history takes place,
> Even when nothing happens.
>
> CHRISTOPHER REID, 'Annals', *Katerina Brac*[1]

With the possible exception of Michael Hofmann, the poets discussed here are all in some ways members of the literary establishment. Raine, Motion and Reid have served as poetry editors for Faber and Faber. All but Morrison are published by Faber. In the 1980s Motion re-established the Chatto poetry list, which published Blake Morrison's poems (as well as those of two other influential literary journalists, Alan Jenkins and Mick Imlah).[2] Morrison, who became for a time literary editor of the *Observer*, edited with Motion *The Penguin Book of Contemporary British Poetry* (1982), an anthology which provided the terms for the discussion of poetry for the next decade. He also wrote *The Movement: English Poetry and Fiction of the 1950s*,[3] a soberly impressive history of that earlier literary generation, which remains the standard work. Motion is the biographer of Philip Larkin,[4] an executor of the Larkin estate, Chair of the Arts Council Literature Panel and (in succession to Malcolm Bradbury) Professor of Creative Writing at the University of East Anglia.

There are many who would view this group of associates with suspicion, as a particularly effective example of the Oxbridge-London mafia in action, carrying off the plum jobs and the prizes. Poetic conspiracy theories are certainly entertaining, but rather than be detained by them here, it will be more interesting to consider briefly what the aesthetics and achievements of this now middle-aged elite appear to be, and what it was in poetry that they represented in the period of their immediate ascendancy and beyond.

Morrison and Motion's introduction to their anthology has, for good or ill, become a central document in the discussion of contemporary poetry. Some of the editors' remarks have become proverbial:

> Now, after a spell of lethargy, British poetry is once again undergoing a transition: a body of work has been created which demands, for its appreciation, a reformation of poetic taste.[5]

> ...a number of gifted English poets, all under forty, have...emerged. Typically, they show a greater imaginative freedom and linguistic daring than the previous poetic generation. Free from the constraints of

immediate post-war life, and not withstanding the threats to their own culture, they have developed a degree of ludic self-consciousness reminiscent of the modernists...they have exchanged the received idea of the poet as the-person-next-door, or knowing insider, for the attitude of the anthropologist or alien invader or remembering exile... It is a change of outlook which expresses itself, in some poets, in a preference for metaphor and poetic bizarrerie to metonymy and plain speech; in others it is evident in a renewed interest in narrative – that is, in describing the details and complexities of (often dramatic) incidents, as well as in registering the difficulties and strategies involved in retailing them. It manifests, in other words, a preoccupation with relativism – and this represents a departure from the empirical mode which was conspicuous, largely because of Philip Larkin's example, in British poetry of the 1950s and 60s. The new poetry is often open-ended, reluctant to point the moral of, or conclude too neatly, what it chooses to transcribe. And it reasserts the primacy of the imagination in poetry, having come to see the imagination not, as did the previous generation, as part of the dark force of modern history (Hitler, Hiroshima, the Nazi and Soviet camps) but as a potential source of tenderness and renewal.[6]

...what we are struck by powerfully is the sense of common purpose: to extend the imaginative franchise.[7]

Having taken issue with part of Morrison and Motion's introduction at the start of this book, I should acknowledge that much of what they say still seems accurate, given the constraints they faced in providing a unified account of the materials. In one sense, the success of their efforts is demonstrated by the fact that their synthesis of observations has become a commonplace in the discussion of poetry among both the friends and the opponents of their work, and part of the vocabulary of those who may not even have read it. But given the time elapsed, what are we now to make of the young English poets whose success they marked or who were emerging at the time, themselves included?

It may be that posterity will show that Craig Raine has suffered from doing The Very Thing at a comparatively early age. The exaggerated importance he gave to the ingenious use of visual simile and metaphor was rapidly given a name – 'Martianism'[8] – which has stuck to the poet whatever he has done since, almost obscuring what his poetry as a whole has consisted of. Rather like Paul McCartney, he has gone on writing, but people are generally less interested in his new material than his early work; and the appeal of his early poems sometimes appears dated in proportion to their distinctiveness, like the syn-drum in popular music. Some of his less guarded comments are also likely to pursue him to the grave, for example: 'Second-rate poets limit themselves to the great safe themes.'[9] This was said, it now seems brashly and enthusiastically, in the context of praising John Berryman for writing about diarrhoea. But it is less to do with Berryman than with Raine's appetite for thematic danger; though his audacity also turns out be something less startling than we might suppose – for example depicting the anus,[10] which is fair enough but hardly a thematic – or perceptual – revolution. Seeing in Raine's practice an analogy to the work of *ostranenie* – 'to make the stone *stony*' – Neil Roberts has commented that 'Our perception of the stone or the arsehole is changed, but we remain in, or are returned to, an empirically safe world in which stones are stony and arseholes are arseholey.'[11]

More seriously, discussion of the early poems seems to have petered out, and the question arises of what Raine has gone on to do. A decade of work saw him produce *History: the Home Movie* (1994),[12] an epic novel-poem of family life and European history. Lack of space forbids a detailed discussion of this enormously ambitious work. The book certainly answers any queries about the continuing fertility of Raine's power of description, if not about the purpose it serves. *History: the Home Movie* does invite doubts, though, about the wisdom of writing the whole thing in short-lined triplets, for though these may legitimately aspire to the momentum of prose, they also seem confining and repetitive. There is certainly audacity in Raine's attempt on the North Face of the long poem, but perhaps he is at bottom a lyric poet, most effective in a smaller compass. His most recent collection of shorter poems, *Clay. Whereabouts Unknown*,[13] certainly offers more of the intimate bare bones of his work.

Although Raine is a poet of the imagination rather than of faith, readers have often commented on the proximity to belief of his lavish and meticulously sensual efforts to know and re-create the world. Douglas Dunn has referred to Raine's 'disbeliever's religion, his quotidian faith',[14] while Neil Corcoran sees Raine's fascination with the visual world as a possible means to 'secular salvation' [15]. More explicitly, Alan Robinson has argued that in Raine 'an impressionable Catholic upbringing has been sublimated ...into an aesthetics of imaginative transubstantiation.'[16]

'Shaman', the fourth part of 'The Prophetic Book', the sequence which opens *Clay. Whereabouts Unknown*, listens to both strains in the poet's spiritual education – maternal Catholicism and his father's less orthodox spiritualism and speaking-in-tongues. First the poem goes back to church:

> Memories of memories of memories:
> fainting after my first communion:
> Father Watson like the Abbé Liszt,

blu-tacked boldly with cysts
all over his sorrowful face,
saying, You can leave the Church,

but the Church will never leave you.
On the back of my hand
a rosary of beaded blood.[17]

This is very plain stuff by Raine's standards. Much of the vigour of his work depends on a kind of serious showing-off, a redemptive demonstration of talents of a worldly kind, something likely to provoke the disapproval of a priest – as may be hinted, among other things, in the beads of blood, priests at one time being great men for wielding the ruler.

Only when Raine begins to itemise Father Watson's resemblances does the poem acquire the momentum we expect: 'The roquefort marble of the font/ was a match for his teeth'; 'his fingers fine but sulphurous// with Senior Service, forty a day,/ kept in a silver case/ he consulted like a breviary...'[18] The reader can enjoy these reminders of Raine's appeal at the same time as seeing them as demonstration models for the adverse critic, whose response to the poet's ingenious observations has long been 'So what?' Perhaps the baldest expression of dissent comes from Andrew Crozier, for whom Raine's work illustrates poetry which 'does not wish to influence the reader's perceptions and feelings in the lived world: its intersection with that world is attenuated and discourages reading back; transformation is confined within the surprises and routines of rhetoric'.[19] Yet surely the melancholy circularity of the imagery of 'Shaman' works to dramatise a theme of cultural and mortal confinement with which we are all ultimately familiar, as though to show that the god, or the religion, is inescapably in the details, the 'memories of memories of memories'.[20] The poem travels further back, from the church to home and into family history, until the poet states:

I am only my father
having a fit on the floor,

leaving the body behind
stretched in a perfect crab,
while gravity stretches my face

and I hurtle to heaven.[21]

The intimacy of this is hardly 'attenuated'. If home is where we start from it is also likely to be, at any rate metaphorically, where we end up. *Clay. Whereabouts Unknown* is Raine's account of the middle way; it is this markedly un-discursive poet's equivalent of Seamus Heaney's *Station Island*,[22] and it attempts a Heaneyesque wedding of form and feeling. As well as in art, Raine has staked his faith in the establishment of his own domestic and family life: the little room of uxoriousness and parenthood may at any rate provide somewhere from which to celebrate the gifts of the present while contemplating extinction. In the title poem of *Rich* (1983), the poet speaks of his wife as the goddess of a bountiful creation: 'I woo her with words/ against the day of divorce.'[23]

At the end of 'Theatre of Trope', his admiring essay on Raine and Christopher Reid, Alan Robinson remarks, alluding to a poem of Yeats's, 'it remains to be seen whether Raine's subsequent poetry will recognise that there's more enterprise in walking naked'.[24] After the near-mannerism of *Rich*, Raine has occupied much of the last decade or so with collaboration and *History: the Home Movie*, developments which could only make readers curious about what his new individual poems would amount to. *Clay: Whereabouts Unknown* is above all concerned with the facts of death and dying which underlie the courtly puns of 'Rich'. This is 'something always known,/ but kept a secret from yourself/ because it can't be helped'.[25] Nor is the experience singular: 'There will be more of this,/ more of this than I had realised'.[26] The new book does show signs of walking naked, and also, at its best, of providing a critique of the poet's methods and imaginative disposition which can also work as an apologia.

The opening poem, spoken as though to an unborn child, offers as a gift a random cross-section through the possibilities of knowledge – names of kinds of stone, breeds of sheep, along with numerous samples of Raine's figurative gift:

> There is so much to celebrate:
> the fine rain making midges
> on a pool, the appalled moon,
> and the crescent moon at morning
> which fades like fat
> in a frying pan, the frail
> unfocused greens of spring.[27]

If some of Raine's earlier poems seemed to favour the list over the argument, this is another factor he builds into 'The Prophetic Book'. The title section could almost be asking its young recipient, like the recent computer software advertisement, 'Where do you want to go today?' While this approach seems suited to the emergent enthusiasm of a child, it begs the question of what larger ordering principle the poet can appeal to, and the question is emphasised by increasingly insistent alliteration. Memorability both exposes doubt and tries to assuage it:

I will pledge you what is here:
a thousand kinds of bread,
each with a shape and a name,
happiness and its haemorrhage,
the homesick hardware store
which can only say home,
Goethe and the gift of death.[28]

Elsewhere Raine attempts more direct treatments of mortality. This asks a good deal both of the poet and his audience. It is a challenge to tact, and Raine has sometimes produced sophisticated vulgarity, loudly pointing at things without quite seeing them. A degree of unease may accompany the reading of Raine's own introductory notes on the cover of the new book, which, he says, concerns 'Friends...people I loved, lives – those difficult, lost masterpieces. In this context my title, an art-historical term, has heart-breaking connotations'. The connotations, surely, are for the reader to judge, while the notion of persons as 'masterpieces' seems improper, elevating (albeit by default) a response to life itself – an extreme example of Raine's objectifying habit. The affectionate compliment ends by sounding misplaced.

The nakedness of some of the poems themselves is of a kind which can initially draw attention to itself rather than the matter in hand. 'Scrap', 'Shut' and 'Death Bed' [29] are unpunctuated pieces, making some use of layout for scoring – practices also employed in recent years by Raine's occasional opponent in criticism, Tom Paulin, whose work, whilst short of Raine's miniaturist music, is rhythmically more sinewy. Both poets seem indebted to Zbigniew Herbert. In 'Death Bed' we read

whistling like a dynamo
this one wide-open nostril

thought on its thermal
drifts

watching   unseeing
we consider the cog in snowflakes
the squirrel's strobe   effect

the famous   caught by cameras
facing arrow flights at Agincourt

Whereas the translated voice of Herbert makes shapes on the air to exercise its own compelling authority, the removal of punctuation can make Raine's verse sound boneless rather than spare, especially in comparison with the nearby 'Retirement', where the Raine couplet makes a lingering music from the combination of formal declaration, repetition and enjambement:

> The world is a beautiful woman
> we live but have ceased to see,
>
> with whom we must learn to linger
> all over again, to prize and to praise
>
> all over again, while there is still time,
> so much time has been lost.[30]

Here the method is at the service of the poem rather than in pursuit of a nervy authenticity to which, for all Raine's manifest and understandable anxiety, the plush furnishing of his imagination does not really lend itself. What matters is not that the work is 'important' culturally or even personally, but that it can stand on its own two feet. In parts of 'The Prophetic Book', along with the wry alarm of 'On My Fiftieth Birthday', plus 'Redmond's Hare' and 'Heaven on Earth'[31], the business of taking stock is handled with an emotional clarity which the reader is bound to respect, while the accompanying disinterestedness, which in earlier days could seem a bit heartless, is here not the demand for recognition from the clever man and the anxious boy but a sign of real weight and substance. *Clay. Whereabouts Unknown* is an uneven book, but some of its significant risks are taken in the poems that succeed, and they make this collection Raine's most interesting to date, testing secular salvation against hard facts. Where once he might have been accused of talking a good poem, he now seems more likely to write one, albeit with less inflated claims to attention.

As a student at Oxford, Christopher Reid was for a time taught by Craig Raine,[32] but despite their obvious common interest in the employment of striking visual comparisons it would be a mistake to suppose that Reid's work is imitative of the older poet. Michael O'Neill crisply indicates a basic difference in temperament:

> Raine's poetic presence is exuberant, edgy, vigorous; Reid's is droll, self-contained, cool. Raine's love poems are erotic, Reid's affectionate. Raine admires Picasso's bold distortions; Reid invokes the intimate interiors of Vermeer and Vuillard... Raine's finest poems are capable of a surprisingly raw directness; Reid's best work is elegantly oblique.[33]

It is tempting to see these differences as class-related. Raine reads like an *arriviste*, while Reid was there in the first place, with nothing to prove (or no one worth proving it to). Reid is from the beginning a manifestly bourgeois poet. His terrain consists of the pleasant interiors, the sheltered gardens and well-tended spaces of bourgeois life. Domestic ease, food, company and reflective leisure are plentifully available, which colours his declaration in 'Utopian Farming':

I love to be here, private,
subversive and free...[34]

Here 'subversion' is not serious but elegantly fanciful: otherwise, arguably, in Reid's terms it could hardly *be* 'subversive'. The comic spirit contains an escape clause. Elsewhere, 'The Imperial War Museum', the second part of 'The Meaning of Morning', a poem which brushes against something more exposed, tends only to confirm its own comfort:

A squirrel sat on the lawn
like a sketchy fleur-de-lys
on a tattered flag
and trembled as it fed –
a prey to shell-shock
from the autumn bombardment.
Goose-stepping pigeons
pecked about the paving-stones,
where orts of reminiscence
fell from our table,
with its empty tent of toast,
gun-turret of black coffee.[35]

A comparatively weak poem like this may sometimes bear a writer's fundamental imprint. The suggestion here – which surely can hardly be intended – is that the world naturally presents itself at the poet's desk (or in this case, his breakfast table) for interpretation and filing. The low-key approach should not be confused with humility. Accordingly, it seems that the analogy with war is set aside as easily as it was taken up, and the reminiscent undertones are hard to credit. It is perhaps Reid rather than Raine who exemplifies the paradox of Martianism: the ingenious, estranging eye tends to domesticate the world, to bring it indoors and tidy it up. As with Raine, it can also appear that self-delighting ingenuity is basically miniaturist and episodic rather than through-composed. In Reid's debut, *Arcadia* (1979), the reader repeatedly experiences a sense that poems are not so much completed as stopped ('At Windsor', 'The Man with Big Ideas', 'Utopian Farming', 'H. Vernon').[36] An ingenious, sometimes enthralling series of images takes the stage, bows and departs without quite exceeding (or arguably, even amounting to) the sum of themselves. This is clearly shown in 'A Holiday from Strict Reality':

Everything that we see
in this gilded paradise
is ours to make use of:
palm-trees on the marine drive,
nature's swizzle-sticks,
stir the afternoon air

to a sky-blue cocktail
of ozone and dead fish.

All day long
the punctilious white yachts
place their set-squares
against our horizon,
as we lie around on mats
and soak up the heat,
cultivating a sun-peel
that grows like lichen.[37]

Inconsequence is of course factored into this poem; indeed, it is the 'purpose' of a beach holiday. The scene's entropic idleness is counterpointed by a single contrast. Whereas the poem is full of life being transformed into things, the beach bum, playing his guitar, 'contemplates the plangent/ hollow of its navel'. Yet the poem closes a bit feebly, with the nostrum that all this will have to be paid for. The problem, perhaps, is that the bill can certainly be covered without difficulty.

A reader responding with asperity to Reid's light-heartedness may feel crass or churlish, as if missing the point, for this Arcadia certainly has seductions to offer, mostly its brilliant details – 'The borborygmus of a dove/ calls from the belly of its bush'; a watch is 'a silver case of fidgety/ wheels, rich with activity'; 'A motor-launch,/ with its jewellery of tyres,/ bobs at the quay/ like a harbour tart.'[38] But if *Arcadia* is also without history – as despite the graveyards and anxious moments it seems to be – its poems need not be finished, and there is accordingly a lack of *urgency* here which in turn makes the embrace of large terms seem slightly odd. The poems can hardly be said to test their own limits, even if, as Reid declares in 'In Medias Res', 'Nothing that we see/ in the park// can quite fend off mythology' and 'the world stands on our table:// imagination.'[39] In 'Maritime Liverpool' Reid describes perching gulls as 'full of velleity', defined by the *OED* as 'the fact of merely willing, wishing or desiring, without any effort or advance towards action of realisation'. The question begged by *Arcadia* is whether Reid can convert this disposition in himself into part of the subject of his poems rather than allowing it to persist as a problem from which they suffer.

There is certainly a reforming tendency at work in his 1982 collection *Pea Soup*,[40] most clearly apparent in the increased enthusiasm for rhyme and the deftly-worked stanza forms in poems such as 'Dark Ages', 'Charnel', 'Kawai's Trilby', 'The Traveller' and the sestets of 'Magnum Opus'.[41] The last is one of several poems concerned with religious sites and the sacred. Dealing with a visit to a cathedral, it naturally invites comparison with 'Church Going',[42] Philip Larkin's earlier examination of the place of religion in a secular age. Neil Corcoran sees Reid's as a poem occurring 'well beyond'[43] Larkin's in the progress of secularism. Even Larkin's affirmation of the durability of 'a serious house on serious earth' is brought into question by the refusal of eye and ear to simply accept either the basic seriousness of the performance of the service, or the connection between the congregation and the underlying doctrine:

The organ, modulating
on currents of reverie,
seemed like accommodating
all secularity,
with grave rumpuses, flytings
of fanfares and fugal whoopee,

when the frilly choir entered,
blasé and epicene.
I recall a young woman who fainted,
my neighbour's atonal keen
and the brute baby that ranted
against the preaching dean.[44]

All of this is what our inculcated respect for what we no longer believe is taught to carefully ignore. Naturally it becomes Reid's subject. It is odd that his alertness leads in the direction of a statement of the obvious – that, taken literally, the 'tall tale' of Christianity may have had its day, that meaning has been evacuated from myth by history. The poem, though full of impressive local features, seems pat in comparison with Larkin's nagging meditation on the durability of wishes as distinct from truths. And as a whole, Reid's venture into formalism in *Pea Soup* tends to suggest that in proving himself equal to the constraints he sets himself he reveals more clearly the want of the imaginative – the *metaphysical* – compulsion at which the poems gesture. He is, albeit at the highest level, versifying the received ideas of the period. What is required is access to inner rather than outer weather, to the workings, for example, of the mind in language, rather than an examination of cultural forms which can seem merely decorative. Aptly, it is with his most "impersonal" book, *Katerina Brac*, that he attempts some of this work.

'Impersonal', that is, because *Katerina Brac* presents the poems of an imaginary poet from central or eastern Europe, and does so in translation – though the 'originals' are naturally unavailable. It has been suggested, moreover, that these 'translations' (despite Brac's uncluttered manner) can seem uncomfortable with the conventions and idioms of English. As Neil Corcoran has pointed out, part of the opening poem, 'Pale Blue Butterflies', sounds distinctly odd:

> I'm sure that I was not alone
> in feeling, as I do each year,
> that this would be the perfect time
> to mend the whole of one's life.[45]

Corcoran refers to the un-English phrase 'to mend the whole of one's life' (as well as the inconsistent use of elision in the first line).[46] It is indeed an odd phrase, made odder by its echo of Stephen Dedalus's question in *A Portrait of the Artist as a Young Man*: '– I have amended my life, have I not?'[47] Stephen himself, we recall, is uncertain of his position in relation to the King's English. Meanwhile the first two lines of the stanza sound faintly like the impossibly neutral utterance regularly attempted by the Queen in her Christmas broadcast to the nation. The 'translation', then, is both clumsy and instantly encrusted by overtones from its host language. The effect is like being shown round the back of a poem, where the threads of its tapestry are knotted or roughly hacked off, where what we see is the opposite of a pattern. This is also like a sort of literary criticism, a primer in rhetoric for postmodernists. At the same time, Reid has effaced or distorted his own skills in order to offer us a heartfelt awkwardness, to create the work of a distinctly minor talent: unavoidably, as we read the poems, we speculate about the absent Katerina, about the central and now finished love affair to which she refers most of her experience, her life in a quiet province, her exhaustion and lack of political curiosity. Michael Hofmann, reviewing the book, commented:

> What does sound 'foreign' is the undisguised animation of every poem, the simplicity as much as the self-delighting verbosity...And there is evidence everywhere of Reid's continuing love-affair with the ridiculous and the inglorious...In his earlier books Reid seems to me to have been more aggressive and critical in identifying the ridiculous: here he is compassionate. The ridiculous emerges in *Katerina Brac* not as a quality that other people or institutions have, but as a condition of existence itself...[48]

Hofmann's approving observations might be recast less sympathetically. It sounds as if what he means is that *Katerina Brac* is a book about the inability to write about history. It may be a problem with sources both in circumstances and temperament. The encoded condition of poetry under a dictatorship may also lend an unearned sense of gravity to poems whose concerns have somehow – through egoism or incapacity, perhaps – evaded full knowledge of the actual conditions. Viewed in this light, *Katerina Brac* would be a reactionary work, though the adjective implies energy of a more decided kind – despite Hofmann's mention of 'animation' – than the poet 'herself' can muster. This would at any rate make sense of the ending of 'Pale Blue Butterflies':

> Later, when the butterflies had gone,
> we loaded our van with the last of the strawberries
> and drove to town
> to be given the official market price.
>
> There followed an unscheduled
> season of summer thunders:
> colossal rearrangements
> somewhere at the back of the mind.[49]

The thunder may be an example of chaos theory (born of the wings of butterflies) but we also infer disturbance of a political kind – a purge, perhaps – not to be spoken of directly, but in some sense not pertinent either to Katerina's life among the strawberry-pickers on the collective farm. Brac's poems are at once bald and muffled. What seems to be her poem about resistance and subterfuge, 'A Box',[50] gives itself away immediately. A love poem, 'The Sea', ends on a note of hesitant banality:

> There were many questions over which we were at odds,
> but none so large or complex or important as the sea.[51]

At times Brac might be writing underwater, such is the narcotic slowness with which she works, wishing only for a private life, something as manifestly dead here as in Pasternak's Russia. The fascinating impasse of her work is one from which her creator has yet to extricate himself.

In Blake Morrison's ambitious first collection, *Dark Glasses* (1984),[52] there is an important set-piece called, 'The Renunciation'. Set in an old bourgeois family house, it concerns age and the passing of power from generation to generation:

> How could we see what we amounted to –
> A glint of eyes as headlights swept away?[53]

Unlike its cousin, James Fenton's 'A Vacant Possession',[54] Morrison's is a populous poem, full of voices rather than ghosts and allegations – *'Peter, Jenny's husband, never forgave her'; 'Simon has a sperm count of ten million – / Almost no chance at all, the clinic said.'* And if the narrator knows that his time and that of his age and the style of his class are at an end, he is an authoritative and elegiac commentator on these facts: 'Every verse is a last verse, concluding/ Sadness. You hear its tone in the chestnuts/ And rookery – how much has been taken.' The poem itself occupies a position analogous to the speaker: it sees how things must be, but cannot entirely cross into the changed world, so that while Fenton is influential on it (as indeed on the title poem), so is Larkin: 'Our lives run down like lawns to a sundial' is worthy of him, and sounds like early Douglas Dunn,[55] and yet the poem is not quite convincing. It feels *constructed*, the work of a conscientious and subtle reader lacking an essential arrogance (something borne out in a different way by the nearby Lowell impersonation, 'Long Days').[56] This impression is strengthened by a companion-piece, 'Grange Boy'. Here sexual preference, rather than age, seems to signal the end of an industrial dynasty. The son of the house tells us: 'I've been getting pamphlets/ In a plain brown envelope and feel like/ A traitor. Strangers have been seen/ By the wicket-gate. Mother keeps to her bed./ English, we hoard our secrets to the end.'[57] The last line adds a needless belt to the poem's braces: if it doesn't apologise, it certainly explains: the poem as a whole seems too schematic, its sexual theme too inexpensively purchased, an off-the-peg correlative more excusable in the inferior art of the dramatist. The poem also echoes, faintly, the last stanza of Larkin's 'Livings, I'[58] – a source poem for the so-called New Narrative poems written by Morrison and by his friend and collaborator Andrew Motion. In addition, the marked clarity, the patterning, the fitting of theme to form, displayed by Morrison's work, provokes an analogy with the novelist David Lodge, whose carpentering is at times (as in *Nice Work*)[59] so exact as to be disturbing, as if the world could be made redundant by a sufficiently clear summary. Curiously, Lodge, like Morrison, has also been a prominent cultural intermediary in English life, a domesticator of ideas.

His second (and, so far, his last) book of poems, *The Ballad of the Yorkshire Ripper* (1987),[60] showed Morrison considerably extending his ambitions. The title poem, a ballad in a hundred stanzas about the serial murderer Peter Sutcliffe, clarifies both his strengths and his limitations. Morrison has written appreciatively about themes of class and language in Tony Harrison's work,[61] and here he goes a stage further than Harrison. Rather than talk about accent, he writes in it and casts the poem wholly in West Yorkshire dialect:

> Cos Sonia, though she nittered,
> and med im giddyup,
> were potterin too long in t'attic
> to mind that owt were up.[62]

The sustained momentum is extremely impressive, as if Morrison has found the form for which he was intended. Description of

Sutcliffe's victims and methods is neither avoided nor indulged, and this is one of the strengths of the speaker Morrison creates – a man with the kind of curiosity about awful detail not generally admitted in polite society, but a man, too, without prurience. His attitude to women, we learn, makes him, and not Sutcliffe, an outcast from his sex and his class:

> An ah look on em as equals.
> But mates all say they're not,
> that men must have t'owerance
> or world will go to rot.[63]

At the same time, he understands – he knows personally – the sexual imperative which his mates use to justify male behaviour, but which they can scarcely distinguish from violence: 'sex is like a stormclap,/ a swellin in thi cells,/ when lightnin arrers through thi/ and tha knows there in't owt else'.[64] Disquiet about this poem, as about the others touched on here, has something to do with the neatness of its resolution: the speaker would, if he could, love the dead women back to life. But 'ah mend em all wi kindness'[65] makes him too clearly the representative of male enlightenment, of the New Man of 1980s journalism. He is kind but strong and, you understand, definitely going equipped. He has been an idea before he has been heard as a voice. As with several of Morrison's themes – national and family decline, treason, embourgoisement, unemployment – the matter of 'The Ballad of the Yorkshire Ripper' has been imagined and processed elsewhere in advance. It is the gossip of the age, the cultural commonplace. The imagination, which should pre-empt and complicate such matters, can have little to add – and the reader can respect Morrison's liberal conscientiousness and considerable skill without feeling enlightened, or challenged, by it. The open-endedness of which Morrison and Motion spoke in their anthology introduction is hard to detect.

When Tony Harrison writes about 'the silence round all poetry',[66] the reader knows that he is referring to those who will not read or write it – those silenced by status and history. There is a silence around Andrew Motion's poetry, too, but it has less to do with history than with mortality: almost everything he has written is touched, in theme or mood, by the silence of the grave. The voices of his poems often seem like the only audible (and thus the only living) presence in his imagined world. Death reaches into life. The sequence 'Anniversaries'[67] records the years spent in a coma by the poet's mother, who never awoke. In the ambitious narrative poem 'Independence'[68] a man mourning his wife's death in childbirth sees out the final days of the British Raj in India. The bodies of the drowned are an early presence, in the title poem of his first book *The Pleasure Steamers* (1978).[69] and recur in poems concerning the sinking of the pleasure-boat *The Marchioness* in the River Thames in 1989. 'Independence' combines two motifs by including a grave drowned by the Monsoon floods. A later book, *Love in a Life* (1991),[70] includes dreams of death and the dead. Yet the dominant note is not desperation or despair. As Edward Larrissy has remarked, Motion's is a poetry of loss and mourning, rather than the despair of which Philip Larkin often wrote.[71] Larkin's biographer seems better able than his subject to accept fate.

Awareness of death is hardly unusual in a poet: William Empson called it 'the trigger of the literary man's biggest gun'.[72] In his sense of mortality, Motion, more than any of the other poets considered in this section, seems 'traditional', inviting reference back through Larkin to Edward Thomas, Housman and Hardy (he has written critical books on Larkin and Thomas).[73] But his methods are by no means conventional. He occupies an interesting historical position: loyal to and confident in the merits of his antecedents, he does not write 'traditionally', though he commands the plangency expected of a lyric poet. He has given much thought to the use of narrative and point of view: if the dramatic monologue has become a habitual mode in modern poetry, he has subjected it to fresh scrutiny.

The poem which first brought Motion to wide attention, 'The Letter', the winning entry in the 1982 *Observer*/Arvon Poetry Competition, exemplifies his early narrative style. Like some other interesting poems of the period, such as Paul Muldoon's 'The Big House',[74] James Fenton's 'A Vacant Possession', and Blake Morrison's 'The Renunciation' and 'Grange Boy', it uses the familiar novelistic setting of rural domesticity (albeit at a less privileged level than the other poems) as a way of focusing a crisis. During the Second World War (perhaps during the Battle of Britain) a young woman leaves her parents' house early to read a letter from her absent lover. She sees a Messerschmitt at such close range that the pilot's face is visible. The plane crashes:

> ...By lunch
> they found where he lay, the parachute
> tight in its pack, and both hands spread
> as if they could break the fall. I still
> imagine him there exactly. His face pressed
> close to the sweet-smelling grass. His legs
> splayed wide in a candid unshamable V.[75]

Philip Larkin, one of the judges for the competition, dissented from the majority decision of his colleagues (Charles Causley, Seamus Heaney and Ted Hughes) to award the First Prize to a poet (the entries being anonymous) who turned out to be Motion, by then a friend of Larkin's. In a letter to Judy Egerton, Larkin commented: 'By now you'll know that the Arvon winner was your friend and mine...Motion. You, and everyone else will think: Larkin looking after his own, but it wasn't so. I couldn't make head or tail of his poem. Could you? My selection wasn't placed.'[76] Later, in a letter thanking Motion for a copy of his book *Secret Narratives* (which included 'The Letter') Larkin elaborated on his difficulties with the younger man's work:

> You will laugh when I say that although I recognise the originality and precise detail of the poems, I am nevertheless baffled by them. I have tried to see the four groups as separate entities and to see a common factor in each, but without much success. I can see individual poems as entities, and indeed as narratives, but they leave me feeling I ought to know more, or be told more. Sorry! I suppose I want them to be better since the tender, sharp observation behind them is so good.[77]

Larkin's expectations of narrative were not those Motion was trying to satisfy. The older poet's discomfort seems to have arisen from the fact that the closure (not that Larkin would have used that term) of 'The Letter', for example, did not keep to the expected terms of its contract with the reader. The poem does not *resolve* its various elements. Readers note, and go on noting, the buried comparison of the dead flier to the absent lover. The young woman, we see, learns in a harrowingly vivid way something about the personal impact of a war which has until now been distant from her experience and masked by the endearments of her lover's letter. And the posture of the dead man is powerfully but imprecisely (rather than ambiguously) suggestive of insult, vainglory and sexuality. Perhaps what baffled Larkin is the way that Motion leaves the young woman as the imperfect interpreter of the incident. She still ponders it many years later, without advancing an interpretation, but returning over and over to the shock of the events. Clearly she is not a poet; nor is she simply the poet's ambassador to the occasion. The poet's expected task, *to make something of this*, to make the material reveal a pattern and yield an understanding for us, is something Motion abjures in favour of a sense of an event which is monolithically influential on the woman's life but to all intents uninterpretable. The very thing Larkin took issue with may be the real point of the enterprise. Such an approach places enormous weight on the speaking voice in the poem, and moves a stage further on from the occluded but gradually clarified suggestiveness of Edward Thomas. It is very different from much of Larkin's work, but it has something in common with an 'unhistorical' monologue such as 'Livings, 1', while in 'Firing Practice' from his 1987 collection *Natural Causes*, Motion's narrator states baldly: 'you realised nothing connected/ with anything, ever'[78] – a sentiment the Larkin of 'Aubade'[79] would have understood.

So consistent is the considering, precise, melancholy voice in Motion's earlier work that it can be difficult to trace the source of one's unease about the most ambitious of the early poems, 'Independence'. In the end, though, it has something to do with the fact that Motion at once knows too much and not enough about his material. Neil Corcoran, concise as ever, argues:

> ...it is still hard to feel that this historical narrative poem manages to situate its period in any very fruitful relation to the present moment of its composition. The elegiac tone in Motion tends to suggest nothing more convinced or complicated about Britain's past than the pain of its loss. In this respect *Independence* is lacking at just the point where...personal emotion should connect with present political fact.[80]

The harshest reader might object that in 'Independence' history serves only as the pretext for the vivid fragments of personal narration. India is "background", a series of names and landscapes and weathers which highlight the individual agony of bereavement and the poem's sense of defeat and disinheritance. The evidence of 'The Letter' suggests that this may in fact be Motion's intention, rather than an inadvertent error – to show how the individual will be, for good or ill, and however impotently, the leading character in the closet drama of his own life, even while dwarfed by the history from which he is being expelled. Viewed in this light, the poem avoids working as apologetics-by-default for the vanished empire – and yet the reader cannot avoid wondering why this period in particular recommended itself, or noticing that Motion's characters so often share a sense that resistance is useless. When another early piece, the memorable 'Inside and Out', situates itself in another historically arrested landscape – the Great War world of 'Vimy, Arras, Bapaume' – admiration for Motion's control of mood is offset by worry at its *completeness* when the narrator comments:

> As if we were ghosts of ourselves
> we waited for darkness, watching it
> deepen to bring us together again
> like shadows, our close definition.[81]

This lyric pessimism is suspiciously attractive, its atmosphere akin to what Americans call a 'white suit' movie, starring Charles Dance.

What is missing is the sense of scale, and the awe, which emerges from the more frankly reactionary world of a book such as Lampedusa's *The Leopard*.[82] But like Lampedusa's, Motion's world, richly detailed, memorably phrased, is – in a phrase from Larkin's 'Ambulances' – 'something very nearly at an end',[83] while his restless technique carries him beyond, and exposes the contours, of his sensibility, so that his poems seem unconvinced of the solidity of contemporary life, and unable to enter it.

Michael Hofmann's *Nights in the Iron Hotel* (1983) and *Acrimony* (1986) [84] seemed to introduce a new tone and attitude to English poetry. The literariness of the work, with its references to Goethe, Thomas Mann, Strindberg, Knut Hamsun, Mario Vargas Llosa, Wilde, Chekhov and Tolstoy (as well as the poet's father, the novelist Gert Hofmann) was not new in itself, though the poet's German background and a flat sombre tone made him of particular interest. What was striking was that a bookish young man's range of reference was allied to a voice which seemed not simply elderly in the manner of young poets but in some way both emotionally short-circuited and urgent – depressed and passive-aggressive, as therapists might say. Hofmann's subjects often involved emotional extremes such as love affairs, broken marriages, infidelity and a vexed relationship with his father; they showed a sour familiarity with life's more dismal outcomes; but his voice was rarely raised or granted any music, while the sentence structure was deliberately prosaic, and the function of the poems often seemed to be to signal the possession of weary knowledge, rather than to seek a further interpretation of experience. (Given all this, his most obvious influence was surprising – Robert Lowell, the most emotionally strenuous of poets.) Furthermore, Hofmann sought to extend the authority of his nihilism beyond the personal into broader areas of culture and politics.

In his essay on *Acrimony* (1986), Alan Robinson concludes a reading of 'From Kensal Rise to Heaven',[85] Hofmann's catalogue of urban odds and ends (political posters, broken pavements, prostitutes' advertisements in telephone booths, blood on the pavement) with a comment which has a wide application to Hofmann's work:

> The problem for the reader is to decide whether the superficial, detached observations imply any cumulative, underlying significance – such as an evaluative judgment that is selectively drawn to our attention – or whether they remain discrete, relatively arbitrary…jottings.[86]

The title might offer some assistance, since it alludes to Chesterton's 'The Rolling English Road':

> For there is good news yet to hear and fine things to be seen,
> Before we go to Paradise by way of Kensal Green.[87]

Chesterton's notion of 'seeing' is scarcely rigorous, but it's a good deal more expansive than Hofmann's. It includes witnessing, experiencing, feeling privileged to have witnessed; and it implies a progressive revelation of meaning. These are possibilities which Hofmann can scarcely entertain, except from a position of complete though not incurious scepticism. He deploys irony pre-emptively: it is the climate of his work. It has ceased to be productive of surprise: 'world' may be 'various' and 'more of it than we think', in MacNeice's words,[88] but there is nothing to discover. We could say it has all been foresuffered, if 'suffering' were not an overstatement of the neurasthenia of Hofmann's poems in general. His irony is not even defensive – 'the poor man's nerve-tic, irony', as Louis Simpson calls it.[89] It has become a form of abjection before the endless boring variety of London's bits and pieces, which are also England's bits and pieces – and this is one of Hofmann's most "political" poems. Its oddments are inseparable from, yet by no means in solidarity with, the poet's exhausted, febrile, distracted manner. Although Hofmann's poem is about the visible, there is no visual *perspective* in the poem: things come indifferently under the poet/speaker's gaze: they could be very nearly anything. The poem is a sort of practical, carried out in the laboratory of the street, examining the idea of society as spectacle. Ends and purposes have retired to such an immense distance as to be, in effect, extinct. The poet knows this and so do we, and we're left to wonder what tiny hoarded energy has enabled Hofmann to write his poem at all. We may also ask what use the reader can serve in this denuded world. Robinson admiringly comments:

> With studied impassivity [Hofmann's] omnivorous gaze unreflectingly assimilates objects and people into a common dehumanisation. Intellectually and emotionally therefore his poems depend largely on what the reader projects into their absences and elisions.[90]

If this is true, the prospect of DIY poetry might not seem much of a bargain. The reader, seeking a point of friction with this fully-furnished but somehow underpopulated world, is likely to look for a more fully dramatised sense of the poet's disengagement from his own materials. Something of this sort can be found in 'Nighthawks',[91] dedicated to Hofmann's friend and fellow poet James Lasdun. Here again Hofmann proceeds from an allusion – to Edward Hopper's 'Nighthawks' (1942), a painting by now so much a classic as to be almost invisible. In his discussion of Hopper's work, Rolf Gunter Renner comments on 'Nighthawks' that 'though the picture derives its social impact from the presentation of the bar and the background stores, it is primarily a screen on to which discrete fantasies can be projected'.[92] Whilst a good deal less erotic than some of Hopper's pictures, it has served for many viewers to evoke a gritty romanticism, a lowlife glamour where none should apparently be; and thus it has become an icon of the popular imagination, living far beyond its original painted means, for instance in the songs of Tom Waits. Hofmann can hardly help seeming to deride such feelings. Hopper himself commented: 'I didn't see it as particularly lonely. I simplified the scene a great deal and made the restaurant bigger.'[93] The effect of this process is to unify the scene, whereas half a century later, Hofmann's vigil is both crowded and solitary (despite his friend's company), both atomised and homogeneous:

Earlier, I watched a couple over your shoulder.
She was thin, bone-chested, dressed in black lace,
her best features vines of hair. Blatant, ravenous,
post-coital, they greased their fingers as they ate.

I met a dim acquaintance, a man with the manner
of a laughing-gas victim, rich, frightened and jovial.
Why doesn't everyone wear pink, he squeaked.
Only a couple of blocks are safe in his world.

Now we've arrived at this hamburger heaven,
a bright hole walled with mirrors where our faces show
pale and evacuated in the neon. We spoon our sundaes
from a metal dish. The chopped nuts are poison.

We've been six straight hours together, my friend,
sitting in a shroud of earnestness and misgiving.
Swarthy, big-lipped, suffering, tubercular,
your hollow darkness survives even in this place...

The branch-line is under the axe, but it still runs,
rattling and screeching, between the hospital
lit like a toy, and the castellated factory –
a *folie de grandeur* of late capitalism.[94]

Simultaneously, Hofmann presents both the passage of time, as one thing after another comes to his attention, and the absence of change enforced by the defining fact of 'late capitalism', where all the supporting cast are versions of the basic human commodity, consuming and (we infer) in turn consumed. A slightly eerie effect of this is to beg the question of whether any necessity animates and organises the poem. Couldn't the stanzas be rearranged to equal effect? If so, where is the poem's authority? In fact, however, while Hofmann is resistant to many forms of rhetorical insurance – rhythm, metaphor, the expression of direct feeling – he has quietly succumbed to the temptations of closure. He leads the reader from the larger scene "inwards" to the sphere of personal relationships (addressing his friend), which he then sites in the reader's mind's eye against the large and heavily symbolic buildings between which the train will eventually 'rattle' away, so that the two poets become the subject of the scene, rather than components in it. There may be nothing deliberate about it, but the trajectory is not without vanity. This would not be so if the public political realm were felt by the poet to hold any substance, or the possibility of change. But if the poem seems objectionable in this way, we should also note that the egoism is of an honest sort. Unpleasant as it may be, the poem suggests, this empty dramatisation of the self, the *poem noir*, is one of the places where 'late capitalism' may be leading. The evidence of popular culture seems to support such a view. If Hofmann writes about compromise, his poems, cold and inert as they can seem, clearly seek to resist it. The antidote to a certain complacent nihilism is a determination to set it down accurately. Above all, perhaps, Hofmann is aware of the belatedness of his response to circumstances: the poem's alienation could be matched at any time since Baudelaire, and the scene reminds Hofmann of Weimar Germany; everything and nothing has changed.

This kind of extremism presents a serious challenge to the poet's determination. If what he says is true, can the work be worth the candle? *Corona Corona* (1993) [95] showed dangerous signs that Hofmann might be lightening up a little. He refers to the Consul Crassus as 'the pioneer of insuranburn'.[96] He supplies a biography of Marvin Gaye seemingly drawn from interviews and PR biog sheets, partly as an instance of the inadvertently interesting deformation of language by the entertainment media:

> Including duets he had fifty-five chart entries.
> His life followed the rhythm of albums and tours.
> He had 'a couple of periods of longevity with a woman'.[97]

America seems like Hofmann's "natural" home: the shabby poolside apartment in 'Freebird' certainly seems familiar, as do the attitudes of a poem about inauthenticity (or the impossibility of authenticity):

> The setting was a blue by pink downtown development,
> Southern hurricane furniture in matchwood:
> live-oaks and love-seats, handymen and squirrels,
> an electric grille and a siege mentality...
>
> ...The frat boy overhead gave it to his sorority girl steamhammer style.
> Someone turned up the Lynyrd Skynyrd,
> the number with the seven-minute instrumental coda.
> Her little screams petered out, *inachevée*.[98]

The Lowell of 'Waking in the Blue', 'Memories of West Street and Lepke', 'Skunk Hour' and 'Water'[99] is in the background here, as (the stanza about sex) is Hofmann's own earlier 'Entr'acte'.[100] Of all the poets considered in this section, Hofmann, for all his tart assurance, seems to have most to discover, and the greatest potential to do so. *Is that all there is?* could now be his signature tune.

23. Simon Armitage and Glyn Maxwell: *Now then, Lads*

For obvious reasons, caution is required in assessing the claims of younger poets. The critic's perspective may be skewed by proximity, so that common preoccupations serve to mask profounder differences or limitations. The poets themselves are still in the relatively early stages of development. And the hunger of journalism for good copy often lends a temporary yet exhilarating urgency to the workaday and worse – a point which has been illustrated several times in the immediate past. With these caveats in mind, readers are still likely to feel that, beginning in the 1980s, poetry has begun to emerge which sets itself apart from that of some of the major figures – such as Larkin, Hughes, Hill and Harrison – touched on in the earlier chapters of this book. Change itself is hardly a novelty, but, for example, poets including Simon Armitage, Glyn Maxwell, Michael Hofmann and Jo Shapcott, among others (including some discussed elsewhere in these pages) differ, both among themselves and from their predecessors, in ways which may require some reconsideration of our ideas of the poetic.

Simon Armitage (born 1963) is perhaps the first English poet of serious artistic intent since Philip Larkin to have achieved wide popularity – that is, an audience, albeit fragmentary and largely unliterary, beyond the denizens of newspaper book review pages. It is possible that he will attain the sort of proverbial status Larkin now occupies. A proof of this would be the entry of a quotation or two into common parlance, alongside 'They fuck you up, your mum and dad', 'Sexual intercourse began/ In nineteen sixty-three/ .../Between the end of the *Chatterley* ban/ And the Beatles' first LP' and 'What will survive of us is love.'[1] If this has not yet happened, it is a sign of Armitage's comparative youth, which he shares with those who will (or won't) promulgate his language in this way. He certainly commands jaunty, memorable rhythms, able, like Larkin's utterances, to weld themselves to the collective mind. The quotability is there if required:

> I said no, no, no, no, no, no, no. OK, come on then.[2]
>
> I have lived with thieves in Manchester.[3]
>
> sometimes he did this, sometimes he did that.[4]
>
> One thing we have to get, John, out of this life.[5]

> I said grapevine, bargepole, whirlpool, chloride,
> concrete, bandage, station, story. Honest.[6]

Such an exercise is no real guide to what the work offers, but it's notable that all these examples bear some resemblance to speech, however ritualised, and to its capacity for real-time improvised summing-up – the fourpenn'orth of one accustomed to thinking on his feet. Armitage also incorporates vocabulary and references, as well as the sense – the tone – of a particular cultural climate (northern, youthful, seemingly classless) which are comparatively new to poetry. The balance of the relationship between the vernacular and the literary has altered since Larkin was at work. Perhaps the former no longer requires the assent of the latter; perhaps there is no longer any functional division between the two, so that 'diction' consists of whatever the occasion requires. Yet Armitage, like many of his contemporaries, is an extremely self-conscious poet. The influence of writers as different as Frank O'Hara and Paul Muldoon has helped him to view the workings of poems and poetry as part of his subject, and thus to place the games and instabilities of postmodernist writing in the current mainstream, though whether this proves to be more than the creation of a further convention remains for his writing to indicate.

Armitage has already written a handful of poems that seem likely to stick, such as 'Lines Thought to Have Been Written on the Night Before the Execution of a Warrant for His Arrest', 'On Miles Platting Station', 'To His Lost Lover', 'Becoming of Age,' and in 'In Our Tenth Year'.[7] There are many others of more ambiguous status, vigorous and amusing and ingenious, which may or may not have something to say a decade hence – including 'Advertisement', 'The Stuff', 'Brassneck', 'Hitcher', 'Great Sporting Moments: The Treble' and 'The Two Of Us'.[8] Clearly, Armitage is ambitious in scale as well as detail, as the sequence 'Book of Matches'[9] and the recent 'Five Eleven Ninety Nine'[10] for example indicate. His prolific first decade in print contains much work to enjoy and some to admire. The inflated market of literary publicity should not disguise the fact that his are real and substantial accomplishments; nor, equally, should it prevent attention being given to the nagging unease to which some of Armitage's work gives rise, or the feeling that he may be part of a beginning rather than an end in himself.

'What this kind of writing most resembles, in fact, is parody,'[11] comments Ian Gregson on 'Ivory', a poem which includes one of the lists in which Armitage's writing is so rich: 'No more blab,/ none of that ragtag// and bobtail business,/ or ballyhoo/ or balderdash//

and no jackassery, or flannel,/ or galumphing.'[12] Although the targets of parody may include pretension, double-talk, delusions of linguistic competence and so on, these are not always the major interest of Armitage's poems for the reader (or, it seems, the author). It can appear that a kind of linguistic automatism, or echolalia – like language running around with its head cut off – has in some instances become both the form and the content of the work, with the effect of short-circuiting further enquiry. This applies even where Armitage appears to move beyond the present day to attempt a historical perspective, as in 'Lines Thought to Have Been Written on the Night Before the Execution of a Warrant for His Arrest':

> Boys, I have a feeling in my water,
> in my bones, that should we lose our houses
> and our homes, our jobs, or just in general
> come unstuck, she will not lend one button
> from her blouse, and from her kitchen garden
> not one bean. But through farmyards and dust bowls
> we will lay down our topcoats, or steel ourselves
> and bare our backs over streams and manholes.[13]

In place of the poignant antitheses of Chidiock Tichbourne's famous Elizabethan anthology poem, 'My Prime of Youth is But a Frost of Cares' (sometimes called 'Lines Supposed to Have Been Written on the Night Before His Execution'),[14] with which this poem invites comparison, Armitage employs the redundancies of second-rate political oratory as a means of interpreting Thatcherism. The result is a poem about political impotence, which plays – very effectively, one might argue – on a rhetoric which is itself the embodiment of an impotence of the imagination. At what point, though, does the poem become, like the dyer's hand, subdued to the element it works in? The fact that irony or something lesser, like knowingness, is endemic, does not guarantee that it will always be purposeful or even active. An ironic, undeluded manner has been the prerogative, the weapon, the defence and the evasive strategy, of postwar youth (who are continually amazed to discover that the past was smart enough to get there before them). It is the language of cool, a pre-emptive comment on the prevailing conditions. It may be that Armitage's popularity with a younger readership owes much to their recognition of themselves in his language, and that they're not looking for anything more at the moment (which would mean that he occupies the place once held by the Liverpool poets, though his work is much more complex than theirs.) Such a consideration may lie behind the heartfelt response of Anthony Thwaite to what seems to him almost a foreign language:

> my chief problem in reading Armitage is that a lot of the time I find it difficult – or impossible – to follow what he is saying. I enjoy the sensation of someone being very bright, streetwise, racy, someone who can mix West Yorkshire idiom with more Parnassian language, and who knows how to turn a line a line and spin a tale. But, particularly with *Book of Matches* (1993), I find that, when I try to write a marginal paraphrase, or a précis, the whole thing too often seems to collapse into banality, when what I think Armitage is after are ironies.[15]

It may be that some of time the banality *is* the irony, that the secret is the lack of a secret. There is more than one Armitage to be found in the poems to date, of course, but the I-speak-your-one-liner version is the most prominent. It may also prove that the horizontal plane of puns and redundancies, and the combinations of jaunty rhythm and "light" half-rhymes in which Armitage has often worked to date will themselves become problematic for him, as he seeks to raise himself by his bootstraps from what could threaten to become an accomplished mannerism, and towards a more inclusive poetry. This is something attempted in different ways in the title sequence of *Book of Matches* (1993) (though some of these poems have an odd affective hollowness); in 'Five Eleven Ninety Nine' from *The Dead Sea Poems* (1995); and, in a more isolated way, in the earlier love poems, 'In Our Tenth Year' and 'To His Lost Lover'.

It is a vague formulation: but there is something I recognise as Northern about Armitage – a guarded flatness and watchfulness that oversee even his most zestful work and make his best poems, which are mainly about love, seem like exceptions to a general rule of sensibility. Paradoxically, even his garrulity is somehow close-mouthed, as if meant to be accessible to a group rather than the generality. Part of what makes it hard to describe this climate more clearly is the sense that his is the work of the battle (though not the war) won, that he has the manner but not the politics of the place and its people. The painful dramatisation of linguistic and class prejudice which lights Tony Harrison's poems like a naval flare is something Armitage never seems to have felt much need to engage with. For him, that looks like the concern of a previous generation or even a past age. 'Great Sporting Moments: The Treble' gives 'the rich' a good doing, but its speaker's allegiance lies at least as much with John Braine as with Karl Marx, and the poem asserts the right of access, not the need for transformation. Similarly, in 'The Two of Us', the war of the nobs and the oiks is to be resolved by Death the Leveller, which is rhetorically very appealing but of little present use:

> …on the day they dig us out
> they'll know that you were something really fucking fine
> and I was nowt.
> Keep that in mind,
>
> because the worm won't know your make of bone from mine.[16]

There is in fact some similarity with Harrison here – with the close of *V.*, where a similar universalising retrenchment takes place. The curious result in Armitage's case is that he both avoids history and looks backwards, which may explain the odd lack of context in his work. His poems about crime and drugs are quite properly dramatic, concerned with particulars, and one infers his principles and his sympathy – but without feeling that he's convinced about the necessity of solidarity, or even its existence. In this regard, he is a perfectly representative Englishman of the times, living in a state of Blairite ideological denial. Where this might lead is interesting to speculate. For instance, though he writes about the city, he is not a city poet: at least half his mind now seems drawn on to the Pennine moorlands which are the terrain of the much older Ted Hughes, the ambiguously "apolitical" poet of elemental themes. This seems to be where Armitage is headed in his best recent work, the prose memoir 'I'm sitting way above the farm' in *Moon Country*.[17]

Even before *Moon Country*, their collaborative book about their visit to Iceland, Armitage was habitually paired with his friend and contemporary, Glyn Maxwell (born 1962), the possessor of a style at least as highly elaborated and considerably more obtrusive. The task of comparison may offer critics occupation for some time to come, but it's worth trying to sketch the links between the poets' work. To do so involves bearing in mind that in a period of media-consciousness such as our own it is extremely difficult (supposing it remains desirable) to separate the work from the life, or the context from the identity. Certainly the juxtaposition of a southerner who read English at Oxford and a Yorkshireman who didn't can hardly help but seem suggestive, though of what is far from clear – perhaps the effacement of old boundaries, and if so, perhaps to neither party's benefit. As poets, in several ways they meet like opposites, though the view of England which emerges from their work has strong basic similarities. Where Maxwell is lush, Armitage is laconic, and where Maxwell is all concealment, Armitage can seem a poet wholly of the surface. What they have in common is the creation of immediately recognisable rhetorics, alert to the possibility of cliché, proverb, ad-speak, slang, popular song and the ironic bracketing of all major terms which is part of the *lingua franca* of everyday postmodernity. This, to recapitulate, is the whole baggage of youth: theirs may be the first rising generation in English poetry which finds no difficulty in placing its speech among the other constituents of poetic language.

In his first two books especially, Maxwell's version of this rhetoric also has strong inflationary, mystificatory tendencies, even when the poem seems to be simply going about its business, as in the opening of 'The Fires by the River':

> Just say you went beside the fires by the river,
> in neither night nor day, insofar as
> violet and lime were the shades of the air that
>   steamed or anchored over
> the slurping water, and this was the River Thames
>   you somehow knew it.[18]

If poetry is language which, in contrast to prose, cannot be ignored in favour of its supposed subject, Maxwell is operating at the extreme end of the spectrum and in a quite specialised way. He is not really a poet of objects, which exist to populate (fairly thinly) a world where thought and feeling are uppermost. If the poet must always unavoidably cast a shadow on the scenery, Maxwell takes pains to point his out: 'Maxwell' is primarily a creature of syntax, register and form. (He records self-deprecatingly that a friend pointed out how unusual 'The End of the Weekend' was in his work, in that only very late on did the Maxwell/poet/narrator put in an appearance. The story is an exaggeration, but nonetheless truthful: in fact the letter 'I' doesn't need to be mentioned for us to sense its presence.)[19] By the time readers of 'The Fires by the River' are dealing with 'insofar' they will still be puzzled by the nonstandard construction 'in neither night nor day', which might have come out of Dylan Thomas or another very different poet, W.S. Graham. Further, while the rest of the long sentence of this opening sestet appears to explain the proposal of the opening clause, in fact it merely reasserts it – a kind of wish-fulfilment for the poet. This might suggest the proximity of the world of fairytale which often seems to border or penetrate Maxwell's work. But the simplicity of such allure is balanced by the obstructions to sense which Maxwell deliberately lays before us. He both invites and rejects participation: the intention seems to be not that we shall see clearly, but that we shall listen to the involutions of the speaking voice problematising the matter in hand, or just beyond the hand's grasp. Again, Maxwell has commented instructively on his methods:

> I sometimes write a stanza in a particular form and see how it works and then write all the other stanzas in that metre. I was using form to process chaotic material in my own mind...My thought in itself isn't organised.[20]

This is admirably frank. If it feeds the detractor's suspicions it also shows Maxwell's self-knowledge. It also seems, however, to indicate a division in his thinking between 'form' and 'material'. Further, it implies a view of form as a container, rather than a mould; which may in turn account for the impression that Maxwell is in the habit of presenting his own problems of expression and construction as gnomic challenges to the reader. Certainly there comes a point when some will ask whether it is really illumination that is on offer or, instead, the idea, or the sound, of it being rehearsed elsewhere.

One might suspect from Maxwell's balder poems, such as 'The Eater',[21] where capitalism seems to be addressing its consumers as prey, that his view of the subject-matter is sometimes less complicated than the orchestration which surrounds it. There may even be a gap between the two, for which the spectacular manner and air of difficulty are a compensation and a disguise. Poems become the evidence of a poet at work, and the poet's dramatic lyrics deal ultimately in abstractions. Among Maxwell's most successful poems are high-performance light verse workouts like 'Video Tale of a Patriot', 'Sport Story of a Winner' and 'Tale of the Crimson Team',[22] all of which serve as witty illustrations of material already familiar to the audience, rather than the rending of the doors of perception at which he seems to be aiming elsewhere. When Maxwell stops playing hard to get, his hospitality to the reader verges on cosiness. Curiously, in one of his least cluttered pieces, the early 'The Last Dessert', which deals with the brutality of a self-made man towards his wife at a dinner party, there can be felt the ancestral presence of John Betjeman, that supremely unchallenging versifier of Metroland, at whose far limit Maxwell's native Welwyn stands:

> She went to fetch it, called and cheered,
> she put it in the sink to see:
> brown and pink and crumbled like
> a failure. She was twenty-three.[23]

But Maxwell's master is clearly Auden, with whom, like Armitage, he has been compared. In 1990 he commented: 'I'm still under the shade of that oak tree...I think it's a good place to grow, at least in the climate as it is now, politically, morally and also poetically. Nobody else has really decided to beat a path to that door it seems to me!'[24] There's a refreshing openness and enthusiasm here, and perhaps it is possible that even so recently it was not everywhere apparent that Auden was proving to be one of the most highly influential poets of the postwar period, setting the terms of reference for much of its most interesting work, including that of Peter Porter, John Fuller and James Fenton. Maxwell approaches the topic with some humility, but his interest marks a far from modest ambition. What might it be that Maxwell is after in Auden? Is it what Leavis disparagingly described as 'that air of knowing one's way about',[25] the cultural assurance and power of synthesis? Is it the air of authority, born of a capacity to travel between exact dramatic detail and external commentary? The seemingly infallible power of diagnosis? The tricks with articles and syntax? The formal gifts? The air of secrecy and conspiracy? The various personal myths? The answer is unclear, and one wonders whether Maxwell himself knows. But his reference to the value of learning from Auden in 'the climate as it is now, politically, morally and also poetically' may mean that he feels the poet should seek the role of the age's representative, which the young Auden acquired and the older Auden elaborated. But would you start from here – that is, from Welwyn Garden City, a place so pacific and frictionless in Maxwell's account of it – even when faced with the Flood – that it could rival Auden's Macao as a place where 'nothing serious can happen'? [26] Welwyn is Maxwell's England-as-afterlife. Ignored, though shaped, by the larger historical and political currents, it lives on into a period where the significant events in 'politics and morals' are felt to occur so remotely from the everyday that the greatest civic virtue is a mild-mannered ironic impotence, not a million miles from the attitudes of the Movement (though Maxwell adds his own element of stage gadzookery). The engine revs, but the poem isn't going anywhere. This is in fact the theme of Maxwell's long poem, 'Out of the Rain', where Welwyn is viewed mythologically through the boozy gaze of the narrator, who sees the Flood, a visitation by a unicorn and the restoration of the status quo, concluding:

> I finish this and put in on the shelf.
> I take it down and send it to myself.[27]

Again, Maxwell has illumination to offer: 'Whatever structure I've given this story it ends by mouthing the words of what it's like to be in a situation in which...in a way you do have almost everything you want but you know that nothing good will ever come of it.' [28]

There may be little the poet can do about his material and his imaginative resource: the margins for change lie elsewhere. What Maxwell has done in his more recent work is to use form and syntax more dynamically and as means of clarification. Parts of *Rest for the Wicked* (1995) show a marked advance on their predecessors. The wit is less of an allegation, the memorability assured:

> You don't forgive what's left of what you loved.[29]

> You note at once that no one is beside you.
> Your neighbour said he'd wave, but so far hasn't.
> 'Our blessings! May our God be there to guide you!'
> Your family never said, and their God isn't.[30]

There is a powerful strain of the Audenesque, too, from sources including the 'Detective Story' (1936)[31] and *The Orators*, for example the invocation to the detectives.[32] The greater concision of poems like 'The Plot and None', 'The Sentence' and 'Six for the Wicked'[33] may owe something to the sonnets of 1938 such as 'Brussels in Winter', 'The Sphinx' and 'A.E. Housman'.[34] 'The Great Detectives' is a brilliant pastiche on Law, art and knowledge, with references to 'Gare du Midi' and 'In Memory of W.B. Yeats'[35] close to the surface:

> No certainties like those of private eyes,
> Once the detecting bug is coughed and caught:
> Wherever Art is made or history taught,
> What isn't Law might just as well be lies
> For all the help it brings in the hot nights
> Before the white steam clears and he alights.[36]

This focused ingenuity, in which Maxwell's hitherto cluttered attempts on the epigram are encouraged, seems a sound basis for development.

Whether either Maxwell or Armitage will manage this will be one of the most interesting poetic questions of the next few years. The matter is not entirely in their hands, of course. David Kennedy, an enthusiastic reader of both poets, offers an ingenious reading of their work in terms of a felt historical lack:

> The poet who comes to maturity in a period when consensus has been irrevocably eroded, history commodified and the relation between values and forms of life derided will...inevitably acquire an impoverished account of how he come [sic] to be as he is and where he is. He may lack, if one can so term it, an historical self and will therefore struggle to develop an imagination whose supply lines to the past are kept open.[37]

Kennedy seems to be thinking of the Thatcher era as the last trump of catastrophe, the moment when the self knows itself to be severed from the various nourishments of identity. His reading is itself arguably unhistorical because of its very clarity. Peculiar as it might seem, there have been worse things than Thatcherism, and England was as ready for Thatcherism as it was fearful of it. The enslavement required electoral connivance. The wave of cultural activity which Kennedy has described and been part of is in no small degree fuelled by Thatcherism – both in opposing it and learning from its methods. Bloodaxe Books, where Armitage, Maxwell, Jo Shapcott and others first found book publication, is in some respects, in the "soft" sense of the current New Labour administration, a Thatcherite enterprise. One could adduce, for instance, its early rejection of the poetic establishment in favour of the energetic creation of a quite different map of what seemed significant to the firm's founder-editor, and its subsequent incorporation in the establishment.

Whatever the details of possible disagreement with Kennedy, the sense of social and imaginative disconnection (and implied political de-commitment) on which Kennedy concentrates is surely traceable in the work of Armitage and Maxwell. Kennedy has propounded the phrase 'the rhetorical imagination' to describe 'a change of emphasis from the latencies and nuances of language to its forms and surfaces.' Even as danger signals flash in the minds of a slightly older constituency, Kennedy makes haste to insist that this is not necessarily a regrettable state of affairs:

> while the rhetorical imagination can be described as the product of an impoverishment, it would be wholly incorrect to assume that it is itself a form of impoverishment. Indeed, one of the paradoxes of the poetry of Simon Armitage and Glyn Maxwell is that carefully husbanded resources of containment and circumspection go hand in hand with exuberant enjoyment, prolific output and a wide range of occasion and inspiration.[38]

But even on this optimistic and in some ways accurate assessment, it is hard not see a process of decline. The reader must wonder if poetry is not in danger of decadence, of becoming in some sense a *genre*, parasitic on its unambiguously serious antecedents, as sword and sorcery novels or the thriller are parasitic on more serious kinds of fiction. Whether this is a problem of poetry itself, or of individual exponents, it's too early to say.

24. Jo Shapcott, Selima Hill, Helen Dunmore: *The Long Haul*

In an issue of *Poetry Review* concerned with the twenty 'New Generation' poets who in 1994 participated in a campaign to raise public awareness of poetry, the name mentioned most often by the poets when they were asked to identify significant influences on their work was that of Elizabeth Bishop.[1] Had such a survey of poets been conducted ten or twenty years earlier, Sylvia Plath's name would surely have figured, but among those whose comments are recorded it is strikingly absent – as it as from Linda France's introduction to her popular anthology *Sixty Women Poets* (1993). France speaks of the guiding force of her anthology as 'women being positive, creative and in charge of their own lives'.[2] The unfortunate resemblance of her phrasing to the breathless clichés of *Cosmopolitan* shouldn't disguise the importance of her point, which is to suggest that the woman poet need not be a casualty or a victim, a lunatic or a suicide, and that her work should prepare itself for the long run. Bishop, though much troubled,[3] survived to enjoy high acclaim, and her reputation, rather than declining as is common in the years after a poet's death, continues to rise – witness the unprecedented interest in her Selected Letters, *One Art*, when they appeared in 1994.[4]

This is not to disparage Plath's achievement, which seems more significant with the passage of time. Nor does the fact there have already been many long-lived, durable women poets affect the point. As Carol Rumens has commented of women writers, '…for a variety of well-documented reasons, our passage into a writing career is often belated, and rarely proceeds uninterrupted'.[5] Thus it is also true that as Jane Dowson puts it, 'Periodisation is frequently, albeit unwittingly, hostile to women because it is built on publishing history'.[6] And poets' work must be available and known to an audience: the concern of France, as of Fleur Adcock and others before her,[7] has been as much with re-presenting poets as of advocating those now emerging.

Seeking to accomplish and accelerate the recognition of her chosen poets, the anthologist may thus have more than one task in hand. In this hectic climate, debate and thoroughgoing disagreement about the role of the anthology, the status of women poets and the best way to mark their achievement, are not far behind. When Carol Rumens, who had already edited one anthology, *Making for the Open* (1985)[8] introduced her second, *New Women Poets* (1990), she remarked:

> the whole notion that women poets can legitimately be grouped together in this way, and that gender is almost a symbolic form of nationality, a line of cohesion and relationship whatever the superficial differences, owes everything to the Women's Movement, and the literary revolution it created. The very fact that such a book as this can be published at all proves the success of that revolution. It seems to me that any amassing of women's voices will amount to a fairly radical critique of current society.[9]

Arguably, Rumens's language – 'the Women's Movement', 'the literary revolution it created', 'a fairly radical critique of society' – might already have sounded slightly belated when she wrote her introduction (though to say this implies no disagreement with her views). From the standpoint of the late nineties it sounds historically remote. The accelerating wave of feminism which emerged from the 1960s was unfortunate in that its arrival turns out to have coincided with the point at which began the decline of the New Left politics in which much of its energy was invested, and which has been followed by the collapse of political discourse into managerialism and moral tinkering. In recent years the language of public discussion, where ideology has little purchase and is automatically derided, has tended increasingly to place disparaging inverted commas around 'the Women's Movement', 'revolution' and anything more 'radical' than a new management style or a haircut. Despite its undeniable successes, the political dimension of feminism, the caucus of the 'symbolic form of nationality', has been eroded – by fashion; by the pressures of commodity capitalism; by the speed with which the media forget recent history; by an impatient desire to be post-something; and by the resulting dissolution of the energies of the collective into the pursuit of individual "fulfilment". Feminism sounds "old-style": who wants to be seen wearing an oxymoron nowadays? Perhaps it was sombre considerations of this kind which provoked Rumens's irritated and revisionist response to the arrival of another anthology of women poets, Maura Dooley's *Making for Planet Alice* (1997):[10]

> In her introduction, Maura Dooley says she wants to see women's poetry become 'part of the main canon of English Literature'. I had a comparable ambition when I edited *Making for the Open* twelve years ago. Now I see how futile it was. Such work is perceived inevitably as a criticism of, and alternative to, the canon. Dooley should realise she has chosen a self-defeating route to her goal, one practically guaranteed never to arrive.
>
> A woman's anthology is *ipso facto* concerned with politics, weasel-words like celebration notwithstanding. And, of course, with economics.

> So let's say it loud and clear: anthologies of poetry by women sell. The publisher gets rich (though the poets and editors do not) and simultaneously earns good conduct stars. Meanwhile the reputation of Women Poets (the glamorous, saleable, product) and the stuff they actually write blurs into an unfathomable if vaguely fashionable mass which may actually prevent individual poets – and more importantly, poems – from emerging.[11]

The 'blurring' may take the form described by Jane Dowson in her account of the emergence and role of women's anthologies:

> There is an understanding that anthologies are consumed by the general reader more than by the specialist, and, consequently, that anthologised poems are somehow marketable and that double-sided concept 'accessible' rather than demanding or innovative.[12]

Despite the violence she does the language here, Dowson makes a significant point about the durability of expectations: the 'understanding' to which she refers affects both production and consumption of anthologies (though not necessarily the poems themselves). Rumens might almost be carrying on Dowson's argument when she turns to the readership of anthologies of women poets:

> As any one not living in Planet Alice must realise, a woman's anthology has a *keep out* notice on it as far as the average male reader is concerned. Men rarely read such books, and never edit them. Women's anthologies are read primarily by women. They could even be viewed as the up-market version of the woman's magazine.[13]

These concerns have something in common with the danger foreseen by Fleur Adcock in the introduction to her 1987 *Faber Book of Twentieth Century Women's Poetry*. Poetry by women, she suggested might 'be shunted into a ghetto, occupying the "Women's" section of the bookshop rather than the poetry section, and taught in "Women's Studies" courses at universities'.[14] Ten years further on, certain features of the 'ghetto' have been brought in cosmeticised form into the economic mainstream – as has been the rule with all forms of cultural dissent, a phenomenon most dramatically illustrated by a comparison with the repeated recuperation of the rebellious energies of popular music. In her exasperation, Rumens seems mistakenly to attribute Linda France's remark about women being 'positive, creative and in charge' to Dooley, but this fits in rather neatly with her magazine comparison, and she may well be right in her suspicions about the marriage of seriousness and saleability. She adds the alarming comment that 'light verse-with-an-edge might be emerging as the quintessential female genre. Sophie Hannah and Eleanor Brown are writing in the tradition re-established in the 1980s by Wendy Cope (though not yet with Cope's finesse) which can be traced back to Dorothy Parker and earlier,

English "bluestocking" wits.'[15] If this prognosis were confirmed, it would be a dismaying state of affairs. Rumens's final point takes us back to the introduction to these essays:

> There was a time, I believe, for splitting the world of the canon open, for bringing in the new voices, the raw and awkward and anarchic. But there is a time, too, for consolidation, stringency, sifting. [*Making for Planet Alice*] would be better if it were leaner. Bloodaxe, of course, would not agree. First we had *Sixty Women Poets* (admittedly representing three generations): now, we have thirty poets representing the first half of the '90s. What will it be next – 2000 Women Poets for the Year 2000? Such profligacy does not benefit women writers: it may in fact ensure that, as far as posterity is concerned, the great and the good will once more, thanks to their gender, be 'hidden from history'.[16]

The mismatch between the radicalism of political desire on the one hand, and the public outcome on the other, is hardly new. Where might Rumens's call for aesthetic 'stringency' direct us? 'Hidden' or not, the most interesting work of women poets in recent years resists the categorisation which might suit the market, and in some ways it has moved ahead of its advocates. If sisterhood is no longer so much in evidence, some very impressive women poets are emerging. Fleur Adcock, Carol Ann Duffy, Carol Rumens herself and Kathleen Jamie are considered elsewhere in these pages, and a fuller account of the matter would have to touch on poets including Ruth Padel, Katherine Pierpoint, Anne Rouse and Eva Salzman.[17] But three poets in particular – Jo Shapcott, Selima Hill and Helen Dunmore – stand out and can help to suggest the variety, the vitality and the refreshing imaginative challenge offered by the work of contemporary women poets.

Jo Shapcott's poem 'Motherland (after Tsvetaeva)' describes a condition of separation in some respects akin to those suggested by Simon Armitage and Glyn Maxwell:

> Language is impossible
> in a country like this. Even
> the dictionary laughs when I look up
> 'England', 'Motherland', 'Home'.[18]

The Russian poet provides her English successor with an index of alienation. 'Motherland', for example, is a term with no currency applied in an English context (if in doubt, try the male equivalent, 'Fatherland', which sounds equally inappropriate). It is as though the poet has not only lost her 'English' bearings but also the idioms in which to name what might once have been the case. The dictionary

> ...insists on falling open instead
> three times out of the nine I try it
> at the word 'Distance' – degree
> of remoteness, interval of space –
>
> the word is ingrained like pain.
> So much for England and so much
> for my future to walk into the horizon
> carrying distance like a broken suitcase.[19]

To refer a translation back to the identity of her own country is typical of Shapcott's bold elegance. After Maxwell's pastel murk and roaring mirrors, and Armitage's laconicism, her poem is limpid, for all the compression of its underlying argument. It is also the case that – paradoxically, since 'Motherland' is in part about exile – Shapcott deals with her imaginative world from within, rather than matching her male colleagues' air of externality. This is partly to do with physical curiosity, as in the weird blending of analysis and reverie in 'In the Bath':

> She loved the water trails over her body curves,
> the classical lines between wet and dry
> making graph patterns which she thought might follow
> the activity in her brain –[20]

Shapcott's poetry is much occupied, as Ian Gregson has suggested, with 'the boundaries of the self shifting, and...with the themes of splits and transformations'.[21] If a male poet is often concerned with naming what has been, a woman poet may also be interested in the process of becoming and adaptation. This might suggest that politically hers is the more active project, since as well as interpretation and assessment there is something else at stake – the formation of identity without limit. Rather than producing redundancy or rodomontade, Shapcott's 'play' is constructive – and it is allied, we may suspect, to a considerable accompanying grasp of theory. The unsettling inventiveness of her work finds a more formally expressed equivalent in this comment from Patricia Waugh:

> There can be no simple legitimation for feminists in throwing off a 'false consciousness' and revealing a true but 'deeply' buried female self. Indeed, to embrace the essentialism of this notion of 'difference' is to come dangerously close to reproducing the very patriarchical construction of gender which feminists have set out to contest...[22]

Such a contention can be seen at work (or rather, in play) in the monologue 'Goat', with its gleeful, mischievous opening:

> Dusk, deserted road, and suddenly
> I was a goat. To be truthful it took
> two minutes, though it seemed sudden...[23]

Shapcott's numerous animal poems, including the Mad Cow series from *Phrase Book*, show little inclination to produce the moral equivalences supplied by fables or the interpretative keys of allegory: they ask to be understood in terms which the poems work to discover as they proceed. The reader – perhaps especially the male reader – has to learn that the poems' excursions are not dependent on reference back to a place of interpretative safety. But this is to make them sound forbidding, when in fact they are in some ways more hospitable than we normally expect poems to be. In 'Goat', the speaker operates with sometimes startling ease in a number of related but different roles – as narrator/explainer, with that unusually welcoming but not ingratiating voice; as the expert user of the world she uncovers; and in the role one of its objects or properties, as surprised and intrigued as her readers. Hers is a world that exists before, instead of, and as well as, familiar categories. Shapcott's multiple perspective is particularly interesting when she writes about love. In the utterly ambiguous 'Matter', it works both to praise and rebuke a lover; to mark and clarify differences between knowledge and possession, experience and analysis, meaning and summary, sex and language; and yet not to exclude:

> Then I think he was searching
> for the particles
> not yet discovered
> but believed to exist.
>
> Then I didn't know
> what time it was any more
> and neither of us knew
> which was inside or outside
> as he reached somewhere
> very deep and fingered gold –
> charms, stranges, tops and gravitons –
> but not the words he wanted
> which only come now.[24]

Animals are also important inhabitants of the poetry of Selima Hill, as an inspection of the contents page of *Trembling Hearts in the Bodies of Dogs: New and Selected Poems*[25] will quickly indicate. The whole of *A Little Book of Meat* (1993)[26] – her books have to read *as* books – takes place down on a farm where 'there are girls growing up into women', who work up 'to their angelic necks in steers and guinea fowl', girls for whom 'the only males are bulls and cobs',[27] but who are to learn differently, like the wife in an earlier poem, 'The Unsuccessful Wedding Night', who lies awake, thinking unhappily:

> It's all because of Buster.
> Of course it's unreasonable,
> he couldn't possibly have come –
> his barking, his midnight walk,
> the way he scratches at the blankets –[28]

Jane Dowson says of this poem that it 'undermine[s] the narratives of romantic love',[29] which seems an almost absurdly obvious remark. Surely, too, the poem is a good deal more interested in the burdensome reality of wishes and longings than in arguing with the conventions. This is borne out by the fact that Selima Hill seems one of the least *embarrassed* poets ever to have found publication: she moves straight to a concern with psychic realities, while the social norms (for example of her parents' generation) may be obstructive but are also somehow insubstantial. The poems are already living another life. It may be true, as she says of women, that

> ...all we're allowed's anxiety like fishbones
> lodged in our throats
> as beauty parlours hum;
> all we're allowed is having pretty faces
> and cold and glittery hearts like water-ices.[30]

But this constraint must take its place alongside the facts:

> Mine's more like a centrally-heated boiler-room,
> evil and warm;
> like kidneys on a plate.[31]

As with Shapcott (and also, more vexatiously, with Medbh McGuckian and Penelope Shuttle) there is a sense in which it is not part of Hill's work to ask the reader to agree to the possible validity of her way of seeing things, for if the poet is a discoverer, her imagination is already landed on the new continent, already *there*, even if its whereabouts are not yet clear. This is not a mannerly, negotiated surrealism, but something like English expressionism. And that may help to account for the feelings of disorientation and irritation initially experienced by some male readers who find themselves turning back at the border to face the possibility that their vocabulary is simply not equipped for the job of reading the resulting poems. The temptation is to fall back on catch-all dismissals – to complain about whimsy and triviality. The first chapter of this book appeared in the magazine *Sunk Island Review*, in the issue entitled 'Spleen', where various writers let rip with their opinions about the state of contemporary poetry. Among the other contributors was Martin Stannard, who found himself so depressed and irritated by the stack of books he'd taken for review that in his 'Open Letter to Michael Blackburn' he gave up all pretence of detachment, for example in writing about Pauline Stainer, Carole Satyamurti, and about Hill's *A Little Book of Meat*:

> Perhaps Selima Hill's *A Little Book of Meat* is not her best book. What I do know is, if you took all the similes out of it you'd have bugger all left. The book bulges with them. There's hardly a poem unburdened by them. If you're not careful they fall out all over the carpet, or if your hands are sweaty, they stick to your fingers, and when someone asks you how you are, you say that you feel like a toilet cistern that's unflushed on the borders of the new Czech Republic. Not because it makes sense, or is apt, but just because. The editors of the Bloodaxe *New Poetry* anthology would have us believe in Hill's 'centrality to the new poetry', but come on, lads: even if we accept such a thing as 'the new poetry' this is a bit much. And as for their other claim, there's very little, if anything, that's 'anarchic' about these poems, unless anarchic poetry is untethered poetry, devoid of control because lack of control, or editorial restraint, is intrinsically good. Subject these poems to close scrutiny, and they show up as thin and unrewarding as gruel.[32]

The epistolary form allows Stannard's heartfelt disapproval full rein without his needing to employ the usual critical devices of example and argument. His ultimate court of appeal is Common Sense, the refuge of reactionary opinion from Larkin and Amis to Auberon Waugh, where self-evident truths expose dissenters as fools and frauds. Does he wish to be included in this company? The effect is to make the world seem smaller, dimmer and less interesting – but only momentarily. His objection to Hill's use of simile, for example, treats as a rhetorical error what really seems to be a device for destabilising the homeliness of everyday comparison:

> – as if LOVE were a dome of glass beneath a lake
> entered through a maze of dripping tunnels
> I hoped and prayed I'd never be found inside.[33]

> because the last night I spent longing for you
> was like spending the night with no clothes on
> in a Daimler full of chows
> with the windows closed,
> I have decided to calm myself down,
> and imagine my head as a tinkly moss-padded cavern
> where nothing happens.[34]

Perhaps the second example, where simile is the structural principle and a sign of unassuageable distress, and where the reader thinks, on reading the last line, 'No chance', is the source of Stannard's annoyance. But if this – this rushing, crowding, ungovernable succession – is what things are *like*, Hill's poems suggest, then what are the things which prompt these comparisons – things including a stable selfhood – anyway? Common sense will not take us very far here, since the similes trace states of mind which are themselves mobile. It is not the kind of poetry which is likely to 'pull itself together', since it's about being pulled apart and living to tell the tale. Part of Stannard's irritation seems to arise from the feeling that in fact it doesn't much matter what he thinks. Take it or leave it, Hill's work seems to suggest.

Hill, like Shapcott, is basically a *dramatic* writer, as too is the quietly but powerfully authoritative Helen Dunmore. Dunmore is at first sight a rather more conventional poet than Shapcott or Hill, and her points of domestic reference – children, home life, marriage – might, in the bizarre way of these things, be taken as limitations. At any rate, her work seems to proceed from a greater assurance about the integrity of the self than that of the other two poets discussed here. It may be useful to view her poetry as a bridge between realism and less readily definable imaginative practices. Dunmore can write directly as a social critic (as in 'Poem for Hidden Women', 'Getting the Strap' or 'When You've Got').[35] She can speak plainly as a moralist, writing about the Gulf War in 'In the Desert Knowing Nothing'[36] and with cold anger in 'Poem on the Obliteration of 100,000 Iraqi Soldiers',[37] where, like Tony Harrison,[38] she describes the terrible photograph of the incinerated Iraqi army lorry driver which appeared in the world's press following the bombardment of the Iraqi retreat during Operation Desert Storm:

> That killed head straining through the windscreen
> with its frill of bubbles in the eye-sockets
> is not trying to tell you something –
>
> it is telling you something.[39]

It is the 'frill of bubbles' that the reader carries unhappily away into memory. The intent accuracy of Dunmore's gaze (and of her treatment of the other senses) does the work which often turns other poets into commentators. Her approach both acknowledges and resists the kind of pessimism Adorno applied to the depiction of modern warfare, when he spoke of 'the withering of experience, the vacuum between men and their fate, in which their real fate lies'.[40]

As the reader grows accustomed to Dunmore's work, what at first seems like a rather conventional modesty is revealed as a powerful disinterestedness which can incorporate difficulty as well as directness. The complex mood of the opening of 'Adders', for instance, makes her lines themselves seem like a place:

> this path is silky with dust
> where a lizard balances across bracken fronds
> and a brown butterfly opens wide
> to the stroke of the sun,

where a trawler feels its way along the sandbanks
and two yachts, helplessly paired, tack far out
like the butterflies which have separated and gone quiet.[41]

If there can be sensed here the background voices of other poets of shore and sea, Anne Stevenson and Elizabeth Bishop, Dunmore has found a dramatic power of her own, which she has also gone on to exploit very successfully in fiction. She operates much closer to familiar realism than Hill or Shapcott, and perhaps the radicalism of her work could best be described in terms of a refusal to see realism as a convention. The background hum of the world is continually about to become a roar, as in 'Poem in a Hotel', where irritation and tedium have come to the edge of something graver and far from merely 'personal':

Waiting. I'm here waiting
like a cable-car caught in a thunderstorm.
At six, someone will feed me, at seven
I'll stroll and sit by the band.

I have never seen so many trombones
taking the air, or so many mountains.
Under them there are tunnels
and a troll's salt-garden.[42]

Perhaps Martin Stannard might have enjoyed his reading better if he had started here. Be that as it may, it seems clear that the female line(s) in poetry currently embody a good deal of its most interesting energy. The male reader may at least hope to find himself not hopelessly strange to the new conditions.

25. Don Paterson, Kathleen Jamie, Robert Crawford, W.N. Herbert: *Scotland! Scotland! Actual/Virtual*

In the concluding chapter of his book *Identifying Poets* (1993)[1] Robert Crawford (born 1959) discusses the presence of ideas of 'home' in numerous poets from Derek Walcott to W.N. Herbert (born 1961). Amongst Crawford's arresting remarks are the following: 'In Scotland we live between and across languages'[2] and 'Homogeneity is the enemy of Scottish culture'.[3] Many writers and readers in Scotland and elsewhere will understand and assent to these formulations, which are examples of the poet-critic making strength out of seeming paradox. For 'between and across' and 'heterogeneity' read: vigour; openness; readiness to meet and relish actual circumstances and to exploit imaginatively the changes they entail; resistance to the desiccations of the imaginary academy of tweedy and deceased pedants in Scotland itself – '*Scots style-sheeters*, prescriptivists who want us all the same'[4] – with which Crawford seems always to be waging war. It is a romantic view – a Heaney-esque free space of the imagination, invested with real powers of definition, an imaginative legislature. It might be designed to dismantle the definition handed down by Eliot from the bench of his judgement and quoted by Douglas Dunn at the opening of the introduction to *The Faber Book of Twentieth Century Scottish Poetry*:

> The first part of the history of Scottish literature is part of the history of English literature when English was several dialects; the second part is part of the history of English when English was two dialects – English and Scots; the third part is something quite different – it is the history of a provincial literature. And finally, there is no longer any distinction to be drawn for the present day between the two literatures.[5]

As an example of language in use, this passage is so boring that readers may feel inclined to check that they have not inadvertently picked up a legal document. Yet the tedious legalism ('the second part is part') has a rhetorical function. It means: *this stuff is true because of the way it's said*. And the discussion of the languages and literature of Scottish people is as much a political act as John Major's recent claim that 'one thousand years of British history'[6] were under threat from the then Labour Opposition's policy on Scottish devolution. His claim was answered by Scottish Nationalists with historical facts about the Act of Union, but these, we may suspect, are not very interesting to the English, who, whether they agree with Major or not, do by and large 'know what he means', and in large numbers take that 'meaning' for the fact, as is the

English habit where other people's business is concerned.

I labour this point in order to suggest that while it may be interesting it's also delusory to propose that a national literature can operate in a platonic condition of hypertextuality, unsoiled by the confusions of the "real world" to which the philistines are always demanding the arts should return (while trying like mad to keep them out of it). The sophistication of the literature itself can seem to be almost excluded from the debate. Consider the barely disguised ferocity of the English reaction to James Kelman's Glaswegian novel *How Late It Was, How Late*,[7] and the hostility of some to reading the poetry of W.N. Herbert because he sometimes writes in Scots (and gets some of it from a dictionary and other parts from his imagination: he's too clever and he makes things up). These responses are of a piece with the arguments about whether Scots MPs should be able to vote at Westminster after devolution – a difficulty which would be the product of English policy, but for which the Scots are mysteriously to blame. *Ours is the best way, in fact the only way*, the English argument goes: the issue is always power.

If the case for a national literature needs to be made beyond as well as inside the nation – as presumably it does – then that literature needs to travel. Irish literature has done this and twentieth-century Scots literature, by and large, has not. MacDiarmid has not been accorded the same weight of attention as Yeats. Douglas Dunn has proposed that 'an undoubted awkwardness has been the relatively limited object lesson conveyed by two of its major figures [MacDiarmid and Edwin Muir] to subsequent writers for whom the available, common language [English] is the obvious and natural one to use. MacDiarmid's English is too much of a special case, while Muir's, though undoubtedly appropriate to the stories he tells, would look archaic in any other context.'[8] But the identity and limits of 'common language' have come to seem less settled in recent years. The different courses followed by Norman MacCaig (1910-96), W.S. Graham (1918-86) and Edwin Morgan (born 1920), and the recognition gradually bestowed on the Gaelic poet Sorley Maclean (1911-96), show difficulty made into opportunity. At the same time as the Scottish novel has been attracting the distorting attentions of the media, Scottish poetry has begun to produce critics worthy of its vigour and linguistic variety – including Dunn, Herbert and Crawford himself. Such commentators, necessarily historically-minded (as well as formalist, in Crawford's case), can do the job of making the 'present strength' of Scottish poetry an international matter. Crawford cites Bakhtin, the presiding genius of his book:

> In the realm of culture, outsideness is a most powerful factor in understanding. It is only in the eyes of *another culture* that foreign culture reveals itself fully and profoundly…A meaning only reveals its depths since it has encountered and come into contact with another, foreign meaning: they engage in a kind of dialogue, which surmounts the closedness, the one-sidedness of these particular meanings, these cultures.[9]

Here perhaps we can seen the source of Crawford's optimism: for a critic who is above all an advocate, otherness may in fact be the ignition of understanding. If this sounds a little like the soft play version of Kipling's two strong men standing face to face, resistance to it may be equally well-intentioned, the inadvertent by-product of goodwill. Witness the tangle of geography and authority in the introductory paragraphs of Anthony Thwaite's chapter 'Scotland and Wales' from the most recent (1996) edition of *Poetry Today* – a book described by its publishers as 'the most authoritative and up to date survey of contemporary British poetry':

> Despite the fact of ease of communication in Britain today – or perhaps partly because of it – there are certain regions that seem very conscious of themselves as entities: the role played by Liverpool and the North-East in the pop movement was significant. But the Celtic awareness in Scotland, Wales and Ireland has become even stronger during the present century, heightened in Ulster by the clash – the physical clash – between separate cultures. The expression of this has been mainly political, but there have been signs in the poetry of these countries too.
>
> Ireland has been the most obvious case…But even in the 1990s there have been passionate – and passionately articulated – manifestations of separateness in Scotland and in Wales. Introductions to recent anthologies of verse from these countries give one texts by which to argue what might be true here, what merely contentious; and, when Scottish and Welsh poets are enlisted into 'British' anthologies, and when these poets appear to take their own stand on their own ground, there is cause for reflection.[10]

Limitations of space have an influence here, as does the apparent obligation of a survey (one offered to students overseas) to appear objective. The effect, though, is to say nothing and everything at once. We slip from English regions of Britain to the countries of Scotland, Wales and Ireland (which is of course not *in* Britain) without a clear distinction between region and country being made. In a sense it is not Thwaite's task to do this, and his writing simply reflects common *English* usage. But at the same time his tolerance sounds that of the interested, sympathetic but ultimately uncomprehending functionary of the imperial state, for whom the old structures of authority necessarily retain their force, since without them his own identity would be mysteriously questioned or even extinguished – though it would of course be no surprise if he could scarcely recognise such a description. The understandable (if, to some readers, startling) corollary of this is the ferocious distrust with which the hand of English friendship might be rejected by an intended recipient who feels English incomers in Scotland are all white settlers, a famous tribe of liars. It seems as if the target of Tom Leonard's 'Unrelated Incidents' must be the liberal as well as the authoritarian:

thi langwij
a thi
intellect hi
said thi lang-
wij a thi intill-
ects Inglish

then whin thi
doors slid
oapn hi raised
his hat geen
mi a fare-
well nod flung
oot his right

fit boldly n
fell eight
storeys
doon thi
empty
lift-shaft[11]

The enemy – as 'Ghostie Men' indicates[12] – is also within Scotland, in the craven Anglicised respectability which Leonard (born 1944), wielding a Glaswegian 'lang- / wij a thi/ guhtr'[13] ('ach well / all livin language is sacred / fuck thi lohta thim')[14] hates as keenly as he hates the English newsreaders ('belt up')[15] and cultural agents who, he says, made poetry 'nothing to do with me'.[16] Scotland must be understood as much in terms of class as of nation (not to mention religion). In contrast to Crawford's oddly frictionless approach – like Dick Barton, with one bound he was free of the English yoke – some other Scottish poets illustrate this in a variety of ways, both as material for poems and in analysing the problems the material presents. At a certain point, the Scot in English company will be burdened with the role of the excluded, the subject, the *described*, the inherently proletarian race, an experience well evoked by Douglas Dunn:

> It's something I was made to feel more in England because I spoke with an accent that, through some sort of mythology, made even working-class people think that a) you were more working-class than them and b) probably more violent with it...People would somehow be suspicious if you quoted Larkin at them, or had an education, or a first-class honours

> degree. 'Who is this?' You get the same tension in Tony Harrison. I've called Harrison's poetry 'The Scholarship Boy's Revenge' – trying to get back at society for the way they demeaned you, through their false expectations, or their willingness to categorise you, and keep you there. Them and Uz, that crazy class system still persists.[17]

This is not quite the same position as that of the Irish. Part of the difference arises from the fact that while the Irish have typically been viewed first as peasants and then as working class, they have been much more readily identifiable to the English in terms of nationalism and (in respect of Ulster) by sectarianism than of class politics. Nationalism is a more compromised activity in Scotland, and while sectarianism is clearly significant, in political terms it has often been averted from the English gaze by socialism. Thwaite's 'Celtic awareness' is hardly designed to indicate, never mind to account for, these complexities.

If the conflict for the Scots working-class writer is seen occurring on two fronts, race and class, both are felt as invasive by the victim. Witness, for example, the extreme discomfort of a gifted younger poet, Don Paterson (born 1963), talking about his poem 'An Elliptical Stylus'. It seems directly autobiographical. It tells of a visit by the poet and his father to buy a new stylus, only to be sneeringly told by the salesman that their record player is too old to be compatible with the item in question:

> We had the guy in stitches: 'You can't...
> er...you'll have to *upgrade your equipment.*'
> Still smirking, he sent us from the shop
> With a box of needles, thick as carpet-tacks...[18]

The poem contains its own alternative version of itself – a poem of comfortable elegiac approbation written by the salesman about his own father – as well as a painfully plain account of the shamed, embarrassed homeward journey of the poet and father, plus, like belt and braces, a damning, mock-reluctant clarification:

> But if you still insist on resonance –
> I'd swing for him, and every other cunt
> happy to let my father know his station,
> which probably includes yourself. To be blunt.[19]

This seems unlikely to slip down as easily as the Bakhtinian critic might appear to suggest. Paterson himself elaborated on the matter in an interview. The poem, he says,

> was intended as a deliberate inversion of the current practice of inviting the audience to 'share' the experience; I'm terrified some well-heeled wee bugger will come up to me afterwards and tell me how much he enjoyed it. I think there are some grudges that have to be renewed annually: poetry is a good way of making palatable things that should

> remain indigestible, making certain kinds of crime easier for both the perpetrator and the victim to live with. There are a lot of sub-Harrison types who see their poetry as lending dignity to the working-class experience, as commemorating it in the proper fashion, when what they're really dealing with is their own embarrassment with their social origins, and their awkwardness in using the language of their superiors. It's depressing to see the working classes patronise *themselves* in this way. But I do worry about talking too openly about this sort of thing –[20]

The 'grudge' described many years ago by Douglas Dunn needs to be renewed as well as nursed, then. But while Paterson accounts honestly for his masonic, secretive inclination about this material, his view can sound like a counsel of despair: steer clear of this, he seems to say, or you will be at risk of definition. His remarks seem to regret the scalding honesty of his own poem – which anyway cannot be un-written, but whose inviolability he doubts in retrospect. In the larger context of the interview he can also be seen to imply the fusion of race and class in his own understanding. His practice in the remainder of his work to date can be seen in the light of Douglas Dunn's advice in 'The Come-On': 'Our honesty is cunning./ We will beat them with decorum, with manners,/ As sly as language is.'[21] (Though it might be pointed out that to the English, when the Scots are not ignorant they can be open to the compensating accusation of being 'sly' – a word which can hardly be used approvingly in England – and too clever by half: it is hard to win against a system whose function is not understanding but exclusion and which feels no *need* to understand.) Paterson could be seen as a perfect pupil of this teaching: the formal accomplishment of his work, where the influence of the mandarin Muldoon is married with a solid-bodied rendering of objects, is emphasised to the point where it becomes an important part of the subject. But what he does *not* write will also exert an effect on his poems.

Paterson's position might seem the inevitable result of a certain kind of sophistication, but we should also consider the very different approach of his contemporary Kathleen Jamie (born 1963), whose work in *The Queen of Sheba* (1994)[22] and since is becoming a poetry of the Condition of Scotland in a much more open and decisive fashion than Paterson might think possible (or desirable). In 'Forget It', Jamie shows that the corollary of cunning silence may be the internalisation of shame, the abolition of history and, in a sense, of the self:

> *We done the slums today!*
> I bawled from the glass
> front door she'd long desired.
> *What for?* bangs the oven shut.
> *Some history's better forgot.*[23]

Such a view, while painfully understandable, assists in the psychological relegation of the history of the conquered to folktales and allegations, the kind of thing which in the neighbouring context of Ulster is bundled under something called 'religion', and is *therefore* a subject – an English speaker implies – in which there is no sense or truth to be discerned. Jamie demurs:

...but this is a past
not yet done; else how come
our parents slam shut; deny
like criminals: *I can't remember, cannae*
mind, then turn at bay: *Why?*

who wants to know? stories
spoke through the mouths
of closes; who cares
who trudged those worn stairs,
or daily ran down the very helix
of her genes, to play
in now rubbled back greens?
What happened about my grandad? Why
did Agnes go? How come
you don't know

that stories are balm,
ease their own pain, contain
a beginning, a middle –
and ours is a long driech
now demolished street...[24]

What is arresting in Jamie is this directness. Here, as in 'Mr and Mrs Scotland are Dead', 'Song of Sunday' and 'The Graduates',[25] Jamie demonstrates that it is the charge of feeling which animates the themes of history and identity – feeling, that is, which is sometimes suborned in order to relegate 'Celtic awareness' to picturesque sentimentality. Her response is a clarifying lyric abrasiveness. She is not alone in these concerns, but brings them to fruition. In 'Glasgow 1956' Gerald Mangan (born 1951) evokes a state of permanent desolation, a determining historical unconscious, from a photograph: 'A grey posy in her hands,/ the bride stands smiling there / for decades, waiting for the click.'[26] Liz Lochhead (born 1947) in the richly dialogic 'The Bargain' turns over a personal dilemma in a Glasgow market at 'packing up time/ with the dark coming early/ and as cold as the river' and finds history there too, in such a way as to make us sympathise with Jamie's tight-lipped adults: 'I wish we could either mend things/ Or learn to throw them away.'[27]

It is a permissible contradiction for the reader both to feel the truth of this weariness and to wonder where a convincingly renewed and enlarged dispensation, a new tense in which to read history, might be found. The classic Scottish theme of the double, the divided self, might be seen recurring at the level of the nation's poetry, for alongside a poetry of resistance, of chill exposure to the political elements, the comic, celebratory and utopian modes can also be seen to flourish, for instance in the work of Crawford and Herbert. This can take the form of urban pastoral, as in Crawford's 'The Glasgow Herald':

> ...At Dalmarnock Power Station the sky enlarged
> Over and over, above towerblocks, beyond the Campsies
> Brushed by works hooters, the lyric blasts of a train.[28]

It can produce apparently affectionate satires, in a baroque revisionist form, like 'Alba Einstein': 'When proof of Einstein's Glaswegian birth / First hit the media everything else was dropped.'[29] The project can also take up the challenge of an affirmation that seems in one way more traditional, while occupying the utopian space of the imagination, as Herbert does in 'Dingle Dell':

> There is no passport to this country,
> it exists as a quality of the language.[30]

Like Crawford, but as it were more emphatically, Herbert writes in both Scots and English. This does not seem to present him with the anxieties experienced by Gaelic-speaking poets such as Iain Crichton Smith (or, in a parallel case, the Irish poet Michael Hartnett). Herbert reads the protean, borderless, promiscuous character of language as a power. In doing so he discards the antiquarian notions of propriety and singularity which have driven his Scots-language foes, the 'style-sheeters'. In their place he unleashes an appetite (his poetry is linguistically gluttonous) for the possibilities of language both in the impure state he finds it in and in the further combinations he can discover for it. In doing this, he proposes in a remark which echoes MacDiarmid, it can be shown that 'Scots is a language capable of doing more than English, capable of doing something different from English that criticises and, ultimately, extends English. That is the spirit in which I write Scots poetry.'[31] Part of the 'something different' may be a vestigial but undimmed apprehension of mystery, felt both as a mental climate and in landscape – something captured in Dunn's description of MacDiarmid's 'The Eemis Stane',[32] of which he writes: 'It is the poem's mysteriousness that is exact, not its meaning.'[33] The spirit of Herbert's own comic-sinister 'The Third Corbie'[34] is in a (circuitous) line of descent from MacDiarmid. In English poetry this capacity has retired almost beyond the margins but in Scotland it makes itself felt as a kind of unstated positive, not only in Herbert, but intermittently in Dunn, Paterson, Jamie and especially in John Burnside. Yet whatever its attractions, it is unavoidably the presence of Scots language, rather than the subject matter, which provokes antipathy among some English readers, who simply dislike reading Scots, and whose objections anticipate negatively the critical challenge Herbert hopes to extend, and which seems offered by the subversive anachronism of lines such as these, from 'The Landfish':

> Ut wiz a muckil boattul
> in whilk a man wiz jammd
> aa bowsie i thi bowfarts wi
> fleesh lyk lubbertie,
> lour-shouthirt wi a lurkit fiss
> crammd i thi neck,
> anely'iz hair free-flarin til
> thi waatir's geck.[35]

If proof were needed, the fact that Herbert's concerns are not themselves simply another kind of bone-sniffing antiquarianism is indicated by the severity of the response of Don Paterson, Herbert's fellow Dundonian. Paterson protests too much:

> The top-down approach that literary Scots adopts alienates more people than it wins over; it's an entirely separate, hieratic diction, one that means absolutely nothing to the vast majority of the population...until we can talk Scots among ourselves I don't see how we can write in it. The trouble is you're still dealing with an essentially rural vocabulary and certain kind of linguistic perversity manifests itself, mainly in the form of post-MacDiarmid lexomania, when you try to bend it to accommodate more sophisticated concerns or abstractions. for which it's ill-suited...I'm just glad that [Herbert] seems to be publishing more stuff in English, as about a thousand times more people will be able to recognise how good he is.[36]

To which one might respond that the evidence of Herbert's poems shows the life, the salty power and flexibility of his Scots – synthetic, rural, or plain invented – which in turn begs questions about the appetites and inclinations of the allegedly excluded audience. It seems unlikely that this debate can die off into mere archival handbagging, because the imaginations which conduct the debate are large and vigorous and their mutual concern has more to do with poetry than with being proved right, and with a response to history rather than the conclusions of the seminar. Out of and alongside such arguments, which are those of democrats rather than reactionary nationalists of the English sort, a multi-vocal nation makes a memorable contemporary poetry. England could do with such clarifying problems.

Afterword: *In Search of the Audience*

Asked to comment on 'the current situation' of poetry, the critic might well feel able to say that there is a good deal of interesting work and some of real distinction appearing. I hope this book will have recommended some of it to new readers and encouraged experienced readers to look again. But if the 'situation' also refers to poetry in relation to audience, it becomes much harder to speak with confidence. Twenty years ago, a book like this might not have seemed the place to deal with the matter at all. But at present that would not seem an entirely responsible reaction, since, like it or not, the idea of the audience must loom fairly large in the thinking of most of those concerned with poetry, given the energy which in recent years has gone into trying to identify and expand the poetic constituency. Could Adrian Mitchell still make his famous claim that 'Most people ignore poetry/ because/ most poetry ignores people'?[1]

Two of the most prominent initiatives have been National Poetry Day and the New Generation Poets promotion, which have certainly generated a good deal of publicity. Whether these efforts or the greater attention paid to poetry in the media have claimed new readers for poetry is hard to say.[2] Looking elsewhere, there is plenty of evidence that, partly as a result of the National Curriculum, there is more concern with poetry in schools at present than previously, though experience suggests that this is likely to be as much the product of externally imposed dogma as of real enthusiasm. Certainly the poetry shelves of bookshops seem generously stocked with anthologies and collections. But there are more frankly contradictory signs as well. In a recent consultative paper on poetry, the Arts Council included a summary of the responses of the public to enquiries about 'the image of poetry'. The contents hold few surprises:

> The general public has a problem with the image of poetry. It was often perceived as out-of-touch, gloomy, irrelevant, effeminate, high-brow and elitist. However, further exploration of such perceptions led to a broadening of the definition of poetry. These broader definitions included verses in greetings cards, rap, music lyrics and the like. Such expanded definitions led people to be more supportive of poetry generally.
>
> The poetry constituency's image of poetry is at odds with that of the general public. The poetry world concentrates primarily, though not exclusively, on contemporary poetry and attributes the increase in poetry book sales, attendance at readings and interest in the art form to this. In contrast, those without an interest in poetry perceived it as consisting of old fashioned, pre-twentieth century work.

> Amongst the general public, contemporary poetry had an even more negative image. On first reflection it was commonly perceived as inaccessible, complex and lacking rhyme and rhythm.[3]

One notes grimly the implied use of the word 'complex' as a criticism, and not for the first time the comment that comes to mind is from Randall Jarrell, who had the whole of the modern period in view:

> Since most people know only about the modern poet that he is *obscure* – i.e. that he is *difficult*, i.e. that he is *neglected* – they naturally make a causal connection between the two meanings of the word, and decide that he is unread because he is difficult. Some of the time this is true; some of the time the reverse is true: the poet seems difficult *because* he is not read, *because* the reader is not accustomed to reading his or any other poetry...If we were in the habit of reading poets their obscurity would not matter; and, once we are out of the habit, their clarity does not help.[4]

Jarrell is careful to point out that this response (or lack of one) doesn't exist in isolation, but is part of modernity as a whole. And it is clear that in our own immediate situation contemporary poetry is not alone in occupying a vague state of public disfavour. Other art forms might well be criticised in this way, and so, with slight adjustments, could science, the law and education. Objection thus encompasses several of the bastions of the Them by whom We are done to from cradle to grave. Yet while there may be some consolation to be had from keeping such company (and the picture itself is nothing new), it is hard not to feel disquiet about the situation of poetry in particular, made as it from the common property of language.

There are those who would argue that poetry is fated – and even fortunate – to remain the preoccupation of a few practitioners and committed readers. Others may be tempted by this position and yet feel that an opportunity is going to waste. Who would actually refuse the possibility of poetry becoming part of the normal cultural experience of the many? Sceptical by training, armed against disappointment, some poets find this an ideal on whose behalf they are prepared to act.

The pursuit of an audience has meant that poetry has had to get used to going out in public in the evenings more often. Poetry readings and poetry-as-performance are by no means novel, though their advocates can sometimes seem unaware of the tradition in which they stand. What is relatively new, however, is the greater degree of organisation and publicity involved, resulting, for example, in nationwide tours and identifiably branded series of events. At the same time, many poets have had to give thought to how best to deliver their work to an audience. There have been benefits in this area: the all-too-frequent experience at poetry readings of yore, held for instance in university lecture theatres, where the somnambulant addressed the catatonic in a religiose torment devised in the interests of 'culture', is certainly rarer now. There are a number of popular performers, such as Roger McGough, Liz Lochhead and Ian McMillan. Perhaps most significant is the rich vein of Black writing whose exponents come into their own in the context of performance, whose poetic roots lie in the spoken at least as much as in the written word, and in song as much as speech. These poets have made the poetry reading a theatrical, celebratory event – witness the popularity of performance poets such as John Agard, Grace Nichols, Linton Kwesi Johnson, Jackie Kay and Benjamin Zephaniah. It is notable that there is a dimension of social and political comment and criticism in these writers' work which makes their live performances into acts of solidarity with audiences for whom the message is often a good deal more urgent than the medium. It is perhaps partly for this reason that the performers tend to somewhat overshadow poets whose work depends on being read on the page, such as Fred D'Aguiar and David Dabydeen (though clearly this is not D'Aguiar's own view of the matter: see his recent review article on Linton Kwesi Johnson).[5] D'Aguiar's work, for instance, is at times thematically very knotty and formally ambitious. 'The Kitchen Bitch', the long narrative poem from his second collection, *Airy Hall* (1989),[6] uses the theme of a journey to the interior (of D'Aguiar's native Guyana) as a means of dealing with politics, power and, implicitly, the workings of the imagination. Worried by its flaws, one none the less admires its readiness for risk. D'Aguiar necessarily situates himself in relation to the modernist fiction of Conrad, and also to his fellow countryman, the novelist Wilson Harris, whose Guyana Quartet exemplifies the kind of difficult, ambitious writing compared with which much performance work can seem like a painless alternative. It is notable that in recent years D'Aguiar himself has devoted much of his energy to prose fiction. Perhaps he finds the medium more amenable than poetry to structural complexity; but perhaps too he finds the climate of reception for prose fiction more hospitable to his imaginative scope.

In seeking an audience, does poetry itself risk not simply change but dilution? The climate seems to favour poems which court popularity by tailoring the work to the market, dealing in crowd-pleasing effects at the expense of more serious artistry. In the seminar room or at the conference such considerations may seem irrelevant: the scholar is always more likely to be drawn to Roy Fisher than Attila the Stockbroker. Yet the larger context in which poetry is produced and received may be changing anyway. The Arts Council's consultative document states: 'Poetry is not a homogeneous entity but a broad continuum ranging from easily understood verse to complex, highly literate works. As such, not all poetry is universally accessible but responses from people outside the poetry world suggested that they would endorse more poetry being presented in a way which made it more easily accessible.'[7] There are two uses of the word 'accessible' in this passage: the first refers to comprehensibility and the second to availability. Poetry will always resist at the margins, and will produce the occasional Heaney or Hughes by whom its marginality is both denied and confirmed. The representative poets will, in Dana Gioia's phrase, serve as 'priests in a town of agnostics'.[8] But it is not hard to see how the vast bulk of what is made available could become the exclusive sphere of what is readily and even immediately comprehensible, with the resulting identification of simplicity (and popularity) with value. Jarrell again: '[The] common reader knows what he likes, but is uncomfortable when other people do not read it or do not like it: for what people read and like is good: that is what good means.'[9] There is undeniably an appetite for greater access and accessibility among many in the poetry world – some poets themselves, promoters, reviewers, cultural hucksters and arts administrators – but it is not clear whether the possible consequences are fully appreciated. A recent article by Mike Higgins from *The Independent* follows the logic of accessibility to its conclusion:

> Over the last ten years, publicists have laboured to imbue poetry with 'relevance'. Mostly, this makeover treatment involved perky day-glo invitations – 'Give yourself a kick up the trochees' – to listen to dungareed doggerel in remote community centres. Nevertheless, the 1990s finds more poetry out in the hurly burly of clubs and pubs. Moreover, one concept looks to have struck a chord with poetry fans and newcomers alike: the slam.
>
> Originating in Chicago in the mid-Eighties, the slam takes the form of competitive performance poetry and seeks to debunk the elitist image of the traditional recital. This democratic attitude is most apparent in the judging process, which is left to the audience: the louder the cheer, the better the performance. 'The idea behind the performance is that it's entertaining,' says Bristol slam organiser Claire Williamson. 'Since we started in 1994, though, there's been more and more emphasis on presentation – an average poem can be performed brilliantly and vice versa.'[10]

Though the journalist's tongue may be firmly in cheek, poems seems almost surplus to requirements in the setting he describes.

The key term is 'entertaining' – the curse-word of residual Leavisites everywhere. More seriously, it is a term which can encompass – and acknowledge – only a small fraction of the experience which poetry can offer; at the same time, its tendency is to deny what lies outside its limits. "Entertainment" has become the core of the culture. It is the homogenising force which drives Radio 3 down-market and makes television drama exclusively realist in style, while also extruding Cilla Black and Bruce Forsyth. Its function is to denature whatever it touches. Its pressure can even be felt in education, in the disguise of 'relevance'. In considering that word, Christopher Middleton cogently sets out consequences applicable to audience (and the poet) as well as to the student in the classroom:

> There is much to be said for the efforts of Humanities teachers who try to make apparently remote matters 'relevant'. But here there is a serious problem. By reducing the otherness of other things...for the sake of relevance, the teacher merely indulges existing egomorphic 'behavioral patterns'. The object of study, once its otherness is denied or ignored, is merely cut to fit the student's condition of mind, his existing frame of reference. No real intellectual transformation, no real structuring refinement of sensibility, no cultivation of instinct, can occur without exertion towards the other...If objects of study are no longer tended for what they are, as intrinsically interesting structures of meaning that can be shared, then they cease to radiate their interior life. The norms of teacher and student remain untransformed and eclipse all features other than those which suit the criteria offered by those norms. If those criteria are such as fail to identify what they cannot measure, and so fail to achieve intelligent contact with the *other reality*, then those criteria are wrong for the educational process.[11]

This seems to me a decisive argument, but I have to acknowledge that it involves a conviction which is probably not popular at present, given the confusion of homogeneity with democracy. It is the conviction that art has something to offer the audience – enlightenment, a sense of wonder, a clarification of feeling, an extension to the map of experience – of which the audience is not already in complete possession. The distinction between art and entertainment is to be sought in this area. Our concern or lack of concern with that distinction will govern our cultural health, not only in the microcosm of poetry but far beyond it.

NOTES

Preface (pp.9-12)

1. Montaigne, 'On Experience', *Essays,* translated by J.M. Cohen (Penguin, Harmondsworth, 1993), p.347.

Introduction: *Who's in Charge Here? (pp.13-20)*

1. Roland Barthes, *Mythologies*, translated by Annette Lavers (Jonathan Cape, London, 1972; Paladin, St Albans, 1973), pp.29-31.
2. Terence Hawkes quoted in James Wood, 'Second Front: to see or not to see', *Guardian* (13 October 1994).
3. Blake Morrison and Andrew Motion (eds.), *The Penguin Book of Contemporary British Poetry*, Introduction p.17, on Dunn and Harrison: 'both writers insist on the strength and value of these alternative traditions, which are provincial and working-class'. The term 'provincial' is never merely descriptive.
4. Andrew Motion, 'The Margin Spread Thickly', *Observer* (16 May 1993).
5. Anthony Thwaite, 'On Consulting Contemporary Poets of the English Language', *Poems 1953-88* (Hutchinson, London, 1989), pp.130-32.

1. Philip Larkin: *If Home Existed (pp.23-33)*

All references to the poetry of Philip Larkin are to *Collected Poems* (hereafter *CP*), edited by Anthony Thwaite (Faber, London, 1988).

1. A. Alvarez (ed.), 'Introduction: The New Poetry or Beyond the Gentility Principle', *The New Poetry* (Penguin, Harmondsworth, revised edition, 1966), pp.29-32.
2. Seamus Heaney, 'Englands of the Mind', *Preoccupations* (Faber, London, 1980), p.169.
3. Philip Larkin, 'Here', *CP,* pp.136-37.
4. Larkin, 'MCMXIV', *CP,* pp.127-28.
5. 'Going, Going', *CP,* pp.189-90.
6. George Orwell, *The Lion and the Unicorn* (Penguin, London, 1982), p.123.
7. David Gervais, *Literary Englands: Versions of 'Englishness' in Modern Writing* (Cambridge University Press, 1993), p.178.
8. Kingsley Amis, 'Lone Voices', *Encounter* (July 1960).
9. John Betjeman, 'In Westminster Abbey', *John Betjeman's Collected Poems* (John Murray, London, 1958), pp. 84-85.
10. James Booth, *Philip Larkin: Writer* (Harvester Wheatsheaf, Hemel Hempstead, 1992), pp.71-72.
11. Larkin, 'The Blending of Betjeman', *Required Writing* (Faber, London, 1983), p.133.
12. *Required Writing*, p.130.
13. 'Essential Beauty', *CP,* pp.144-45.

14. 'Afternoons', *CP*, p.121.
15. Tom Paulin, 'She Did Not Change: Philip Larkin', *Minotaur: Poetry and the Nation State* (Faber, London, 1992), pp.233-34.
16. Orwell, *1984* (Penguin, Harmondsworth, 1954), p.65.
17. *Coming up For Air* (Penguin, Harmondsworth, 1962), p.180.
18. Robert Pinsky, 'Larkin in Prose', *Poetry and the World* (Ecco Press, New York, 1988), p.28
19. Larkin, 'Ambulances', *CP*, pp.132-33.
20. 'The Building', *CP*, pp.191-93.
21. 'The Old Fools', *CP*, pp.196-97.
22. Orwell, *The Lion and the Unicorn* (Penguin, London, 1982), p.54.
23. Larkin, 'Here', *CP*, pp.144-45.
24. 'The Importance of Elsewhere', *CP*, pp.144-45.
25. 'To the Sea', 'Livings', 'The Building', 'The Old Fools', 'Show Saturday' and 'Aubade', *CP*, respectively pp.173, 186, 191, 196, 199, 208.
26. 'To the Sea', *CP*, p.173.
27. 'Show Saturday', *CP*, p.199.
28. Eric Homberger, *The Art of the Real* (Dent, London, 1977), p.36.
29. Larkin, 'Going, Going', *CP*, pp.189-90.
30. Orwell, *The Lion and the Unicorn*, p.36.
31. Larkin, 'Friday Night in the Royal Station Hotel', *CP*, p.199.
32. Douglas Dunn, 'Nights of Sirius', *The Happier Life* (Faber, London, 1972, p.15), reprinted in *Selected Poems 1964-1983* (Faber, London, 1986), p.39.
33. W.H. Auden, 'August for the people and their favourite islands…', *The English Auden*, edited by Edward Mendelson (Faber, London, 1977), p.155.
34. Andrew Swarbrick, *Out of Reach: The Poetry of Philip Larkin* (Macmillan, London, 1995), p.132.
35. Larkin, 'Waiting for breakfast, while she brushed her hair', *CP*, p.20.
36. Larkin in the *Listener*, 17 August 1972, cited in *An Enormous Yes* edited by Harry Chambers (Peterloo, Calstock, 1986).
37. 'The Winter Palace', *CP*, p.211.
38. 'Forget What Did', *CP*, p.184.
39. 'Solar', *CP*, p.159.
40. 'Livings II', *CP*, p.186.
41. Thom Gunn, 'Sunlight', *Collected Poems* (Faber, London, 1993), pp.223-24
42. Larkin, 'High Windows', *CP*, p.165.
43. W.B. Yeats, 'Politics', *Last Poems* (1936-1939), *Collected Poems of W.B. Yeats* (Macmillan, London, 1950), pp.392-93.
44. Booth, *Philip Larkin: Writer*, p.168.
45. Swarbrick, *Out of Reach*, p.136.
46. John Clare, 'I Am', *ll.*13-18.
47. Auden, 'Plains', *Collected Poems,* edited by Edward Mendelson (revised edition, Faber, London, 1991), p.565.

2. Ted Hughes: *Time Not History* *(pp.34-40)*

1. Ted Hughes, *The Hawk in the Rain* (Faber, London, 1957).
2. Hughes, *Lupercal* (Faber, London, (1960) 1970), p.15.
3. Robert Lowell, *Life Studies* (Faber, London, (1956) 1972), p.15.
4. David Lodge, *Language of Fiction* (Routledge, 2nd edition, 1984), p.249.
5. Kingsley Amis, *Lucky Jim* (Penguin, Harmondsworth, 1961), p.14.
6. Ian Hamilton, *A Poetry Chronicle* (Faber, London, 1973), p.165.
7. A. Alvarez, *Beyond All This Fiddle* (1968); *The Savage God* (1971).
8. Donald Davie, *Encounter* (November 1956), p.70.
9. Amis, *Socialism and the Intellectuals* (Fabian Tract No.304, Fabian Society, London, 1957).
10. Zbigniew Herbert, 'To the Hungarians', *Selected Poems*, translated by John and Bogdana Carpenter (Oxford University Press, 1977), p.28.
11. Tom Paulin, 'Laureate of the Free Market', *Minotaur* (Faber, London, 1992), p.268.
12. Hughes, *Gaudete* (Faber, London, 1970), p.9.
13. *Wodwo* (Faber, London, 1967), p.9.
14. Paulin, 'Laureate of the Free Market', *Minotaur,* p.254.
15. Paulin, p.252.
16. Paulin, p.260.
17. Hughes, *Rain-Charm for the Duchy* (Faber, London, 1992).
18. *Shakespeare and the Goddess of Complete Being* (Faber, London, 1992).
19. *Rain-Charm,* p.60.
20. *Rain-Charm,* p.60.
21. *Rain-Charm,* p.58.
22. *Rain-Charm,* p.29.
23. T. S. Eliot, 'The Metaphysical Poets', *Selected Essays* (Faber, London, 1951), p.288.
24. Hughes, *Rain-Charm,* p.33.
25. *Rain-Charm,* p.54.
26. *Rain-Charm,* p.24.
27. Patrick Kavanagh, 'Epic', *Selected Poems*, edited by Antoinette Quinn (Penguin, London, 1996), pp.101-02.

3. Geoffrey Hill: *The England Where Nobody Lives* *(pp.41-48)*

Unless otherwise indicated, all references to the poetry of Geoffrey Hill are to *Collected Poems*, hereafter *CP* (Penguin, London, 1985).

1. John Haffenden, *Viewpoints: Poets in Conversation* (Faber, London, 1981), p. 93.
2. Thomas Carlyle, from *Past and Present* in *Selected Writings* edited by Alan Shelston (Penguin, Harmondsworth, 1986), p.266.
3. A.S. Byatt, *The Virgin in the Garden* (Vintage, London, 1994).
4. Byatt, *The Virgin*, pp.319-20.
5. D.J. Taylor, *After the War: The Novel and England since 1945* (Flamingo, London, 1994), p.92.

6. Tom Paulin, 'A Visionary Nationalist: Geoffrey Hill', *Minotaur: Poetry and the Nation State* (Faber, London, 1992), p.281.
7. Byatt, *The Virgin*, pp.143-44.
8. Paulin, 'A Visionary Nationalist: Geoffrey Hill', *Minotaur*, p.282.
9. T.S. Eliot, 'The Metaphysical Poets', *Selected Essays* (Faber, London, 1951), p.288.
10. Geoffrey Hill, 'Funeral Music' 2, *CP*, p.71.
11. Hill, 'Funeral Music' 3, *CP*, p.71.
12. '"I in Another Place", Homage to Keith Douglas', *Stand*, 6 no.4 (1964), pp.6-13.
13. Keith Douglas, 'How to Kill', *Complete Poems*, edited by Desmond Graham (Oxford University Press, 1987), p.112.
14. Douglas, *Alamein to Zem Zem* (Penguin, Harmondsworth, 1969), p.207.
15. Neil Corcoran, *English Poetry Since 1940* (Longman, Harlow, 1993), p.125.
16. Hill, 'Our Word Is Our Bond', *The Lords of Limit* (André Deutsch, London, 1984), p.155.
17. John Bayley, 'The Tongue's Satisfactions', *Agenda*, 30 nos.1-2 (Spring/Summer 1992), p.11.
18. Hill, 'Funeral Music' 4, *CP*, p.73.
19. Corcoran, *English Poetry*, p.125.
20. Hill, *Collected Poems*, p.199.
21. Corcoran, *English Poetry*, p.125.
22. Clive Wilmer, 'An Art of Recovery', *Agenda*, 30 nos.1-2 (Spring/Summer 1992), p.141.
23. Hill, 'The Stone Man', from 'Soliloquies', *King Log*, *CP*, p.85.
24. Andrew Waterman, 'The Poetry of Geoffrey Hill', *British Poetry since 1970: a Critical Survey*, ed. Peter Jones and Michael Schmidt (Carcanet, Manchester, 1980), p.87.
25. Waterman, *British Poetry*, p.88.
26. Hill, 'Old Poet with Distant Admirers', from 'Soliloquies', *King Log*, *CP*, p.86.
27. Waterman, *British Poetry since 1970*, p.85.
28. Waterman, *British Poetry since 1970*, p.94.
29. Hill, v, 'The Crowning of Offa', *Mercian Hymns*, *CP*, p.109.
30. vii, 'The Kingdom of Offa', *Mercian Hymns*, *CP*, p.111.
31. Waterman, *British Poetry*, p.94.

4. Tony Harrison: *Showing the Working* *(pp.51-64)*

Unless otherwise indicated, all references to the poetry of Tony Harrison are to *Selected Poems*, hereafter *SP* (Penguin, London, revised edition 1987).

1. Introduction by Rosemary Burton to *Tony Harrison*, edited by Neil Astley (Bloodaxe, Newcastle upon Tyne, 1991), p.14.
2. *A Language for Life* – Report of the Committee of Inquiry appointed by the Secretary of State for Education and Science under the Chairmanship of Sir Allan Bullock FBA (HMSO, London, 1975).

3. Unless otherwise indicated, Harrison, 'Them & [uz]', *SP*, p. 122.
4. 'Oh, Moon of Mahagonny!', *SP*, pp.201-2.
5. Stephen Spender, 'Changeling', *Tony Harrison,* edited by Neil Astley (Bloodaxe, Newcastle upon Tyne, 1991), p.223.
6. Harrison, 'Illuminations,' II, *SP*, p.147.
7. Blake Morrison, 'The Filial Art', *Tony Harrison*, p.57.
8. Morrison, 'Labouring', *Tony Harrison*, p.219.
9. Harrison, 'Lines to My Grandfathers, II', *SP*, p.178.
10. Morrison, 'Labouring', *Tony Harrison*, pp.219-20.
11. Harrison, edited by Carol Rutter, *Permanently Bard: Selected Poetry* (Bloodaxe, Newcastle upon Tyne, 1995), p.29.
12. 'Wordlists' I, *SP*, p.117.
13. 'Me Tarzan', *SP*, p.116.
14. 'Thomas Campey and the Copernican System', *SP*, p.13.
15. Rutter (ed.), *Permanently Bard*, p.126.
16. Harrison, 'Wordlists' III, *SP*, p.119.
17. 'Them & [uz]' I, *SP*, p.122.
18. Stephen Spender, *Tony Harrison* edited by Neil Astley, p.222.
19. Luke Spencer, *The Poetry of Tony Harrison* (Harvester/Wheatsheaf, Hemel Hempstead, 1994), p.16.
20. Harrison, 'Me Tarzan', *SP*, p.116.
21. 'On Not Being Milton', *SP*, p.112.
22. 'The Rhubarbarians', *SP*, p.113.
23. 'The Queen's English', *SP*, p.136.
24. 'Bookends' II, *SP*, p.127.
25. 'Continuous', *SP*, p.143.
26. Rick Rylance, 'On Not Being Milton', *Tony Harrison*, p.116.
27. Harrison, *SP*, p.155.
28. Spender, *Tony Harrison* edited by Neil Astley, p.224.
29. Harrison, 'Marked with D.', *SP*, p.128.
30. Richard Hoggart, *The Uses of Literacy* (Penguin, Harmondsworth, 1957), pp.87-94.
31. Harrison, 'The Nuptial Torches', *SP*, p.60.
32. Jeffrey Wainwright, '1815', *Selected Poems* (Carcanet, Manchester, 1985), p.40.
33. Harrison, 'On Not Being Milton', *SP*, p.112.
34. Anthony Thwaite, *Poetry Today: A Critical Guide to British Poetry 1960-1984* (Longman, London, 1985), p.120.
35. Harrison, 'Them & [uz]' II, *SP*, p.123.
36. 'A Cold Coming', *The Gaze of the Gorgon* (Bloodaxe, Newcastle upon Tyne, 1992), pp.48-54.
37. Douglas Dunn, 'New Light on Terry Street', *Selected Poems*, (Faber, London, 1986), p.4.
38. Spencer, *The Poetry of Tony Harrison,* pp.81-82.
39. 'Classics Society', SP, p.120.
40. Harrison, *v.*, *SP*, p.236.
41. Spencer, *The Poetry of Tony Harrison*, p.92.

42. George Saintsbury, *A History of English Prosody from the Twelfth Century to the Present Day* (3 vols, London, 1906-10), vol.3, p.32, quoted in Derek Attridge *The Rhythms of English Poetry* (Longman, Harlow, 1982), p.150.
43. Spencer, *The Poetry of Tony Harrison*, p.92.
44. Harrison, *v.*, *SP*, p.236.
45. *v.*, *SP*, p.236.
46. James Shirley, 'The Glories of Our Blood and State', *The Penguin Book of Renaissance Verse*, edited by H.R. Woudhuysen (Penguin, London, 1993), p.663.
47. Roger McGough, 'Streemin', *In the Glassroom* (Cape, London, 1976), p.9.
48. Thomas Gray, 'Elegy Written in a Country Churchyard', *ll.*15-16.
49. Harrison, *v*, *SP*, p.236.
50. *v*, *SP*, p.237.
51. Terry Eagleton, 'Antagonisms: *v*', *Tony Harrison*, edited by Neil Astley, p.350.
52. Harrison, *v.*, *SP*, p.249.
53. *v.*, *SP*, p.246.
54. *v.*, *SP*, p.242.
55. Larkin, 'Church Going', *Collected Poems,* edited by Anthony Thwaite (Faber, London, 1988), p.97.

5. Douglas Dunn: *Ideology and Pastoral* *(pp.65-80)*

1. Douglas Dunn, 'Broughty Ferry', *Northlight* (Faber, London, 1988), p.24.
2. Dunn, 'Dimensions of the Sentient' (interview) in *Poem, Purpose and Place: Shaping Identity in Contemporary Scottish Verse* (Polygon, Edinburgh, 1992), p.184
3. 'Syndrome', *The Happier Life* (Faber, London, 1972), p.33.
4. Dunn, 'Preserve and Renovate', *Dante's Drum-kit* (Faber, London, 1993), p.95.
5. Andrew Marvell, 'An Horatian Ode upon Cromwell's Return from Ireland', *l.*32.
6. Dunn, 'Social Realism and Romantic Sleep', quoted by Anthony Thwaite in 'Allegiance to the Clyde' in the *Times Literary Supplement* (2 October 1981), p.1125.
7. Sean O'Brien, 'Dunn and Politics' in *Reading Douglas Dunn*, edited by Robert Crawford and David Kinloch (Edinburgh University Press, 1992), p.66-79.
8. Dunn, 'Back and Forth: Auden and Political Poetry', *Critical Survey,* 6 no.3 (1994), pp.325-35.
9. 'Back and Forth', *The Critical Survey*, p.331.
10. Robert Crawford, 'Secret Villager' in *Reading Douglas Dunn*, p.119.
11. Dunn, 'Barbarian Pastorals', *Barbarians* (Faber, London, 1979), pp.13-30.
12. *St Kilda's Parliament* (Faber, London, 1981).

13. W.H. Auden, 'Letter to Lord Byron', *The English Auden*, edited by Edward Mendelson (Faber, London, 1977), p.190.
14. Dave Smith, jacket note on Douglas Dunn, *Selected Poems* (Ecco Press, New York, 1989).
15. Dunn, interview in *The Printer's Devil*, A, 1990, p.30.
16. Interview in *Poem, Purpose and Place*, p.185.
17. *Secret Villages* (Faber, London, 1985).
18. *Ploughman's Share* ('Play for Today', BBC 1, 27 February 1979).
19. *Northlight* (Faber, London, 1988) and *Dante's Drum-kit* (Faber, London, 1993).
20. Blake Morrison and Andrew Motion, Introduction, *The Penguin Book of Contemporary British Poetry* (Penguin, Harmondsworth, 1982), p.17.
21. Dunn, 'Preserve and Renovate', *Dante's Drum-kit*, p.95.
22. Seamus Heaney, 'Digging' and 'Follower', *Death of a Naturalist*, pp.13 and 24-25 respectively.
23. Dunn, 'Horses in a Suburban Field', *Terry Street*, p.43.
24. 'The Garden', *The Happier Life*, pp.11-12.
25. Fontenelle, 'Discours sur la nature de l'églogue' cited in *The New Princeton Encyclopedia of Poetry and Poetics* (Princeton University Press, 1993), p.887.
26. Dunn, 'Saturday', *St Kilda*, p.36.
26. 'Muir's Ledgers', *Northlight*, p.37.
28. 'The Apple Tree', *St Kilda*, p.16.
29. 'Ratatouille', *St Kilda*, p.85.
30. 'The Terry Street Fusiliers', *Terry Street*, p.19.
31. 'The Happier Life', *Happier Life*, p.42.
32. Michael Longley, 'Peace', *Selected Poems* (Penguin, London, 1986), p.169.
33. Dunn, 'Gardeners', *Barbarians*, p.17.
34. 'In the Grounds', *Barbarians*, p.44.
35. 'The Come On', *Barbarians*, p.14.
36. 'Warriors', *Barbarians*, p.44.
37. 'The Dark Crossroads', *Northlight*, p.62.
38. 'The Harp of Renfrewshire', *St Kilda*, p.30.
39. Gerard Winstanley, *The Law of Freedom and Other Writings* edited by Christopher Hill (Penguin, Harmondsworth, 1973), p.77.
40. William Shakespeare, *Richard II*, II.i.60 and *King Lear*, II.iii.18.
41. Dunn, 'Galloway Motor Farm', *St Kilda's Parliament*, p.26.
42. 'An Address on the Destitution of Scotland', *St Kilda*, p.19.
43. W.H. Auden, 'Consider', *CP*, p.61.
44. Dunn, 'The Apple Tree', *St Kilda*, p.16.
45. 'The Happier Life', *Happier*, p.42.
46. 'A Snow Walk', *Northlight*, p.42.
47. Interview, *Printer's Devil*, A, pp.21-22.
48. 'Remembering Lunch', *St Kilda*, p.44.
49. 'Realisms', *Love or Nothing*, p.19.

50. 'Let God Not Abandon Us': On the Poetry of Derek Mahon, *Stone Ferry Review*, 2 (Winter 1978), pp.7-30.
51. Philippe Jaccottet, *Selected Poems*, translated by Derek Mahon (Penguin, London, 1988), p.44.
52. Derek Mahon, 'Matthew V. 29-30', *Poems 1962-1978* (OUP, Oxford, 1979), p.69.
53. Dunn, 'Loch Music', *St Kilda*, p.79.
54. 'Daylight', *Northlight*, p.11.
55. Tony Harrison, 'Them & [uz]' II, *Selected Poems* (Penguin, London, 1987), p.123.
56. Dunn, Interview, *Printer's Devil*, A, p.19.
57. Tom Leonard, 'thi lang-/wij a thi/guhtr' quoted in Robert Crawford, *Identifying Poets: Self and Territory in Twentieth Century Poetry* (Edinburgh University Press, 1993), p.169.
58. Dunn, 'Dressed to Kill', *Dante's Drum-Kit*, pp.129-45.
59. 'Here and There', *Northlight*, p.26.
60. 'Audenesques for 1960', *Dante's Drum-Kit*, pp.89-91.
61. W.H. Auden, 'The Cave of Making', *CP*, p.691.
62. Auden, 'Dichtung und Warheit', *CP*, p.647.
63. Dunn, 'Audenesques for 1960'.
64. Auden, 'XXIV (to Christopher Isherwood)' *The English Auden*, edited by Edward Mendelson (Faber, London, 1977), p.155-57.

6. Ken Smith: *I Am Always Lost in It* *(pp.89-96)*

1. Ken Smith, *Tender to the Queen of Spain* (Bloodaxe, Newcastle upon upon Tyne, 1993), p.38
2. *The Oxford Companion to 20th Century Poetry* edited by Ian Hamilton (Oxford University Press, 1994), p.122.
3. Smith, 'The Botanic Garden Oath', *Terra* (Bloodaxe, Newcastle upon Tyne, 1986), p.66.
4. *The Pity* (Cape, London, 1967).
5. Interview with Sean O'Brien, *Words* (1987).
6. Philip Larkin, 'MCMXIV', *Collected Poems* edited by Anthony Thwaite (Faber, London, 1986), pp.127-28.
7. Smith, 'Family Group', *The Poet Reclining: Selected Poems 1962-80* (Bloodaxe, Newcastle upon Tyne, 1982), p.13.
8. See 'Roads in the North between Two Seas', *Terra*, pp.36-39.
9. 'The Bee Dance' from 'As it Happens', *Wormwood* (Bloodaxe, Newcastle upon Tyne, 1987), p.41.
10. 'Departure's Speech', *Terra*, p.87.
11. *Burned Books* (Bloodaxe, Newcastle upon Tyne, 1981).
12. 'Another Part of His Childhood', *Poet Reclining*, p.50.
13. 'Hawkwood', *Terra*, pp.8-32
14. Smith, *Fox Running* (Rolling Moss Press, London, 1980); the text quoted here is from the revised and extended version in *The Poet Reclining* (1982).
15. 'Fox Running', *Poet Reclining*, p.136.

16. 'Fox Running', *Poet Reclining*, p.165.
17. *Terra*, p.53.
18. 'Mr Mayhew's Visit', *Terra*, p.54.
19. *Terra*, p.55.
20. 'In Silvertown, chasing the dragon', *Terra*, pp.87-89
21. 'The meridian at Greenwich', *Terra*, p.55.
22. 'Wormwood', *Wormwood*, p.13.
23. *Wormwood*, p.48.
24. *The heart, the border* (Bloodaxe, Newcastle upon Tyne, 1990), p.13.

7. Seamus Heaney: *The Space Made by Poetry* *(pp.99-106)*

The following chapter is indebted to Bernard O'Donoghue's remarkable book *Seamus Heaney and the Language of Poetry* (Harvester/Wheatsheaf, Hemel Hempstead, 1994).

1. Philip Larkin, *Required Writing* (Faber, London, 1983); Ted Hughes, *Winter Pollen* (Faber, London, 1994); Thom Gunn, *Shelf-Life* (Faber, London, 1993).
2. Robert Pinsky, *Poetry and the World* (Ecco Press, New York, 1988); Dana Gioia, *Can Poetry Matter* (Graywolf Press, St Paul, 1992).
3. See Michael Parker, *Seamus Heaney: the Making of the Poet* (Macmillan, London, 1993), p.120: 'the Paisleyite *Protestant Telegraph* welcomed "the departure of the well-known papist propagandist" at last heading for "his spiritual home in the popish republic"'.
4. Seamus Heaney, 'The Flight Path', *Spirit Level* (Faber, London, 1996), p.25.
5. Heaney, 'Sounding Auden', *The Government of the Tongue* (Faber, London, 1988), p.120.
6. Randall Jarrell, 'The Age of Criticism', *Poetry and the Age* (Faber, London, [1953] 1996), p.63.
7. 'Mossbawn' in *Preoccupations: Selected Prose 1968-1978* (Faber, London, 1980), p.27.
8. Tony Harrison, 'Blocks', *Permanently Bard* (Bloodaxe, Newcastle upon Tyne, 1995), p.50.
9. W.H. Auden, 'The Watershed', *Collected Poems*, edited by Edward Mendelson (Faber, London, 1991), p.32.
10. Heaney, 'Sounding Auden', *The Government of the Tongue*, p.123.
11. Ted Hughes, 'Myth, Metre, Rhythm', *Winter Pollen: Occasional Prose* (Faber, London, 1994), p.365.
12. Heaney, 'Englands of the Mind', *Preoccupations*, p.150.
13. See 'The Fire i' the Flint', *Preoccupations*, p.81 and (implicitly) 'Sounding Auden', *The Government of the Tongue*, p.109.
14. 'Fireside', *Wintering Out* (Faber, London, 1972), p.76.
15. 'Bogland', *Door into the Dark* (Faber, London, 1969), p.56.
16. John Haffenden, *Viewpoints: Poets in Conversation* (Faber, London, 1981), p.71.
17. Parker, *Seamus Heaney*, p.41.

18. O'Driscoll: See note 3 to chapter 11 on Peter Reading.
19. Introduction to *The Penguin Book of English Pastoral Verse*, edited by John Barrell and John Bull (Allen Lane, London, 1975), quoted in 'In the Country of Convention: English Pastoral Verse', *Preoccupations*, p.174.
20. Anthony Thwaite, *Poetry Today: A Critical Guide to British Poetry 1960-1995* (Longman, Harlow, 1996), p.98.
21. Heaney, *An Open Letter*, Field Day Pamphlet No. 2 (Field Day Theatre Company, Derry, 1983).
22. *The Penguin Book of Contemporary British Poetry*, edited by Blake Morrison and Andrew Motion (Penguin, Harmondsworth, 1982).
23. Heaney, 'Englands of the Mind', *Preoccupations*, p.169.
24. 'The Main of Light', *The Government of the Tongue*, pp.15-22.
25. Heaney, 'The Placeless Heaven: Another Look at Kavanagh', *The Government of the Tongue*, pp.3-14.
26. 'The Fire i' the Flint', *Preoccupations*, pp.79-97.
27. 'The Murmur of Malvern', *The Government of the Tongue*, pp.23-29; 'The Schooner Flight', Derek Walcott, *Collected Poems* (Noonday Press, New York, 1986), p.350.
28. 'Englands of the Mind', *Preoccupations*, p.169.
29. 'The Murmur of Malvern', *The Government of the Tongue*, p.29.
30. 'The Murmur of Malvern', *The Government of the Tongue*, p.23.
31. 'Englands of the Mind', *Preoccupations*, p.48.
32. 'The Redress of Poetry', *The Redress of Poetry* (Faber, London, 1995), p.1.
33. Sir Philip Sidney: see 'An Apology For Poetry', *The Oxford Authors: Sir Philip Sidney*, edited by Katherine Duncan-Jones (Oxford University Press, 1989), pp.215-26.
34. Frost, 'The Figure a Poem Makes', *Modern Poets on Modern Poetry*, edited by James Scully (Fontana, London, 1966), p.55.
35. 'The Government of the Tongue', *The Government of the Tongue*, p.92.

8. Derek Mahon: *The World as Exile* *(pp.97-103)*

Mahon's revisions of poems and titles through successive selections have left some readers marooned unhappily between the versions they know and those they're now offered. Changes of title have in themselves been the object of scholarly study. While the poet is at liberty to take liberties with his own poems, on a more modest basis I have referred to books and versions I have found most useful or interesting.

1. Derek Mahon, 'Entropy', *Lives* (Oxford University Press, 1972), pp.30-31.
2. Mahon, 'The Last of the Fire Kings', *Poems 1962-78* (Oxford University Press, 1979), pp.64-65.
3. John Kerrigan, 'Ulster Ovids', *The Chosen Ground* (Seren, Bridgend, 1992).
4. *The Chosen Ground*, p.259.

5. Mahon, *Poems 1962-78*, p.81 and pp.84-86.
6. *Light Music* (Ulsterman Publications, Belfast, 1977).
7. 'After Cavafy', *Lives*, p.24.
8. 'Gypsies Revisited', *Poems 1962-78*, p.29.
9. 'Ecclesiastes', *Poems 1962-78*, p.3.
10. 'Teaching in Belfast', *Poems 1962-78*, pp.31-32
11. 'The Snow Party', *Poems 1962-78* (Oxford University Press, 1979), pp.63-64.
12. 'A Stone Age Figure Far Below', *Poems 1962-78*, pp.46-47.
13. Seamus Heaney, 'Place and Displacement: Reflections on Some Recent Poetry from Northern Ireland', *Contemporary Irish Poetry*, edited by Elmer Andrews (Macmillan, London, 1992), p.130.
14. Mahon, 'The Sea in Winter', *Poems 1962-78*, p.114.
15. *The Hunt by Night* (Oxford University Press, 1982); *Antarctica* (Gallery Press, Oldcastle, 1985).
16. *The Hudson Letter* (Gallery Press, 1995), p.37.
17. 'A Terminal Ironist: Derek Mahon', *Writing to the Moment: Selected Critical Essays 1980-1996* (Faber, London, 1996), p.84.
18. 'A Mythological Figure', *Poems 1962-78*, p.10.
19. 'The Banished Gods', *Poems 1962-78*, p.78.
20. *Night Crossing* (Oxford University Press, 1968).
21. *Night Crossing*, p.14.
22. *The Hudson Letter*, p.39.
23. *The Hudson Letter*, p.40.
24. *The Hudson Letter*, p.42.
25. *Poems 1962-78*, p.80.
26. *The Hudson Letter*, p.43.
27. 'April on Toronto Island', *Night Crossing*, p.30.

9. Paul Durcan: *Look at it This Way* *(pp.115-21)*

Unless otherwise indicated, all quotations are taken from *A Snail in My Prime: New and Selected Poems* (Harvill, London, 1993).

1. Durcan, 'The Woman with the Keys to Stalin's House', *Snail*, p.140.
2. 'The Repentant Peter', *Snail*, pp.208-09.
3. Brendan Kennelly, *The Book of Judas* (Bloodaxe, Newcastle upon Tyne, 1991), p.11.
4. Durcan, 'The Divorce Referendum, Ireland 1986', *Snail*, p.122.
5. Edna Longley, *The Living Stream* (Bloodaxe, Newcastle upon Tyne, 1994), p.214.
6. Durcan, 'Wife Who Smashed Television Gets Jail', *Snail*, p.22.
7. *Christmas Day* (Harvill, London, 1996), p.40. 'Me and Bobby McGhee' is a country and western song by Kris Kristofferson, containing the lines 'Freedom's just another word for nothin' left to lose./ Nothin' ain't worth nothin' but it's free.'
8. Bernard O'Donoghue, *The Oxford Companion to Twentieth Century Poetry*, edited by Ian Hamilton (Oxford University Press, 1994), p.140.

9. Durcan, 'Poem Not Beginning with a Line by Pindar', *Snail*, p.196.
10. Longley, *The Living Stream*, p.215.
11. Durcan, 'Fjord', *Snail*, p.186.
12. R.F. Foster, *Modern Ireland 1600-1972* (Penguin, London, 1989), p.563.
13. Durcan, 'Teresa's Bar', 'Sister Agnes Writes to Her Beloved Mother', 'The Woman Who Keeps Her Breasts in the Back Garden' and 'Hommage à Cézanne', all *Snail*, pp.15, 42, 76 and 160 respectively.
14. Longley, *The Living Stream*, p.216.
15. Durcan, 'Divorce Referendum, Ireland 1986', *Snail*, p.122.
16. Longley, *The Living Stream*, p.216.
17. Durcan, 'Hymn to a Broken Marriage', *Snail*, p.101.
18. 'The Pièta's Over', *Snail*, p.111.
19. Richard Kearney, 'Myth and Modernity in Irish Poetry', *Contemporary Irish Poetry*, edited by Elmer Andrews (Macmillan, London, 1992), p.42.
20. *Contemporary Irish Poetry*, pp.53-54.
21. Durcan, 'The Haulier's Wife Meets Christ on the Road Near Moone', *Snail*, p.87-92.

10. Roy Fisher: *A Polytheism with No Gods* *(pp.112-122)*

Unless otherwise indicated, quotations from Roy Fisher's poems are taken from *The Dow Low Drop: New & Selected Poems* (Bloodaxe Books, Newcastle upon Tyne, 1996).

1. Raymond Williams, *Keywords* (Fontana, London, 1976), p.257.
2. Theodore Adorno and Max Horkheimer, 'The Culture Industry: Enlightenment as Mass Deception', translated by John Cumming in *The Cultural Studies Reader*, edited by Simon During (Routledge, London, 1993), p.37.
3. Roy Fisher, 'Reply to Paul Lester' in Paul Lester, *A Birmingham Dialogue* (Protean Pubs, Birmingham, 1986), pp.21-29.
4. Fisher, 'Six Texts for Film, 1: Talking to Cameras', *Birmingham River* (Oxford University Press, 1994), p.11.
5. Louis Zukofsky, in 'An Objective', *Preposition: The Collected Critical Essays* (University of California Press, London, 1981), p.12.
6. Fisher, *Birmingham River*, p.11.
7. Ian Gregson, *Contemporary Poetry and Postmodernism* (Macmillan, London, 1996), p.172.
8. Fisher, 'Birmingham River' 1, 'Talking to Cameras', *Birmingham River*, p.11.
9. 'Handsworth Liberties', *Poems 1955-1987* (Oxford University Press, (1988), p.120.
10. 'Lullaby and Exhortation for the Unknown Hero' from 'City', *The Dow Low Drop*, p.17.
11. Donald Davie, 'Roy Fisher: An Appreciation', in *Thomas Hardy and British Poetry* (Routledge, London, 1973), p.168.

12. Fisher, 'By the Pond' from 'City', *The Dow Low Drop*, p.20.
13. Friedrich Nietzsche, *The Twilight of the Idols*, translated by R.J. Hollingdale (Penguin, London, 1990), p.48.
14. Charles Olson, in *The Poetics of the New American Poetry* (The Grove Press, New York, 1973), p.151.
15. Neil Corcoran, 'Varieties of Modernism' in *British Poetry Since 1940* (Longman, Harlow, 1993), pp.171-73.
16. Thom Gunn, 'In Praise of Cities', *Collected Poems* (Faber, London, 1993), pp. 59-60.
17. Fisher, 'Wonders of Obligation', *The Dow Low Drop*, p.136.
18. *The Thing about Joe Sullivan: Poems 1971-1977* (Carcanet, Manchester, 1978), reprinted in *The Dow Low Drop*, pp.93-124; *City* (Migrant Press, Worcester, and Ventura, CA, 1961), *The Dow Low Drop*, pp.13-30; 'Handsworth Liberties', in *Poems 1955-1987; A Furnace* (Oxford University Press, 1988).
19. Anthony Thwaite, *Poetry Today: A Guide to British Poetry 1960-1984* (Longman, London, 1985), p.92.
20. *Contemporary Poets of the English Language*, edited by Rosalie Murphy, 4th edition (St James Press, London and Chicago, 1970), p.374.
21. Fisher, Preface, *A Furnace*, p.vii.
22. *The Dow Low Drop*, pp.72-73.
23. Craig Raine, *A Martian Sends a Postcard Home* (Oxford University Press, Oxford, 1979), pp.1-2.
24. *The Dow Low Drop*, pp.73-74.
25. W.H. Auden, from 'The Age of Anxiety', *Collected Poems*, edited by Edward Mendelson (Faber, London, 1991), p.466.
26. John Bayley, 'W.H. Auden' in *The Romantic Survival: a Study in Poetic Evolution* (Chatto and Windus, London, 1957), pp.151-52.
27. Bayley, *The Romantic Survival,* pp.151-52.
28. Fisher, *Collected Poems 1955-1987* (Oxford University Press, 1988), pp.142-43.
29. *Poems 1955-1980* (Oxford University Press, 1980), pp.60-61.
30. *The Dow Low Drop*, pp.78-79.
31. From 'An Interview with Roy Fisher' by Jed Rasula and Mike Erwin in *Nineteen Poems and an Interview* (Pensnet, Staffordshire, 1975), p.25.
32. *The Dow Low Drop*, pp.151-52.

11. Peter Reading: *The Poet as Thatcherite* *(pp.123-31)*

Unless otherwise indicated, quotations are taken from *Collected Poems, 1: Poems 1970-84* (Bloodaxe, Newcastle upon Tyne, 1995), hereafter called *CP1*, and *Collected Poems, 2: Poems 1985–96* (Bloodaxe, Newcastle upon Tyne, 1996), hereafter called *CP2.*

1. Tom Paulin, *Minotaur: Poetry and the Nation State* (Faber, London, 1992), p.287.
2. Reading, 'Thanksgiving', *CP1*, p.97-98.

3. Dennis O'Driscoll, 'No-God and Species Decline Stuff': The Poetry of Peter Reading, *In Black and Gold: Contiguous Traditions in Post-War British and Irish Poetry,* edited by C.C. Barfoot (Radopi, Amsterdam & Atlanta, Georgia, 1994), pp.199-218.
4. *Essential Reading: Selected Poems*, selected and edited by Alan Jenkins (Secker, London, 1986).
5. O'Driscoll, 'No-God', p.199.
6. Charles Tomlinson, quoted in 'Roy Fisher: an Appreciation' in Donald Davie, *Thomas Hardy and British Poetry* (Routledge & Kegan Paul, London, 1972), p.165.
7. Patrick Kavanagh, 'Epic', *Selected Poems*, edited by Antoinette Quinn (Penguin, London, 1996), pp.101-02.
8. Heathcote Williams, *Whale Nation* (Cape, London, 1988).
9. O'Driscoll, 'No-God', p.202.
10. Aristotle, *On the Art of Poetry* in *Classical Literary Criticism* (Penguin, Harmondsworth, 1965), pp.43-44.
11. Reading, from *C* in *CP1*, p.280.
12. Martin Seymour-Smith, 'Peter Reading', *The Oxford Companion to Twentieth Century Poetry* edited by Ian Hamilton (Oxford University Press, 1994), p.443.
13. Reading, *CP1*, Introduction by Isabel Martin, p.17.
14. For 'arthropods', see *Evagatory*, *CP2*, pp.229 & 240.
15. 'going on...', *Going On* in *CP2*, p.70; 'well, you has to live' in *Ukulele Music, CP2*, p.45.
16. Louis MacNeice, 'Autumn Journal', IV, *Collected Poems*, edited by E.R. Dodds (Faber, London, 1966), p.106.
17. Reading, *Ukulele Music*, *CP2*, p.42.
18. *For the Municipality's Elderly* (Secker, London, 1974).
19. 'Letter in Winter', *CP1*, p.31.
20. 'Severn at Worcester', *CP1*, p.36
21. 'Early Closing', *CP1*, p.39.
22. 'New Year Letter', *CP1*, p.47.
23. 'St James's', *CP1*, p.57-58.
24. 'Juvenilia', *CP1*, p.43.
25. 'Juvenilia', *CP1*, p.43.
26. 'Luncheon', *CP1*, p.86.
27. *The Prison Cell and Barrel Mystery* (Secker, London, 1976).
28. 'The Prison Cell and Barrel Mystery', *CP1*, p.95.
29. 'Duologues', *CP1*, p.100.
30. 'Soiree', *CP1*, p.101.
31. 'Severn at Worcester', *CP1*, p.37.
32. *Ukulele Music*, *CP2*, p.39.
33. *Stet* (Secker, London, 1986).
34. *Stet, CP2*, p.108.
35. Paulin, 'Junk Britain: Peter Reading', *Minotaur,* pp.285-94.
36. Reading, *Ukulele Music* in *CP2*, p.19.

12. Peter Porter: *A Planet in the Mind* *(pp.132-38)*

All references are to Peter Porter's poems are to *Collected Poems* (Oxford University Press, 1983) unless otherwise indicated.

1. Peter Porter, 'Beast and the Beauty', *CP*, p.12.
2. 'John Marston Advises Anger', *CP*, p.17.
3. Bruce Bennett, *Spirit in Exile* (Oxford University Press, 1991).
4. Diana Watson-Taylor, interview in *Spirit in Exile* (Oxford University Press, 1991), p.72.
5. Terry Eagleton, 'New Poetry', *Stand*, 14 no.2 (1972), p.77.
6. Porter, 'John Marston Advises Anger', *CP*, p.17.
7. A. Alvarez, *The New Poetry* (Penguin, Harmondsworth, 1962; 1966).
8. Alvarez, *The Shaping Spirit* (Arrow Books, London, 1958), p.89.
9. W.H. Auden, 'Lay Your Sleeping Head My Love', *Collected Poems* (Faber, London, 1976, revised 1991), p.157.
10. Alvarez, *The Shaping Spirit*, p.90.
11. Porter, 'Soliloquy at Potsdam', *CP*, p.41.
12. 'Septimius Severus at the Vienna Gate', *CP*, pp.47-48.
13. 'Vienna', *CP*, p.49.
14. Thom Gunn, 'Confessions of the Life Artist, 1', *Collected Poems* (Faber, London, 1993), p.159.
15. Simon Raven, *Close of Play* (Anthony Blond, London, 1962).
16. Porter, 'The World of Simon Raven', *CP*, p.53.
17. Raven, Preface to *Alms for Oblivion*, (Anthony Blond, London, 1962-78).
18. Anthony Powell, *A Dance to the Music of Time* (10 vols, Heinemann, London, 1951-75).
19. Porter, *After Martial* (Oxford University Press, 1972).
20. 'V.x', *After Martial*, *CP*, p.317.
21. Bruce Bennett, *Spirit in Exile.*
22. Raven, *Fielding Grey* (Anthony Blond, London, 1967).
23. Porter, IV.xviii, *CP*, p.315.
24. 'Dreamtime', *CP*, p.223.
25. 'Madame de Meurteil on "the loss of an eye"', *CP*, p.51.
26. 'John Marston Advises Anger', *CP*, p.17.
27. Anthony Thwaite, *Poetry Today: A Critical Guide to British Poetry 1960-1995* (Longman, Harlow, 1996), p.71.
28. Thwaite, *Poetry Today*, p.71.
29. Andrew Sinclair, *The Breaking of Bumbo* (Penguin, Harmondsworth, 1961); Derek Raymond, *The Crust on Its Uppers* (London, 1962).
30. Porter, 'The Cost of Seriousness', *CP*, p.255.
31. 'Walking Home on St Cecilia's Day', *CP*, p.13.
32. 'To Make It Real', *CP*, p.204.
33. 'Soliloquy at Potsdam', *CP*, p.41.
34. 'The Historians Call Up Pain', *CP*, p.30.
35. 'Europe: An Ode, *CP*, pp.127-29.
36. 'John Marston Advises Anger' and 'Elegy', *CP*, pp.17 and 120 respectively.

37. T.S. Eliot, 'A Game of Chess', II, *The Waste Land* in *Collected Poems* (London, Faber, 1963), pp.66-69.
38. Porter, 'Short Story', *CP*, p.122.
39. Alan Brownjohn, 'Sea Pictures', *The Observation Car*, (Hutchinson, London, 1990), pp.1-18.
40. Bennett, *Spirit in Exile*, p.122.
41. Porter, 'The Sanitized Sonnets', *CP*, p.141.
42. *The Last of England* (Oxford University Press, 1970).
43. 'The Last of England', *CP*, p.119.
44. Alan Jenkins in *The Oxford Companion to Twentieth-Century Poetry* edited by Ian Hamilton (Oxford University Press, 1994), p.427.

13. Peter Didsbury: *Getting Some Things Down* *(pp.139-46)*

1. Peter Didsbury, 'A Daft Place', *The Butchers of Hull* (Bloodaxe, Newcastle upon Tyne, 1982), p.45.
2. Peter Didsbury and I discussed this poem when it appeared in *Penguin Modern Poets 24* (Penguin, Harmondsworth, 1974), p.75.
3. Didsbury, 'In Belgium' and 'In Britain', *The Butchers of Hull*, p.49 and p.48 respectively.
4. 'The Pub Yard at Skidby', *The Butchers of Hull*, p.13.
5. 'The Globe', *The Classical Farm* (Bloodaxe, Newcastle upon Tyne, 1987), pp.64-65.
6. 'The Autumn', *The Butchers of Hull*, p.30.
7. 'The Experts', *The Butchers of Hull*, p.14.
8. 'Scenes from a Long Sleep', *The Classical Farm*, p.33.
9. 'Venery', *The Butchers of Hull*, p.55.
10. 'Mappa Mundi', *The Classical Farm*, pp.28-29.
11. Didsbury told me (27 August 1997) that an article by Raymond Gardner in *The Guardian* (19 April 1975), coinciding with Ashbery's visit to the Cambridge Poetry Festival, sparked his interest in Ashbery.
12. 'The Globe', 'The Hailstone', 'Glimpsed among Trees', 'The Classical Farm' and 'Eikon Basilike', *The Classical Farm*, pp.64-65, 60, 47, 40 and 38-39 respectively; 'The Shore' and 'Part of the Bridge', *That Old-Time Religion* (Bloodaxe, Newcastle upon Tyne, 1994), pp.9 and 14 respectively.
13. At various times since 1970 Didsbury has expressed an enthusiasm for the work of these poets. There is an unpublished Didsbury poem called 'Christopher Middleton in September'.
14. Christopher Middleton, from an interview in *The Poet Speaks* edited by Peter Orr, reprinted in *The Penguin Book of British Poetry since 1945* (Penguin, Harmondsworth, 1970), p.389.
15. John Osborne, 'The Sage of Ventnor Street', *Bête Noire* 6 (1988), pp.7-41; David Kennedy, *New Relations: The Refashioning of British Poetry 1980-94* (Seren, Bridgend, 1996), throughout. Ian Gregson, *Contemporary Poetry and Postmodernism: Dialogue and Estrangement* (Macmillan, Basingstoke, 1996), pp.222-25 and 231-32.

16 Osborne, 'The Sage of Ventnor Street', *Bête Noire,* 6, p.28.
17. Didsbury, 'A Winter's Fancy', *The Classical Farm*, pp.16-17.
18. 'A Shop', *The Classical Farm*, p.51.
19. Osborne, 'The Sage of Ventnor Street', *Bête Noire,* 6, p.7.
20. See *Poetry Book Society Bulletin* (Spring 1994).
21. Osborne, 'The Sage of Ventnor Street', *Bête Noire,* 6, pp.32-40.
22. Didsbury, 'The Drainage', *The Butchers of Hull*, pp.40-41.
23. 'Common Property', *That Old-Time Religion*, p.43.
24. 'The British Museum', *The Classical Farm*, p.63.
25. 'The Surgery', *The Classical Farm*, p.23.
26. 'Next', *That Old-Time Religion*, p.56.
27. 'The Hailstone', *The Classical Farm*, pp.60-61.

14. Fleur Adcock: All the Things Men Do *(pp.148-153)*

1. Clive Wilmer, *Poets Talking* (Carcanet, Manchester, 1994), p.32.
2. Fleur Adcock, *The Eye of the Hurricane* (Reed, Wellington, 1964).
3. Adcock, *Tigers* (OUP New Zealand, Wellington, 1967).
4. *Selected Poems* (Oxford University Press, 1983; reissued 1991).
5. Wilmer, *Poets Talking* (Carcanet, Manchester, 1994), p.30.
6. Adcock, 'Note on Propertius', *Selected Poems*, p.1.
7. 'Instructions to Vampires', *Selected Poems*, p.6.
8. 'Beauty Abroad', *Selected Poems*, p.4.
9. 'Advice to a Discarded Lover', *Selected Poems*, pp.15-16.
10. Alan Robinson, *Instabilities in Contemporary British Poetry* (Macmillan, London, 1988), p.187.
11. Wilmer, *Poets Talking*, p.30.
12. Adcock, 'A Day in October', *The Inner Harbour* (Oxford University Press, 1979), p.36.
13. 'Against Coupling', *Selected Poems*, pp.33-34.
14. 'Mornings After', *Selected Poems*, pp.34-36.
15. 'Dreaming', *Selected Poems*, p.120.
16. 'Street Song', *Selected Poems*, pp.120-21.
17. 'Across the Moor', *Selected Poems*, p.121.
18. 'Declensions', *Selected Poems*, p.102.
19. Peter Porter, 'Last of the Dinosaurs', *Collected Poems* (Oxford University Press, 1983), p.77.
20. Adcock, 'The Ex-Queen among the Astronomers', *Selected Poems*, pp.73-4.
21. Robinson, *Instabilities in Contemporary British Poetry*, p.189.
22. Wilmer, *Poets Talking*, p.32.

15. Carol Rumens: *The Room You Are In* *(pp.154-59)*

1. Carol Rumens, *Unplayed Music* (Secker, London, 1981).
2. Rumens, *Thinking of Skins: New and Selected Poems* (Bloodaxe, Newcastle upon Tyne, 1993).
3. 'A Marriage', *Unplayed Music* in *Thinking of Skins*, p.57.

4. 'A Marriage', *Thinking of Skins*, p.57.
5. 'Before These Wars', *Thinking of Skins*, p.61.
6. 'A Woman of a Certain Age', *Thinking of Skins*, p.118.
7. 'A Woman of a Certain Age', *Thinking of Skins*, p.118.
8. James Vinson and D.L. Kirkpatrick (eds.), *Contemporary Poets of the English Language*, 4th edition (St James Press, London and Chicago, 1985), pp.732-33.
9. 'A New Song', *Thinking of Skins*, p.111.
10. Neil Corcoran, *English Poetry Since 1940* (Longman, Harlow, 1993), p.230.
11. Rumens, 'In the Craft Museum', *Thinking of Skins*, p.119.
12. 'Ballad of the Morning After', *Thinking of Skins*, p.107.
13. *Star Whisper* (Secker, London, 1983).
14. 'Star Whisper', *Thinking of Skins*, p.66.
15. 'The Hebrew Class', *Thinking of Skins*, p.71.
16. 'The Hebrew Class', *Thinking of Skins*, p.71.
17. 'A Day in October', *The Inner Harbour* (Oxford University Press, 1979), p.36.
18. Rumens, 'Outside Oswiecim', *Thinking of Skins*, p.87.
19. Douglas Dunn, 'The Deserter', *Selected Poems* (Faber, London, 1988), p.198.
20. Michael Longley, 'Ghetto', *Gorse Fires* (Secker, London, 1991), p.40.
21. Rumens, 'Surrey', *From Berlin to Heaven* (Chatto, London, 1989), pp.27-28.
22. 'A Lawn for the English Family', *Thinking*, p.147.
23. Douglas Dunn, 'In the Grounds', *Selected Poems*, pp.101-02.
24. Rumens, 'Our Early Days in Graveldene', *Thinking of Skins*, pp.144-45.
25. Tom Paulin, *Minotaur* (Faber, London, 1992), pp.233-34.
26. Rumens, 'Our Early Days in Graveldene', *Thinking of Skins*, pp.144-45.

16. Carol Ann Duffy: *A Stranger Here Myself* *(pp.160-68)*

1. Carol Ann Duffy, 'Originally', *The Other Country* (Anvil, London, 1990), p.7.
2. Duffy, 'Ash Wednesday 1984' and 'Words of Absolution', *Standing Female Nude* (Anvil, London, 1985), pp.14 and 32 respectively.
3. 'Originally', *The Other Country* (Anvil, London, 1990), p.7.
4. 'Saying Something', *Standing Female Nude*, p.18.
5. 'I Remember Me', *Standing Female Nude*, p.16.
6. 'Politico', *Selling Manhattan* (Anvil, London, 1987; new edition 1997), p.35.
7. 'The Good Teachers', *Mean Time* (Anvil, London, 1993), p.16.
8. 'In Mrs Tilscher's Class', *The Other Country*, p.8.
9. 'The Captain of the 1964 Top of the Form Team', *Mean Time*, p.7.

10. 'Like Earning a Living', *Mean Time*, p.17.
11. 'The Good Teachers', *Mean Time*, p.16.
12. A.S. Byatt, *Still Life* (Chatto, London, 1985).
13. Byatt, *The Virgin in the Garden* (Chatto, London, 1978).
14. Byatt, *The Game* (Chatto, London, 1978).
15. Duffy, 'Litany', *Mean Time*, p.9.
16. 'Education for Leisure', *Standing Female Nude*, p.15; 'And How Are We Today', *Selling Manhattan*, p.27; 'Psychopath', *Selling Manhattan*, p.28.
17. 'Dear Norman', *Standing Female Nude*, p.41; 'Warming Her Pearls', *Selling Manhattan*, p.58.
18. M.M. Bakhtin, *The Dialogic Imagination* (University of Texas Press, Austin, 1976), quoted in Ian Gregson, *Contemporary Poetry and Postmodernism*, Macmillan Press, London, 1996), p.99.
19. Duffy, 'A Provincial Party, 1956', *Standing Female Nude*, p.40.
20. Alan Robinson, *Instabilities in Contemporary British Poetry*, (Macmillan, Basingstoke, 1988), p.196-97.
21. Gregson, *Contemporary Poetry*, p.105.
22. *Contemporary Poetry*, p.105-06
23. Hans Magnus Enzensberger, 'The Industrialisation of the Mind', *Dreamers of the Absolute: Essays on Ecology, Media and Power* (Century Hutchinson, London, 1988), p.7.

17. Paul Muldoon: *The Advanced Muldoon* *(pp.171-80)*

1. Muldoon, Interview with Sean O'Brien, July 1994.
2. Interview with Sean O'Brien, July 1994.
3. 'A Trifle', *Quoof* (Faber, London, 1983), p.30.
4. Tim Kendall, *Paul Muldoon* (Seren, Bridgend, 1996), pp.91-92.
5. Kendall, *Paul Muldoon*, pp.91-92.
6. Viktor Shklovsky, 'Art as Technique' in *Russian Formalist Criticism: Four Essays*, translated and edited by Lee T. Lemon and Marion J. Reis (Lincoln, Nebraska, 1965), pp.5-22.
7. Michael Donaghy, 'A Conversation with Paul Muldoon', *Chicago Review*, 35 no.1 (Autumn 1985), p.85.
8. John Haffenden, *Viewpoints* (Faber, London, 1981), p.135.
9. Seamus Heaney, 'Punishment', *North* (Faber, London,1975), p.37.
10. Muldoon, 'Gathering Mushrooms', *Quoof* (Faber, London, 1983), p.7.
11. 'Dancers at the Moy', *New Weather* (Faber, London, 1973), p.20.
12. Donaghy, *Chicago Review*, pp.77-78.
13. Heaney, 'The Other Side', *Wintering Out* (Faber, London, 1972) pp.34-36.
14. Muldoon, 'The Sightseers', *Quoof*, p.15.
15. 'Duffy's Circus, *Mules* (Faber, London, 1977), p.51; 'Cuba', *Why Brownlee Left* (Faber, London, 1980), p.13.
16. 'The Boundary Commission', *Why Brownlee Left*, p.15.

17. 'October 1950', *Why Brownlee Left*, p.9.
18. John McGahern – see *The Dark* (Faber, London, 1965) and *The Barracks* (Faber, London, 1963).
19. Heaney, *Preoccupations* (Faber, London, 1980), p.211.
20. Muldoon, 'The More A Man Has, the More A Man Wants', *Quoof*, p.58.
21. Edna Longley, *Poetry in the Wars* (Bloodaxe, Newcastle upon Tyne, 1986), p.15.
22. Roland Barthes, *Writing Degree Zero*, translated from the French by Annette Lowers and Colin Smith (1953, Hill and Wang, New York, 1968), p.48.
23. Clair Wills, 'The Lie of the Land: Language, Imperialism and Trade in Paul Muldoon's *Meeting the British*', *The Chosen Ground: Essays on the Contemporary Poetry of Northern Ireland* edited by Neil Corcoran (Seren, Bridgend, 1992), p.146.
24. Wills, *Improprieties and Politics and Sexuality in Northern Irish Poetry* (Oxford University Press, 1993), p.202.
25. T.V.F. Brogan in *The New Princeton Encyclopedia of Poetry and Poetics*, edited by Alex Preminger and T.V.F. Brogan (Princeton University Press, Princeton, 1993), p.1054.
26. Brogan in *The New Princeton Encyclopedia of Poetry and Poetics*, p.1060.
27. Donaghy, *Chicago Review*, p.81.
28. Ian Gregson, *Contemporary Poetry and Postmodernism* (Macmillan Press, London, 1996), p.53.
29. Baudelaire, *Intimate Journals* translated from the French by Christopher Isherwood and edited by W.H. Auden (Beacon Press, Boston, 1957), p.56.
30. Kendall, *Paul Muldoon*, p.134.
31. Muldoon, 'Immram', *Why Brownlee Left*, pp.38-47; 'Madoc – A Mystery' (Faber, London, 1990) pp.13-261; 'Yarrow', *The Annals of Chile* (Faber, London, 1994). pp.39-189.
32. 'Something Else', *Meeting the British* (Faber, London, 1987), p.33. Heaney, 'Away From It All', *Station Island* (Faber, London, 1984), pp.16-17.
33. Kendall, *Paul Muldoon*, p.133.
34. Louis Simpson, 'To the Western World', *People Live Here: Selected Poems 1949-1983* (Boa Editions, Brockport, NY, 1983), p.59.
35. Muldoon, 'Meeting the British', *Meeting the British*, p.16.
36. 'Yarrow', *The Annals of Chile*, pp.39-189.
37. Kendall, *Paul Muldoon*, p.149.
38. 'Incantata', *The Annals of Chile*, p.19.
39. Peter Porter, 'An Exequy', *Collected Poems* (Oxford University Press, 1983), pp.246-49.
40. Henry King, 'An Exequy. To his Matchlesse never to be forgotten Friend', *Penguin Metaphysical Poets*, edited by Helen Gardner (Penguin, Harmondsworth, 1966), pp.110-13.

41. Porter, 'Public and Private' in 'Contemporary Poetry', *New Writing 5* (Vintage, London, 1996), p.279.
42. Porter, p.275.
43. Kendall, *Muldoon*, pp.227-28.
44. Kendall, p.229

18. Tom Paulin: *The Critic Who Is Truly a Critic* *(pp.181-88)*

1. Tom Paulin, Introduction, *Writing to the Moment: Selected Critical Essays 1980-1996* (Faber, London, 1996), p.ix.
2. Alan Robinson, 'The Civil Art: Tom Paulin's Representations of Ulster', *Instabilities in Contemporary British Poetry* (Macmillan, Basingstoke, 1988), p.116.
3. *The Faber Book of Political Verse,* edited by Tom Paulin (Faber, London, 1986). For example Big Joe Williams, 'President Roosevelt', p.396; Charlie Patten, '34 Blues', p.388; John Cooper Clarke, 'evidently chickentown', p.462.
4. *Contemporary Poetry Meets Modern Theory*, edited by Anthony Easthope and John O. Thompson (Harvester Wheatsheaf, Hemel Hempstead, 1991), p.99.
5. Paul H. Fry, *A Defence of Poetry: Reflections on the Occasions of Language* (Stanford University Press, Stanford, California, 1995), Chapter 1, 'Non-Construction: History, Structure and the Ostensive Moment in Literature', p.13.
6. Paulin, 'Theory', *Writing to the Moment*, p.279.
7. 'Trotsky in Finland', *Selected Poems 1972-90* (Faber, London, 1993), p.34.
8. 'The Fuse and the Fire', *Writing to the Moment*, p.89.
9. 'The Fuse and the Fire', *Writing to the Moment*, p.85
10. See R.A. Foster, *Modern Ireland 1600-1972* (Penguin, Harmondsworth, 1989), Chapter 12, 'Enthusiasm Defying Punishment: Revolution, Republicanism and Reaction', pp.259-86.
11. Neil Corcoran, *English Poetry Since 1940* (Longman, Harlow, 1993), p.215.
12. Edna Longley, *Poetry in the Wars* (Bloodaxe, Newcastle upon Tyne, 1986), p.192.
13. Bernard O'Donoghue, 'Involved Imagining: Tom Paulin', *The Chosen Ground: Essays on the Contemporary Poetry of Northern Ireland*, edited by Neil Corcoran (Seren, Bridgend, 1992), p.176.
14. Paulin, 'Paisley's Progress', *Writing to the Moment*, pp.30-31.
15. 'A Visionary Nationalist: Geoffrey Hill', *Minotaur: Poetry and the Nation State* (Faber, London, 1992), p.282.
16. 'Desertmartin', *Selected Poems*, p.43.
17. Longley, *Poetry in the Wars*, p.192.
18. See O'Donoghue, 'Involved Imagining', throughout.
19. Paulin, 'Responsibilities', 'A Just State' and 'Under the Eyes', *Selected Poems 1972-1990*, pp.18, 11 and 3 respectively.

20. 'Argument from Design', 'Off the Back of a Lorry', 'Manichean Geography II', 'S/He', 'To the Linen Hall', *Liberty Tree* (Faber, London, 1983), pp.31, 33, 34, 44, 48 and 77, respectively.
21 Anthony Thwaite, *Poetry Today* (Longman, London, 1996), p.107-08.
22. Dunn, *St Kilda's Parliament* (Faber, London, 1981), Notes, p.87.
23 Thwaite, *Poetry Today*, p.108.
24. Paulin, 'The Fuse and the Fire', *Writing to the Moment*, p.88.
25. 'The Fuse and the Fire', *Writing to the Moment*, p.94.
26. Derek Mahon, 'Light Music': 18, *Poems 1962-78* (Oxford University Press, 1979), p.96.

19. Ciaran Carson: *These Things Are What We Are* *(pp.189-97)*

1. Ciaran Carson, 'Two to Tango', *First Language* (Gallery Press, Oldcastle, 1993), p.18.
2. 'Queen's Gambit', *Belfast Confetti* (Gallery Press, Oldcastle, 1989/ Bloodaxe, Newcastle upon Tyne, 1990), p.35.
3. Walter Benjamin, Introduction to *Reflections*, translated from the German by Edmund Jephcott, edited by Peter Denetz (Schocken, New York, 1986), p.xvii.
4. Declan Kiberd, *Inventing Ireland: The Literature of the Modern Nation* (Vintage, London, 1996), p.600.
5. Neil Corcoran, 'One Step Forward, Two Steps Back: Ciaran Carson's *The Irish For No*' in *The Chosen Ground: Essays on the Contemporary Poetry of Northern Ireland*, edited by Neil Corcoran (Seren, Bridgend, 1992), p.225.
6. Carson, *The Irish for No* (Gallery Press, Dublin, 1988/Bloodaxe, Newcastle upon Tyne, 1989), p.46.
7. William Shakespeare, 'Sonnet 116', *ll.*2-3.
8. Benjamin, 'A Berlin Chronicle', *Reflections*, pp.3-60.
9. Carson, *Belfast Confetti*, p.81.
10. Benjamin, 'A Berlin Chronicle', *Reflections*, p.5.
11. Carson, *Belfast Confetti*, p.80.
12. Corcoran, *The Chosen Ground*, p.221.
13. *The Chosen Ground*, p.216.
14. Paul Muldoon, 'Yarrow', *The Annals of Chile* (Faber, London, 1994), pp.39-189.
15. Carson, *Belfast Confetti*, pp.72-75.
16. *Belfast Confetti*, p.72.
17. *Belfast Confetti*, p.73.
18. *Belfast Confetti*, p.74.
19. *Belfast Confetti*, p.74.
20. *Belfast Confetti*, p.67.
21. John Milton, *Prose Works*, vol.3 , p.334, quoted by Edna Longley in *The Living Stream*, p.88.
22. Tom Paulin, 'The Crack', *Writing to the Moment: Critical Essays 1980-1996* (Faber, London, 1996), p.96.

23. Carson, 'Loaf', *Belfast Confetti*, pp.15-18.
24. Baudelaire, 'Correspondances', *The Complete Verse*, vol.1. translated by Francis Scarfe (Anvil Press, London, 1986), p.61; Carson, Correspondences', *First Language* (Gallery, Oldcastle, 1993), p.39.
25. 'Eesti', *Opera Et Cetera* (Bloodaxe, Newcastle upon Tyne/Gallery Press, Oldcastle, 1996), p.7.
26. W.R. Rodgers, 'Epilogue', *Poems,* edited and introduced by Michael Longley (Gallery Press, Oldcastle, 1993), p.106.
27. Carson, 'Grass' and 'Two to Tango', *First Language*, pp.16 and 18 respectively.
28. 'Dresden', *The Irish for No*, p.11.
29. 'Two to Tango', *First Language*, p.20.
30. 'Two to Tango', *First Language*, p.19.
31. Carson, 'Bagpipe Music', *First Language*, p.74.
32. 'Drunk Boat', *First Language*, p.34.
33. 'The Ballad of *HMS Belfast*', *First Language*, p.74.
34. 'Opus 14', *First Language*, p.31.
35. 'Opus Operandi', *First Language*, p.60.
36. Mick Imlah, 'Abandoned Origins', *Times Literary Supplement*, 4 September 1987, p.946.
37. Paul Muldoon, 'Ma', *Mules* (Faber, London, 1977), p.23; 'Immram', 'Anseo', 'Promises, Promises', 'Why Brownlee Left', *Why Brownlee Left* (Faber, London, 1980), pp.23, 20, 24 and 22 respectively; *Quoof* (Faber, London, 1983).
38. Muldoon, *The Prince of the Quotidian* (Gallery, Oldcastle, 1994).
39. 'Letters from the Alphabet' and 'Opera', pp.11-36 and 67-92 respectively, *Opera Et Cetera*.
40. 'Letters from the Alphabet', 'I', *Opera Et Cetera*, p.19.
41. 'Letters from the Alphabet', 'A', *Opera Et Cetera*, p.1.

20. Matthew Sweeney: *A Separate Peace* *(pp.198-204)*

1. Seamus Heaney, 'Elegy', *Field Work* (Faber, London, 1979), p.31.
2. Matthew Sweeney, *A Dream of Maps* (Raven Arts Press, Dublin, 1981), *A Round House* (Allison & Busby, London, 1982), *The Lame Waltzer* (Allison & Busby, London, 1985), *Blue Shoes* (Secker, London, 1989) and *Cacti* (Secker, London, 1992).
3. Sweeney, 'No Answer', *Blue Shoes*, p.34.
4. 'A Daydream Ahead', 'Calais' and 'The Shadow Home', *Blue Shoes*, pp.12, 14 and 17 respectively.
5. 'The Burglar', *The Flying Spring Onion* (Faber, London, 1992), p.69.
6. 'A Couple Waiting', *Blue Shoes*, p.11.
7. 'Dog on a Chain', *Blue Shoes*, p.4.
8. 'On My Own', *Blue Shoes*, p.19.
9. 'Pink Milk', *Blue Shoes*, p.36.
10. Patrick McCabe, *The Dead School* (Picador, London, 1995).
11. Sweeney, 'The Man with the Budgie on His Back', *Blue Shoes*, p.31.

12. 'The Women', *Blue Shoes*, p.16.
13. 'The U-boat', *Blue Shoes*, p.23.
14. 'Symmetry', *Blue Shoes*, p.35.
15. 'A Postcard of a Hanging', *Blue Shoes*, p.25.
16. 'Where Fishermen Can't Swim' and 'Tube Ride to Martha's', *Blue Shoes*, pp.9 and 50 respectively.
17. Robert Frost, '"Out, Out–"', *Selected Poems*, edited with an introduction by Ian Hamilton (Penguin, Harmondsworth, 1973), p.89.
18. Sweeney, 'Monkey', *Cacti*, p.37.
19. 'Asleep in a Chair', *Cacti*, p.41.

21. John Fuller and James Fenton (*pp.207-18*)

All quotations from John Fuller are taken from *Collected Poems* (Chatto, London, 1996), hereafter referred to as *CP*, unless otherwise stated.

1. A. Alvarez, 'Introduction: The New Poetry or Beyond the Gentility Principle', *The New Poetry* (Penguin, Harmondsworth (1962), revised edition, 1966), p.21.
2. *Conductors of Chaos: A Poetry Anthology* edited by Iain Sinclair (Picador, London, 1996).
3. *The Penguin Book of Contemporary British Poetry* edited by Blake Morrison and Andrew Motion (Penguin, Harmondsworth, 1982); *The New Poetry,* edited by Michael Hulse, Michael, David Kennedy and David Morley (Bloodaxe, Newcastle upon Tyne, 1993).
4. Charles Bernstein, 'In the Middle of Modernism, in the Middle of Capitalism, on the Outskirts of New York', from *A Poetics* (Harvard University Press, Cambridge, Mass., 1992), pp.90-91.
5. Peter Forbes, 'How the Century Lost its Poetry, *Poetry Review*, 86 no.1 (Spring 1996), p.4.
6. 'Introduction', *Postmodernism: A Reader,* edited by Patricia Waugh (Edward Arnold, London, 1992), p.3.
7. Peter Porter, 'Tending Towards the Condition', *Collected Poems* (Oxford University Press, 1983), p.189.
8. Frank O'Hara, 'Personism: A Manifesto', *The Poetics of the New American Poetry*, edited by Donald M. Allen and Warren Tallmann (Grove Press, New York, 1973) pp.353-55.
9. Randall Jarrell, 'Changes of Attitude and Rhetoric in Auden's Poetry', *The Third Book of Criticism* (Faber, London, 1975), pp.115-50.
10. John Fuller, 'A Footnote to Ovid' *CP*, p.41.
11. Tony Harrison, 'The Nuptial Torches', *Selected Poems* (Penguin, London, revised edition 1987), pp.60-62.
12. Fuller, 'Girl With Coffee Tray', *CP*, p.3.
13. 'Band Music', *CP*, p.5.
14. 'Edwardian Christmas', *CP*, p.4.
15. 'In a Railway Compartment', *CP*, p.5.
16. Alan Jenkins, 'Politics', *In the Hot-House* (Chatto, London, 1988), pp.36-37.

17. Jenkins, *Harm* (Chatto, London, 1994).
18. Fuller, 'Alex's Game', *CP*, p.6.
19. See Waugh, *Postmodernism*, Introduction, p.1.
20. Anthony Thwaite, *Poetry Today: A Critical Guide to British Poetry 1960-1984* (Longman, Harlow, 1985), p.54.
21. Fuller, 'In The Corridor', *CP*, pp.270-71.
22. Reprinted in *The Memory of War and Children in Exile: Poems 1968-1983* (Penguin, Harmondsworth, 1983), pp.81-84.
23. Jorge Luis Borges, 'The Lottery in Babylon', *Labyrinths* (Penguin, London, 1970), pp.55-61.
24. Fenton, 'The Pitt-Rivers Museum', *Poems 1968-1983*, pp.81-84.
25. William Empson, 'Homage to the British Museum', *Collected Poems* (Chatto, London, 1969), p.35.
26. Neil Corcoran, *English Poetry Since 1940* (Longman, Harlow, 1993), p.246.
27. Fenton, 'A German Requiem', *Poems 1968-1983*, pp.11-19.
28. 'A Vacant Possession' and 'Nest of Vampires', *Poems 1968-1983*, pp.47-49 and 44-46 respectively.
29. 'Letter to John Fuller', *Poems 1968-1983*, p.67.
30. Ian Gregson, *Contemporary Poetry and Postmodernism: Dialogue and Estrangement* (Macmillan, Basingstoke, 1996), p.65.
31. Alan Robinson, *Instabilities in Contemporary British Poetry* (Macmillan, London, 1988), pp.8-9.
32. Fenton, 'A Staffordshire Murderer', *Poems 1968-1983*, pp.58-61.
33. Robinson, *Instabilities*, p.4.
34. Frank Kippax, *Fear of Night and Darkness* (Harper Collins, London, 1994), p.9.
35. Fenton, 'A Staffordshire Murderer', *Poems 1968-1983*, p.60.
36. 'A Staffordshire Murderer', *Poems 1968-1983*, p.59.
37. Gregson, *Contemporary Poetry and Postmodernism,* p.80.
38. Gregson, p.69.
39. W.H. Auden, 'Bucolics', *Collected Poems*, ed. Edward Mendelson (Faber, London, 1991) pp. 556-69.
40. Fuller, 'England', *CP*, pp.410-11
41. A.S. Byatt, *Babel Tower* (Vintage, London, 1997), p.16.

22. Craig Raine, Christopher Reid, Blake Morrison, Andrew Motion, Michael Hofmann: *Middlemen* *(pages 219-40)*

1. Christopher Reid, 'Annals', *Katerina Brac* (Faber, London, 1985), p.17.
2. Blake Morrison, *Dark Glasses* (Chatto, London, 1984); Alan Jenkins, *In the Hothouse* (Chatto, London, 1988); Mick Imlah, *Birthmarks* (Chatto, London, 1988).
3. Morrison, *The Movement* (Oxford University Press, 1980).
4. Andrew Motion, *Philip Larkin: A Writer's Life* (Faber, London, 1993).
5. Morrison and Motion (eds.), *The Penguin Book of Contemporary Poetry*, Introduction, p.11.

6. Morrison and Motion, p.12.
7. Morrison and Motion, p.20.
8. The term 'Martian' was first used in print by James Fenton in the *New Statesman*, 20 October 1978, p.520.
9. Interview with John Haffenden in *Viewpoints*, edited by John Haffenden (Faber, London, 1981), p.181.
10. Raine, 'Arsehole', *Rich* (Faber, London, 1983), p.26.
11. Neil Roberts, 'Dance of Being: The Poetry of Peter Redgrove' in *British Poetry from the 1950s to the 1990s: Politics and Arts*, ed. Gary Day and Brian Docherty (Macmillan, London, 1997), p.90.
12. Raine, *History: the Home Movie* (Penguin, London, 1994).
13. *Clay. Whereabouts Unknown* (Penguin, London, 1996).
14. Douglas Dunn, 'The Topical Muse: on Contemporary Poetry', Kenneth Allott Lectures No.6, *Liverpool Classical Monthly* (University of Liverpool, 1990), p.20.
15. Neil Corcoran, *English Poetry Since 1940* (Longman, Harlow, 1993), p.237.
16. Alan Robinson, *Instabilities in Contemporary British Poetry* (Macmillan, Basingstoke, 1988), p.47.
17. Raine, 'The Prophetic Book', iv, 'Shaman', *Clay*, pp.12-13.
18. 'The Prophetic Book', iv, 'Shaman', *Clay*, p.13.
19. Andrew Crozier, 'Thrills and Frills: Poetry as Figures of Empirical Lyricism' in *Society and Literature 1945-1970*, edited by Alan Sinfield (Methuen, London, 1983), p.230.
20. Raine, 'The Prophetic Book', iv, 'Shaman', *Clay*, p.12.
21. 'The Prophetic Book', iv, 'Shaman', *Clay*, p.16.
22. Seamus Heaney, *Station Island* (Faber, London, 1984).
23. Raine, 'Rich', *Rich*, p.17.
24. Robinson, *Instabilities in Contemporary British Poetry*, p.48.
25. Raine, 'The Prophetic Book', vi, 'Chest of Drawers', *Clay*, p.20.
26. 'For Hans Keller', *Clay*, p.53.
27. 'The Prophetic Book', i, *Clay*, p.4.
28. 'The Prophetic Book', i, *Clay*, p.5.
29. 'Scrap', 'Shut' and 'Death Bed', *Clay*, pp.26, 30 and 35 respectively.
30. 'Retirement', *Clay*, p.39.
31. 'On My Fiftieth Birthday', plus 'Redmond's Hare' and 'Heaven on Earth', *Clay*, pp.47, 51 and 29 respectively.
32. See Haffenden (ed.), *Viewpoints*, p.183.
33. *The Oxford Companion to Twentieth Century Poetry*, edited by Ian Hamilton (Oxford University Press, 1994), p.448.
34. Reid, *Arcadia* (Oxford University Press, 1979), p.16.
35. *Arcadia*, p.33.
36. *Arcadia*, pp.17, 18, 15 and 25 respectively.
37. *Arcadia*, p.13.
38. 'The Gardeners', 'Verge Escapement with Fusee', 'Maritime Liverpool', *Arcadia*, pp.7, 41 and 20 respectively.
39. 'In Medias Res', iii and xvii, *Arcadia*, pp.45 and 50 respectively.

40. *Pea Soup* (Oxford University Press, 1982), p.16.
41. 'Dark Ages', 'Charnel', 'Kawai's Trilby', 'The Traveller' and 'Magnum Opus', *Pea Soup*, pp.30, 17, 27, 48 and 15 respectively.
42. Larkin, *Collected Poems*, ed. Anthony Thwaite (Faber, London, 1988), p.97.
43. Corcoran, *English Poetry Since 1940*, p.239.
44. Reid, 'Magnum Opus', *Pea Soup*, p.16.
45. 'Pale Blue Butterflies', *Katerina Brac*, p.10.
46. Corcoran, *English Poetry Since 1940*, p.242.
47. James Joyce, *A Portrait of the Artist as a Young Man* (Penguin, Harmondsworth, 1992), p.166.
48. Michael Hofmann, 'Compassionate Ridicule', *Poetry Review* 75 no.4 (1986), p.48.
49. Reid, 'Pale Blue Butterflies', *Katerina Brac*, p.10.
50. 'A Box', *Katerina Brac*, p.32.
51. 'The Sea', *Katerina Brac*, p.34.
52. Morrison, *Dark Glasses* (Chatto, London [1984], revised and expanded 1989).
53. 'The Renunciation', *Dark Glasses*, p.12.
54. Fenton, *The Memory of War and Children in Exile: Poems1968-1983* (Penguin, Harmondsworth, 1983), pp.47-49.
55. See Dunn, 'Five Years Married', *The Happier Life* (Faber, London, 1972), p.46: 'We have been waltzing in the foggy meadows/At the edges of cliffs, in outmoded evening dress./ Our lives are out of date...'
56. Morrison, 'Long Days', *Dark Glasses*, pp.16-17.
57. 'Grange Boy', *Dark Glasses*, p.15.
58. Larkin, 'Livings, I', *Collected Poems*, p.186.
59. David Lodge, *Nice Work* (Penguin, Harmondsworth, 1989).
60. Morrison, *The Ballad of the Yorkshire Ripper* (Chatto, London, 1987).
61. See 'The Filial Art' and 'Labouring: Continuous', collected in *Tony Harrison*, edited by Neil Astley (Bloodaxe, Newcastle upon Tyne, 1991), pp.54-60 and 216-20 respectively.
62. Morrison, *Yorkshire Ripper*, p.28.
63. *Yorkshire Ripper*, p.24.
64. *Yorkshire Ripper*, p.23.
65. *Yorkshire Ripper*, p.36.
66. Tony Harrison, 'On Not Being Milton', *Selected Poems* (Penguin, London, 1987), p.112.
67. Motion, 'Anniversaries' appears in an abbreviated form in *Dangerous Play: Poems 1974-1984* (Penguin, Harmondsworth, 1985), pp.77-81.
68. 'Independence', *Dangerous Play*, pp.19-38.
69. *The Pleasure Steamers* (Carcanet, Manchester, 1978).
70. *Love in a Life* (Faber, London, 1991).
71. *The Oxford Companion to Twentieth Century Poetry* edited by Ian Hamilton (Oxford University Press, 1994), p.367.
72. William Empson, 'Ignorance of Death', *Collected Poems* (Chatto, London, 1969), p.58.

73. Motion, *The Poetry of Edward Thomas* (Routledge, London, 1980); *Philip Larkin* (Methuen, London, 1982).
74. Paul Muldoon, 'The Big House', *New Selected Poems 1968-1994* (Faber, London, 1996), pp.23-24.
75. 'The Letter', *Dangerous Play*, pp.12-13.
76. *Selected Letters of Philip Larkin 1940-1985*, edited by Anthony Thwaite (Faber, London, 1992), p.640.
77. *Selected Letters of Philip Larkin*, pp.694-95.
78. Motion, 'Firing Practice', *Natural Causes*, p.44.
79. Larkin, 'Aubade', *Collected Poems*, pp.208-09.
80. Corcoran, *English Poetry Since 1940*, p.253.
81. Motion, 'Inside and Out', *Dangerous Play*, p.54.
82. Giuseppe Tomasi di Lampedusa, *The Leopard*, translated by Archibald Colquhoun (Collins Harvill, London [1958], 1992).
83. Larkin, 'Ambulances', *Collected Poems*, p.132.
84. Hofmann, *Nights in the Iron Hotel* (Faber, London, 1983); *Acrimony* (Faber, London, 1986).
85. 'From Kensal Rise to Heaven', *Acrimony*, pp.34-35.
86. Robinson, 'Waiting for the End: Absences in the Poetry of Michael Hofmann', *Instabilities in Contemporary British Poetry*, p.50.
87. G.K. Chesterton, *Wine, Water and Song* (Methuen, London 1943), p.22.
88. Louis MacNeice, 'Snow', *The Collected Poems*, edited by E.R. Dodds (Faber, London, 1979), p.30.
89. Louis Simpson, 'There Is', *People Live Here: Selected Poems 1949-1983* (Boa Editions Limited, Brockport, 1983), p.62.
90. Robinson, 'Waiting for the End: Absences in the Poetry of Michael Hofmann', *Instabilities in Contemporary British Poetry*, p.49.
91. Hofmann, 'Nighthawks', Hofmann, *Acrimony*, p.30-31.
92. Rolf Gunter Renner, *Edward Hopper 1882-1967: Transformation of the Real*, translated by Michael Hulse (Benedikt Taschen, Köln, 1990), p.80.
93. Renner, p.80.
94. Hofmann, 'Nighthawks', *Acrimony*, pp.30-31.
95. *Corona, Corona* (Faber, London, 1993).
96. 'Lament For Crassus', *Corona, Corona*, p.3.
97. 'Marvin Gaye', *Corona, Corona*, p.15.
98. 'Firebird', *Corona, Corona*, pp.20-21.
99. Lowell, 'Waking in the Blue', 'Memories of West Street and Lepke', 'Skunk Hour', *Life Studies*, (Faber, London, 1977), pp.95-96, 99-100 and 103-04 respectively; 'Water', *For The Union Dead*, (Faber, London [1964], 1985), p.3.
100. Hofmann, 'Entr'acte', *Acrimony*, p.27.

23. Simon Armitage and Glyn Maxwell *(pp.241-50)*

1. 'Philip Larkin, This Be The Verse', 'Annus Mirabilis', 'An Arundel Tomb', *Collected Poems*, edited by Anthony Thwaite (Faber, London, 1988), pp.180, 167 and 110 respectively.

2. Simon Armitage, 'Great Sporting Moments: The Treble', *Kid* (Faber, London, 1992), p.57.
3. Armitage, 'It Ain't What You Do It's What It Does to You', *Zoom* (Bloodaxe, Newcastle upon Tyne, 1989), p.20.
4. 'Poem', *Kid*, p.29.
5. 'November', *Zoom*, p.47.
6. 'The Stuff', *Zoom*, p.68-69.
7. 'Lines Thought to Have Been Written on the Night Before the Execution of a Warrant for His Arrest', *Kid*, p.60; 'On Miles Platting Station', *Zoom*, p.10; 'To His Lost Lover' and 'Becoming of Age,' *Book of Matches* (Faber, London, 1993), pp.51 and 55 respectively; 'In Our Tenth Year', *Kid*, p.47.
8. 'Advertisement' and 'The Stuff', *Zoom*, pp.50 and 68 respectively; 'Brassneck', *Kid*, p.5; 'Hitcher', *Book of Matches*, p.46; 'Great Sporting Moments: The Treble', *Kid*, p.57; 'The Two Of Us', *The Dead Sea Poems* (Faber, London, 1995), p.32.
9. *Book of Matches*, pp.3-32.
10. 'Five Eleven Ninety Nine', *Dead Sea Poems*, pp.36-57.
11. Ian Gregson, *British Poetry and Postmodernism* (Macmillan, London, 1996), p.118.
12. Armitage, 'Ivory', *Zoom*, p.74.
13. 'Lines Thought to Have Been Written on the Night Before the Execution of a Warrant for His Arrest', *Kid*, p.60.
14. *The Penguin Book of Renaissance Verse 1509-1659*, edited by H.R Woudhuysen (Penguin, London, 1993), p.630.
15. Anthony Thwaite, *Poetry Today* (Longman, Harlow, 1996), p.154.
16. Armitage, 'The Two of Us', *The Dead Sea Poems*, p.32.
17. Simon Armitage and Glyn Maxwell, *Moon Country* (Faber, London, 1996), p.142-59.
18. Glyn Maxwell, *Out of the Rain* (Bloodaxe, Newcastle upon Tyne, 1992), p.16.
19. Maxwell, Interview with David Kinloch, *Talking Verse*, edited by Robert Crawford, Henry Hart, David Kinloch and Richard Price (*Verse*, St Andrews and Williamsburg, 1995), p.139.
20. *Talking Verse*, p.142.
21. 'The Eater', *Out of the Rain*, p.18.
22. 'Video Tale of a Patriot', 'Sport Story of a Winner' and 'Tale of the Crimson Team', *Out of the Rain*, pp.30, 28 and 92.
23. 'The Last Dessert', *Tales of the Mayor's Son* (Bloodaxe, Newcastle upon Tyne, 1990), p.32.
24. *Talking Verse*, p.141.
25. F.R. Leavis, 'Retrospect 1950', *New Bearings in English Poetry* (Penguin, Harmondsworth [1932], 1950), p.167.
26. W.H. Auden, 'Macao', *Collected Poems*, edited by Edward Mendelson (Faber, London, 1991), p.176.
27. Maxwell, 'Out of the Rain', *Out of the Rain*, pp.42-62.
28. *Talking Verse*, p.139.

29. 'The Night is Young', *Rest for the Wicked* (Bloodaxe, Newcastle upon Tyne, 1995), p.35.
30. 'As You Walk Out One Morning', *Rest for the Wicked*, p.18.
31. Auden, *Collected Poems*, p.151.
32. *The English Auden*, edited by Edward Mendelson (Faber, London, 1977), pp.66-67
33. Maxwell, 'The Plot and None', 'The Sentence' and 'Six for the Wicked', *Rest for the Wicked*, pp.56, 47 and 49 respectively.
34. Auden, 'Brussels in Winter', 'The Sphinx' and 'A.E. Housman' *Collected Poems*: pp.178, 175 and 182 respectively.
35. 'Gare du Midi' and 'In Memory of W.B. Yeats', *Collected Poems*, pp.180 and 247 respectively.
36. Maxwell, 'The Great Detectives', *Rest for the Wicked*, p.72
37. David Kennedy, *New Relations* (Seren, Brdgend, ,1996), pp.58-59.
38. Kennedy, p.59.

24. Jo Shapcott, Selima Hill, Helen Dunmore *(pp.251-60)*

1. *Poetry Review*, 84 no.1 (Spring 1994).
2. *Sixty Women Poets*, edited by Linda France (Bloodaxe, Newcastle upon Tyne, 1993), Introduction, p.18.
3. See Brett C. Millier: *Elizabeth Bishop: Life and the Memory of It* (University of California Press, Berkeley, 1993).
4. Elizabeth Bishop, *One Art: the Selected Letters*, edited by Robert Giroux (Chatto, London, 1994).
5. *New Women Poets*, edited by Carol Rumens (Bloodaxe, Newcastle upon Tyne, 1990), Introduction, pp.11-12.
6. Jane Dowson, 'Anthologies of Women's Poetry', in *British Poetry from the 1950s to the 1990s: Politics and Art*, ed. Gary Day and Brian Docherty (Macmillan, Basingstoke, 1997), p.239.
7. See *The Faber Book of Twentieth Century Women's Poetry*, edited by Fleur Adcock, (Faber, London, 1987); *The Bloodaxe Book of Contemporary Women Poets*, edited by Jeni Couzyn (Bloodaxe, Newcastle upon Tyne, 1985).
8. *Making for the Open: Post-Feminist Poetry*, edited by Carol Rumens (Chatto, London, 1985).
9. Rumens, *New Women Poets*, Introduction, p.12.
10. *Making for Planet Alice: New Women Poets*, edited by Maura Dooley (Bloodaxe, Newcastle upon Tyne, 1997).
11. Carol Rumens, 'My Leaky Coracle', *Poetry Review*, 86 no.4 (Winter 1996-97), p.26.
12. Dowson in *British Poetry from the 1950s to the 1990s: Politics and Art*, pp.237-38.
13. Rumens, 'My Leaky Coracle', *Poetry Review*, p.26.
14. *The Faber Book of Twentieth Century Women's Poetry* edited by Fleur Adcock, Introduction, p.2.
15. Rumens, 'My Leaky Coracle', *Poetry Review*, p.27.
16. 'My Leaky Coracle', *Poetry Review*, p.27.

17. See Ruth Padel, *Angel* (Bloodaxe, Newcastle upon Tyne, 1993), *Fusewire* (Chatto, London, 1996); Katherine Pierpoint, *Truffle Beds* (Faber, London, 1995); Anne Rouse, *Sunset Grill* (Bloodaxe, Newcastle upon Tyne, 1993), *Timing* (Bloodaxe, Newcastle upon Tyne, 1997); Eva Salzman, *The English Earthquake* (Bloodaxe, Newcastle upon Tyne, 1992), *Bargain with the Watchman* (Oxford University Press, Oxford, 1997).
18. Jo Shapcott, 'Motherland' *Poetry Review*, 83 no.3 (Winter 1992), p.7, and also in *Motherland* (Gwaithel and Gilwern, Gladestry, 1996), p.12.
19. Shapcott, 'Motherland' *Poetry Review*, Vol.83 No.3, p.7.
20. *Phrase Book* (Oxford University Press, Oxford, 1992) p.28.
21. Ian Gregson, *Contemporary Poetry and Postmodernism: Dialogue and Estrangement* (Macmillan, Basingstoke, 1996), p.239.
22. Patricia Waugh, 'Modernism, Postmodernism, Feminism: Gender and Autonomy Theory' in *Postmodernism: A Reader* (Edward Arnold, London, 1992), p.189.
23. Shapcott, 'Goat', *Phrase Book*, p.11.
24. 'Matter', *Phrase Book*, p.19.
25. Selima Hill, *Trembling Hearts in the Bodies of Dogs* (Bloodaxe, Newcastle upon Tyne, 1994).
26. Hill, *A Little Book of Meat* (Bloodaxe, Newcastle upon Tyne, 1993).
27. 'Little Sisters', *A Little Book of Meat*, p.10.
28. 'The Unsuccessful Wedding Night', *Trembling Hearts in the Bodies of Dogs*, p.39.
29. Dowson in *British Poetry from the 1950s to the 1990s*, p.248.
30. Hill, 'Do It Again', *A Little Book of Meat*, p.60.
31. 'Do It Again', *A Little Book of Meat*, p.60.
32. Martin Stannard, 'An Open Letter to Mike Blackburn', *Spleen, Sunk Island Review* 10 (1995), p.26.
33. Hill, 'Don't Let's Talk About Being in Love', *A Little Book of Meat* p.13.
34. 'Sleepless Nights', *A Little Book of Meat*, p.15.
35. Helen Dunmore, 'Poem for Hidden Women', *Short Days, Long Nights: New and Selected Poems* (Bloodaxe, Newcastle upon Tyne, 1991), pp.88-90; 'Getting the Strap' and 'When You've Got', *Recovering a Body* (Bloodaxe, Newcastle upon Tyne, 1994) pp.27 and 62.
36. Dunmore, 'In the Desert Knowing Nothing', *Recovering a Body*, p.23.
37. 'Poem on the Obliteration of 100,000 Iraqi Soldiers', *Recovering a Body*, p.24.
38. Tony Harrison, 'A Cold Coming', *Guardian* (18 March 1991), and collected in *The Gaze of the Gorgon* (Bloodaxe, Newcastle upon Tyne, 1992), p.48-54.
39. Dunmore, 'Poem on the Obliteration of 100,000 Iraqi Soldiers', *Recovering a Body*, p.24.

40. Theodor Adorno, *Minima Moralia*, trans. E.F Jephcott (New Left Books, London, 1974), p.55.
41. Dunmore, *Recovering a Body*, p.29.
42. *Recovering a Body*, p.13.

25. Don Paterson, Kathleen Jamie, Robert Crawford, W.N. Herbert: Scotland! Scotland! Actual/Virtual *(pp.261-69)*

1. Robert Crawford, *Identifying Poets* (Edinburgh University Press, 1993).
2. Crawford, *Identifying Poets*, p.161.
3. 'Homogeneity is the enemy of Scottish culture', *Identifying Poets* edited by Robert Crawford (Edinburgh University Press, 1993), p.162.
4. *Identifying Poets*, p.162.
5. T.S. Eliot, 'Was There a Scottish Literature', *The Athenaeum*, 1 Aug. 1919, quoted in 'Language and Liberty', *The Faber Book of Twentieth Century Scottish Poetry,* edited by Douglas Dunn (Faber, London, 1992), p.xvii.
6. Will Hutton, *The State To Come* (Vintage, London, 1997), p.2.
7. James Kelman, *How Late It Was, How Late* (Secker, London, 1994).
8. Dunn, 'Language and Liberty', *The Faber Book of Twentieth Century Scottish Poetry*, p.xxxiv.
9. M.M. Bakhtin, 'Response to a question from the *Novy mir* editorial staff', *Speech Genres*, 6-7, quoted by Crawford in *Identifying Poets*, p.12.
10. Anthony Thwaite, *Poetry Today* (Longman, London, 1996), p.85.
11. Tom Leonard, 'Unrelated Incidents', *Intimate Voices* (Vintage, London, 1995), p.86.
12. Leonard, 'Ghostie Men', *Intimate Voices*, pp.103-21.
13. 'Unrelated Incidents', *Intimate Voices*, p.86.
14. 'Ghostie Men', *Intimate Voices*, p.120.
15. 'Unrelated Incidents', *Intimate Voices*, p.88.
16. 'Poetry', *Intimate Voices*, p.36.
17 Dunn, 'Interview with the Devil', *The Printer's Devil,* A, p.24.
18. Don Paterson, 'An Eliptical Stylus', *Nil Nil* (Faber, London, 1993), p.20.
19. Paterson, 'An Eliptical Stylus', *Nil Nil* (Faber, London, 1993), p.21.
20. Paterson, Interview with Raymond Friel, *Talking Verse* edited by Robert Crawford, Henry Hart, David Kinloch and Richard Price (*Verse*, St Andrews and Williamsburg, 1995), p.193.
21. Dunn, 'The Come On', Selected Poems 1964-1983 (Faber, London, 1986), p.100.
22. Kathleen Jamie, *The Queen of Sheba* (Bloodaxe, Newcastle upon Tyne. 1994).
23. Jamie, 'Forget It', *Penguin Modern Poets 9* (Penguin, London, 1996), p.145.

24. 'Forget It', *Penguin Modern Poets 9*, pp.146-47.
25. 'Mr and Mrs Scotland are Dead', *The Queen of Sheba*, p. 37; 'Song of Sunday' and 'The Graduates', *Penguin Modern Poets 9*, pp.143-44 and 149.
26. Gerald Mangan, 'Glasgow 1956', *Waiting for the Storm* (Bloodaxe, Newcastle upon Tyne, 1990), p.9.
27. Liz Lochhead, 'The Bargain', *Dreaming Frankenstein and Collected Poems* (Polygon, Edinburgh, 1985), pp.117-20.
28. Crawford, 'The Glasgow Herald', *Talkies* (Chatto, London, 1990), p.54.
29. 'Alba Einstein', *A Scottish Assembly* (Chatto, London, 1990), p.53.
30. W.N. Herbert, 'Dingle Dell', *Forked Tongue* (Bloodaxe, Newcastle upon Tyne, 1994), p.40.
31. Quoted in *Identifying Poets*, p.7.
32. Hugh MacDiarmid, 'The Eemis Stane', *Sangschaw* (1925) in *Selected Poems* edited by David Craig and John Manson (Penguin, Harmondsworth, 1970), pp.21-22.
33. Dunn, 'Language and Liberty', *The Faber Book of Twentieth Century Scottish Poetry*, p.xx.
34. Herbert, 'The Third Corbie', *Cabaret McGonagall* (Bloodaxe, Newcastle upon Tyne, 1996), pp.42-45.
35. 'The Landfish', *Forked Tongue*, p.70.
36. Paterson, Interview, *Talking Verse*, p.192.

Afterword *(pages 270-74)*

1. Adrian Mitchell, 'Most People', *Heart on the Left: Poems 1953-1984* (Bloodaxe, Newcastle upon Tyne, 1997), p.110.
2. According to *A Consultative Green Paper on Support for Poetry in the English Arts Funding System* (Arts Council of England, London, 1997), Appendix 3, p.31: 'The consumer market for poetry has increased slightly in recent years, with 5 per cent of adults claiming to have bought at least one poetry book in 1994 (compared with 1 per cent in 1989).'
3. Arts Council, Appendix 3.
4. Randall Jarrell, 'The Obscurity of the Poet', *Poetry and the Age* (Faber, London, 1996) pp.1-2.
5. Fred D'Aguiar, 'Wan Way Tickit', *Poetry Review*, 87 no.3 (Autumn 1997), pp.14-15.
6. *Airy Hall* (Chatto and Windus, London. pp.45-63.
7. Arts Council, Appendix 3, p.8.
8. Dana Gioia, 'Can Poetry Matter', in *Can Poetry Matter? Essays on Poetry and American Culture* (Graywolf Press, Saint Paul, 1992), p.1.
9. Jarrell, 'The Age of Criticism', *Poetry and the Age*, pp.60-61.
10. Mike Higgins, 'Slamming Verse in the face of the Pub Crowd', *Independent*, 'Eye' (21 November 1997), p.6.
11. Christopher Middleton, *Bolshevism in Art* (Carcanet, Manchester, 1971), pp.145-46.

INDEX

Index compiled by Stephanie J. Dagg